St. Louis Community College

Forest Park
Florissant Valley
Meramec

Instructional Resources
St. Louis, Missouri

To the people, clan mothers,
and chiefs of the Six Nations Confederacy.

Hiawatha Belt. The belt recorded the formation of The Iroquois League of Nations.

EXILED
IN THE LAND
OF THE FREE

Clear Light Publishers

Santa Fe

Democracy, Indian Nations, and the U.S. Constitution

Oren Lyons, John Mohawk,

Vine Deloria, Jr., Laurence Hauptman,

Howard Berman, Donald Grinde, Jr.,

Curtis Berkey, Robert Venables

Foreword by Peter Matthiessen
Preface by Senator Daniel K. Inouye

First Edition

Library of Congress Catalog Card Number: 91–072479

Library of Congress Cataloging-in-Publication Data

Exiled in the land of the free: democracy, Indian nations, and the U.S. Constitution / John Mohawk . . . [et al.]; preface by Sen. Daniel K. Inouye, foreword by Peter Matthiessen.
    p.   cm.
Includes notes and index.
ISBN 0–940666–15–4: $24.95
   1. Indians of North America—Government relations. 2. United States—Constitutional history. 3. United States—Civilization—Indian influences.
4. Iroquois Indians—Politics and government.
E93.E965 1991
973'.00497—dc20   91–72479
                                                       CIP

Editors: Oren R. Lyons and John C. Mohawk

Printed in the United States of America
Typeset in Melior by Rick Heide, Redwood City, CA
Back cover: David Calabaza, Comanche Dance, San Juan Pueblo, 1991.
Photo by Marcia Keegan

Acknowledgments

This volume had its genesis in meetings and discussions between newspaper publisher Thomas E. Worrell, Jr., and Oren R. Lyons, associate professor of American Studies at the State University of New York at Buffalo. These discussions took place over a period of several months in 1987 on the topic of the United States Constitution and the American Indian. The result was that Mr. Worrell agreed to sponsor a proposal to develop a book on the subject. The Five Rings Corporation then generously provided grants to enable the authors to research and write the articles. Oren Lyons recruited John C. Mohawk, his colleague at SUNY, Buffalo, and editor of *Daybreak* magazine, as co-editor of the book.

The editors would like to express gratitude to all the people who made this book possible. At the top of this list, of course, is Thomas Worrell, Jr. Special thanks must go to Timothy Kolly and Susan Olsen of Worrell Enterprises for the many hours they spent reading, commenting upon, and negotiating the many details of the book. The project benefited greatly from their unflagging energy and unselfish commitment to style and clarity.

We also want to thank the faculty of the American Studies Department at the State University of New York at Buffalo, especially professors Charles Keil and Lawrence Chisholm, whose advice and assistance proved invaluable. Acknowledgment is due also to the office of the Faculty of Arts and Letters at SUNY, Buffalo, and to the SUNY at Buffalo administration for making space available for the project which produced this volume and for their overall support of the work.

Gregory Chester provided helpful assistance by reading and commenting on the first draft of the articles. Others offered invaluable assistance in a number of ways. A special acknowledgment is owed to the people at Computer Time, Inc., in Getzville, New York, who several times went beyond the call of duty to provide timely help managing the computer files.

Our thanks are also extended to Senator Daniel K. Inouye for his generous contribution of a preface, and to Peter Matthiessen for his foreword. Each has added greatly to the value of the book for this and future generations.

Finally, recognition is due to Marcia Keegan and Harmon Houghton at Clear Light Publishers for their enthusiasm for the project and for commitment to bringing the book to the public. The book could not have been produced without their help, or that of managing editor Dennis H. Dutton and copy editor Ann Mason.

There are several others who also deserve recognition and thanks, but who cannot be mentioned by name on this very short list. To all those who assisted us, in whole or in part, we extend our deepest gratitude.

John C. Mohawk
Oren R. Lyons

Contents

Illustrations

Preface

In November of 1986, I assumed the position of chairman of the Senate Select Committee on Indian Affairs. At that time, like many other Americans, I knew very little about the contributions that this nation's first Americans have made to the fabric of our society. I was soon to learn that the ignorance regarding the native people of America is pervasive.

Apparently, few Americans are aware that the fundamental structure of our democratic form of government has its origins in the Iroquois Confederacy. Many may not know that the debates of the Continental Congress contain many references to the Indian nations. Few know that it was the Indians who enabled General George Washington and his troops to survive the winter at Valley Forge. It is not well known that Indian people fought side by side with the soldiers of the American Revolution, nor is it well known that American Indians have served in the armed forces of the United States in every military action since the time of the revolutionary war, in numbers proportionally far greater than any other ethnic group in the United States.

Many Americans have no idea that historians and anthropologists suggest that prior to European contact, there were a minimum of 10 million, and as many as 50 million native people residing in the land that subsequently became the United States. And because the period known as the Indian wars era is not typically documented in basic history primers, it may well be that most Americans are unaware that the effort to control areas of land then occupied by the Indians decimated the Indian population so effectively that there were approximately only 250,000 Indian people remaining in the United States at the end of the Indian wars era.

Nor is the fact well known that Indian people once exercised dominion over 550 million acres of land, and that through conquest, and all too frequently misrepresentation, those lands were systematically taken from the Indians, so that today they are left with less than 50 million acres.

The Indian nations entered into 800 treaties with the United States. These were solemn and sacred documents which promised the Indians that "as long as the rivers flow, and the sun rises in the east," the lands and resources that had been secured to them would be protected in perpetuity. In exchange for the cession of vast amounts of land, the Indians were promised that the Great White Father in Washington, D.C., would provide them health care and education for all the generations to come.

The Indian people lived up to the commitments they made in those treaties. They sacrificed their ancestral homes, the lands upon which they hunted and fished and gathered berries and roots for their subsistence. They were and remain today people who revere the Mother Earth and her bounty, people who were environmentalists and conservationists long before those terms gained common currency.

However, those 800 treaties were only honored unilaterally. The United States Senate refused to ratify 430 of them, even though the government charged the Indians with having to live up to the terms of those treaties. Even more tragically, of the 370 treaties that were ratified, the United States proceeded to violate provisions in every one.

Perhaps it is because there are many chapters in what we term "American" history which record atrocities and cruelties of the worst kind imposed upon the native people of America that our history books evidence a reluctance to view American history from the perspective of native people.

So it is with much enthusiasm that I commend this book, *Exiled in the Land of the Free,* to the American people. Our children and our children's children should know the true story of our country. They should read from those pages of history of which we can be proud, and they should also know that there are a people of this nation upon whose ancestral lands we now reside—a people who sacrificed their homelands so that we could build a country called America, a people who, despite the great adversity we thrust upon them, gave generously of themselves in every respect.

This is a chapter of history we must all have the opportunity to learn, and a chapter that we, as Americans, must never forget.

Senator Daniel K. Inouye

Foreword

A great myth that has been used to justify and to sustain the seizure of North and South America from native peoples is that what was "discovered" on this continent by Europeans was a vast wilderness, a "new world," The New World: fresh, virginal, unaltered by human hands. And in consequence of believing in the unspoiled nature of the land found here, all culture on this continent was considered then, and is considered now by many, to have been transplanted from the "advanced" civilization of Europe, the "Old World."

In fact, that pristine realm of unbroken virgin forest, clear blue rivers, and immortal silence that Europeans found here on and after Columbus's appearance in 1492 may actually have ended forever upon the arrival of hunters out of Asia not less than forty thousand years ago and perhaps a good deal more. (Many Native American traditionalists maintain that the original nature of the Americas had begun its change even earlier, when the ancestors emerged into this world ages ago through sacred springs and underground caverns—pathways from previous worlds, previous existences.)

The "New World" was not new, not virginal, nor was it a wilderness when Europeans came. For the Native Americans it was home—profoundly loved, respected, and honored; its geography intimately known; and its bountiful resources put to use in knowing ways by people fully inhabiting its spaces.

Nor were this land's inhabitants primitive, far less savage, without culture. Certain Native American civilizations, such as the Mayas and the Incas, built cities more massive architecturally than any in the Old World, not excepting the Greek, Roman, East Indian, and Chinese. Other Indian nations, such as the Haudenosaunee (or Iroquois), were so politically sophisticated that the rebellious colonists did not hesitate to borrow ideas from them in drawing up our United States Constitution. In addition, many staples of material culture first developed by the Indian peoples, among which corn, the potato, manioc, cotton, and tobacco are only the best known, transformed the agriculture not only of Europe, but of Eurasia and Africa.

In the first centuries of settlement, the stronger tribes were sought as allies in territorial and trade disputes between the European kingdoms. The Indian nations remained powerful and sovereign, and were dealt with as such in any number of official documents and treaties, some of which (despite the brutal exile of the Indians in their own land, so starkly documented in this book) have never been invalidated. It was only when the power of the colonists increased and the rightful inhabitants grew weaker and less numerous that their sovereignty was called into question—why grant them sovereignty when through force of arms (and lies and alcohol and pox-infected blankets and strategic massacres) their ancient claim on these good lands could be denied them? Even those who were never defeated in their wars with the United States—the Miccosukee Seminoles, for example—were finally subjugated by the missions and bureaucracies.

To justify betrayal, usurpation, and rapine—not to speak of atrocious cruelty and murder—it became desireable to denigrate the native peoples, even the hospitable and faithful allies, as subhuman beings, nomadic savages, with no geographic, political, or moral claim upon their territories. After all, the Indians claimed no "ownership" of the earth and air and water, an unnatural concept (as we usurpers recognize very late, to our great cost) that they were wise enough to reject. How could they do otherwise, since they were at one with their Mother Earth, which most tribes treated in a profound and spiritual way that had been lost to all but a few "traditional" Europeans in the very farthest corners of that continent.

Such critical points and many others are well documented in this excellent compilation, which deserves wide circulation in this country and throughout the world. As is pointed out in the stirring introduction, "European footsteps were planted, not on virgin soil, but in Indian towns." Most tribes encountered by the white men, even on the coasts, had been "standing on the land" for generations, with a strong agriculture—the Hopis, Pueblos, Algonquians, and others—or an advanced fishing culture—the Inuits, the Pacific Northwest peoples, the powerful Calusas of south Florida—all of them distinguished by vibrant traditions of art and oral literature. Such traditions were combined with hunting and wild gathering, as with the Plains tribes, who adapted feral Spanish horses to develop in a single century a hunting culture as various and splendid in its artifacts as any ever known before on earth.

Underlying all Indian claims for our attention, and all of the arguments in this fine book, is the issue of Indian sovereignty—or rather, the *principle* of sovereignty, since the American government has never permitted it to become an "issue." Among the hundreds of Indian nations (too many of them vanished now, or all but gone), only the Six Nations of the Iroquois were able to retain even minimal sovereignty (the Six Nations issue their own passports, and their young men are not obliged to fight our wars, though many do).

Despite the hysteria of whites in the affected regions, the Indian nations harbor no ambition or intent to take back all or even most of the land that was guaranteed them in that heap of broken treaties, but only to reestablish this *principle* of sovereign right as a legal basis for fair and reasonable claims on certain public lands administered by the state and federal agencies. Since the Indian peoples are legally (and in common justice) entitled to far more land than they are asking for, why not return to them the dignity of sovereignty as well?

Peter Matthiessen
Sagaponack, New York

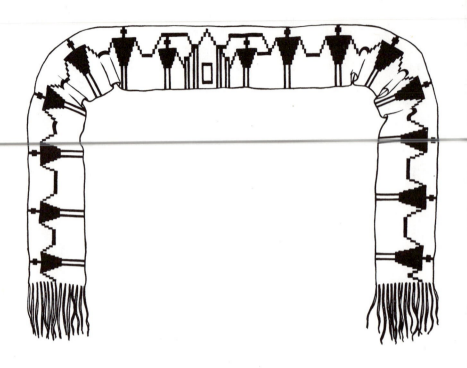

Washington Covenant Belt. The belt was used as a covenant of peace between the
thirteen original colonies and the Six Nations.

Introduction

John C. Mohawk
Oren R. Lyons

This book provides a new interpretation of an aspect of early United States history. It proposes, in a collection of essays written by eight scholars and Native American leaders, that American Indians influenced the development of democratic tradition in Western culture and provided some inspiration for the writing of the United States Constitution and Bill of Rights.

There remains a perception in popular consciousness and even in the minds and writings of scholars who should know better that the so-called Indians whom Columbus discovered in 1492 were "savages": childlike, unsophisticated, godless, lacking in social organization, technology, government, higher thought, and other hallmarks of civilization. Columbus is seen, on the other hand, as the representative of a civilization whose rapid advances in science, technology, and philosophy made it the inevitable, and somehow proper and desirable, power over the indigenous and "inferior" peoples of the Americas.

To the contrary. Long before Columbus made contact with the Native Americans of the "New World" (so off course that he thought he was discovering land on the opposite side of the globe) some Native American civilizations had developed vast irrigation networks that rivaled those of Rome; they had domesticated crops that would eventually save Europe from starvation; they had developed medical and psychotherapeutic knowledge that made medieval Europe's medical model of "humours" and its use of leeches as a form of treatment look primitive; they had advanced astronomical calendars; they had a body of literature, both oral and in some cases written, that is only today finally being recognized as the equal of any found in the world; and they had developed highly sophisticated forms of representative government in which freedom was not only prized, but was the foremost principle.

Conquest was one of the primary goals of Columbus and of Europe in its exploration of the world, and conquest—of indigenous peoples and their lands—is what occurred. But there is an ironic twist to this domination: the conquerors were themselves conquered. For along with the exportation of gold and slaves from the New World, something else was exported, a product which had been created through numerous interactions between American Indians and the colonists: democracy. This export item, perhaps Native America's greatest contribution to the world, toppled European monarchies and ultimately resulted in the formation of the United States of America. Yet, this contribution by

America's original people is seldom recognized.

American history has long been written as a kind of Eurocentric mythology, standing in considerable contrast to the summary given above. Until the late 1970s, mainstream historians propagated the view that everything significant about America began in 1492 or thereafter and that the story of America was of the triumph of European peoples bringing civilization and prosperity to the vast "wilderness" that was the Americas. That view reflected a kind of utopian vision, long present in Western thought in a variety of tendencies, which presented Western civilization as an adventure of discovering the perfection of human potentials, and which projected an ideology that would enable the West to solve all the problems of humankind. Indeed, the idea that Western civilization is in the vanguard of this potential of human societies may be the most prominant factor in the many streams of thought which compose the intellectual history of the West.

Eurocentric historians generally have reinforced this view to one degree or another. Historians who uncritically subscribe to this kind of ideology are likely to construct history by carefully selecting patterns of facts which lend it support and to disregard or even deny patterns of facts which are in any way contradictory. Few of these historians have seriously questioned whether the West is indeed moving toward a perfect society or whether a perfect society is even possible. This may explain, in part, why American historians have accepted changes, even dramatic and ecologically destructive changes, as inevitable, and ultimately positive.

When a civilization thinks it holds the key to the solution of humankind's problems, sometimes such a civilization may also think it is justified to "break a few eggs," and in Western history that has meant sometimes exterminating a few species of plants or animals, human cultures, or whole populations of distinct peoples. Such developments might be seen as regrettable, but they are rarely seen as the result of ideologies. The story of the Americas, as most Americans understand it, is one of European peoples who journeyed across the oceans and transformed the Americas (and other places) into new Europes, where cultures of the Old World were transplanted and perpetuated. Eurocentric historians have adopted a point of view, usually unconsciously, that peoples different from themselves are peoples who are not embarked on the same adventure, that indeed they are often obstructions to this process of human perfection. They have never thought of themselves as utopianists whose ideologies about peoples and "races" different from their own have caused (and have rationalized) tremendous destruction.

Many modern historians mark the commencement of significant change in that tradition of history with the 1977 publication of Francis

Jennings's *The Invasion of America: Indians, Colonialism, and the Cant of Conquest* (1975). This book lays groundwork for challenging the thesis that European societies were transplanted to new geography with practically no cultural consequences resulting from contact with non-Europeans. Instead, the European invasion of North America is described as an invasion of its indigenous peoples. European footsteps were planted, not on virgin soil, but in Indian towns, and the story of early exploration and settlement is about the interaction of peoples and not, as it had previously been portrayed, the story of the peopling of a practically unoccupied continent. Indeed, Jennings argues that had there been no Indians in North America during the sixteenth and seventeenth centuries, it is possible European penetration would have been impossible or would have taken much longer than it did.

A number of books by historians who have reinvestigated and reinterpreted the historical record have greatly extended our knowledge of cultural interactions and transformations that contributed to the modern world. Robert Berkhofer, Jr.'s *The White Man's Indian* (1978) proposes that the idea and images of the Indian were a European invention. European writers were uncertain of the identities of Indians relative to European culture, but they were clear about one point: they knew who the Indian was not. The Indian was not the European, and in many historical writings and in popular thought of the time the Indian is widely treated as an "other." Berkhofer records a history of attempts to locate the Indian in that context through centuries of European and Euro-American images created of the Indian which were intended to strengthen an identity of the Euro-American as the representative of civilization, progress, and the future.

Tzvetan Todorov, in *The Conquest of America* (1982), continues that investigation with a review of the Spanish conquest and the Black Legend (which asserted the brutality of the conquest). The Spanish invasion of the Caribbean and the mainland was marked with an incredible ferocity that was recorded by the sixteenth-century Spanish historian Bartolome de Las Casas. Las Casas was horrified by Spanish cruelty, and he reported with vigor the excesses of the conquistadors. Todorov investigates Las Casas's writings with a view to understanding Spanish treatment of "the other" as a mirror of Spanish civilization of the time. Previous generations of historians had reported the Spanish conquest as an event on the road to modernity with little reflection on the cost in human lives and suffering and the general trends in Western culture which those costs implied.

Another critique of the West's treatment of "others," including American Indians, is Richard Drinnon's *Facing West: The Metaphysics of Indian-Hating and Empire-Building* (1980). Drinnon argues that the North American expansion of Euro-American civilization was facilitated by a tradition of inventive slander designed to cast the "other" as a less than admirable being, and that American historians played a major role in justifying and reinforcing the kind of aggressive behavior which made the idea of "manifest destiny" sound so logical to nineteenth-century ears. A significant element of this work proposes that many major American historians have been anything but neutral observers of facts but were, instead, human beings shaped by their time, subject to the prejudices and viewpoints of their age and, as such, cast as willing if sometimes unwitting propagandists. Drinnon proposes that this tradition influenced American behavior toward peoples of the American continent and across the Pacific, and ultimately peoples of the Philippines and Viet Nam.

Conservative historians have argued that revisionists have added nothing new to the record. Recent books, however, have mounted persuasive arguments that ample evidence exists to challenge the view that modernity was an exclusive invention of Western culture brought about by European and Euro-American ideas, policies, and practices which were developed independently and/or in isolation from influence by other cultures.

Some historians, for example, argue that cultural change and transformation have been as much or more a result of random fortune as a consequence of design. William Cronon's *Changes in the Land: Indians, Colonists, and the Ecology of New England* (1987) argues that a major factor in European success during the seventeenth century involved changes that were brought about by the introduction of new biological patterns from Europe to New England. Weeds, domestic animals, aggressive plants, and other factors tended to alter patterns the Indians had counted on for centuries as the basis of their subsistence. Furthermore, although the New England colonists depicted the Indians as nomadic hunter-gatherers who had no tradition of individual or group land rights, they were well aware that the Indians had landholding patterns not entirely unlike English concepts of private property, and it was well established that these Indians were sedentary, not nomadic. Biological pressures, most often quite independent of human intent and generally unnoticed by previous American historians, contributed to an environment of change that helped to facilitate English expansion.

Alfred W. Crosby, Jr.'s *Ecological Imperialism: The Biological Expansion of Europe, 900–1900* (1986), develops the theme of the role of technology and biology in world history. Crosby's work builds partly on the work of historian William McNeill (*Plagues and Peoples*, 1976) and his own earlier book, *The Columbian Exchange: Biological Consequences of 1492* (1973). *Ecological Imperialism* proposes that some major events in history, including the Spanish invasion of the Canary

Islands and the conquest of Mexico, are best understood in the light of the effect of smallpox and other epidemic diseases introduced by Europeans to populations which had no previous exposure. These diseases had tremendous consequences, sometimes destroying entire populations in the Americas and the newly "discovered" islands. The role of disease organisms in military conquest and European expansion has long been mentioned but was previously underreported and certainly not viewed as a significant trend in the history of the modern world.

Other books have challenged the previously established view of world history in new and exciting ways. Edward Said's *Orientalism* (1978) challenges the European academic tradition of Oriental studies. Said argues that European academics have created fictional images of Orientals (i.e., non-Western "others" of the Old World) as part of the process which justified (and justifies) European colonialism. The process, he states, has been entirely self-serving.

Martin Bernal's *Black Athena: The Afroasiatic Roots of Classical Civilization* (1987) argues that nineteenth-century European classical scholars collaborated to deny the contributions of Middle Eastern and North African cultures to classical Greek civilization because they were inserting a theory of race into the story of the origins of civilization, and they did not want to acknowledge contributions by Semitic and African peoples. *Black Athena* is a powerful indictment of the ethnocentric tradition of history which has been used to promote racist assumptions by simply eliminating the contributions to modernity of non-Western peoples. The story of this elaborate effort to distort history helps to explain why the issue of non-Western origins and influences on Western culture is so important.

Jack Weatherford's *Indian Givers: How the Indians of the Americas Transformed the Modern World* (1988) may be the most direct and concrete challenge to that tradition of history which ignores the contributions of American Indian cultures to the development of modernity. Weatherford argues that the modern world is a product of the confluence of world cultures and that European society was profoundly transformed as a result of contact and interaction with the Indians of the Americas. *Indian Givers* credits the American Indians with developments in agriculture that provided necessary elements for the foundation of the industrial revolution. Weatherford states that American Indian gold and silver provided the necessary base for the monetary system that gave rise to the world money economy. He also proposes that the tradition of democracy was strongly influenced by American Indian cultures. *Indian Givers* identifies American Indian contributions to modernity in broad strokes, with a powerful array of facts interwoven with excellent social history.

The idea that American Indian cultures influenced the West's democratic tradition and provided ideas and possibly inspiration for the process which culminated in the creation of the United States Constitution has been strongly resisted by some of the established anthropologists and historians who write about American Indian and Iroquois history. Most of this opposition has been in the form of informal and oral statements made at conferences or in letters which cite such things as "poor scholarship" on the part of the proponents of this theory, without specifying exactly what was in error. As is common in debates of this kind, proponents and opponents seem to have proposed the full spectrum of possibilities. Professor Gregory Schaaf has maintained that the United States Constitution appears to have been modeled after the Iroquois tradition of the Great Law of Peace. By contrast, a number of prominent scholars have argued that American Indians in general and the Iroquois in particular had no influence on the Constitution and that American Indians provided little or no inspiration for the development of democratic thought and tradition in the West.

One of the arguments against Indian influence on the thinking of the American colonists has been that the colonists feared and hated Indians, referred to them as "savages," and therefore would never have adopted or been influenced by Indian thinking. To accept this reasoning would be to conclude that people never get ideas from a different culture which they dislike, a proposition which is both overly simplistic and historically inaccurate.[1] All cultures have borrowed from other cultures, and whether they liked or disliked those cultures is irrelevant. Geographer George F. Carter states:

> No civilization arose in isolation, as the flowing genius of a single people. Great civilizations illustrate that genius lies in the ability of a group of persons to assemble ideas borrowed from far and wide into some new pattern suited to their needs, tastes, and opportunities.[2]

That cultural diffusion exists does not prove any of the proposals around the issue at hand, but it would seem to disprove the assertion that it could not have happened.[3]

Professor Erik M. Jensen, in a law review article responding to an article by Professor Gregory Schaaf, has committed to print some of the strongest arguments against American Indian influence on Western democratic thought and the Constitution.[4] Jensen attacks Schaaf's lack of primary authority:

> To have a plausible theory connecting Iroquois ideas to the United States Constitution, a historian—one might expect—would cite discussions of the Iroquois Confederacy at the Constitutional Convention.

Schaaf and others cannot do that for one simple reason: there were no such discussions.[5]

To be completely accurate, one might say that no record of such discussions survives in the primary documents unearthed thus far, and that such documentation may not exist. However, to limit evidence of the Confederacy's influence to the documents produced at the Constitutional Convention is to argue that all discussions and experiences of the men at the convention which took place prior to that time were irrelevant and that everything that shaped their thinking is present in a few documents. When considering the possible, probable, or compelling influences American Indians had on the culture of the men at the convention, this is an indefensible proposition. Speaking of the limitations of the literary record in terms of understanding the impact of cultural diffusion, McNeill states:

> *The literary record . . . tends to divide humankind into separate and more or less watertight compartments. Everyone who depends on texts for evidence will be impelled to overlook or minimize the borrowing across cultural and literary boundaries that did, in fact, occur. Only when art history and the material remains uncovered by archeology are made to supplement literary testimony can a juster estimation of the role of borrowing in times past be hoped for, and even that leaves many gaps. . . . All we can hope for is history written with a keen sensitivity to the possibility and probability of borrowing, material and immaterial alike.*[6]

Those who deny that American Indian cultures influenced and even inspired the colonists' ideas about democracy and the way in which they structured their government are arguing that these developments were the product of independent invention. Independent invention is at least as difficult to prove as cultural diffusion, and is quite rare in human history. The northeastern American Indians articulated a great respect for the rights of the individual and organized themselves into confederacies, and the colonists concerned themselves with both of these issues. Although American historians have strained to find European roots for these ideas, it was not necessary to look abroad, and although some people were reading about the Greek democracies, the ancient Greeks had failed to inspire movement in this direction in the previous millennium. Historians and anthropologists who deny American Indian influence in this process are proposing something not only unlikely but probably unprecedented: that an independent invention occurred which was purely coincidental and entirely isolated from the indigenous societies at hand. Professor Jensen's argument, for example, denies the possibility of cultural diffusion:

> The argument of those who have hypothesized relationships between the Great Law of Peace and the U.S. Constitution relies not on direct connections, for which there is no evidence, but on osmosis. As phrased by Onondaga Nation Chief Oren Lyons, the transference of democratic ideals to the white man "was a process of association, of years of meetings, discussions, wars, and peace."[7]

Most historians and legal scholars do not read the anthropological material about diffusion. Whenever two cultures come into contact, an immense amount of information changes hands immediately. Some of this information exchange takes place nonverbally, and some of it is poorly understood in the terms it is offered. Such interactions are always enormously complex and the outcome unpredictable. There is also a pattern of unconscious, or perhaps subconscious, learning that goes on. Borrowing is easier than inventing, and people are always looking for ways to do things that work. On the one hand, Europeans borrowed many things from the American Indians; on the other hand, almost everything they borrowed was altered to fit a context different from that of its origins. In some cases, the thing borrowed was transformed so much it became almost unrecognizable in its altered form. Sometimes, when a people perceive that they need something, borrowing and invention go on at the same time, often at a dramatic pace.

Peoples very often develop selective memories about the origin of the elements of their culture, preferring to believe that their ancestors invented rather than borrowed the things of which they are proud. It is also important to note that sometimes very basic values of American Indians did not transfer, probably because the colonists felt no need for these things at the time. The colonists, for example, did not emulate Iroquois ideas about communal property rights or women's rights. Indeed, the list of the things that did not transfer is very long.

If we can assume, as many historians and anthropologists have done, that cultural diffusion can and does take place, we are then faced with the question of whether there were channels by which the ideas or practices might have transferred. The argument of this book is that such channels existed in abundance, that the colonists were in need of ideas to replace European theories of government, and that transference of ideas from American Indians to the people who now are known as Americans did take place.[8]

The publication of *Exiled in the Land of the Free* comes at an opportune time. Five years ago the people of the United States celebrated the bicentennial of the writing of the United States Constitution. More recently, in late 1991, we celebrated the 200th anniversary of the writing of the Bill of Rights. And this year we celebrate—or mourn, or examine, as it may be—the 500th anniversary of Christopher Columbus's "discovery" of America.

The publication is timely also in light of recent world events. The breakaway of republics in the Soviet Union has been hailed by politicians and pundits in this country as the end of the "evil empire" and the beginning of democracy in that part of the world. In this country, however, the original inhabitants of America—the Native Americans— remain remarkably unaffected by the documents of freedom for which this nation is justifiably acclaimed, and remarkably underrepresented and mistreated by the executive, legislative, and judicial branches of government they undoubtedly helped inspire.

This is perhaps the ultimate irony—that American Indians have made significant, even indispensable contributions to the development of democracy in the West, and in the United States of America in particular, but have received few of the rights and privileges they helped give birth to. This book, we hope, will begin a rectification of that injustice.

"The American Indian in the Past" by Oren R. Lyons recounts the history of the European invasion through aboriginal eyes and notes that there was a preexisting and vigorous political tradition in North America which the colonists had been associated with. The American Indian culture which most directly and for the longest period of time caught the attention of the people who founded the United States was the Six Nations or Iroquois Confederacy, known to themselves as the Haudenosaunee. Lyons, an Onondaga chief and professor of American Studies, recounts part of the story of their first contact with Europeans during the early seventeenth century in the form of an Iroquois tradition known as the "Two-Row" treaty. As the story will illustrate, the Iroquois had a refined theory of international relations which they applied to the first Europeans they encountered and which they continue to urge upon the United States to this day.

John C. Mohawk's "Indians and Democracy: No One Ever Told Us" investigates how American Indian intellectual contributions to Western culture could have been disregarded. It concludes that a tradition of Eurocentric history has worked to overlook the implications of preexisting American Indian democratic traditions and the evidence that the Founding Fathers were aware of these traditions. This chapter also focuses on the existing mythological antecedents of democratic thought which claim democratic origins in Greek and Roman culture and the French Enlightenment, and concludes that although some of the founders of the American republic may have been influenced by some of these writings, the creation of the United States was a step in a new direction, one that had at least some aboriginal American roots.

Robert W. Venables's "American Indian Influences on the America of the Founding Fathers" explores the views of American indigenous peoples found in the literary and artistic traditions of the West and finds a well-established if somewhat imprecise history of ideas and opinions woven into the fabric of the West's imagination. Within the colonies themselves, the American Indian was even more significant.

Howard R. Berman's essay, "Perspectives on American Indian Sovereignty and International Law, 1600 to 1776," illustrates that the Europeans negotiated with the Indian nations using approximately the same rules as they used to negotiate with European sovereign nations. By the time of the American Revolution, there had been in North America more than a century and a half of history of European nations conducting what can only be termed international relations with North American nations. This well-established tradition was inherited by the new United States.

Curtis G. Berkey's "United States–Indian Relations: The Constitutional Basis" seeks to discover the context and original intent of the words in the United States Constitution which refer to American Indians. Berkey makes a clear and forceful argument that the Founding Fathers used the words they meant to use, that the people who gathered in Philadelphia in 1789 viewed American Indian nations as separate sovereignties and constructed language in the Constitution to reflect their view. Berkey looks carefully into the wording of each section and into the record which provides the context for the wording in the first serious exercise of its kind.

Donald A. Grinde, Jr.'s "Iroquois Political Theory and the Roots of American Democracy" investigates the culture of the constitutional era and the ideas of the individuals gathered at the Constitutional Convention in Philadelphia in 1789, discovering that Indians were the toast of the time. Several significant personalities in this period, including Benjamin Franklin and John Rutledge (who chaired the draft committee), were confirmed "Indian buffs" who shared a passion for Indian thought and traditions. Grinde offers evidence that this tendency influenced some of the ideas found in the Albany Plan of Union, the Articles of Confederation, and the United States Constitution.

Vine Deloria, Jr., eminent historian and author, reviews how the United States treated the American Indian under the United States Constitution during the nineteenth century in "The Application of the Constitution to American Indians." Deloria's writing is animated and confrontational. His review of nineteenth-century American legal history as applied to American Indians should be required reading for law students contemplating a career in American Indian law.

In "Congress, Plenary Power, and the American Indian, 1870 to 1992," historian Laurence M. Hauptman reviews the history of the Indians of the United States during the twentieth century. American Indians are generally seen as historic figures and rarely as contemporary peoples with problems and aspirations. Hauptman explains the struggles and ambitions of contemporary American Indians.

It is hoped that *Exiled in the Land of the Free* will inspire readers to reassess the impact of Native Americans upon the course of United States history and that these essays will encourage scholars to reevaluate the methodology traditionally used to write American historical accounts. Furthermore, it is hoped that this book will help reclaim for Native Americans a position of honor in the history of nations.

1.
The American Indian in the Past

Oren R. Lyons

I am Dekanawideh and with the Five Nations confederate lords I plant the Tree of the Great Peace. I plant it in your territory Adodarhoh and the Onondaga Nation, in the territory of you who are fire keepers.

I name the tree the Tree of the Great Long Leaves. Under the shade of this Tree of the Great Peace we spread the soft, white feathery down of the globe thistle as seats for you, Adodarhoh and your cousin lords.

. . . There shall you sit and watch the council fire of the Confederacy of the Five Nations.

Roots have spread out from the Tree of the Great Peace . . . and the name of these roots is the Great White Roots of Peace. If any man of any nation outside of the Five Nations shall show a desire to obey the laws of the Great Peace . . . they may trace the roots to their source . . . and they shall be welcomed to take shelter beneath the Tree of the Long Leaves.

The smoke of the confederate council fire shall ever ascend and shall pierce the sky so that all nations may discover the central council fire of the Great Peace.

I, Dekanawideh, and the confederate lords now uproot the tallest pine tree and into the cavity thereby made we cast all weapons of war. Into the depths of the earth, down into the deep underearth currents of water flowing into unknown regions, we cast all weapons of strife. We bury them from sight forever and plant again the tree. Thus shall all Great Peace be established and hostilities shall no longer be known between the Five Nations but only peace to a united people.

Paul A. Wallace, The White Roots of Peace[1]

"It is a given that winners write the history books." So spoke Wilber E. Garrett, editor of *National Geographic* magazine in a March 1988 editorial. It is also a given that time modifies the passions of the moment, and time is the factor needed to distill the events of history, whether it be the history of the earth or the history of human life upon the earth.

The history of humankind in North and South America can be divided into two parts: the history of the aboriginal peoples of the Western Hemisphere prior to the landfall of Western man, and the history of North and South America after the voyages of Columbus. These histories can be likened to an iceberg: four-fifths of its height and seven-eighths

The Great Tree of Peace, planted by the Iroquois prophet Deganawidah to foster peace among the five founding nations of the Iroquois Confederacy, or Haudenosaunee—the Mohawk, Oneida, Cayuga, Seneca, and Onondaga. (Lithograph of painting, The Tree of the Great Peace by Oren Lyons, courtesy of the Onondaga Savings Bank.)

of its mass lie beneath the surface of the water. We can see Western occupation above the surface and visible. The aboriginal peoples' time is below the surface and invisible.

This five-hundred-year occupation by Western man contrasts with the conservative estimate of twelve thousand years of aboriginal occupation to illustrate a historical iceberg. Only one twenty-fourth of human history in North and South America occurs after the landfall of Columbus; the twenty-three twenty-fourths that is aboriginal history is largely invisible.

The point is that history is still being written in the passions of the times and being written subjectively by the "winners." This writer reflects the indigenous part of the historical iceberg. With the passage of time, the histories of the indigenous peoples of the Western Hemisphere are emerging, and recognition is being given their accomplishments: the advanced engineering and food plant development of the Incas; the Mayans' profound knowledge of astronomy and the calendar; the desert agriculture of the Anasazis and the Hopis; the technologies of arctic survival of the Inuits; the political confederations of the Lakotas and other North American native peoples; and the principles of freedom and democracy inherent in the traditions of the Haudenosaunee and other Indian nations.

The observance of the quincentenary of Christopher Columbus's arrival in the Americas is an appropriate time to discuss these matters, especially since the observance comes so closely after the bicentennial of the United States Constitution and its Bill of Rights. This is a time for assessment, reflection, and enlightenment.

Columbus believed he had reached Asia in 1492. He designated the native peoples he found "Indians," and for years the Spanish continued to believe they were in Asia. This was a mistake that may have been grounded in biblical scriptures, which made no mention of a Western Hemisphere or of the peoples and nations that existed there. These were the times of the Inquisition, and it was imprudent to challenge the infallibility of the Holy Scriptures. This posed a problem, for, if the Bible was the complete word of God to mankind, why were these continents and peoples absent from its pages?

Prehistoric is a term that has been used to describe the peoples of the Western Hemisphere prior to Columbus. The inference is that there was no human history until the white man arrived. This, of course, is not true (and is, in fact, impossible); and many historians, anthropologists, ethnologists, and archaeologists have made a rich living writing about the extraordinary civilizations of indigenous peoples in this hemisphere. Yet, numerous civilizations that were here in 1492 are positioned in Western history as though they came into existence as inert props in the story of Western expansion.

Most Americans think of American Indians in terms of the Plains Indians, and popular images often portray Indians in Plains dress, complete with the familiar feathered headdress of the Lakota people. The Lakotas are, of course, a significant presence in North America, but the popular images of Indians are a reflection of the way history is presented.

At the moment of contact and conflict peoples are spotlighted briefly and their images are frozen forever in time. The last time the spotlight was intensely focused on an Indian people in North America was during the wars on the Great Plains, and American people do not generally know what happened after that. Many Americans are surprised to learn that there are still Indians east of the Mississippi River because historians and the popular media have simply ignored the fate of peoples after the spotlight has dimmed. The scope of information that is presented to us as the relevant body of evidence we need in order to understand the world we live in is the product of the attitudes, ideas, and beliefs of the generations of peoples before us.

Historian Olive Patricia Dickason has observed that

> [t]he writing of history is a montage of attitudes and beliefs that is often predicated upon cultural perspectives that are fitted to concepts pervasive and flexible to the politics of the writers.[2]

Dickason also noted that "sometimes an idea becomes identified with a particular nation at a certain period, although it may have had quite different origins, both as to time and place."[3] Many historians have recounted their stories as a celebration of how things came to be the way they are, incorporating a powerful ideology of progress that proposes human history as a story of mankind's inexorable advance toward a more perfect society and projects all changes with few exceptions as part of this process. The tradition of historical presentation in the West has had a strong tendency to select events in a way that constructs a story supportive of this largely unspoken thesis. It is this careful selection of events that has been a major factor in the distortion by omission that characterizes much of what is considered accepted history. Although historians claim to be scientific in the sense that they are neutral in their selection and presentation of history, each generation has an obligation to reevaluate the process of selection and to interpret for itself the rules that construct a foundation for a version of reality.

Professional historians have tended to be vigorous gatekeepers. Although their experiences in research may be limited to a narrow area of investigation, they often claim a right to determine for the following generation which pieces of information are relevant and which are not. In that way they are among the principal agents of socialization in the West.

Columbus's reports of his voyages, and the growing realization that the peoples and lands therein described were previously unknown, posed a dilemma to Christian civilizations. The immediate implications of Columbus's accounts are difficult to grasp in our time. If the lands Columbus described were indeed new lands, and the new peoples were not "Indians" in the sense that the Americas were not India, the inescapable conclusion had to be that the traditional knowledge of the universe was incomplete. When a people must conclude that the sources of information upon which they evaluate reality are incomplete, two obvious choices are available. The first involves the inevitable psychological denial that the accepted sources of information are incomplete, and the second involves embarking on a journey to find the missing information.

Operating from a position of denial, European philosophers and scholars sought to prove that the Bible and the classics were complete after all and that the clues had simply been overlooked. This explains the vigor with which people tried to prove that the Americas were lands mentioned in the classical accounts of areas beyond the Pillars of Hercules, and that the American Indians were descendants of the Lost Tribes of Israel or the descendants of survivors of sunken continents. Jeffrey Goodman states that

> [t]he day Columbus set foot in the New World was the day the Western world got off on the wrong foot concerning Indian origins. Columbus, believing that the natives he met were East Asiatics, promptly and permanently dubbed them "Indians," initiating a series of misconceptions about the first Americans that lasts to this day.[4]

Until fairly recently a significant number of people in the United States were thoroughly convinced that the American Indians were descendants of the Lost Tribes of Israel, and at least one modern religious group, the Mormons, incorporated that theory into its own cosmology. Goodman believes that this tradition of inserting the origins of the American Indians into Western mythology has had a long history:

> During the twentieth century, the boldest and most imaginative combatants in the quest of fixing the origins of the Indian entered the arena: a fervent group arguing that the first Indians were survivors of the Lost Civilizations of Atlantis and/or Mu. This last theory, which at times has been the most popular of all, is particularly difficult to debate since these alleged great civilizations are supposed to have flourished on continental remnants that have since

sunk beneath the sea, the last remnant disappearing some 11,000 years ago. . . .[5]

A tension existed from the first moment the West encountered the expanding information about new lands and new peoples. That tension has abated somewhat over the centuries but, as the following writings will attest, it has not disappeared.

The eighteenth-century Enlightenment was influenced by the information flowing into Europe from distant lands and peoples. It opened the door to the modern intellectual world, and the American Indian was an important key to that development. Generally, historians have been slow to give recognition to the role played by non-Western peoples in this story.

If traditional (European/Euro-American) treatment of American Indian history and traditions is flawed, the conventional treatment of the themes of the European invasion of the Americas is similarly distorted. The accepted nineteenth-century version of North American history is that Europeans found a wild and unsettled land inhabited by primitive indigenous nomads. These nomads were then confronted by an advanced civilization that carried the seeds of modernism and that transformed the land from a veritable wasteland into a productive and progressive civilization. If American Indian or other non-Western cultures contributed to this process of modernity, their contributions were largely overlooked, understated, or denied.

Modernity is the product of the confluence of many cultures and has its origin in many places in the world. Two of these places are the Tigress and Euphrates valleys and Egypt because it is there that a major development took place which cannot be ignored. Sumerian civilization was the birthplace for new diseases previously unknown:

The Old World's civilized peoples had herds of cattle, sheep, goats, pigs, horses, and so forth. They lived with their creatures, sharing with them the same water, air, and general environment, and therefore many of the same diseases. The synergistic effect of these different species living cheek by jowl—humans, quadrupeds, fowl, and the parasites of each—produced new diseases and variants of old ones. Pox viruses oscillated back and forth between humans and cattle to produce smallpox and cowpox. Dogs, cattle and humans exchanged viruses or combined different viruses to produce three new maladies for each other: distemper, rinderpest, and measles. Humans, pigs, horses, and domesticated fowl in contact with wild birds shared and still share influenza, periodically and perpetually producing new virulent strains for each other.[6]

The history of Western civilization is not only one of empires and emperors, but also of the incubation over several millennia of a myriad of diseases that swept populations periodically. Most of these diseases were to play a major role in the expansion of Western civilization because they would infect peoples who had never come in contact with such diseases and who had therefore never had a chance to develop even the rudiments of immunity to them. Since that evolution,

> *the common individual's immune system, adjusted and tuned by heredity and experience to a particular environment, has been chronically obsolescent. One's immune system is tuned to one's part of the world, but human greed, aggression, curiosity, and technology chronically thrust one into contact with the rest of the world.[7]*

Caravans passed between the Roman Empire and China in the second century, A.D., trading goods and infections as well. Measles and smallpox probably became established in the Mediterranean at about that time, and initially had devastating effects.

In the mid-fourteenth century there were numerous areas of the world that had not been in contact with the civilizations of the Old World, including the Canary Islands, many of the islands of the Pacific, New Zealand, Australia, and others. The entire Western Hemisphere was one of these areas.

Because the peoples of the Americas were separated geographically from the peoples of Europe, Africa, and Asia, they had thus been isolated from the diseases of those continents for thousands of years. Although the Americas had developed civilizations, those civilizations did not domesticate and could not have domesticated the same animals that were an apparent part of the evolution of the epidemic diseases which had for centuries plagued Europe, Africa, and Asia. Because the peoples of the Americas had domesticated few species of birds and animals, the spiral of exchanged disease organisms did not occur in the Western Hemisphere. No catastrophic plagues awaited Europeans on America's shores.

The Crusades set the stage for a chapter in western European history that has been understated in most histories about the conquest of the Americas. These religious wars were an attempt by European civilization to colonize the Middle East. European armies achieved temporary success in those lands but were eventually repulsed by the indigenous peoples, who had a shared history and similar if not identical disease organisms. European colonization of the Holy Land was frustrated in part by malaria and other disease organisms to which Europeans had little resistance.

Activity in the East whetted European appetites for spices and trade goods not available in western Europe and thus stimulated trade. The difficulty encountered in moving armies across the Mediterranean was one of the factors which stimulated a further development of sailing technology that would later prove invaluable in the assault on the great oceans of the world. The thirst for profits found in trade combined with improved sailing technology to set into motion Spanish and Portuguese quests for sea routes to India and China.[8] The story of the Norseman Leif Ericsson and his attempt at colonizing Vinland five centuries before Columbus remains intriguing and incomplete. There are artifacts and curious archaeological finds that indicate he or his Norsemen may have penetrated as far inland as Iowa. But that part of North American history is not central to this story.

Exploration brought surprises. In 1336, Lanzarote Malocello landed on the Atlantic island that bears his name (Lanzarote Island) and announced the rediscovery of the Canary Islands. Soon other Europeans discovered Madeira Island in the Azores group, and the stage was set for the process of colonization that would change the world order.

These changes began with the colonization of the nine uninhabited mid-Atlantic islands known as the Azores. By 1439, feral sheep were known to inhabit Madeira, doubtless left ashore by sailors who sought to put the islands to some use. That year the king of Portugal issued permits for people to settle there, and ten years later people were shipping wheat and dye products from the Azores to the mainland.[9]

In 1420, Portuguese settlers arrived to colonize Porto Santo and Madeira. On Porto Santo

> Bartholemeu Perestrello, captain donatory of Porto Santo (and, incidentally, future father-in-law of Columbus), set loose on his island where the likes of such had never lived before a female rabbit and her offspring; she had given birth on the voyage from Europe. The rabbits reproduced at a villainous rate and "overspread the land, so that our men could sow nothing that was not destroyed by them." The settlers took up arms against these rivals and killed great numbers, but in the absence of local predators and disease organisms adapted to these quadrapeds, the death rate continued to lag far behind the birth rate. The humans were obliged to leave and go to Madeira. . . .[10]

Madeira was completely covered by forest. The Spanish quickly chopped and burned the forests to the ground and set about the business of developing a cash crop for the European market. The product that was to catapult Madeira into the world market and colonization into courtly popularity was sugar. Sixty to seventy thousand kilograms of sugar were shipped to the mainland in 1455. Sugar was shipped to England the following year. By the turn of the century Madeira was the sugar capital of the world, and the slave plantation era, a significant evolution in the history of the modern world, was under way.

Long before the success of Madeira, European attention had turned to the Canary Islands, occupied by an indigenous population estimated at 80,000 Gaunches. The invasion, initiated by French and Castilian forces, began in 1402 at Lanzarote and lasted until September 1496. Although they did not possess firearms or even metal weapons, the Gaunches put up a desperate and, by Spanish accounts effective, struggle for their freedom and survival. Epidemics—possibly measles, perhaps smallpox, or maybe some other of the formidable arsenal of mainland diseases to which this isolated island people had no prior immunity— swept their ranks and reduced their numbers. Epidemic was probably the major factor in their defeat. The Gaunches were not only defeated but were rendered extinct as a people. Many of their few survivors were carried as slaves to the plantations at Madeira and other islands of the Azores, where the Gaunches, as a distinct people, vanished from the face of the earth. They were the first recorded victims of the European expansion to new worlds. The Gaunches

> stood in opposition to this initial sally, like pickets deployed out in front of trenches held by Aztecs, Zapatecs, Araucanians, Iroquois, Australian Aborigines, Maori, Fijians, Hawaiians, Aleuts, and Zunis.[11]

The Spanish, as we have seen, were engaged in the process of colonization and conquest for ninety years before Columbus entered the Caribbean. To make the journey to the Americas and back, sailors needed to know more about the patterns of winds over the great oceans; and Columbus had enough information to develop a theory about how to cross and re-cross the Atlantic and made a couple of fortunate but informed guesses that produced success. He arrived, as every North American school child knows, in 1492. European intentions in the Caribbean are pretty transparent in light of the history of the Canary Islands. The Spanish arrived in the New World with a blueprint for conquest that had been mapped out over several generations, and Cortez lost little time putting the lessons learned in the Canary Islands to work.

One of the great mysteries of history is the relatively swift conquest of Mexico. How could the Spanish, who were relatively few in number, quickly overwhelm the formidable numbers and military traditions of the Indians of Mexico? Spanish armor and cannon were obvious advantages, and the mounted soldier undoubtedly dominated Indian foot warriors, but disease was the major factor in the collapse of the Aztec military. The

Aztecs repulsed the Spanish army initially but were crushed by a pox.[12] The emperor of the Incas also fell to disease, an event that demoralized his army and paved the way for the Spanish victory.

The European invasion of the Americas and the stunning conquests over the Aztecs and Incas greatly accelerated a trend in European economic expansion that had been growing for several hundred years. It was a trend stimulated by Aztecan and Incan gold:

> *The appearance of the Spanish treasure in Europe was one of the most momentous occurrences in early modern European history. From 1530 to the end of the century, in a seemingly unending flood, silver and (to a lesser extent) gold poured from the great Mexican and Peruvian mines. From 1600 on, the supply began to taper off; by 1660, it had largely ceased. In this hundred and thirty years, something like 18,000 tons of silver and 200 tons of gold had been officially recorded in the Spanish assay offices. Only a part of this precious stream remained in Spain. A goodly part of it went out to the Orient and thus made possible a great increase in the trade with the Far East. Another goodly part moved into the commercial life of western Europe generally, so that in time France, Holland, and England also profited from the Spanish discoveries.[13]*

It was not long before Spanish treasure attracted the envy of other nations, especially England. In 1570, Spain was the wealthiest and most powerful nation in the world, with an empire greater than that of Rome at its zenith. During this period English and Spanish relations deteriorated, and English privateers (the Spanish called them pirates) brazenly raided Spanish galleons and brought the treasure home. Spain was sufficiently outraged at this turn of events that in 1588 she mounted the famous Spanish Armada against England. The Armada was a disaster, in world history a defeat on the scale of that suffered by the Persians at Marathon. Before the defeat of the Armada, French and English settlement in the New World was very dangerous because such colonists were viewed by the Spanish as intruders. In fact, the first French colonists in the New World were slaughtered by the Spanish military.[14] And there is a theory that the first English settlements may have been attacked and destroyed by the Spanish. However, following the Armada it was much safer for England to establish colonies on the East Coast of North America and by 1609 the first English colonies appeared. Spanish power declined, partly as a result of failure in battle at sea but also as a result of an epidemic that raged in Spain from 1596 to 1602.[15]

The impact of this influx of wealth and increased volume of trade in England continues to be analyzed by historians. The expansion of trade that characterized these centuries and that was aggressively led by Italy and then Spain and Portugal created merchants in England as well. At least as early as the beginning of the sixteenth century, and probably earlier, English merchants began to invest their surplus profits in landed estates.

As a result, the old order of a landed aristocracy that derived wealth from the labors of peasants was replaced, sometimes dramatically, by a new order of investment-motivated landowners who believed that there were more profitable ways to use land than allowing small farmers to use a portion of it to grow food and fibers that were in large part consumed by the producers.

Whereas the ancient system, based on an exchange between lord and peasant, was centered on labor as payment for use of land, the emerging economy devalued that exchange, and increasingly the landowner sought money in place of labor in exchange for use of land. In turn, the widespread use of money made possible (some would say inevitable) the tradition of profit seeking. Services could be purchased. Michael Wood describes the new forces thus:

> Many scholars have seen the rise of the yeoman class—whose interests were strongly identified with making money from the exploitation of property—as the beginning of a different form of class system and economy in England; this was R.H. Tawney's opinion in his famous book Religion and the Rise of Capitalism, which was based on a study of the agrarian collapse in the sixteenth century and the rise of the capitalist spirit. Certainly dramatic changes took place in the countryside in the period 1450 to 1550, with thousands of villages being deserted—often deliberately depopulated—by new landowners who were buying up the old monastic and ecclesiastical estates which had been built up since the tenth century.[16]

The methods employed to remove the poor tenants from their lands forecast English behavior toward Indians in the Americas. English courts heard the pleadings of poor landholders who argued their right to continued possession of their land. The courts occasionally agreed with the aggrieved tenant; if they had not, the court system would have been so clearly an instrument of the landowners it would have had no legitimacy in the eyes of the commoners. Sir Thomas More, however, notes that these tenants could be removed by other means; sometimes "by coueyne and fraude or by violent oppression they be put besydes it, or by wrongs and injuries they be so weried that they be compelled to sell all."[17] The literature of the time affirms that these enclosures cast many small farmers into poverty. These people contributed to the growing numbers of landless poor in England, and became the subject of considerable discussion for at least three centuries. Moreover, some of these landless poor were pressed into service as indentured servants and became colonists in America. The evictions of the poor caused such hardship and resulting frustration that in 1549 England experienced a peasant revolt. Enclosure was

> a revolution of the rich against the poor. The lords and nobles were upsetting the social order, breaking down ancient law and custom, sometimes by means of violence, often by pressure and intimidation. They were literally robbing the poor of their share in the common, tearing down the houses which, by the hitherto unbreakable force of custom, the poor had long regarded as theirs and their heirs'. The fabric of society was being disrupted; desolate villages and the ruins of human dwellings testified to the fierceness with which the revolution raged, endangering the defenses of the country, wasting its towns, decimating its population, turning its overburdened soil into dust, harassing its people and turning them from decent husbandmen into a mob of beggars and thieves. Though this happened only in patches, the black spots threatened to melt into a uniform catastrophe.[18]

The pressures of enclosure on the poor in England continued to rage a generation after the first pilgrims settled at Plymouth, as witnessed by the 1649 petition by Gerrard Winstanley that reads in part:

> For though you and your Ancestors got your Propriety by murther and theft, and you keep it by the same power from us, that have an equal right to the Land with you, by the righteous Law of Creation, yet we shall have no occasion of quarreling (as you do) about that disturbing devil, called Particular Propriety: For the Earth, with all her Fruits of Corn, Cattle, and such like, was made to be a common Storehouse of Livelihood to all Mankinde, friend and foe, without exception.[19]

Englishmen had witnessed Spanish colonization in the Canary Islands and the Azores, and by 1565 they began talking about applying the idea of colonization in Ireland.[20] English investors were recruited to a plan for the settlement of Englishmen in Ulster:[21]

> The problems raised by colonization . . . involved establishing title to property and clearing the indigenous population from the lands they and their ancestors had occupied for hundreds of years.[22]

The English colonizers soon discovered things about the Irish personality they had overlooked for centuries. English propaganda arose out of Ireland that the indigenes were not Christian after all (they were, in fact, Catholic) but were pagans of a sort. Furthermore, *if [they] themselves were suffered to possess the whole country as their septs have done for many hundred of years past, they would never (to the end of the world) build houses, make townships or villages or manure or improve the land as it ought to be, therefore it stands neither with Christian policy nor conscience to suffer so good and fruitful a country to lie waste like a wilderness.*[23]

Much of the early seventeenth-century New England history of Indians, and especially the Indians' rights to the land, has roots in the struggle for land between rich and poor and the process of enclosure in England, as well as the experience of colonization in Ireland. English colonists in North America argued that the Indians were nomads and had no tradition of land ownership, although they knew in fact that the Indians of the Connecticut River did have traditions of land ownership very much like their own.[24]

Other rationalizations that succeeded in Ireland were readily transferred to the Americas, for example the fact that the Indians were not Christians;[25] and the argument that the Indians should not be allowed to keep the land because they were not making the best (i.e. English-style) use of the land was applied in New England exactly as it had been applied in Ireland. The practice of inventing rationalizations to provide legalisms for taking land and employing violence to remove people from land was an English way of doing things at least a couple of generations before the first English colonies appeared in the Americas, and that practice was to be used against North America's Indians.

The English arrived to find the area around the Connecticut River reduced in population by disease that had wiped out the Patuxet people. The English immigrants were very fortunate because the sole survivor of the Patuxet people, Squanto, had been kidnapped years before and had sailed with English sailors. He spoke English, and he taught the new immigrants what they needed to know to survive. This accomplished, Squanto suddenly caught a fever and died.[26] English ideologues of the time tended to view epidemic diseases among the Indians as the workings of divine providence: " 'Thus was God pleased to smite our enemies,' said John Mason, 'and to give us their land for an Inheritance.' "[27] Microscopic and sub-microscopic organisms obviously have no politics, but organic causes of diseases were not understood in the seventeenth century. (English ideologues of a later generation were slower to explain in terms of divine providence the fate of English soldiers in Africa, who died at a rate of fifty percent per year.)

During most of the sixteenth century, France was still an insignificant player in the race to colonize the Americas. France was mired in a series of religious conflicts, crises in leadership, and economic depressions.

One trend that emerged during this time, however, was a dramatic rise in literacy and in the popularity and availability of the printed word. Although French writers were leading the continent's literati, the Crown was struggling to unite the country under an evolving absolute monarchy while engaged in a long war with Spain and another with Italy.

During this period France suffered a series of setbacks to her colonial ambitions on the North Atlantic coast. French fishing vessels arrived there as early as 1500, plying their trade off Newfoundland. There were attempts to explore the Gulf of St. Lawrence in 1506 and 1508, and rumors of an unsuccessful colony on Sable Island in 1518.[28] Verrazano led the first official exploration in 1524, and in 1534 Jacques Cartier explored the Gulf of St. Lawrence, reaching the La Chine rapids and present-day Montreal the next year. He founded a colony at Stodacona (Quebec) in 1541, but the colonists suffered famine that winter, and the site was abandoned the following summer. No French colony was established in Acadia for the next fifty years.

Although a French expedition under Marquis de la Roche landed two shiploads of colonists on Sable Island in 1598, the effort failed, and five years later the survivors were rescued; several other attempts were made but were unsuccessful. Then in 1608, Champlain succeeded in establishing a trading settlement at Quebec, and the following year he accompanied a war party of Hurons and Algonquins to the Lake of the Mohawks (now called Lake Champlain). There Champlain and his Indian allies attacked a party of Mohawks, winning the field but alienating the Iroquois, who, with the availability of firearms, would prove to be the best organized and most militarily successful Indians in the Northeast woodlands. The French colonists, more than colonists from other major countries, joined the Indians on the Indians' terms. Voyageurs left their trading settlements and set out for Indian country, where they learned Indian languages and took Indian wives. French Jesuits came to the continent to find and convert the Indians. Unlike the Spanish priests, who were mainly concerned with conversion after the Indians had been brutally subdued, or the English clergy, who during most of the seventeenth century made few concentrated attempts to proselytize the Indians, the Jesuits were determined in their mission. They risked life and limb (and often lost both) in their efforts to spread the word of God, and in the process they left invaluable records of their experiences.

In 1613, the Jesuits began publishing their *Jesuit Relations*, which were immensely popular in France; and profits from the books helped promote the work of the Jesuit order, spurring the priests on to keep sending reports. Some Jesuits saw nothing positive about the cultures and peoples they encountered, while others were captivated by the innocence and integrity of the Indians. Some of the Jesuit writings are surprisingly humble and candid. Unlike many of the sixteenth-century Spanish writers on Indian affairs who set off a philosophical revolution about man and nature, the Jesuits brought the stories about adventures with Indians to France in great detail and complexity. Some Jesuit writers elaborated on the theme of the "noble savage," and pointed to numerous advantages of Indian life, including examples of the freedom of the individual. In general, the Jesuit writings helped to inform a growing intellectual movement in France that would build upon the ideals of egalitarianism and the dignity of the individual.

Other French writers also advanced these ideals with their accounts of the Indians. One of these was the Baron de Lahontan, whose *New Voyages to North America* appeared in 1693 while France was in the grip of an economic depression. His work appeared in English in 1703 and was, for decades, one of the important works on North America. Lahontan helped promote a positive view of the "savage":

> in alleging I am a Savage myself, and that that makes me speak so favourably of my Fellow-Savages. These Observators do me a great deal of Honour, as long as they do not explain themselves, so as to make me directly of the same Character with that thinking: For in saying that I am of the same temper with the Savages, they give me without design, the Character of the honestest Man in the World.[29]

Lahontan asserted that the respect for and rights of the individual were ideas learned from the Indians. In Europe the French intelligentsia had been deeply affected by generations of French writers in the Americas, and on the American frontier the English had had five generations of firsthand experience with the Indians.

We know surprisingly little about what North America looked like when the first Europeans stepped ashore. Europeans brought more than language and customs with them. They brought a dazzling array of crops, animals, pests, viruses, microbes, weeds, and technologies, all of which transformed the Americas dramatically. The result of that on-slaught, as we do know, was that many Indian peoples disappeared, some at the hands of the invaders but many victims of the new diseases. It is very probable that prior to 1492 North America contained much larger populations of Indians than has previously been thought. Many areas were completely depopulated before Europeans encountered them—by diseases that spread from group to group among the Indians faster than the invaders themselves.[30]

The imported plants, weeds, plant diseases, bugs, feral animals, and other European biotica were certainly disseminated beyond the boundaries of organized colonial society. It is well known, but not very well emphasized, that significant numbers of European colonists also left the confines of those societies. Europeans escaped into the forest and "went Indian," adopting the dress, customs, and language of their new nations. While certain chilling depictions were drawn of North America's natives, something quite remarkable was being experienced by some of the colonists on the land:

> *One fact disturbed: whites would run off to join Indian tribes, or would be captured in battle and brought up among the Indians, and when this happened the whites, given a chance to leave, chose to stay in the Indian culture. Indians, having the choice, almost never decided to join the whites.*[31]

This aspect of American history has received less emphasis than it deserves. Time and again colonists found their way into Indian societies. Sometimes they fled indentured servitude and were taken in by Indians, sometimes they were captured in raids, and sometimes they were rescued by Indians from the forest. However they came into the Indian country, many soon adapted, adopting new languages, dress, and names. Many of these people were quite young, a fact that has been used to explain the phenomenon that very few of them, when offered the opportunity to return to colonial society, opted to leave their newfound friends and relatives, the Indians. They had, in fact, "voted with their feet." It is equally interesting that very few Indians, once captured by whites and given an opportunity to return to their people, chose to stay with the whites. Almost all Indian captives of the colonial period chose to return to the Indians. The most logical explanation for this phenomenon is that, given the choice of two worlds, people turned their backs on the hierarchical society of colonial America to join the egalitarian and community spirited Indians.

Stories about these people have rarely been included in the "accepted" histories,[32] and we are generally left with a distorted picture of cultural isolation between Indians and whites. On the eve of the American Revolution, ninety percent of English colonials lived in rural areas. To survive, the frontiersmen were forced to dress like Indians in buckskins and coonskin hats, eat Indian foods, and hunt like the Indians. There is ample evidence that many traveled among the Indians and took Indian wives. Although the literature is sparse about their lives and the roles they played, we know that some of these people came to know more about Indian customs and organizations than modern anthropologists know. Liberated by distance from both England and the governments of the colonies, frontiersmen embraced a love of liberty and equality and a skepticism toward authority that have become an American tradition. A few generations later de Tocqueville observed:

*Amongst the novel objects that attracted my attention during my
stay in the United States, nothing struck me more forceably than
the general equality among the people . . . it creates opinions, gives
birth to new sentiments, founds novel customs, and modifies whatever
it does not produce. . . . I perceived that this equality of condition
is the fundamental fact from which all others seem to be derived
and the central point at which all my observations constantly terminated.*[33]

The American colonists had absorbed some of this spirit on the eve
of the revolution. It was, as de Tocqueville observes, their expectation
of equality that made them a distinctive people. This expectation of
equality helps to explain why so many volunteers were recruited into a
rebellion against the Crown over taxes many of them did not even pay.
Boston may have been incensed over public policy and taxation, but it
was the rhetoric of freedom that found a sympathetic ear among the
broad spectrum of people who were called upon to shoulder arms against
the king.

An ideology as complex as the Western democratic tradition was
predictably influenced by many historical factors. American scholars
have generally credited the cultures of Greece, Rome, France, and
England with providing the ideological basis for the development of the
democratic tradition, and the width of the Atlantic Ocean for giving it
room to grow. It is widely accepted in contemporary American thought
that the Magna Carta was a significant document in this development,
and there is no question that the Anglo-American intelligentsia of the
eighteenth century cultivated an interest in the classics. Some of the
Protestant traditions also found a democratic tradition in the story of
the New Testament, and there were democratic tendencies forming on
Europe's mainland. All of these factors undoubtedly influenced events
in North America in 1775. Although this tradition of discovering
European roots for all of the developments that created the modern
world continues to be strong in the twentieth century, some modern
historians are crediting the Indians of the Americas with critical contributions to world history and modernity.

Indian gold and silver, as mentioned, formed the monetary basis for
the modern world economy, but the most lasting and dramatic source
of wealth lay in the plant products developed in the Americas by the
Indians. When the Old World encountered the Indian world, important
exchanges took place which created the modern world. Old World technologies encountered New World products to create the foundation of
the industrial revolution. One of those products was probably the potato.
The potato was grown extensively in South America, especially among

the people known to the English-speaking world as the Incas. It was a crop that produced more calories per acre than any grain, was much more resistant to blight, birds, insects, and weather than were grains, and required considerably less labor to produce. In Europe potatoes formed the foundation of a food culture that freed peasants from subsistence chores to do industrial labor. In addition to freeing the peasants, the potato also freed some water-driven grain mills for other duties.

The chore for which water power was destined involved another crop from the Americas—cotton. It was the longer strand cotton that made mechanized spinning of cotton possible. Further, machine-spun cotton brought the proliferation of cotton mills, creating in Europe an industry that would form the basis for machine-driven production.

Indian agricultural products are generally acknowledged, but Indian agricultural technology is seldom considered, understood, or reported in conventional histories. When the Europeans arrived in America, they found many foodstuffs that would change the complexion of the world. They took these foodstuffs from the hands of Indians who had cultivated and transformed them over centuries into a dazzling variety of foods adapted to diverse conditions of soil and weather.

The significance of this exchange should not be underestimated. About sixty percent of all the food grown in the world today was developed by American Indians. The two food plants that had the most direct impact on European (and indeed world) population growth were maize and potatoes, but there are many others that also had considerable impact, such as peanuts, cassava, peppers, squash, beans, and sunflowers.

The colonization of the Americas and the engagement with her peoples also opened an intellectual floodgate that stimulated dramatic changes in the way Europeans viewed the world. The Old World ontology was effectively swept away by these events. New ideas about human potential poured into Europe and Anglo-America from previously unheard of peoples and places.

European and Euro-American historians usually describe American history as a story of Europeans and Anglo-Americans evolving to a democratic tradition from inspirations that had exclusively European roots. Missing from their accounts is the story of how egalitarian American Indian societies stimulated the thinking of European philosophers of the Enlightenment, the intellectual movement that provided American colonists with some of the foundations for their rebellion against the English monarchy.

A significant northeastern North American Indian nation which had remained relatively unacculturated with its political institutions generally intact and its philosophies of governance largely undisturbed was the Haudenosaunee—known first to the English as the Five Nations and, after the Tuscarora Nation joined the Confederacy around 1721, as the Six Nations or Iroquois Confederacy. The Americans, as the colonists were now known, had engaged in numerous councils with the Haudenosaunee over a period of several generations, and many American statesmen and politicians were familiar with Haudenosaunee oratory and ideas about confederation. Significant numbers of Americans, including no less than George Washington, had marched into battle beside Seneca and Onondaga fighters during England's struggles with France, and it is impossible to believe that they did not know at least some Indian customs and ideas about political organization.

Colonial history of the sixteenth century is replete with the dialogue of countless meetings between the colonies and representatives of the Haudenosaunee and other Indian nations. These meetings were conducted in the style of Indian nations, and often strings and belts of wampum were exchanged to validate statements, promises, and agreements. In the spring of 1776, John Hancock, president of the Continental Congress, ordered a large wampum belt to be made and carried by their delegate, George Morgan, to the peace meeting at Fort Pitt in July, to illustrate the importance of peace between the colonies and the nations of the Great Lakes.[34]

It is known that American colonists had enough contact with Indians to be acquainted with most of the basic facts about Indian governments. They could not, and did not, fail to notice that the Indians maintained a fairly stable and violence-free society even though they had no police or state organs of coercion. In fact, freedom from coercion was one of the characteristics of Iroquois society that most impressed the European mind. It affirmed a growing belief among Americans that coercion was not, as it had been presented to them, a necessary service performed by the state to protect people, but instead was a tool used by the state to control people.

It was also noted that Indians generally (and the Haudenosaunee were no exception) enjoyed free speech. Indeed, Indian decision-making processes at the local level required the free input of information and advice for these processes to work at all. Any proposal brought to the Haudenosaunee was carried to each of the nations, where it was discussed in either clan or general meetings; the sentiments of the nation were then carried by the principal chiefs to the confederate council, known as the Grand Council. The ancient custom that established the council also delegated to the council the power to act in the interest of all the confederated nations, and the chiefs had the authority to negotiate details of a proposed agreement according to their own judgment and in line with political reality.

Haudenosaunee political organization demonstrated that a form of participatory democracy was possible on a fairly large geographic scale.

Among the Haudenosaunee the privileges of individuals or groups of viduals to make economic decisions which would affect the whole subject, in theory, to intervention and rejection by the governing l __y. Charles Beard, a historian writing in the early to mid-twentieth century, noted that a significant number of the Founding Fathers were land speculators. Consequently, they were, quite naturally, not motivated to create a political system that might be contradictory to their private interest. Thus, the United States Constitution is a compromise. It seeks to take the applicable principles of the visible Indian democracy and to construct around those principles practices that would preserve private property interest.

It is interesting to note that Americans such as Benjamin Franklin and John Rutledge were what would be called in a later time "Indian buffs." However, some of the papers that might have helped clarify the extent to which some of these individuals were influenced by their experiences with the Indians in general and the Haudenosaunee in particular are lost to us. A manuscript on Indian languages by Thomas Jefferson was lost in a robbery; and John Rutledge's papers were destroyed in a fire. It is possible that more evidence will surface in the future, but enough exists to demonstrate that people who framed the United States Constitution came into contact with Indians who had a tradition of democratic thought at the exact moment events made such thought popular. Motive and opportunity were both present to enable some of those thoughts to be transferred from the Indians to the Americans.

The Haudenosaunee political organization did not originate from a struggle for democratic rights. There is no evidence in the oral tradition that an oppressive oligarchy or dictatorship had arisen in their country, and the Iroquois tradition of government is an effort to solve problems quite different from those facing the American colonists in 1775. The unifying ideology the Haudenosaunee embraced was that peace was an attainable objective.[35] Historians will note that they sometimes went to war, even wars of conquest, in ways that contradict that ideology, and that at moments groups broke away from the Confederacy to follow their own inclinations. It is not unusual that cultures develop principles and ideas which they follow imperfectly or, at times, not at all.

The *Gayaneshakgowa*, the Iroquois Great Law of Peace, is nevertheless important in human history. It is the earliest surviving governmental tradition in the world that we know of based on the principle of peace; it was a system that provided for peaceful succession of leadership; it served as a kind of early United Nations; and it installed in government the idea of accountability to future life and responsibility to the seventh generation to come. All these ideas were prevalent among the Haudenosaunee before the arrival of the white man, according to the oral history of the elders of that society.[36]

This oral history relates that the League was organized prior to the landfall of the white man. It was the inspiration of a prophet the Iroquois of today call The Peacemaker. The Peacemaker and a principal disciple, Hayanwatah, known to some as Hiawatha, set about the work of establishing a union of peace under principles the Haudenosaunee understand to be the natural laws of the universe.

These people lived at a time of dark despair and chaos. Their story recounts a period when humans had cast aside the rules of coexistence, a period when bloodlust and vengeance overshadowed the goodness in human beings. It was a time of what we today would call civil war, when brothers hunted brothers, when head-hunting was common, and when men and women sought vengeance for wrongs, real and imagined.

The Peacemaker, we are told, was born among the Huron people and arrived first in the land of the Ganienkehaka, the People of Flint, known to the English as the Mohawks. Legend relates that he crossed Lake Ontario in a stone canoe and, upon landing, asked the first person he met for directions to the fiercest human being in that land. When he found that man, a cannibal, he set about the business of reasoning with him.

There are many stories about the career of The Peacemaker, but the central story recounts his relentless efforts to persuade men who had been dedicated to a life of revenge and blood feuds to abandon that path and to bring peace to the land. He began by arguing that the Maker of Life (or Great Creator) could not have intended that humans would kill one another and that violence, especially organized violence, must be contradictory to the purposes of life. Further, The Peacemaker said that humans have the gift of intelligence and that all humans ultimately desire that their people should live and prosper in peace and safety.

The true purpose of human political organization, The Peacemaker argued, must be to oppose violence. This, he said, can be accomplished when men of healthy minds and bodies unite to create a just world in which human abuse is abolished forever, and in which war is abandoned as a way of settling disputes. Force, he asserted, is justified only when it is necessary to halt aggression and to create the conditions we might call a truce that could be used to create a road to peace.

In addition, The Peacemaker proposed that a council be formed to provide a forum in which violence would henceforth be replaced with thinking, and disputes would be settled with words. He believed that the ultimate extension of the glorification of warfare would be the destruction of all the people of the earth, and that the only hope for mankind was the application of clear thinking to situations resulting from rage and warfare.

The first encounter The Peacemaker had with a woman was at the lodge of Jakohnsaseh, of the Erie or Cat Nation. She welcomed him to her

Tadodaho, spiritual leader of the Great Council of the Haudenosaunee, past and present. Left: The Council of Todadaho at the Time the League Was Formed, with Tadodaho seated at left (painting by Ernest Smith, 1936, courtesy of the Rochester Museum and Science Center); right: Chief Leon Shenandoah, current Tadodaho, spiritual and temporal leader of the Haudenosaunee (photograph by Marcia Keegan).

lodge and said that all men were welcome there to rest and refresh themselves. She said that this was a place of neutrality, and men who were enemies could eat together here in peace, their weapons of war outside the lodge. The great Peacemaker explained his mission and his message of peace, and she was the first to accept it. Later on she played a very important role in the development of the Great League of Peace.

The Peacemaker worked first among the Mohawks. During this time he was united with Hayanwatah, an Onondaga man respected for his gifts of oratory and leadership. The Mohawks honored Hayanwatah by making him a member of their nation and one of their nine leaders. When the Mohawks were organized according to The Peacemaker's principles, Hayanwatah and The Peacemaker journeyed to the Oneidas, a sister nation to the west, where they continued their mission. The Oneidas also agreed to the principles these men taught, and The Peacemaker helped to identify nine leaders among them. And then Hayanwatah and The Peacemaker journeyed to the next westward nation, to the Onondagas.

The most feared and respected of the Onondagas was Tadodaho, who was reputed to be a fierce warrior and, according to some, a sorcerer. Most of the Onondagas agreed to the proposal by The Peacemaker and Hayanwatah, but Tadodaho arrogantly refused to accept their ideas, preferring to remain a power unto himself. The Peacemaker and Hayanwatah were discouraged at his rejection but continued their mission among the people we know today as the Cayugas. Eventually, the mission to the Cayugas was successful, and the two journeyed to the most powerful of the nations of the Finger Lakes, the People of the Great Hill, known to the English as the Senecas. At first they also encountered difficulties among the Senecas but were eventually able to convince their leaders to join their plan.

Now, of the five nations who had been recruited, only Tadodaho and his followers remained uncommitted. Repeated efforts to convince Tadodaho to join their effort failed. Finally, in despair, they went back to the Seneca country, where they encountered Jakohnsaseh again. She became a counselor to the process of unity, presenting a plan to The Peacemaker and Hayanwatah to overcome the resistance of the powerful Tadodaho. For her role in advancing the cause of The Peacemaker, she is known in history as the Peace Queen or, more appropriately, the Mother of Nations.

Their offer to Tadodaho was uncomplicated. They gathered a huge force of fighters from the enlisted nations and organized a flotilla of canoes at the north end of Onondaga Lake. From there they sent messages to Tadodaho asking for a meeting. Tadodaho kindled a council fire and received them. They arrived at the head of the flotilla and commenced negotiations, telling Tadodaho that he could become the spiritual leader of the Great Council if he chose to embrace the law that would bind the members of the new confederation together. The alternative was that Tadodaho would be a major obstacle to the foundation of the Great Peace and that, as an obstacle to peace, he would be consigned to oblivion. It was, to use a phrase popular in another era, an offer he could not refuse. Finally, Tadodaho agreed to their proposal but not because of mere coercion. In the imagery of the day The Peacemaker and Hayanwatah "combed the snakes from Tadodaho's hair," an expression that means he was converted to their way of thinking and embraced wholeheartedly the Great Law of Peace.

The Peacemaker's vision extended to all the peoples of the earth then known to him. He erected a symbolic tree that has come to be called the Great Tree of Peace. This tree was intended to symbolize the law and would be visible from a great distance to all nations. Under the great long leaves of this tree (the Great Law of Peace) people would find protection from arbitrary violence. The Great Law of Peace was to be international in character. If a people were invaded, the nations were to gather together to provide a show of force to dissuade the invader and to urge that the dispute be taken to a council where the injuries that had caused the dispute could be discussed and an amicable settlement reached. If the invader continued his aggression, war would ensue but only until the aggressor agreed to peace; a truce would then be automatic. Further, there would be no wars of conquest. If the aggressor continued to pursue violence as a means of conquest, the war would continue until the aggressor was vanquished or exhausted.

Even following the unconditional conquest of an invader, the conquered were to enjoy rights. There would be no collection of spoils from those who were conquered. There would be no requirement that a conquered people adopt the religion of their conquerors. The aggressors would be required to disarm, but otherwise they would be left in control of their country, and the dispute would be taken to the Great Council, where it would be resolved.

The five founding nations—Mohawk, Oneida, Cayuga, Seneca, and Onondaga—were to find strength in unity, and The Peacemaker symbolized this unity with arrows. First he held forth a single arrow and demonstrated how easily it was broken. Then he held forth five arrows bound tightly together. These, he demonstrated, could not be broken. This is the origin in Haudenosaunee political history of the symbol of the bundle of arrows. The Peacemaker also described a symbolic eagle that was to circle high above the Great Tree. This eagle was to use its keen eyesight to spot trouble from afar and to warn the Confederacy of any developing conflict.

In addition, The Peacemaker spoke of four pure roots which spread from the Great Tree in the four cardinal directions. These White Roots of Peace were to extend to all the peoples of the earth, offering to them a path to the Great Tree, to the law that would provide a way to settle disputes. Then the leaders of the clans (which were also extended families, but in the structure of the Confederacy operated as political units) gathered beneath the tree to counsel for peace, harmony, and the survival of humanity. The Peacemaker called these political leaders Hoyane, which loosely translated means, He-Does-Good; and the English called them sachems or chiefs. There were, and still are, fifty of them.

The political philosophy of The Peacemaker created the foundation for the unity of the Five Nations. This sense of unity went far beyond the idea that a confederation could create safety in numbers. In addition, The Peacemaker argued that human emotions such as rage and grief, although natural, confuse peoples' ability to think clearly. Consequently, according to this tradition, Hayanwatah assembled strings of fresh water snail shells for the purpose of consoling people who had suffered a loss in death, and a ceremony of condolence was conducted to help such people recover their ability to think clearly and to make the clan (the political unit) whole again. This ceremony of condolence soon became a national ceremony performed when a dead leader was to be replaced.

The Peacemaker unified the nations of the Confederacy into one nation under an ideology that was complex but whose symbols were easy to grasp. The longhouse, which had been a dwelling in which extended families resided, became the symbol of a nation: the sky was compared to its roof; the earth was like its floor; and the fires burning inside were like the nations stretching east to west. The people of a nation hold fast to the idea of a unified nation, and The Peacemaker introduced ideas to promote that sense of unity, admonishing the people of the clans across the nations that they are all brothers and sisters, and creating a folk law that the people of a certain clan of the Mohawks could not marry the people of the same clan of the Onondagas or any of the nations because brothers and sisters do not marry. These were powerful ideas which created customs that survive to this day.

This new nation met at Onondaga, where the Great Tree was planted and the fifty chiefs met in council. There, The Peacemaker taught that peace is not simply the absence of violence but can only exist through the vigorous efforts of clear-thinking people to eradicate injustice in the world. In order to promote peace, the practice of attacking hunters who had strayed into the territories claimed by one of the member nations of the Haudenosaunee was, in effect, outlawed by the Great Law of Peace, which declared that the deer belonged to the Creator, not to political units. Under the terms of the ideology of this tradition, those who entered

Haudenosaunee territory were required only to observe the rules of the Great Law of Peace.

In summary, The Peacemaker facilitated what can be described as a revolution. He caused the power of the warrior leaders to be subordinated to the workings of a council of elders whose purpose was to promote peace within the framework of a true confederacy. At the same time, the member nations were encouraged to continue practicing their local laws and customs as before. Some of these laws—such as the laws involving payment for crimes by the perpetrator or his/her clan to the victims or the victim's clan—were similar to some European practices in an earlier time. Other practices, much encouraged by the Great Law of Peace, involved democratic traditions that already existed among the nations, and that were similar to governmental traditions of many northeastern Indian nations. Each of the communities of the Haudenosaunee controlled its internal affairs independently of the Confederacy Council, while the Confederacy Council was restricted to controlling affairs of a national or international character.

Among the Haudenosaunee participatory democracy meant that on some level every individual had a right to voice an opinion and to agree or disagree on actions to be taken. Every effort was made by the local chiefs (who were often not sachem or Confederacy chiefs) to maintain harmony or at least minimize internal hostility. Because the Confederacy was organized to meet external threats and not as an organ of internal control, it had no organs of repression. In fact, the Confederacy Council had no coercive power whatsoever over its people. There was no permanent army, no police force, no insane asylums, and no jails. This meant that communities were free to disagree with the decisions of the Confederacy Council, especially on trade issues. For example, some of the western Seneca villages in historic times continued to trade with France after the Confederacy Council had made a trade agreement with England. Under this democratic system, they were free to do so.

Some historians have argued that the Confederacy ceased to exist following the American Revolution. Although the Confederacy Council stood neutral during the war, men from two of the Six Nations, the Oneida and Tuscarora, fought on the side of the Americans. Some of the men of the other nations had supported the British. As a result of this time of turmoil, there was a period of a few years in which the Confederacy Council did not meet. However, when they did meet, they agreed to adopt the principles of the Great Law of Peace once again. Although this was indeed a dark hour in Haudenosaunee history, people who argue that the Confederacy ceased to exist fail to understand the noncoercive nature of the Confederacy vis-a-vis its members and the fact that disruption is not the equivalent of cessation. (No one, for example, seems to seriously argue that the United States ceased to exist during or because of the Civil War.)

The earliest treaties or agreements with Europeans have been handed down in oral traditions and memorialized with a wampum belt known as the Gaswentah or Two-Row Wampum. Of special significance for an understanding of the Haudenosaunee principles of friendship and peace in connection with early white colonists is the oral tradition of the earliest treaties. In essence, these treaties, which the Haudenosaunee associate with the principle of the Silver Covenant Chain, extended to the Europeans the Haudenosaunee principle of respect for the laws and customs of different cultures. The Silver Covenant Chain is a promise that the Haudenosaunee will not interfere in the internal affairs of the European people, and reciprocally that Europeans will not interfere in Haudenosaunee internal affairs. The modern American idea of states' rights is a correlative to this principle.

Haudenosaunee oral tradition contains the following version of the Silver Covenant Chain:

> The Indian said, "Now that we have agreed, we should hold our hands together and we should agree to have something that will represent this agreement." The white man said, "that is true, we should have something that will represent this agreement. I suggest we use an iron kettle to bind our agreement and that we put the kettle in the ground for safe keeping."
>
> The chiefs had a council on the subject and they decided that the iron kettle will not do because iron will rust if it is put underground. They also did not approve of a kettle. They thought it would be better if they had a pipe and a chain to represent the peace and friendship between them. They thought of having the pipe and chain made of gold, but gold tarnishes, and they did not want anything that would tarnish. They decided the pipe and chain should be made of white gold.
>
> This will not tarnish, nor will it rust. The Mohawk interpreter understood what they meant and turned to the white man and told the white man what the chiefs had said.
>
> "We will use the white gold for the pipe and chain," the Indian said. "This will not rust when put underground. In future days to come we will sit together and renew our agreement, and if there is any dust on the chain we will polish it anew.
>
> "Now the links on the chain will represent certain things. The first link will mean friendship. The second link will mean peace. The third link will mean that it will always be the same between us."

That is how it was agreed upon by the two parties at that time. The chiefs then explained to the white man, through the interpreter, how they would abide by their agreement.

"Our Creator has made rivers," they said, "lakes, and big waters. Our brother the white man has made a big boat to travel on these waters. The Indian has also made boats to travel on these waters. The two parties will each put their boats parallel to each other. The white man's boat will be on the left, and the Indians' boat will be on the right. Each party will put his laws and religion into his boat. We have different laws and religion and from this time on and forever they will be separated. The white man's boat will carry his laws and religion, and the Indians' boat will carry Indian laws and religion."

The white man agreed and said, "To travel on these waters I use the sails to move me about." He then asked the Indian about the Indian boat.

The Indian said, "My boat is made of Gaswentah [literally the river, figuratively the River of Life], which is very fast and will last as long as the world will last."

The white man said, "I will now ask you what will happen if your people like my boat and get into it."

The Indian replied, "If ever anyone of my people will step into your boat and will like your religion and your laws, that person will never be able to come back into my boat. In the future there may be a person who will have their feet in both boats. This person we will call Two Minded [a person with two minds who can't make up their mind which is right]. I believe in the future your people will get into my boat, but they will only be in the boat to see if it is true and how strong my boat is. (Emphasis added.)

"I believe in the future days to come your people and my people will have feet in each vessel. There is a day coming when a strong wind will blow, and the water will move and cause our boats to separate further and will cause the people who have their foot in each boat to fall into the water between the two boats. The currents of the water will take them away, and there is not a person born this side of the sky that can bring them back. They will be lost forever. That is what is going to happen in the future days to come."

The white man replied, "Now that we have agreed, what shall we do that will bind us to our agreement?"

The Indian answered, "We shall hold hands, and we will go by what our Creator has made. First, he has put the sun in the sky. We will hold our hands together as long as the sun shines. Second, our Creator has planted grass, and we will hold our hands as long as the grass grows. Third, our Creator has planted shrubs and trees, and he has made the rivers to travel downstream. We will hold our hands together as long as the rivers go downstream. Fourth, we do not know how long the earth will last, so we will hold our hands together and keep our agreement as long as the earth will last.

"We have now finished our agreement on one thing," the Indian continued. "In the future days to come we will be meeting to settle on some issue, and you will know me by the way I dress, and I will know you by the way you dress."

The white man stated he will write the agreement on paper so he will have something to remind him and so that our future families will know what we have agreed upon.

The Indian responded, "It is good what you think we should do. The Creator has also given us a way and that is the wampum, so I will use the wampum. In the future days to come we will be meeting to renew our agreement or on any issue."

The white man said, "It will be up to you when we polish the chain again."[37]

The ideas and principles expressed in the Silver Covenant Chain and other traditions of the Haudenosaunee have been central to our relations with other nations and states, whether Indian, European, or American. In these traditions, there is a recognition that peoples are distinct from each other. However, since the beginning of our memory this distinctiveness has been seen as a foundation for mutual respect; and we have therefore always honored the fundamental right of peoples and their societies to be different. This is a profoundly important principle, and one which, even in the twentieth century, humans continue to struggle to realize.

2.
Indians and Democracy: No One Ever Told Us

John C. Mohawk

If I am right in urging the overthrow of the Aryan Model and its re-
placement by the Revised Ancient one, it will be necessary not only
to rethink the fundamental bases of "Western Civilization" but also
to recognize the penetration of racism and "continental chauvinism"
into all our historiography, or philosophy of writing history. . . .

Martin Bernal, Black Athena[1]

The earliest depictions of America by European and American artists are of a dark-skinned, full-bodied woman wearing a feathered headdress and a skirt of feathers or tobacco leaves; she is a symbol of fecundity. Over the years the image changes. She becomes somewhat more lithe, and lighter in complexion. Around the beginning of the nineteenth century, America takes on increasingly European features. Later during that century she becomes an idealized classical Greek in features as well as dress. During this time the idealized image of America was transformed from an Indian woman to a Greek goddess.

Art often reveals the transformation of images over the centuries. The transformation of the image of America from a stylized Indian woman to a Greek goddess parallels an evolution in thinking that took place over a period of three centuries. This chapter reviews the effects of this transformation on the presentation of history over five centuries, focusing especially on how non-Western peoples are represented.

The American Indian was idealized and reviled at various moments in history by historians, novelists, and artists. During the sixteenth and seventeenth centuries the Indian was sometimes seen abstractly by Europeans as a benevolent human being and sometimes as an innocent or wise child of nature, even while most also believed both the Indian and his culture to be expendable, even inevitably and tragically doomed.

Historians have been powerfully influenced by the ideas and attitudes the West has constructed to explain who the Indian was/is in relation to the European. Most of the history has been created to tell a story, not of the Indian, but of the European; and this history informs us more about these European attitudes and ideas than it does about the reality of the Indian.

The earliest European arrivals were, not surprisingly, fascinated with the world they found. They wrote glowing and often fanciful accounts of the peoples and places they encountered. Throughout this period the histories invariably glorified the European, and within a short time the glorification of the European required the denigration of a vastly complex panorama of cultures all lumped, for the purpose of convenience, under the rubric "Indian." Although the Americas were (and continue to be) home to a vast number of distinct cultures and peoples, an attempt to create a universal personality for the Indian was practically a requirement of early histories.

The other chapters in this book offer ample evidence to support an argument that American Indians exerted significant influence on the development of modern American culture. The great body of such evidence has been in existence and available for a long time. This fact raises a significant question: How could such information exist for so many years with so few people aware of it? Why are historians, anthropologists, and constitutional scholars in the late twentieth century unaware of these influences and unwilling to accept them?

Clues may be found in the story of evolving ideologies of the West. The West, in this definition, embraces the cultures of western Europe, defined loosely in the late first millennium as Latin Christendom. In the mid-eleventh century these cultures experienced a struggle for power when the heads of the Roman Catholic church declared spiritual authority over the secular emperors and proceeded to excommunicate one of them. This movement (which historian Harold Berman has called the Papal Revolution) gave birth to the Crusades and revitalized a tendency in the West to construct an identity for itself based on an idealized continuity with the cultures of the ancient world, especially those of Greece and Rome. But this tendency represented more than simply maintaining historical continuity:

> [A]s a historical culture, a civilization, the West is to be distinguished not only from the East but also from "pre-Western" cultures to which it "returned" in various periods of "renaissance." Such returns and revivals are characteristic of the West. They are not to be confused with the models on which they drew for inspiration. "Israel," "Greece," and "Rome" became spiritual ancestors of the West primarily by a process of adoption: the West adopted them as ancestors. . . . The West, from this perspective, is not Greece and Rome and Israel but the peoples of Western Europe turning to the Greek and Roman and Hebrew texts for inspiration and transforming those texts in ways that would have astonished their authors.[2]

This ideology arose as a proposed "renaissance," as part of a strategy that united Europe under the Roman Catholic church. Prior to the late eleventh century, western Europe viewed itself as a citadel of Christianity under attack from all sides.[3] Pope Gregory VII changed that when he sought to bring the rulers of Europe under the authority of the church by deposing Emperor Henri IV.[4] Gregory VII sought to transform Europe from a disunified collection of rural principalities into a unified political and military force able to organize a crusade to defend Christianity in the East. Although Gregory VII was unable to generate sufficient support for this plan, by 1095

> his successor and devoted follower, Pope Urban II, succeed[ed] in launching the First Crusade. One may say, then, that it took a long time—over twenty years—to accomplish this change, which literally turned Europe around and united it in a collective military and missionary expedition to the East.[5]

Two aspects to the story of the Crusades are of interest here. First, the Crusades united Europe for the purpose of conducting wars against non-European peoples. The papal wars provided Europe with an identity as organizers of armies of a Christian God with a mandate as righteous aggressors in foreign lands:

> These first crusades were the foreign wars of the Papal Revolution. They not only increased the power and authority of the papacy but also opened a new axis eastward to the outside world and turned the Mediterranean Sea from a natural defensive barrier against invasion from without into a route for Western Europe's own military and commercial expansion.[6]

Second, the story of the Crusades illustrates a trend in ideological development that came to characterize the West:

> It is a hallmark of the great revolutions of Western history, starting with the Papal Revolution, that they clothe their vision of the radically new in the garments of a remote past, whether those of ancient legal authorities (as in the case of the Papal Revolution), or of an ancient religious text, the Bible (as in the case of the German Reformation), or of an ancient civilization, classical Greece (as in the case of the French Revolution), or of a prehistoric classless society (as in the case of the Russian Revolution). In all of these great upheavals the idea of a restoration—a return, and in that sense a revolution—was connected with a dynamic concept of the future.[7]

Berman identifies this trend to extremely creative (and sometimes fanciful) revitalizations of ancient and remote civilizations and cultures as characteristic of revolutions in the West. Certainly revitalizations of this nature are an appealing device to facilitate dramatic change, but such ideas can be used outside a framework of the usual definition of revolution. During the Crusades the papacy used the images of ancient Israel, Rome, and Greece to create a common identity for Christian Europe that facilitated military invasions of Palestine.

By the late fifteenth century, the power of the papacy to dictate to the monarchs of Europe had declined, but the identity of the European as a distinct entity existed even before the term "European" came into common usage to denote a specific cluster of peoples. One might even argue that the Crusades were essential in developing a kind of community, a sort of proto-nationalism, among Europeans and that thereafter wars among Europeans were, in some sense, civil wars. The Christian civilization of the fifteenth and sixteenth centuries that conquered the Americas was characterized by an ideology of the Christian right to dominate non-Christian peoples of the world, an ideology that had been used as a rationalization for sending armies across the Mediterranean four centuries earlier. Matiaz de Paz, professor of theology at Salamanca (Spain, 1512), was from what we might call the "old school" of canonical law:

> Paz held that the pope, as Vicar of Christ on earth, enjoyed direct temporal jurisdiction over all the world, a view which was certainly not general and which his fellow Dominican Cardinal Torquemada had expressly denied half a century earlier. . . . Paz cited and approved the opinion of thirteenth century Henry of Susa, the Cardinal-Bishop of Ostia, better known among students of canonical law as Ostiensis, that when heathens were brought to a knowledge of Christ, all the powers and rights of dominion held by these heathens passed to Christ, who became the Lord over the earth in both the spiritual and temporal sense. Christ delegated that supreme domination to his successors, first St. Peter and then the popes.[8]

Most people are unaware that the indigenous peoples of the Americas played a role in the development of the modern world. American history was long presented as a story about a migration of European peoples to a "new continent," where, given new opportunities, they forged the foundations of a modern world. The process of creating this world was presented as based almost entirely on European foundations with little or no influence or contributions from non-Western cultures.[9]

The Spanish of the late fifteenth and early sixteenth centuries possessed a vision of the world formed by traditions and experiences specific to their time. When confronted with the realities of the Indians of the New World, they sought answers to their questions according to Old World beliefs about how the world came to be the way it was. There has been a strong tendency among historians to examine the record and, where the evidence is inconsistent with the story they wish to tell, to construct motives, to omit inconvenient facts, and to draw conclusions based more on the constructions than on the available evidence.

Modern historians have begun, during the twentieth century, to recount and analyze the almost unspeakable violence of the Spanish conquest. Bartolome de Las Casas, a priest who accompanied the conquistadors, was horrified by the violence and wrote accounts of the treatment of the Indians that depicted Spanish cruelty in detail:

> The Spaniards cut off the arm of one, the leg or hip of another, and from some their heads at one stroke, like butchers cutting up beef and mutton for market. Six hundred, including the cacique, were thus slain like brute beasts. . . . Vasco ordered forty of them to be torn to pieces by dogs. . . . Some Indians they burned alive; they cut off the hands, noses, tongues and other members of some, they threw others to the dogs; they cut off the breasts of women.[10]

Under the Spanish, Indian populations diminished dramatically as a result of what must be the most startling crime in recorded human history. Todorov emphasizes the proportions of this crime:

> [I]t will be recalled that in 1500 the world population is approximately 400 million, of whom 80 million inhabit the Americas. By the middle of the sixteenth century, out of these 80 million, there remain ten. Or limiting ourselves to Mexico: on the eve of the conquest, its population is about 25 million; in 1600, it is one million.
> If the word genocide has ever been applied to a situation with some accuracy, this is here the case. It constitutes a record not only in relative terms (a destruction on the order of 90 percent or more), but also in absolute terms, since we are speaking of a population diminution estimated at 70 million human lives. None of the great massacres of the twentieth century can be compared to this hecatomb.[11]

There are many explanations for the decline in Indian population, including introduction of epidemic diseases, loss of will to live under the cruel slavery of the conquistadors, wartime casualties, and casual murder. However, the most prominent reason was the absence of Spanish value for Indian life. Except for economic considerations, such as one might have for a horse or a fig tree, Indians were unimportant. Slaves could be replaced. What was legitimate was Christian Spain and Spanish civilization.

The "discovery" of the peoples of the Americas created a paradox for Christian orthodoxy. The classics and the Holy Scriptures, according to the ideology of the day, were intended by God to provide all the information Christian man would need on earth:

> For the orthodox believer, the Christian cosmogony that explained the origin and history of all humankind also had to explain the

Indians' presence and state of society in the Western Hemisphere. It even determined—or allowed—the questions that could be asked once Europeans realized that the lands discovered by Columbus constituted not a part of Asia but a whole new world unknown, or at least unmentioned, in the Scriptures and classical authors. . . . If Native Americans were unknown to Biblical and classical authorities, were they a part of the human race at all? [12]

Bartolome de Las Casas was the historian of the Spanish conquest of the Indies and Mexico. His accounts of the brutalities of the hidalgos embarrassed the Spanish Crown sufficiently that it called for a debate to be held before the Council of the Indies in Valladolid in 1550. The debate was to determine whether or not the Indians were true human beings.

People who live in the modern era may have difficulty understanding that the Spanish enquiry into the humanity of the Indians was a serious intellectual question at the time. The two figures who engaged the question have become famous in Western tradition. Las Casas, who defended the Indians, became their patron saint, while Dr. Juan Gines de Sepulveda, who argued the conquistadors' right to treat the Indians as beasts, is sometimes called the father of modern racism. One of his arguments in support of seizure of Indian property and persons was consistent with the views of Professor Matiaz de Paz:

. . . one of the important points argued at great length before the fourteen long-suffering members of the junta as they sweltered through the September heat of Valladolid was the interpretation of the fourteenth chapter of St. Luke, wherein the Lord commanded his servant, "Go out into the highways and hedges, and compel them to come in, that my house may be filled." Sepulveda maintained that this command justified war against the Indians in order to bring them into the Christian fold. [13]

Two of Sepulveda's distinct but interrelated arguments were that Spain was justified in making war on Indians because Spain had a mandate to bring the Indians, at whatever cost to the Indians, into the Christian fold, and that it was Spain's duty to bring to the Indians Christian civilization. The Indians, Sepulveda argued, lacked civilized behavior: The Indians are inferior in these characteristics, he declared, as children are to adults, as women are to men. Indians are as different from Spaniards as cruel people are from mild people, as monkeys from men. [14]

Sepulveda further argued that the Spanish colonial policy that was enslaving and destroying millions of Indians was not cruel but was instead beneficial to the Indians:

> Sepulveda ... emphasized the fact that the tutelage of the inferior
> Indians by the superior Spaniards would result in their Christianiza-
> tion eventually. Here he was applying, in a Christian world, the
> Aristotelian doctrine that the superior governors should rule in the
> interest of the Indians. . . . He represents that curious and not wholly
> amalgamated mixture of Aristotelianism and Christianity that is
> observed in the thought of many a Renaissance figure.[15]

The Spanish did not generally view their role in the conquest as a
cruel and unwarranted aggression against foreign peoples because, regardless of their public statements, they did not view Indians as fully
human.[16] They saw themselves as a people who were extending civilization to new parts of the world and who were enjoying a renaissance
inspired, at least in theory, by the Greeks of antiquity. People incapable
of experiencing this renaissance because their culture did not relate to
Greek thought and culture were not, in this framework, complete human
beings.[17]

The Valladolid debate was unique. It centered on the legitimacy of
Las Casas's claim that the Indians were human beings. In actual practice,
Spanish conquistadors knew the Indians were biologically human; witness the rapine lust visited upon Indian women.[18] Rather, what was
being debated was the question of whether the Indians were to be accorded the status of *legitimate* humans in the eyes of the church and
state. The matter under discussion revolved around a kind of feudal
property right. Were the Indians the *property* of the conquistadors to
do with as they pleased, or were they more correctly under the spiritual
hegemony of the Roman Catholic church?

Las Casas argued that the Indians were true human beings possessing
souls and, consequently, they were properly the charges of the church.
He amassed an array of evidence that drew on his experience with the
civilizations of Mexico, which had developed universities and an impressive knowledge of astronomy, among other things. All of this evidence was
offered to demonstrate that the Indians, although ignorant of Christian
civilization, were intelligent enough to understand and accept it. Appealing to the Crown's self-interest, Las Casas urged that the Indians
should be viewed as a potential asset to the state because they could be
socialized to be loyal citizens and as such would be much more valuable
than as chattels to the conquistadors. The proper agent of this socialization, he argued, was the church.[19] It is important to note, however, that
Las Casas did not assert that Indian cultures, or even civilizations per
se, had a legitimate right to a continued existence.

Sepulveda's argument relied heavily on Greek philosophy, specifically
the writing of Aristotle. Aristotle had posited that everything that can

possibly exist does exist somewhere in the universe. Although Aristotle was actually arguing that the civilized Persians and other peoples of Asia Minor who had been brought to Greece should not be kept as slaves because they were civilized, he in fact laid the groundwork for an argument which Sepulveda developed to justify the enslavement of the American Indians.[20] Aristotle's idea was that there exist in the world civilized humans and beasts of burden, and somewhere there exists all things in between, including humans who were, like beasts of burden, *natural* slaves.[21] Sepulveda urged that when they encountered the American Indian, Spaniards had found humans who fit

> the Aristotelian doctrine of natural slavery: that one part of mankind is set aside by nature to be slaves in the service of masters born for a life of virtue, free of manual labor.[22]

Not surprisingly, the church entered the debate on the side of Las Casas. Pope Paul III issued a bull, *Sublimis Deus*, stating that the Indians were not to be treated as "dumb brutes, created for our service" but "acknowledging that the Indians as true men not only are capable of receiving the Christian faith but, as we have been informed, eagerly hurry to it . . . we command that the aforesaid Indians and all other nations which come to the knowledge of Christians in the future must not be deprived of their freedom and the ownership of their property."[23]

The Council of the Indies and the Spanish Crown eventually adopted a version of Pope Paul III's view of the proper treatment of Indians as official, although in fact treatment of Indians in Spanish colonies improved little if at all. The outcome of the Spanish conquest and the Valladolid debates was that the Indians were not seen as legitimate peoples in the eyes of the Spanish and could become legitimate only if they accepted Christianity and Spanish culture. In short, for the Indian to become *real* in European eyes, he must abandon much of that which defined him as Indian.

In effect, the European invented the term "Indian" to mean a kind of "other." The indigenous peoples of the Americas identified themselves as distinct peoples such as Diné or Haudenosaunee or any of hundreds of other distinct peoples. There is no evidence that they conceived of themselves as a hemispheric whole or continental whole in the way Europeans soon came to be known. In the beginning, the Europeans identified these peoples as the "Americans," but that usage eroded after generations of people of European descent were born on American soil. What survived was the idea of "the Indian."

The term was more than a geographic misnomer. It denoted a people who inhabited a place and was strongly identified with a moment in time. The Indian was the "other," the person on shore when the European first arrived in a ship. He was a person about whom the European knew nothing; therefore he was a person without history. The European did not know who the Indian was, so the Indian became the person the European was not. This created a situation in which the identity of the Indian was unclear to the European and over the centuries produced a

> curious timelessness in defining the Indian proper. In spite of centuries of contact and the changed conditions of Native American lives, Whites picture the "real" Indian as the one before contact or during the early period of that contact. . . . If the Indian changed through the adoption of civilization as defined by Whites, then he was no longer truly Indian according to that image, because the Indian was judged by what Whites were not.[24]

Conversely, the white man was judged to be that which the Indians were not. If the white man should change through adoption of things Indian, he was then no longer a white man. There was no room in this idealized framework of absolutes for adaptation and transformation. The historical evidence shows that the white man did in fact change after arrival in the Americas. Acculturation was a two-way street or, more accurately, the process of a complex interaction of cultures that produced other cultures which were variations of each. However, the fact that Europeans and their descendants adopted customs, traditions, and even modes of thought from other cultures posed a serious dilemma in depicting history while trying to maintain the idea of a direct evolution of culture from the ancient world to the modern.

The ethnocentrism that blinded the conquistadors to the legitimacy of everything and everyone not European is a central element in the history of the West:

> If there is one concept that has a privileged place in the ethnocentric image through which Western peoples see themselves in relation to others, it is the concept of civilization. On it is based the whole concept of "History," the distinction between "pre-history" and "History," and therefore the relegation of most other peoples to a shadowy, undefined area situated "outside History." The concept permits the arrangement of diverse peoples into a civilization honors list with Europe always placed at the top. It is in its name that an apparently legitimate base is proclaimed for an evolutionist interpretation of the development of peoples, and which in turn valorizes certain criteria, such as urbanization and writing as "advanced" on a scale of evolution.[25]

Students of world history are correct to point out that Europeans also massacred other Europeans, although on a less dramatic scale, and that a lack of respect for human life is not uncommon throughout history. There is, however, a persistent pattern of behavior of Western peoples that is evidenced throughout history, one that was prevalent during the Spanish conquest and especially in Sepulveda's arguments at Valladolid. This pattern of behavior is the tendency for Western peoples to question and deny the legitimate existence of peoples and cultures different from their own, and it has motivated a construction of history around themes which legitimize these ethnocentric assumptions. Much of Western history is written, in essence, as though other peoples do not exist:

> This concept of Civilization is the very basis of History as written by Westerners. In fact "History" refers only to the past of (so-called) "civilized" peoples.[26]

Some characterizations of the Indian, as described in the early nineteenth century, illustrate this ethnocentrism. In Rev. Charles A. Goodrich's *History of the United States* we find:

> There was little among them that could be called society. Except when roused by some strong excitement, the men were generally indolent, taciturn, and unsocial. The women were too degraded and oppressed to think of much beside their toils. . . . Their language, also, though energetic, was too barren to serve the purposes of familiar conversation. In order to be understood and felt, it required the aid of strong and animated gesticulation, which could take place only when great occasions excited them.[27]

This language challenges the imagination of the reader. Imagine a communal people who possessed no *society*, and whose language was so barren they could not carry on conversations. And further:

> Their treatment of females was cruel and oppressive. They were considered by the men as slaves, and treated as such. Those forms of decorum between the sexes, which lay the foundation for the respectful and gallant courtesy, with which women are treated in civilized society, were unknown among them. Of course, females were not only required to perform severe labour, but often felt the full weight of the passions and caprices of the men.[28]

This is a particularly interesting statement about the Indian, considering that it was written at a time of chattel slavery in America, a time when black women were absolute slaves who often felt much of the weight of the caprices of white men and little of their respectful and gallant courtesy. Moreover, in 1823, the year this book was published, white women had no right to own property, had no right to wages they earned working in the factories (wages which belonged, legally, to their husbands), and had no right, of course, to vote or hold political office. They were not, in that sense, fully recognized human beings. Women, even white women, were subjected to a pattern of treatment consistent with Sepulveda's opinion about women and children.

A significant body of American history is written in the spirit of these passages. Ethnocentrism slanders the "other" while telling an idealized version of the "self," although both are products of the imagination. Goodrich is, however, clear about the images of the story he and others are fashioning about how the world came to be the way it is:

> At the commencement of this period, our history presented us with a continent, over whose surface an interminable wilderness had for ages cast its deep and solemn shade. If we approach the shore, and look through the gloom that gathers over it, the scenes which strike the eye are Indians at their war dance, or perhaps flames curling round some expiring captive or wild beasts mangling their prey.
>
> Passing from this point of time to the close of our period, a space of eighty-two years, the prospect is greatly changed. We now see smiling fields and cheerful villages in the place of dismal forests; instead of beasts of prey, we see grazing herds; instead of the kindling faggot, we witness the worship of Jesus Christ; and instead of the appalling war whoop, we listen to the grateful songs of David. In the beautiful words of scripture, the wilderness has begun to blossom as the rose, and the desert is becoming vocal with the praises of God.[29]

This history recalls themes promoted at Valladolid by Sepulveda. There is a vision of what Indians, who are not like us, must be. We have a fanciful construction of the role of women in Indian societies (and no sense that Indian societies were diverse, complex, and sophisticated). There is a message that the inferior Indian has been replaced by a superior people who have been mandated by God to subdue the wilderness. The slander directed at Indian cultures was necessary in the process of expansion because

> [t]o invade and dispossess a people of an unoffending civilized country would violate morality and transgress the principles of international law, but savages were exceptional. Being uncivilized by definition, they were outside the sanctions of both morality and law.[30]

What this essentially means is that Indians were sufficiently different from whites to be regarded as *less than* persons and not protected by any moral or legal standards.[31] Accordingly, the United States embarked on the Removal Policy in 1824, the year following the publication of Goodrich's *History*. Under this policy the United States tried to remove all Indians east of the Mississippi to an Indian country west of that river.

About 100,000 Indians were rounded up and forced to march westward; an estimated one-quarter to one-third died enroute or shortly after.[32]

One of the heroic stories of that dark period was that of the Cherokees who suffered great losses of human life on their forced march to Oklahoma. Once settled in their new home, they began to reestablish their nation, and within a few decades had rebuilt their towns and a capital at Tahlaquah, which included a courthouse and other public buildings. Then, when Oklahoma was admitted to the union in 1907, the Cherokee Nation suffered a loss of their government and their institutions for a second time.

Historian Francis Jennings provides insight into how ethnocentric thinking has been used to rationalize the destruction of Indian political organization by arguing it never even existed:

> In myth, however, the Euroamerican pleads "not guilty" to killing tribal government. He could not have committed such a crime, he says, because the victim never lived. . . . The logic is simple, faulty, and compelling as that of most other fallacies: Civilization is that quality possessed by people with civil government; civil government is Europe's kind of government; Indians did not have Europe's kind of government; therefore Indians were not civilized. Uncivilized people live in wild anarchy; therefore Indians did not have any government at all. And therefore Europeans could not have been doing anything wrong—were in fact performing a noble mission—by bringing government and civilization to the poor savages.[33]

The identity offered to the Indian was and remains a catch-22 because there has never been an offer of unequivocal legitimacy. Legitimate Indian governments could not have been destroyed because legitimate Indian governments never existed. By the same token genocide could not have taken place because the peoples and populations who were killed or allowed to expire under oppression were never legitimate peoples. The very identity of the Indian in European and Euro-American eyes was, and to a considerable degree remains, a formula leading to oblivion.

During the nineteenth century an ideology of social evolution appeared that valued human cultures in a hierarchical model that ranged from primitive to civilized. The model drew from a dramatically expanded information base but offered a view of non-Western cultures that was strikingly similar to the one proposed by Sepulveda three centuries earlier. There was, however, a contradiction between what was in fact happening and the theory about man's rise to civilization. The model stated that humans evolved from barbarism to civilization. If civilization was the current and desirable mode, any adoption of a custom from some place other than the (imagined) origins must be seen as a kind of dilution of the process, a throwback. However, if Americans (nee Europeans) adopted Indian customs or thinking, this theory of man's "rise" to civilization must be flawed.

The idea that American Indians made contributions to American culture and society is not new. It would have been a strange thing indeed, to paraphrase a quote by Benjamin Franklin, had the English colonists, following several generations of intense association with Indians, not been influenced by Indian thought and culture.

English colonists were influenced by the Indians from the first, but they generally failed to recognize the influences. The story of the first Thanksgiving, the commemorative of which would become a national holiday a century and a half after the event, is an example. In George F. Willison's account we find:

> Indian summer soon came in a blaze of glory, and it was time to bring in the crops. All in all, their first harvest was a disappointment. Their twenty acres of corn, thanks to Squanto, had done well enough. But the Pilgrims failed miserably with more familiar crops. Their six or seven acres of English wheat, barley, and peas came to nothing, and Bradford was certainly on safe ground in attributing this either to "ye badnes of ye seed, or lateness of ye season, or both, or some other defecte." Still, it was possible to make a substantial increase in the individual weekly food ration which for months had consisted merely of a peck of meal from the stores brought on the Mayflower. This was now doubled by adding a peck of maize a week, and the company decreed a holiday so that all might, "after a more special manner, rejoyce together." [34]

The account continues with a description of Indians invited to the feast that lasted three days. No record is left that turkeys were consumed at the event, although it is stated that the Indians brought a considerable quantity of game (deer). The pilgrims' own accounts admit they were horticultural (among other disciplines) students of Squanto, the Indian without whose help the new colony could have easily failed. From the written account we are left to conclude that the pilgrims invented the idea of the feast and that it came about because "the company decreed a holiday." Although it is known among ethnohistorians that unacculturated horticultural Indians of the Northeast woodlands generally hold a ceremonial of thanksgiving at the same time of year (sometimes lasting three days), it has not generally been conceded that the pilgrims may have borrowed the idea of this holiday from the Indians and that Thanksgiving may have originally been an Indian ceremonial adopted by newcomers to the land.

Earlier accounts of the Thanksgiving tradition provide some more information about its origins. These accounts tell of colonists conducting religious services during which they gave thanks to their God for being delivered safely or for food or for good weather. However, there are other aspects of the Thanksgiving tradition that are equally important. This celebration occurred in the fall after harvest; it was annual; and it involved a feast.

It seems very likely that the Thanksgiving of the pilgrims was a blend of English and Indian customs. The pilgrims *adapted* the Indian custom of a celebration of the harvest and the fruits of the hunt to their own culture, but while the Indians generally celebrated with elaborate dances, the pilgrims did not dance.[35] In fact, the pilgrims were probably motivated to omit any reference to Indian influences regarding their festival because the nearby Massachusetts Bay Colony was vehemently opposed to any heathen practices and would probably have made life uncomfortable for anyone adapting an Indian practice.

As we celebrate it today, Thanksgiving has been completely adapted to modern culture. Although there is no documented evidence that turkey and cranberries were eaten at the original feast, they may have been added as a result of "folk memory." In any case, both are believable additions. In modern re-creations of the first Thanksgiving in many American schools, the Indian is present but relegated to the background, invited to attend the pilgrim ceremony and grateful, we must presume, to be fed by the prosperous English colonists. These re-creations should bring the Indians to the foreground and provide the information that Thanksgiving probably was the Indians' idea, since it was their custom. Indeed, the first newspaper in English-speaking America, the *Publick Occurrences* of 1690, which was suppressed after one issue, carried news about "some Christian [Indians] who had 'newly appointed a day of Thanksgiving' for a 'very Comfortable Harvest.' "[36]

Edward H. Dance observed that "[o]ne of the easiest ways of telling an untruth is to speak nothing but the truth with something vital omitted."[37] Sometimes the witnesses to an event omit something vital because they fail to notice the details of the event. Such may be the case concerning the origins of the tradition of Thanksgiving.

Sometimes the Indians held solutions to problems the English sorely needed but were unable to find. Francis Jennings contrasts the French and the English attitudes towards Indians found in the documentation:

> [T]he Catholic imperative for converting and including the heathen compelled Catholics to learn something about them in order to do the holy work effectively, while the Protestant principle of elitism worked out in practice to exclusionism and indifference. The difference in

attitude is sharply illustrated by contrasting approaches to Indian medicine. New England's Puritan missionaries had so closed their minds that after nearly three decades at their task they knew nothing of Indian medicine. Surviving today is a "Drug List" prepared for the use of Massachusetts troops in "King Philip's War"; it contains not a single medicinal product of American origin. In Canada, however, Jesuit Father Le Mercier carefully distinguished between the Hurons' prayers to the devil and their natural remedies, and he asked for instruction in the remedies. Such contrasts explain why the Jesuit Relations are today an invaluable mine of ethnological information in spite of bias and cant. There is nothing comparable in Protestant literature until we reach the reports of Moravian missionaries in the mid-eighteenth century.[38]

Historians have collaborated in this ethnocentrism through their tendency to find only what they want to find and to ignore things that are inconsistent with the dominant ideology of humankind's evolution toward civilization. The idea that Western culture exclusively contributed to modernity was consciously cultivated by social scientists, who have engineered the training of historians since at least the time of the French Revolution. That revolution quite understandably traumatized European aristocracy, causing a reaction which sought to avoid repetition of the French model of revolution by developing an ideology that denigrated everything which informed it. During the nineteenth century historians (primarily German historians) then sought to re-create history on an Aryan model. Greece was embraced as the fountainhead of Western civilization. Speaking to the issue of how study of ancient Greece became institutionalized in northern Germany in the years 1790 to 1830, Bernal states:

> *It is precisely at this critical period that the new discipline of Philologie or Altertumswissenschaft (Science of Antiquity) was established as the pioneer discipline in the modern sense. It was the first to establish clear-cut meritocratic networks of student-teacher relationships. Seminars or departments capable of maneuvering to secure as large a portion of state funding as possible, and journals written in a professional jargon designed to maintain barriers between the practitioners of the discipline and the lay public.*[39]

These roots of the study of ancient Greece are important to our discussion about American Indian contributions to modern culture because they set into motion trends in historiography that must be witnessed to be understood. History as a modern profession was profoundly influenced by its German roots. The German historians sought to prove not only that Greece was *the* fountainhead of Western culture but that Greeks were *pure* Indo-Europeans (Aryans).

However, there is ample evidence that ancient Greek culture borrowed heavily from cultures of Semitic Anatolia and Egypt. But Anatolia and Egypt proved inconvenient ancestors to an ideology that sought to celebrate the purity and superiority of the Aryan race and culture. The European historians of the early nineteenth to mid-twentieth centuries solved that problem by denying that non-Western influences existed. Instead, they produced a revised ancient Greek history which embodied a fanciful reconstruction of classical Greek accomplishments; moreover, their work laid a foundation for the developing argument that Aryans constituted a superior race and that this superior race developed a superior culture traceable to a superior biology. This ideology of a superior race was eventually constructed to exclude specific groups and especially the Semitic Jews. Under the Aryan model of history Aryan culture could not have any Semitic ancestors. The idea that Egypt could have contributed to the development of Western culture was equally unacceptable. Western culture could have no black ancestors. These nineteenth-century anthropologists, historians, geographers, and other social scientists provided the intellectual environment that fostered developments in the twentieth century:

> The atmosphere became even harsher in the 1920s. Anti-Semitism intensified throughout Europe and North America following the perceived and actual centrality of Jews in the Russian Revolution. There had always been Jewish bankers and financiers to blame for economic crises and national frustrations; now in the Bolshevik party the previously vague image of a Jewish conspiracy to subvert and overthrow Christian morality and order seemed to have taken visible form.
>
> Such feelings were not restricted to Germany, or to vulgar extremists like the Nazis. All over Northern Europe and North America, anti-Semitism became the norm in "nice society," and "nice society" included the universities.[40]

None of this discussion is intended to deny that sixteenth-century Europeans were inspired by the writings of the ancient philosophers of Greece and Rome. When Sepulveda mounted a legal defense of the exploitation of the Indians by the conquistadors, he turned to the writings of Aristotle to substantiate an ideology of "natural" slavery. Although it can be stated in defense of Aristotle that Sepulveda took his ideas entirely out of context and applied them to situations Aristotle could hardly have imagined, the nationalism and ethnocentrism found in ancient Greek writings provided a rich source of material for a later western European ideology that sought to rationalize genocide, slavery, and the generally inhumane treatment of Indians and other non-Western peoples in Spanish America. Although the Spanish were the first to articulate the ideology of racism, by the eighteenth century racism based on skin color was evident in England

> alongside the increasing importance of the American colonies, with their twin policies of extermination of the Native Americans and enslavement of African Blacks. This racism pervaded the thought of Locke, Hume and other English thinkers. Their influence—and that of the new European explorers of other continents—was important at the university of Göttingen, founded in 1734 by George II, Elector of Hanover and King of England, and forming a cultural bridge between Britain and Germany. It is not surprising, therefore, that the first "academic" work on human racial classification— which naturally put Whites, or to use his new term, "Caucasians," at the head of the hierarchy—was written in the 1770s by Johann Friedrich Blumenbach, a professor at Göttingen.[41]

Many American historians were strongly influenced by people who received their credentials in Germany during this period. However, it is not necessary to find that connection to illustrate the point because the "father of anthropology" and an author of League of the Haudenosaunee, Lewis Henry Morgan, was quite explicit about his ideology in another book, Ancient Society, or Researches in the Lines of Human Progress from Savagery through Barbarism to Civilization:

> The Aryan family represents the central stream of human progress, because it produced the highest type of mankind, and because it has proved its intrinsic superiority by gradually assuming the control of the earth.[42]

League of the Haudenosaunee is considered by some to be the authoritative book on the Iroquois and a foundation work in the development of scientific anthropology. As the title implies, in Ancient Society, Morgan developed a fully articulated theory of social evolution. He writes:

> They commenced their career on the American continent in savagery; and, although possessed of inferior mental endowments, the body of them had emerged from savagery and attained the Lower Status of barbarism; . . . It gives us a measure of time they had fallen behind the Aryan family in the race of progress: namely the duration of the Later Period of Barbarism, to which the years of civilization must be added.[43]

Morgan issued a call to people who read his book to go forth and gather anthropological data to study this disappearing "Period of Barbarism."[44] Cultural anthropology was organized as a discipline to gather information about non-Western peoples that would be used to elaborate on the ideology of the biological and cultural inferiority of those peoples. The importance of Morgan's work is that it informs us about European intentions and ideology.[45] His scientific construction around European superiority and Aryan supremacy made his work popular.

It is said that whether or not history repeats itself, there is no doubt that historians repeat each other. During the nineteenth century professional historians made a conscious effort to find the origins of all of Western culture and modern civilization in the Aryans. In effect, nineteenth-century historians created the Greeks as the fountainhead of that culture by consciously omitting references to the Semitic or Egyptian origins of mathematics, philosophy, and literature.

When historians trained in the Aryan model wrote about the origins of Western culture, they spoke from a tradition that has simply ignored the legitimacy of non-Western peoples and the contributions those peoples made to an ancient world that had influenced their own culture. In the nineteenth century, classical historians did this consciously, and a parallel history of conscious omission of the significance of American Indians has been practiced in mainstream American history. It has been widely illustrated in American texts that official Soviet histories include references to inventions and discoveries the Western democracies claim as their own, and that the Peoples Republic of China has been known to airbrush people who have fallen from official grace from photographs of the Chinese Revolution. Although the inference has been that this kind of dishonest, selective history cannot happen in the West, clearly it does:

> Nineteenth-century histories generally presented the Indian as obstacle to White expansion. Thus historian W.P. Webb, when writing of The Great Plains, was most interested in examining the societies of the occupying Indians in detail, but "only those features of [them] that throw light on the later history of the plains."[46]

Webb's treatment of Indians was typical of the period. Most of these historians found discussion about Indians in

> a section entitled "The Taming of the West," or something similar, so that the native population, as Daniel Boorstin observes, is lumped together with "the inclement weather, the wild animals, and the unknown distances, among the half-predictable perils of a wilderness." After the West has been won and the Indians "dealt with,"

*one is lucky to find more than a couple of additional references to
Indian affairs, these probably being a line on the Wheeler Howard
Act of 1934, plus a rueful observation that, in Nye and Morpurgo's
phrase, the red man's "assimilation into the pattern of American
culture is still a problem."* [47]

Historians' interest in Indians actually declined during the early
years of the twentieth century. Its revival might be dated around the
early 1960s. From the beginnings of formal American history until the
1960s, mainstream American historians recounting the history of the
country reported very little about American Indians. This tradition
among historians has, however, begun to improve in recent years:

> *Since 1975 a virtual revolution in scholarship has transformed and
> informed the interpretation of Anglo-Indian relations in colonial
> North America. . . . The historians' unflagging fascination with the
> origins and evolution of English colonial institutions and societies
> produced two mature "schools," or broad overviews, for interpreting
> the period. But while both the England-focused Frontier school in-
> creased our knowledge of Whites in the colonial era, each approach
> ignored or distorted the considerable contributions of Native Ameri-
> cans who had strongly influenced London policy-makers and New
> World frontiersmen alike over the centuries.* [48]

A "virtual revolution in scholarship" is needed to revise and re-
interpret a history that was founded on ideas that American Indians and
other non-Western (and often simply non-male, non-Anglo) peoples are
insignificant. The insignificance of these peoples was at the core of the
disciplines of history and cultural and physical anthropology when they
were organized.

The tendency of the classical historians to overlook or understate
the significance of certain groups in history has pervaded practically
all historical writing in the West. It is so pervasive that practically all
history of non-Western peoples built on this model was and continues
to be colored to some degree by its assumptions. For example, the history
of the origins of American democratic traditions was written during the
nineteenth century when the ideology of Aryanism was at its zenith. This
is the most significant explanation of why American Indians were not
cited as influential in the formation of the ideas of democracy or in inspir-
ing the United States Constitution. To most of these historians, it is unacceptable that Indians might have played a role in the democratic tradition.

If the terms "law" and "government" have any application to peoples
whose origins are found outside the Western tradition, it must be conceded
from the evidence that the Iroquois have a long history of possessing

both. To argue against this conclusion one would be forced to define "law" as meaning only Western law as it arose during and following the eleventh century.

The antecedents of these ideas, we have long been told, were the democratic Greeks, the Romans, and the English. This chapter has already dealt with the classical origins of eighteenth-century culture. The English sources most commonly cited are the Magna Carta and the Glorious Revolution of 1688. The Magna Carta, upon close examination, will be seen to be an agreement between a monarchy and a struggling oligarchy. The Revolution of 1688 was not about democracy:

> *After the Restoration and the Glorious Revolution of 1688 . . . England settled down in the eighteenth century to government by Parliament. While the king was by no means a mere figurehead, he did not attempt to interfere with the advances of enclosure. Parliament was more than a committee of landlords; urban commercial interests had at least some indirect representation through the system of rotten boroughs. Local government, with which the peasants came directly in contact, was even more firmly in the hands of the gentry and titled aristocracy than it had been before. As the eighteenth century advanced, the transaction of public business in the parishes, some 15,000 of which formed the cells of the English body politic, came to be conducted more and more behind closed doors, losing whatever vestiges of a popular and democratic character that it may have had during the Middle Ages.*[49]

During the American Revolution, only one person in twenty could vote in England.[50]

The biological and cultural exchanges between the indigenous peoples of the Americas and the rest of the world was not a one-way street. The cultures of the peoples of Europe were transformed dramatically from the moment of contact and continue to be transformed. Since 1492, new cultures have evolved. The modern United States culture is properly a creole culture, a blend of many cultures from all over the world, and the population may soon reflect a new reality. With current trends, sometime during the next century the majority of Americans will have a non-European ancestry.

The origins of European-style government, as practiced in the eighteenth century, are clearly found, not in ancient civilizations, but in medieval times. Feudalism is defined by relationships involving obligations of military service for use of land. The social system of knights and serfs was a kind of military dictatorship in which the commoners had no rights to land and could not negotiate the conditions under which they labored or lived.[51] From the point of view of the peasants, it was a patently oppressive system,[52] a predecessor of the conditions suffered by slaves in later centuries under chattel slavery. A characteristic of this form of government was that the sovereigns acted, and were expected to act, in ways that promoted their personal fortune.[53]

The words used to describe social, political, and economic relationships of this era indicate the totality of the system. A *sovereign* is essentially a person of supreme authority. Such a person was often called a lord, a word that refers not only to an individual but even to a supreme being in the universe. It was the custom of the times, enforced by a military class, that the sovereign owned everything—all the persons and property—of the realm.[54] Under feudalism the idea of rights or appeals against the powers of the state as manifested in the whims of the individual lords of the manor simply did not exist as a remedy for the peasant.

The knights often owed allegiance to a monarch under a system of ascending hierarchies, but under true feudalism such allegiances could often not be enforced by monarchs due to military realities. Castles were formidable fortresses in the days prior to the invention of siege cannon. Even a monarch, who could muster a large army, could not always feed such an army long enough to besiege a recalcitrant or traitorous knight. Feudal Europe was characterized by rural fiefdoms of petty military dictators who enjoyed some autonomy from the monarchies. Feudalism, then, was a condition that preceded the formation of nation-states; when military technology shifted sufficiently to enable monarchies to unite the feudal manors into nation-states, feudalism came to an end.[55]

The transformation of Europe from a collection of small rural feudal manors to unified and politically homogeneous nation-states was under way by the late fifteenth century, but it was far from complete. Feudalism began to decline with the rise of trade. Trade promoted growth of population centers and rising classes of traders and others who were not part of the agricultural system that defines feudalism. In turn, trade and the growth of towns stimulated an increased use of money in transactions, a custom that gradually led to the formation of professional armies and promoted discussion about how and when force should be applied. The merchant classes became distinct powers in Europe, eventually able to ally with sovereigns and princes or stand independent of each as sovereign city-states.

An in-depth discussion of the rise of the bourgeois class and its role in the formation of nation-states is beyond the scope of this discussion. It is significant, however, that this development was crucial to the European expansion that was to follow. Christopher Columbus borrowed money from Genoese bankers to finance his explorations.

At the time when America was "discovered," monarchs were attempting to consolidate their power in the form of nation-states. Their allies and their enemies, depending on circumstances, were competing monarchies, recalcitrant but powerful principalities, and powerful bourgeois interests. European political history during these centuries is the story of how these forces interacted in the events that followed to create a modern European political landscape.

Although there were many important developments during these centuries, we shall concentrate on political events in two countries: France and England. In England, the landed aristocracy engaged in a long struggle with succeeding monarchs, a struggle distinctly audible in the Magna Carta and evidenced in the Glorious Revolution of 1688. The result was that the aristocracy succeeded in maintaining some authority and rights vis-a-vis the monarchy. England did not become an absolute monarchy; it was an oligarchy, a government of privileged property-owning classes. Government in England was based on those classes and the success those classes had in controlling the power to tax.[56]

During the seventeenth century in France, under the guidance of Cardinal Richelieu, the Crown wrested the power of taxation away from the aristocracy. Control of the power of taxation created the foundation of the absolute monarchy, a model followed by most of Europe during that century. The first true European nation-states were direct descendants, albeit on a grand scale, of the political systems that had evolved under feudalism. There were differences, to be sure, but the political theories behind them were very much alike.

In order to gain an understanding of American Indian contributions to the West's democratic tradition, these contributions need to be discussed in the context of the tradition itself. Long before 1492, Europeans had dreamed of and postulated an ideal world as a contrast to their own, a kind of Eden on earth where men were free from toil and oppression. That idea was expressed at least as early as Plato and Homer, and continued to inform the imaginations of medieval philosophers.[57] News of Columbus's voyage, supported by the glowing descriptions in his reports of the natives of the Caribbean, convinced some writers that he had happened upon this land of legend.

Images were then produced of a people living in prosperity and freedom such as had been associated with a mythical European golden age, and it was thought that such conditions could be emulated, thus ushering in a new golden age. The hypothesis, which was clearly a projection of European imaginations upon an as yet only barely realized "other," quickly centered on a discussion of nature. The Indian represented, in this discussion, humankind as a product of nature and thus as a reflection of possibilities that contradicted the strictly controlled and hierarchically structured world of European experience. If nature could produce noble humans who lived happily in freedom from want and oppression, nature should be glorified. The American Indian was to become an exhibit in the debate about nature that would inform and influence both conservative and liberal tendencies in the West for centuries.

It is important to realize that this glorification of nature was highly idealized and a product of an inspired imagination. The Americas

> *presented opportunity for humanitarians dissatisfied with the economic and political absolutism that burdened Europe's peasantry. They would describe the New World not as it was, but as Europe should be. . . . They would create a model that would serve to hurry the return of that Golden Age to Europe by demonstrating that greed and envy could be banished from men's natures. Their image would be a land of abundance and liberty too tempting to resist.*
>
> *What an ideal land they invented! There Nature's bounties were so abundant that none need labor: partridges so heavy they could not fly, turkeys the size of sheep, fish in such plenty that six hundred could be caught with a single cast of a net. There a perfect society had been achieved, unmarred by want or evil.*[58]

The new Eden, as represented by the Americas and American Indians, placed the Indian as an exhibit in Europe's political debate with strong ramifications about government. At the center of the debate was an argument about the fundamental qualities of nature. If people are free, happy, and prosperous in nature, then slavery, and even hierarchical government, along with its inherent structures of privilege, must be seen as not only unwise but actually a crime against nature itself. The liberal philosophers and dreamers, most of whom had never seen either the Americas or American Indians, proceeded to project this idealized vision of American Indian societies. Nature was, in effect, cast as the opposite of European hierarchical society; nature represented the spirit of what Europe was not. If Europe was authoritarian, nature was libertarian. If Europe had jails, nature had no jails, no secret police, no one to order anyone around. And if Europe had starving people, nature provided in abundance.

Writers presented the American Indian, a designated human representation of nature, as having the attributes of nobility necessary for them to appeal to European sensibilities. Thus, for a time the Indian was idealized as a type who could do no wrong, a kind of super person who did not lie, cheat, or steal, and who conducted himself according to the European ideals of dignity in every way. This idealized Indian was different only in the sense that he had no European vices. That American Indians might have been profoundly different in ways Europeans had never imagined, was unimportant. The Indian represented a powerful liberal ideal—nature as refuge from oppression.

However, the Spanish Crown to which Columbus reported was less interested in idealized nature than it was in establishing profitable colonies and developing trade. Civil authorities moved quickly to find economic opportunities in the colonies. Instead of seeing idealized nature, the conquistadors who arrived in the Americas saw peoples who resisted efforts to generate Spanish wealth. Indian intransigence was considered an obstacle to be overcome with force, and they soon vilified the Indian as an uncooperative and sometimes dangerous creature, an opinion which was readily carried to the new lands they encountered. The conservative opinion, reflected in Sepulveda's presentations, was consistent with the European debate about the evils versus the advantages of hierarchical organization, colonization, empire building, and exploitation of people and nature.

Over the centuries the pendulum would swing back and forth between philosophers who vilified or glorified nature, and the Indian would find favor or disfavor accordingly. At the beginning of the seventeenth century European philosophers arrived at the idea that there might be more than one kind of Indian—a "good" one and a "bad" one.[59] This tradition of creating types of Indians according to changing European values, using comparisons to everything from cannibalism to Victorian morals, is a tendency that seems to have persisted over a period of centuries among philosophers and popular writers.

Philosophers may have posited an ideal of human freedom from oppression in the sixteenth century, but political fortunes in Europe were favoring increased centralization, and with it increased oppression:

> [A]bsolutism in the seventeenth century transformed France and Western Europe. The building of the absolutist state meant the razing of the decentralized feudal structures, which had served, not unlike the medieval buttress, by dispersing the weight of governance. The ideal of the united state replaced the ideal of united Christendom. Class structure, economics, religious thought and even art and entertainment were brought to the service of the monarch as the custodian of the state.[60]

In this environment of an absolute monarchy arose that intellectual tradition that is most often identified as the inspiration of the West's democratic tradition, the Enlightenment. In this context, the Enlightenment is easily misunderstood. Enlightenment philosophers sought to define and inform despots about ways to govern justly rather than challenging the idea of despotism itself. It was probably out of an instinct of self-preservation that they did not challenge the authoritarianism of the era.[61]

The most powerful idea of the period was the assertion of the existence of the boundless sovereignty of the state, and the concurrent idea that the citizen is the servant of the state. The spirit of absolutism, under which the fundamental idea of law is subservient to the will of the state, is captured in the statement, "*L'état c'est moi*," attributed to Louis XIV.[62] In that environment,

> [t]he meliorism that dominated the thought and work of the philosophers of the Enlightenment had little patience with democratic ideas or experiments. They looked upward for progress, to monarchs wise enough and morally sensitive enough and strong enough to impose reforms on a society held in bondage by tradition and ignorance.[63]

English philosophers of the seventeenth century have been presented as early contributors to the democratic process. Seventeenth-century England was a period of struggle for power between a divine right monarchy and an elite of old blood and new money. The Glorious Revolution of 1688 was a major defeat for the monarchy that resulted in a

> kind of parliamentary absolutism resting on an aristocratic constitution which sanctified property and held Parliament supreme. Until the nineteenth century the aristocracy of England, without a trace of authentic democratic practice, led a government more aptly called oligarchic than democratic. . . . If the "glorious revolution" assured freedom, it was freedom for men of property.[64]

An oligarchy is a government of the privileged elite. People paid good money for seats in Parliament, where they expected and found opportunities to make even more money. Such was the condition of English government after 1688, the date of the Glorious Revolution. The philosopher of that revolution, John Locke, is credited as being a kind of founding father of democratic thinking. Di Nunzio states that this is misleading and that

> Locke's democracy is more a matter of subsequent reputation—a reputation enhanced by the successful adaptation of his ideas to the American revolutionary experience. . . . Locke became a democrat after, not before, the American experience. . . . Locke attacked divine right absolutism, but for an alternative Locke looked not to democracy but to the leadership of the aristocratic and propertied classes.[65]

Although later historians were to assert that the Enlightenment formed the foundation of the thinking which would lead to democratic governments, it is interesting that no important political thinker of the seventeenth century proposed a government representative of the population to be governed.[66] Equally curious, given the intellectual foundations of the Enlightenment, none found democracy a compelling argument among the Greeks or Romans either, although all were "renaissance men." Later political theorists who were constructing an Aryan model of history were left to make that connection.

As has been discussed, during some periods European thinkers extolled the virtues of the American Indian, and during other periods the important philosophers ignored or vilified the same images. In the era of romanticism this pendulum of opinion moved in a positive direction. The romanticists, most prominently Jean Jacques Rousseau, portrayed the Indian idealistically. Rousseau wrote in the tradition of the golden age and at a time when men such as Benjamin Franklin were formulating their views about the world. Although he may not have spoken in favor of democracy, Rousseau did express strong views about social justice and equality, arguing that European society was headed in the wrong direction and that they "might be persuaded to abandon their headlong quest for worldly goods if they learned of more primitive societies where all were well-fed and contented. The American Indian was the nearest approximation to this happy ideal, and would serve as the example."[67] Rousseau's *Discourse on the Origin of Inequality among Men* appeared in 1755. In it he stated that "Indians enjoyed equality and plenty; Europeans were in chains."[68] It is clear that at the critical moment of the birth of a democratic ideal in England's American colonies, major European thinkers had connected Indians with the idea of equality.

The American colonists, meanwhile, were not burdened with the same problem of distance and absence of accurate information about Indians suffered by Rousseau and his peers. The Americans were dealing and associating with Indians quite frequently. Donald Grinde's chapter in this book contributes greatly to our knowledge of the period, providing an enormous amount of detailed information about the texture of the times. From Benjamin Franklin to Thomas Jefferson, the Founding Fathers were dramatically more familiar with Indian customs and lifestyles than has previously been acknowledged; and they celebrated that familiarity in a plethora of ceremonies and brotherhoods dedicated to the image of the American Indian, which generally have been unreported in mainstream American history. Grinde's work establishes the fact that the climate of the times drew American intellectuals to the Indian camp fire, that some people were strongly in favor of Indian models for subsequent American governments, and that these people knew quite a lot more about the subject than we have previously been led to suspect.

Yet, one of the modern arguments against Indian "influences" on the democratic process is that the Founding Fathers could not have known about Indian government because no one had published anything about the subject, as though primary cultural transference occurs only through academic or popular publishing and not through personal experience. Undoubtedly the American experience had many roots, and no single influence "caused" the tradition.

Some contemporary anthropologists and other professionals assert that influence cannot be said to exist unless causation is demonstrated in the documentary record. What they are asserting, of course, is that they would like to make rules about what constitutes admissible, relevant evidence; and the rules they would impose are constructed to disallow the use of evidence which supports that something happened without leaving a heavy imprint in the documentary record. This argument about rules of admissible evidence tends to contradict the widely accepted observation that human beings think about and learn from their experiences with people of other cultures, and that when they see people doing things that work or that they find attractive, they often adopt the "new" practices or adapt them to their own use.

Perhaps the strongest argument that the democratic tradition originated without American Indian influence is the argument that democracy gradually grew out of the experience of isolation from the mother country. According to this theory, the colonists, ashore thousands of miles from England, were forced to make decisions for themselves. In that environment, the logical thing was to get together and make decisions as a group, a crude form of participatory democracy. This is an attractive argument, and doubtless has at least some merit, but it does present problems.

If isolation from England is the primary, indeed the *only* motivation for a tradition that locates the sovereignty of the nation in the people and reallocates power, in theory, to the masses and not to a monarchy or oligarchy, then Englishmen in other parts of the world, similarly isolated from the mother country, could be expected to also initiate a democratic tradition. But did they? Did a democratic tradition arise in Australia, New Zealand, Canada, South Africa, or anywhere else where European settlers prospered? With apologies to the Canadians, New Zealanders, and others who may have a modern democracy, their European forebears added nothing to the history of democracy. To the extent democracy exists in those lands, it is an import and can be traced to influences in thinking stirred by the United States.

Isolation was surely a factor in the origin of democracy (one can hardly imagine a successful revolution in nearby eighteenth-century Ireland), and had the American Revolution been unsuccessful, it is doubtful Jefferson and the others would have been much more than an obscure footnote to British history. Despite the isolation, however, there was considerable class structure and oppression in the English colonies in America during the colonial period. This is reflected in the fact that in 1713 poor colonists shot the lieutenant governor of Massachusetts because they were starving.[69] And although some scholars have argued that colonists in the decades preceding the American Revolution enjoyed more freedom than any Western population in the world, it is noteworthy that John Locke's constitution for South Carolina was so oligarchical that only eight men in the whole colony owned enough property to qualify as candidates for governor.[70]

While there were democratic practices in the colonies, the idea of democracy gained a lot of momentum with the revolution. It was an idea that remained unique to the Americas for a considerable time without a European counterpart. The major Western thinker who penned a theory of the rights of all citizens to participate in government was Thomas Jefferson in the American Declaration of Independence. Jefferson began by asserting that the Creator had endowed all humans with certain inalienable rights, and that the purpose of government was to protect those rights. His words contradicted the essence of existing European theories of governance:

> *In the context of the Declaration, the concept of the state is superfluous. Sovereignty resides in the people who establish government to serve them.*[71]

Jefferson's Declaration contains the idea of universal adult suffrage long before anything close to it would be realized in the United States. Implicit in it is also the idea that governments exist for the benefit of all, not the privileges of the few or, in the case of absolute monarchies, the one. Although strong arguments can be made that the United States has practiced these ideas imperfectly, the origin of these ideas is clearly rooted in exchanges with the Indians.

During the eighteenth century there was a confluence of ideas, practices, and traditions in North America, resulting in the rise and development of a democratic tradition which was then articulated by American political philosophers of the revolution and translated later into some of the principles of the United States Constitution and its Bill of Rights. There is considerable evidence that one of the streams which significantly contributed to that confluence involved the indigenous cultures of the Americas, and future scholars will undoubtedly find additional evidence. Perhaps from these roots will develop thinking about democracy and the democratic traditions that can continue to benefit all human beings.

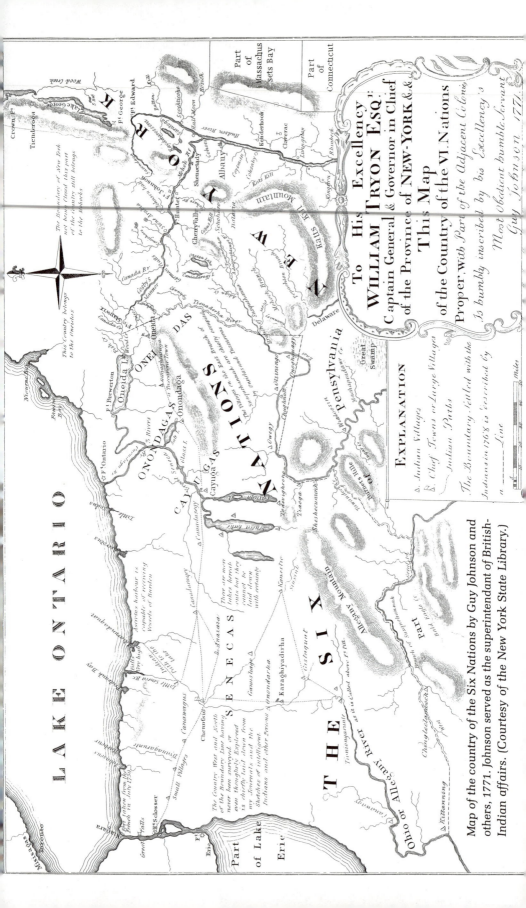

Map of the country of the Six Nations by Guy Johnson and others, 1771. Johnson served as the superintendent of British-Indian affairs. (Courtesy of the New York State Library.)

3.
American Indian Influences on the America of the Founding Fathers

Robert W. Venables

Introduction

"The Mohawks are come!" cried thousands of demonstrators as they surged out of Boston's Old South Meeting House, just as the sun set on 16 December 1773. The air was punctuated with war whoops. As the mob marched toward the waterfront, at their head were groups of men—the Sons of Liberty—all disguised as "Mohawks." Arriving at Griffin's Wharf, the "Mohawks" boarded three ships while the crowd cheered them on. They broke open the holds, hoisted the tea chests stored within the decks, and used hatchets to chop gaps into the wooden chests to be sure the tea would be exposed. Then they dumped the broken chests holding more than 90,000 pounds of British tea into the waters of Boston Harbor. About £19,000 worth of tea—a small fortune—could be seen the next morning floating on the surface of the water, formed into irregular rows by the tide and winds.

The masquerade as Mohawks was more than disguise. These Sons of Liberty were making a symbolic statement: like the Mohawk Indians, they, too, had been born in America. In their use of the symbol of the Mohawk, they were not alone. In New York City a month before, a public protest had been signed, "The Mohawks." Both in Massachusetts and New York, the Sons of Liberty were proclaiming their separate identity. In a word, one could not be more "American" than to be "Mohawk."

The use of an American Indian as a symbol of America was common: on maps, in fine arts such as sculpture and painting, on fine porcelain, and even on wallpaper an American Indian had come to symbolize the Western Hemisphere. So it was fitting that when it came time to celebrate the ratification of the new United States Constitution, New York City mounted a parade down Broadway on 23 July 1788, which included Indians both in person and symbolically. The parade consisted of seventy-six groups marching in ten divisions, all with banners, and some with floats. Since the United States Constitution had come into existence while New York State still debated its entry into the new union, the pro-Constitution crowd was celebrating the new nation even as it was exhorting its own state to ratify. Among the marchers were furriers, reminders of how important the fur trade was to New York; appropriately, they were marching alongside Indians.

The float built by the upholsterers was especially rich with symbolism. On the float was a seven-foot-high "federal chair," flanked on one side by a boy holding a sword and balance scale symbolizing "justice," and on the other by a boy wearing a liberty cap and holding a large paper upon which were written the words "Federal Constitution." Seated on the "federal chair" was a boy dressed as a genie representing "wisdom," while two other "genies," who both symbolized achievement, bore the motto "The reward of virtue." From street level, the crowd could read the words of a verse on the float:

> *None but the virtuous, wise and great,*
> *The Federal States shall e'er dictate*
> *Virtues genii, wisdom show*
> *That laurels are the worthies due.*

But the upholsterers knew that New York had not ratified the Constitution, and was therefore still outside the new union. Thus, another boy, dressed as an American Indian, had been placed on the float near the "federal chair," holding up a banner which read:

> *May the Federal Constitution be supported*
> *as is the canopy and chair of state.*[1]

The word *American*, which the patriots used to emphasize their separation from England, was originally synonymous with the word *Indian*. In the seventeenth century, had anyone asked Captain John Smith at Jamestown or Miles Standish at Plymouth how the Americans were faring, both would have reported on the local Indian nations. Smith and Standish were, after all, Englishmen. And it is useful to recall that originally even the Sons of Liberty were protesting for the rights of Englishmen, even as they proclaimed themselves Americans. The change in meaning had come around the middle of the eighteenth century when the word *American* was co-opted along with the land. By the time of the American Revolution, the English colonists were calling themselves—and becoming known in Europe as—the "Americans."

To be an American was to be separate and different from a European. American Indians symbolized this separateness, difference, and independence by the obvious fact of their location on a different continent. Equally important, however, American Indians were seen as free from the feudal heritage of Europe, where monarchs ruled and where nobles, by birth, dominated society. American Indians especially symbolized two qualities: life and liberty. Thus, during the Philadelphia Convention, Gouverneur Morris noted on 5 July 1787: "liberty and life . . . they possess both in the savage state in the highest perfection."[2]

In addition to life and liberty, the colonists fought their War of Independence against Britain for a third reason: the protection of their private property. By the time the Philadelphia Convention was convened in 1787, many citizens in the newly independent United States felt that life, liberty, and property required a reorganized and centralized government.

Of all the conflicting interests represented at Philadelphia, the greatest conflict was how to balance life and liberty, so well represented by "the savage state," with property. Too great an emphasis on property would have smacked of the corruption that had ossified the European societies and against which the colonists had rebelled. Yet, property also had its positive aspect: political, social, and economic stability. In the chaotic 1780s, such stability seemed very attractive to the new United States.

Given these conflicting impulses of life and liberty on the one hand, and property on the other, it is not surprising that at one moment the Founding Fathers could extol the virtues of the savage state—life and liberty—and at the next moment move to establish checks, balances, and separations of powers that would ensure the survival of property—prosperity.

In seeking to understand the philosophical influences of Native Americans on the newly independent United States, one discovers not a replication of an American Indian political or ethical system, but rather an admittedly selective borrowing.

When the subject in America was liberty from European tradition, images of American Indians were called upon to provide noble examples. When the subject was property, the newly independent United States too often fell back upon variations of European political structures. The Founding Fathers admitted as much. The complete context of the statement above is an example.

When Morris spoke the words quoted above, he was addressing the very specific issue of how the United States could expect settlers who moved west of the Appalachian Mountains to unite with the eastern states, joining the older states within one government. Since the Founding Fathers correctly assumed that the western states would eventually have a greater population than the East, the problem was how to protect the East's greater property. Morris's answer reflects the clear competition of the ideas of life and liberty on the one hand, and property on the other:

> [W]hen the Western Country is settled . . . we must take care that we don't establish a Rule wh. will enable the poor but numerous Inhabs. of the western Country to destroy the Atlantic States—Men don't unite for liberty or Life, they possess both in the savage state in the highest perfection; they unite for the protection of property.[3]

Fortunately for an author writing about symbols, among the Founding Fathers' favorite haunts in Philadelphia was a tavern and inn called the

Indian Queen. Here they often discussed the day's proceedings. On 27 July 1787, the convention's drafting committee gathered at the Indian Queen under the chairmanship of South Carolina's John Rutledge to define the structure of a draft of the Constitution which the committee could then present to the entire convention. According to historian Richard Barry, Rutledge opened the meeting by reading aloud a singularly "American" political idea: an English translation of the Iroquois' oral tradition of the founding of the Iroquois Confederacy. Rutledge wished to stress, as Barry wrote in his controversial 1942 biography *Mr. Rutledge of South Carolina* (New York: Duell, Sloan and Pearce), that the people and government of the United States were native-born and did not need to be shackled by European precedents. Rutledge was also setting the tone for what became the most eloquent section of the entire Constitution, the Preamble. The Preamble would emphasize a point made by the founders of the Iroquois Confederacy, whose history Rutledge referred to: political power came from "we, the people."

This concept, "we, the people," certainly had its European precedents. Some of these were claims to ancient glory in Greece and Rome. The Founding Fathers agreed that these ancient glories faded whenever power was transferred from the people to a tyrant or overly centralized government. Other European precedents for power being vested in "the people" were based on religious beliefs such as those of John Calvin. But far more vividly than any past history, American Indians were living proof that human societies could and did live in liberty. John Locke, the seventeenth-century Englishman, and other philosophers would take this proof from *real life* and combine it with their own European traditions. What evolved was a philosophy which inspired the Enlightenment and the American Revolution. Prior to and during the American Revolution, the concept of power originating among the people would be expressed in political writings and in documents such as the Declaration of Independence, the Virginia Constitution of 1776, and the Articles of Confederation.

The philosophies and experiences of the Founding Fathers represented a synthesis of European cultural baggage and American firsthand experience. A pervasive part of that firsthand experience involved the colonists' long interaction with American Indian societies in diplomacy, in trade, and in war. In the case of the Iroquois, the English colonial experience had been cooperation with the Iroquois, whose Confederacy was allied with the English colonies. Then, during the American Revolution, the Iroquois divided as did their English colonial counterparts, as some took up the Patriot cause and some took up the cause of the British.

The effect of Native American political ideas on the new United States did not result in a replication of an Indian political system. Rather, the revolutionary generation, which won its independence from Britain and then formed "a more perfect union" under the Constitution, was itself a synthesis of the old and the new, the European and the uniquely "American." Woven within the warp and weft of this synthesis were the philosophical threads of uniquely American Indian ideas.

Yet somehow, when retrospectives of the Constitution are written, scholars and the general public fondly refer to the Magna Carta and to other European precedents, but not to Iroquois and other American Indian influences. The Magna Carta certainly influenced the course of events that, slowly over the centuries, evolved in English history to include more modern liberties. However, the Constitution is not simply a replication of the pact between King John and his nobles in A.D. 1215. There is general agreement that the Magna Carta was only one influence among many.

Since replication is not required in order to sanctify a European idea as having influenced the Constitution, the same standard should be applied to those ideas and influences which reflect the contributions of the American Indians. Ideas of Amerian Indian origin thus belong in the history books alongside influences such as the Magna Carta, as all are part of the synthesis that led to the United States Constitution.

In addition, Native Americans were also significant players in the specific historic events in the 1780s which prompted the Philadelphia Convention to formulate the United States Constitution. Therefore, this essay, which begins by considering philosophical and cultural influences, concludes with a review of the context of Indian-white history as it relates to the formulation of the United States Constitution.

Philosophical and Cultural Influences of Indian Nations on the Founding Fathers

> General Washington will be the Chief.
> Alexander Hamilton, 1787

The philosophical influences exerted upon the Founding Fathers can be analyzed within the contexts of two broad themes: the pervasive influences of American Indians on the cultures of Europe and Europe's colonies following Columbus's first voyage in 1492; and the direct influence of American Indians upon the philosophical and political ideas during the Age of Enlightenment. These Enlightenment ideas influenced both Europe and the European colonies in North America.

Europeans viewed American Indians, even those of Mesoamerica, as living at an earlier stage of human development than themselves. Thus, they stereotyped the Indians north of Mexico as people of the woods, in French *sauvage* and in English "savage." This term, whatever its original meaning, has come to mean "cruel." However, when Europeans were originally observing the true nature of the American Indians, they drew conclusions based on one of two premises. The first perspective was the Europeans' belief that American Indians were "noble savages," while the second held that they were "brutal savages."

The term "noble savage" was originated by the English playwright John Dryden to describe primitive Europeans in *The Conquest of Granada* (1670):

> *I am as free as nature first made man*
> *Ere the base laws of servitude began*
> *When wild in woods the noble savage ran.*[4]

The term was then applied to American Indians and other indigenous peoples whom the Europeans were encountering throughout the world.

The Enlightenment thinker Jean Jacques Rousseau's *Discourse upon the Origin and Foundation of the Inequality among Mankind*, published in 1755, contrasted this noble savage with "civilized man":

> *Savage man and civilized man differ so much at the bottom of their hearts and in their inclinations, that what constitutes the supreme happiness of the one would reduce the other to despair. The first sighs for nothing but repose and liberty; he desires only to live, and to be exempt from labor; nay, the ataraxy of the most confirmed Stoic falls short of his profound indifference to every other object. Civilized man, on the other hand, is always in motion, perpetually sweating and toiling, and racking his brains to find out occupations still more laborious; he continues a drudge to his last minute; nay, he courts death to be able to live, or renounces life to acquire immortality. . . . In fact, the real source of all those differences is that the savage lives within himself, whereas social man, constantly outside himself, knows only how to live in the opinion of others . . . in short, ever asking others what we are, and never daring to ask ourselves. . . .*
>
> *It has cost us much trouble to make ourselves so miserable. When on the one hand we consider the immense labors of mankind, so many sciences brought to perfection, so many arts invented, so many powers employed, so many abysses filled up, so many mountains leveled, so many rocks rent to pieces, so many rivers made navigable, so many tracts of land cleared, lakes emptied, marshes drained, enormous buildings raised upon the earth, and the sea covered with ships and sailors; and on the other weight with ever so little attention the real advantages that have resulted from all these works to mankind; we cannot help being amazed at the vast disproportion observable*

between these things, and deplore the blindness of man. . . .

Among other Stories I remember one concerning the Chief of some North-American Indians brought about thirty Years ago to the Court of London. A thousand Things were laid before him, in order to find out what Present would be acceptable to him, without hitting upon any one thing that he seemed to like [until] at length, he was observed to take up a Blanket, and seemed to take great Pleasure in wrapping himself up in it. You must allow, said the Europeans about him, that this, at least, is an useful Piece of Furniture? Yes, answered the Indian, I think it almost as good as the Skin of a Beast. And even this he would not have allowed, had he wore both under a Shower.[5]

In contrast with the noble savage, the image of the brutal savage allowed Europeans to justify their expansion into territories occupied by inhabitants who were "unworthy," "inferior," or so "cruel" as to make them expendable. The contrasting images of the noble/brutal American Indian have been examined in books by many scholars, but nowhere are they examined with a greater range and perception than in the work of Hugh Honour. Honour detailed the major themes in his stunningly illustrated 1975 book *The New Golden Land: European Images of America from the Discoveries to the Present Time.* Honour's outstanding survey was also presented as a traveling art exhibition and catalog, both entitled *The European Vision of America.* The exhibition opened at the National Gallery of Art in Washington, D.C., on 7 December 1975, and then traveled to the Cleveland Museum of Art and to the Grand Palais in Paris. Among the more striking paintings chosen by Honour to illustrate how Europeans viewed American Indians, three from the sixteenth century are especially notable.

The first painting is by the Portuguese Master of Viseu, *The Adoration of the Magi,* dated by Honour as circa 1505. In this work, the future founder of Christendom, the baby Jesus, is held by his mother Mary and attended by Joseph in the right foreground. Approaching from the left are the Three Wise Men, whom Honour describes as follows:

The place traditionally occupied by the black Magus has been taken by a coppery-skinned Brazilian. He wears a feathered headdress. . . . Only in one respect does he differ from the image of the American Indian which was soon to become conventional—his nakedness is covered with a richly patterned shirt and breeches, presumbably to make him presentable to the Holy Family. Few savages could appear more gentle, courteous, and eminently human. . . .

[The painting conveys] the charming notion that one of the Wise Men might have followed the star all the way from Brazil to Bethlehem.[6]

In addition to portraying Indians as noble, the Portuguese Master of Viseu stressed an important element on the "noble" side of the noble/ brutal equation that might best be characterized as the "common cause." The common cause was an attempt to bridge the European and American Indian cultures on both sides of the Atlantic by perceiving universals that transcended racial and cultural differences. Finding a common cause was not illogical when it is recalled that John Dryden first used the term "noble savage" in reference to primitive Europeans, and that the term was eventually extended to include American Indians and other indigenous people like the Hottentots of South Africa.[7] In seeking to establish a common cause, the Europeans believed or hoped that American Indians shared universals and—whatever their political social, technological, and economic differences—a human equality.

At its most self-serving, this common cause allowed Europeans to believe it would not be impossible, and in fact it would be logical, to "convert" the Indians to the white approach to religion, economics, and politics. At its most positive, it fostered an interaction based on respect and was a precursor to twentieth-century pluralism and ethical relativism. In the case of the painting portraying an American Indian as one of the Three Wise Men, the common cause was a spiritual one, that of Christianity. Its foremost exponent was Bartolome de Las Casas, a sixteenth-century Spanish priest whose crusade to force Europeans to view American Indians as equal human beings raised philosophical issues which are still relevant. In his arguments, Las Casas attempted to prove the ultimate human common cause, that "all mankind are one."[8]

The common cause theme became political in the work of a Dutch artist, circa 1540 to 1550: Jan Mostaert's *A West Indian Scene*. In this fantasy-battle painting, Spanish soldiers storm a terraced cliff defended by naked men. In the background is a "window rock" not unlike those found in the American Southwest. Hugh Honour summarizes four art historians' detailed analyses of this painting, including the strong possibility that the painting is a fanciful but telling re-creation of the storming of a Pueblo Indian town by Coronado in 1540. Honour notes that whether the incident portrayed a battle by Coronado or Cortez in Mexico—or even some other event—the painting is in any case a parable with clear political overtones, because both Holland and the New World chafed under the imperialist yoke of Spain.[9]

In addition to the religious and the political common cause, Europeans also evolved an intellectual common cause with Indians. This interpretation was especially dominant during the Enlightenment, and Enlightenment philosophy was used in turn to justify much of the American Revolution and the United States Constitution.

On the other hand, the opposite perception of American Indians—
that American Indians were "brutal"—is exemplified by a painting
which stands in direct contrast spiritually with the painting just mentioned that portrays the American Indian as one of the Three Wise Men.
This work, selected by Hugh Honour as the prime early example of this
attitude, is an anonymous Portuguese artist's vision of the *Inferno*, circa
1550. In this gruesome painting, European men and women from all
walks of life are tortured in hell—even a monk boils in a giant kettle
along with a priest/scholar and three others. In this scene of the damned,
demons of various shapes employ the most brutal of torture instruments.
Seated on a red throne supervising the entire sadistic orgy is the devil—
wearing the feathered headdress and costume of a Brazilian Indian, a
costume similar to that of the red wise man.[10] Since the embodiment of
evil in European thought is the devil himself, the image of the Indian
in the painting by the anonymous Portuguese artist stands dramatically
at the opposite pole of the image in the first painting, *The Adoration of
the Magi*. It also represents the precise opposite of the idea of the common cause: the Europeans' common enemy.

By almost always relating American Indians to their own needs and
viewpoints, Europeans developed only an ethnocentric appreciation of
Indian cultures. They still sought a single answer in attempting to come
to grips with a race they had never encountered before: Indians would
either become assimilated into the Europeans' world, or they would be
cast out like the devil himself.

As the Europeans attempted to make common sense out of a race
their Christian religion of universal truth had somehow omitted, some
Europeans chose to force American Indians into a mold that Christianity
and the European perspective *had* admitted and discussed: that of the
monstrous races, the "wild men." Some of these "wild men" were perceived as being no more than human beings unfortunate enough to be
living as fur-clad hunters far beyond the influence of anything the Europeans would count as "civilization." But many of the monstrous or wild
races had especially unusual characteristics. Perhaps the best-known
among these is the one-eyed Cyclops encountered by the ancient Greek
Ulysses in Homer's *The Odyssey*, an example which also demonstrates
that the roots of these mythical beings lie in the pre-Christian ancient
world of the Mediterranean.

John Block Friedman, in *The Monstrous Races in Medieval Art and
Thought*, reviews them all, including: headless people whose eyes, nose,
and mouth are embedded in their chests; Panotii, "whose ears reach to
their feet and serve as blankets," and who are so shy that "when they
see travelers they unfurl their ears and fly away as if with wings"; and
Sciopods, "one-legged but extremely swift" creatures who spend their

days lying on their backs protecting their heads from the sun with a single great foot."[11] Often these wild men had unusual sexual appetites. Friedman also notes that many of the monstrous or wild people were said to live in India. Thus, he concludes his study by relating these myths to the European

> *discoveries of new peoples in the Americas, who replaced the races of the East in the European consciousness, assuming not only the name "Indians" but also the burden of many traditional attitudes toward "monstrous men."*
>
> *. . . These qualities in New World monsters, however, were dealt with . . . by an important Aristotelian thinker of the sixteenth century, Juan Gines de Sepulveda, who in 1550 engaged in a famous argument with Bartolome de Las Casas on the correct methods of propagating Christianity and Spanish capitalism in the New World. . . .*
>
> *Sepulveda stressed as part of his argument the Indians' sinful or perverted sexuality and their unchecked appetites, clearly modeling these New World savages upon the Old World wild men.*
>
> *Sepulveda has in effect exported late medieval attitudes towards the races and transmogrified the Indians of the America into . . . wild men. . . . They provided a ready and familiar way of looking at the native people of the New World.*[12]

How pervasive this view of American Indians was is indicated on a 1544 map drawn to illustrate Jacques Cartier's entry into the St. Lawrence River Valley. A lone Indian is portrayed on the map, perhaps an Algonquian but perhaps, too, this is the first painting of an Iroquois, as Cartier had extensive dealings with the Iroquois along the St. Lawrence. The Indian is dressed in the fur costume that symbolized a medieval "wild man." On the same map are a pair of unicorns; but if the French mapmaker's imagination was vivid, so was his sense of Cartier's mission: behind Cartier stand three pikemen, and lest anyone doubt the vision of Canada's future, a French peasant toils behind a horse-drawn plow. The Indian—the wild man—sits in the north, looking away from the French figures.

While most Americans have heard the story about how the Dutch purchased Manhattan Island from the local Algonquian Indians in 1626, giving in exchange for goods "the value of sixty guilders," it would surprise most to learn that the term the Dutch used when writing back to Holland about the American Indian sellers of Manhattan, was the term *wilden*.[13]

The sexual behavior of the "wild men" and the "monstrous races" was often described as being excessive or perverse because these expressions of sexuality went far beyond acceptable Christian standards. Of course, one of the reasons the European culture perpetuated myths of wild men in the first place was to describe examples of what *not* to be, and by setting a negative example, to encourage proper Christians to adhere to the opposite behavior. But myth encountered fact after 1492, and myth won out. Differing sexual practices among American Indians were condemned as befitting only wild men. The residue of the myth perpetuated the Europeans' sense of their own moral superiority, as the Europeans adhered to what they regarded as a higher standard of sexual behavior.

A residue of the old wild man myth may have surfaced at the Philadelphia Convention. On 9 August 1787, the delegates were discussing how long a residence period the Constitution should require before immigrants were admitted to full citizenship, when Gouverneur Morris spoke to the issue. James Madison records that Morris said:

> the lesson we are taught is that we should be governed as much by our reason, and as little by our feelings as possible. What is the language of Reason on this subject? That we should not be polite at the expense of prudence. There was a moderation in all things. It is said that some tribes of Indians, carried their hospitality so far as to offer strangers to their wives and daughters. Was this a proper model for us? [14]

Delegate Rufus King's notes record a slightly different version:

> Liberal and illiberal are relative and indefinite Terms. The Indians are the most liberal of any People, because when Strangers come among them, they offer their wives and daughters for their carnal amusement. [15]

Whatever Morris actually said—he left no record of this speech himself—it is interesting to note that Madison's notes do not record the words that Rufus King did write down: "relative and indefinite terms." Such words in King's notes indicate that Morris was a "moral relativist." But Madison records that "there was a moderation in all things" and implies that the Indians' example was not "a proper model."

Whatever Morris really *said*, Madison *heard* Morris give a variation on the old medieval wild man story. What is especially interesting is that in a discussion of the residency requirement for immigrants, a Founding Father would use a titillating example far from the immediate subject. It is this negative interpretation of Indian sexuality which seems to be the residue of the titillating tales of the libidinal wild men. Or perhaps it was simply Gouverneur Morris telling an eighteenth-century version of a locker room story.

By the seventeenth century, American Indian images were familiar all over Europe. The figure of an Indian, male or female but always wearing a feathered headdress, had come to be the symbol of the Western Hemisphere. Hence Indian figures could be found on a pewter tankard in early seventeenth-century Nuremberg; in Giovanni Lorenzo Bernini's sculptural figure *The River Plate* for his *Fountain of the Four Rivers* in Rome (1651); painted or carved in both Catholic and Protestant churches, as the full-length sculpture beneath a pulpit in Bruges (1690); on seventeenth- and eighteenth-century Gobelins tapestries; and on eighteenth-century Meissen porcelain teapots. French and English royalty enjoyed ballets with characters dressed as Indians—the Indian costume of Indigo Jones for the English court of King James I, circa 1613, is among the most outstanding. English composer Henry Purcell wrote *The Indian Queen* (1695). French composer Jean-Philippe Rameau's opera ballet, *Les Indes Galantes* (1735 to 1736), includes characterizations of the Incas of Peru and of North American Indians, as well as Turks and Persians, who were regarded as exotic and hence, for art's sake, within the mental boundaries of "the Indies." What is especially remarkable about Rameau's *Les Indes Galantes* is that it ends with a symbol of peace well understood in the French court: a *Danse du Grand Calumet* (Dance of the Large Peace Pipe). Engravings of American Indians were popularly distributed, and the ceilings and walls of the homes of the wealthy bore paintings of American Indians. American Indian motifs, in other words, could be found throughout Europe.

Accounts of European encounters with Native Americans began with Columbus and never ceased. In addition to those Europeans who actually traveled to the Americas, European writers who remained on the eastern side of the Atlantic nevertheless wrote commentaries on what they believed was the philosophical impact of encountering a race unknown to Europeans before Columbus. One such writer was the Englishman Sir Thomas More, whose 1516 fiction *Utopia* discusses the interrelationships between two worlds which have just discovered each other. While the term "utopian" has come to mean a well-ordered social paradise on earth, its implications for the future of Europe's relations with Indians put its author closer to another contemporary, Machiavelli; for as More discusses the rights a visitor has to a newly found foreign land according to the philosophy of the Utopians:

> If the natives will not dwell with them [the Utopians] and accept their laws, they drive them out of the land they have taken for themselves. If the natives resist or rebel, they make war upon them. For they consider it a just war that is fought to dispossess people from land which they do not use and keep others from using.[16]

One of the more perceptive commentaries on the European invasion of the Americas was made by a Frenchman, Michel de Montaigne, who wrote on many subjects in his fascinating book *Essays*, completed in 1588. Like many other Europeans, he was intrigued by the implications of contact with the Indians and their "new" world because he believed such observations revealed, through contrast and comparison, as much about the nature of European society as they did about the Americas. Montaigne also raised a question still provocative today: would the European "discovery" of the Western Hemisphere ultimately prove to have a beneficial or devastating effect on humans throughout the world? Montaigne believed that the Europeans were more advanced and had a superior civilization when compared to American Indians. However, in his essay "On Experience," he specifically admires the Indians of Mexico for what he perceives as their stoicism, which was

> the first lesson that the Mexicans teach their children. When they come forth from the mother's womb, their elders greet them with these words: "Child, you have come into the world to endure. Endure, suffer, and be silent."[17]

Montaigne's essay "On Cannibals" deals with Brazilian Indians whom he had interviewed in 1562 while the Indians were visiting Rouen, France, with a white man who had lived in their homeland for "ten or twelve years." Montaigne writes:

> I do not believe, from what I have been told about this people, that there is anything barbarous or savage about them, except that we call barbarous anything that is contrary to our own habits. . . . These people are wild in the same way as we say that fruits are wild, when nature has produced them by herself and in her ordinary way.[18]

Significantly, Montaigne would become one of the philosophers most admired by the eighteenth-century Enlightenment philosopher Voltaire, and the paragraph quoted above is paraphrased by no less a Founding Father than Benjamin Franklin. Franklin, talking about the Iroquois rather than the Brazilian Indians of Montaigne's essay, wrote in 1783, while he was in Montaigne's homeland: "Savages we call them, because their manners differ from ours, which we think the Perfection of Civility; they think the same of theirs."[19]

Listening to the Brazilian Indians' accounts of their existence, and of their white companion's viewpoints, Montaigne summarized the concepts which would become known as the "state of nature":

> These [Brazilian Indian] nations, then, seem to me barbarous in the sense that they have received very little moulding from the human

intelligence, and are still very close to their original simplicity. They are still governed by natural laws and very little corrupted by our own. They are in such a state of purity that it sometimes saddens me to think we did not learn of them earlier, at a time when there were men who were better able to appreciate them than we. . . .

This is a nation, I should say to Plato, in which there is no kind of commerce, no knowledge of letters, no science of numbers, no title of magistrate or of political superior, no habit of service, riches or poverty, no contracts, no inheritance, no divisions of property, only leisurely occupations, no respect for any kinship but the common ties, no clothes, no agriculture, no metals, no use of corn or wine. The very words denoting lying, treason, deceit, greed, envy, slander, and forgiveness have never been heard. How far from such perfection would he find the republic that he imagined: "men fresh from the hands of gods."[20]

Regarding the practice of bloody warfare and cannibalism among these Brazilian Indians, Montaigne noted that:

I am not so anxious that we should note the horrible savagery of these acts as concerned that, whilst judging their faults so correctly, we should be so blind to our own. I consider it more barbarous to eat a man alive than to eat him dead; to tear by rack and torture a body still full of feeling, to roast it by degrees, and then give it to be trampled and eaten by dogs and swine—a practice which we have not only read about but seen within recent memory, not between ancient enemies, but between neighbours and fellow citizens [during the civil wars between French Catholics and French Huguenots] and what is worse, under the cloak of piety and religion—than to roast and eat a man after he is dead. . . .

We are justified therefore in calling these people barbarous by reference to the laws of reason, but not in comparison with ourselves, who surpass them in every kind of barbarity.[21]

Montaigne also recorded what the Brazilian Indians had to say about France:

[T]hey [the Indians] have a way in their language of speaking of men as halves of one another—that they had noticed among us some men gorged to the full with things of every sort while their other halves were beggars at their doors, emaciated with hunger and poverty. They found it strange that these poverty-stricken halves should suffer such injustice, and that they did not take the others by the throat or set fire to their houses.[22]

In his essay "Of Vehicles" (or, "Of Coaches"), Montaigne referred to all the Americas and wrote, "Our world has lately discovered another," including the Aztecs of Mexico and Incas of Peru. Montaigne poignantly concluded that the greater virtue of the Indians ultimately brought about their destruction at the hands of far less virtuous Europeans:

> But as to religious conduct, obedience to the law, goodness, liberality, loyalty, and honest dealing, it was greatly to our advantage that we had not as much as they. By excelling us in these virtues they ruined, sold, and betrayed themselves. . . .[23]

Montaigne's admiration of the Aztecs did not prevent him from believing that their fall to the Europeans was inevitable, just that it was tragic that their fall was to sixteenth-century Europeans and not to the ancient Greeks or Romans:

> When I reflect on the indomitable courage with which so many thousands of [Aztec] men, women, and children so often advanced and flung themselves against certain dangers, in defence of their gods and their liberty; and on their noble persistence in withstanding every ordeal and hardship, even death, rather than submit to the domination of the men who had so shamefully deceived them— some, when captured, preferring to pine away from hunger and fasting rather than accept food from the hands of their enemies, who had won by such foul means—I can see that if anyone had attacked them with equality of arms, experience, and numbers, it would have been as perilous a war as any that we know of, or even more perilous.
>
> Why did not so noble a conquest fall to Alexander, or to the ancient Greeks and Romans! Why did not this vast change and transformation of so many empires and peoples fall to the lot of men who would have gently refined and cleared away all that was barbarous, and stimulated and strengthened the good seeds that nature had sown there, not only applying to the cultivation of the land and the adornment of cities the arts of this hemisphere, in so far as they were necessary, but also blending the Greek and Roman virtues with those native to the country?[24]

Montaigne believed that the base motives behind the Spanish conquest of the Aztecs and the Incas had resulted in the "fairest part of the world turned upside down for the benefit of the pearl and pepper trades":

> What a compensation it would have been, and what an improvement to this whole earthly globe, if the first example of our behaviour offered to these people had caused them to admire and imitate our

*virtue, and had established between them and us a brotherly inter-
course and understanding! How easy it would have been to turn to
good account minds so innocent and so eager to learn, which had, for
the most part, made such good natural beginnings! On the contrary,
we have taken advantage of their ignorance and inexperience to bend
them more easily to treachery, lust, covetousness, and to every kind of
inhumanity and cruelty, on the model and after the example of our
own manners. Who ever valued the benefits of trade and commerce at
so high a price? So many towns razed to the ground, so many nations
exterminated, so many millions put to the sword, and the richest
and fairest part of the world turned upside down for the benefit of
the pearl and pepper trades. Mere commercial victories! Never did
ambition, never did public hatreds drive men, one against another,
to such terrible acts of hostility, and to such miserable disasters.*[25]

Perhaps the most significant American Indian motif in any European
art form was created by William Shakespeare. Shakespeare was an interested observer from England's side of the Atlantic of the English colonies
at Roanoke, which failed, and at Jamestown, which was nearly failing.
He was also stirred by the drama of an English shipwreck in 1609 on
the uninhabited island of Bermuda. Shakespeare's last play, *The Tempest*
(1611), reflects his universal perception of the crisis arising from the
contact between any colonial settlers and any indigenous people. Shakespeare's characters are universal because they are drawn from many
sources, but one major source was the English reports of the American
Indians and their homelands.

D. G. James, in his *Dream of Prospero* (Oxford: Oxford University
Press, 1961) outlines how Shakespeare came in contact with accounts
of Roanoke and North Carolina, largely through his patron, the Earl of
Southampton, who was a stockholder in the Jamestown venture. James
also suggests that Shakespeare had seen John White's portfolio of water-
colors of North Carolina Indians. Included in this portfolio was a full-
length portrait of Wingina, a leader of the Roanokes who was assassi-
nated in cold blood while treating for peace.

The heroine of *The Tempest*, Miranda, calls the island upon which
she and her companions are stranded a "brave new world." This small
island is complete with a native population of one, a character named
Caliban, born of a witch named Sycorax. Caliban is not strictly a symbol
only of American Indians. He is instead Shakespeare's composite
"primitive" and indigenous human—one part medieval wild man, with
a strong libido, and one part magic.

At the beginning of *The Tempest*, Shakespeare reveals that Miranda's
father, Prospero, originally intended to share the "brave new world"

equitably with Caliban in exchange for teaching Caliban European civilization. By 1611, English idealism had failed to overcome greed. The English had been no more successful in avoiding violence than had the Spaniards, whose methods of conquest were well known. As for the American Indians, the English had discovered that they were not naive, natural humans one step beyond the boundaries of the Garden of Eden. They were instead capable of the full range of human virtues and vices.

Thus, despite Prospero's original and best intentions, Caliban proves to be less than a perfect cohabitor of the new world, and is soon enslaved by Prospero. Poor Caliban is stripped of all but a small portion of his land—Caliban's "reservation."

Shakespeare presents the universal reasons for this classic dilemma of the conquered and the conquerors in Act I, Scene II, during an exchange between Caliban, Prospero, and Miranda. In the following, note how Miranda calls Caliban "savage"; how Caliban, like a medieval wild man, has an unbridled urge to seduce Miranda; how a European education/perspective is offered to Caliban; and how alcohol is introduced to Caliban.

CALIBAN

This island's mine by Sycorax [the witch] my mother
Which thou takest from me. When thou camest first,
Thou strokest me and made much of me; wouldst give me
Water with berries in't [wine]; and teach me how
To name the bigger light, and how the less,
That burn by day, and night; and then I loved thee
And showed thee all the qualities o' the isle,
The fresh springs, brine-pits, barren place, and fertile,
Cursed be I that did so! All the charms
Of Sycorax—toads, beetles, bats light on you!
For I am all the subjects that you have,
Which first was mine own king; and here you sty me
In this hard rock, whiles you do keep from me
The rest o' the island.

PROSPERO

Thou most lying slave,
Whom stripes [whipping] may move, not kindness! I have used thee
In mine own cell [room] till thou didst seek to violate
The honor of my child [Miranda].

CALIBAN

O ho, O ho! Woud't had been done!
Thou didst prevent me; I had peopled else
This isle with Calibans.

MIRANDA

[Some editors say these are Prospero's lines]

Abhorred slave
Which any print of goodness will not take,
Being capable of all ill! I pitied thee,
Took pains to make thee speak, taught thee each hour
One thing or other. When thou didst not, savage,
Know thine own meaning, but wouldst gabble like
A thing most brutish, I endowed thy purposes
With words that made them known. But thy vile race,
Though thou didst learn, had that in't which good natures
Could not abide to be with. Therefore wast thou
Deservedly confined into this rock, who hadst
Deserved more than a prison.

CALIBAN

You taught me language, and my profit on't
Is, I know how to curse. The red plague rid you
For learning me your language![26]

By portraying the failure of even a highly motivated European (Prospero) to live by his preconceived ideals, Shakespeare dramatizes the reality of colonization. Caliban's only alternative to submission is also realistic: during the play, Caliban allies with other Europeans against Prospero, an alliance which Prospero's enemies bind by plying Caliban with wine. (In fact, during the 1560s, the Guale Indians of coastal Georgia allied with French soldiers against the Spanish.) By the end of the play, however, this alliance proves a farce and a failure (as indeed the Guale-French alliance had). Caliban looks to Prospero for forgiveness (as the Guale Indians surrendered to the Spanish): "I'll be wise hereafter, / And seek for grace." The implication is that Caliban will again become submissive to Prospero, and Caliban's only compensation will be a European education and patronizing praise. Since Caliban has also failed to win Miranda, his singular race is doomed to die out, leaving the Europeans supreme in the "brave new world."

The 1734 *Essay on Man* by the English poet Alexander Pope eloquently presents, in four epistles, the major themes of the Enlightenment, including the dependence on reason, not faith or intuition. Within this poem, Pope stereotypes the "noble savage." Although Pope oversimplifies American Indian religious beliefs, his view is nevertheless poignant and sympathetic, especially in his reference to heaven as a place where American Indians will regain the lands lost to base European conquerors. Indeed, among those wishing to denigrate American Indians, this stereotyped Indian has become known by the name "Lo," a personal name obtained through a perverse twist on Pope's first line, "Lo, the poor Indian. . . ." However, by attempting to belittle and turn around the following words of Pope's poem, those embarrassed by its pro-Indian and anti-imperialist sentiments actually conceded how powerful Pope's lines have always been:

> Lo, the poor Indian! whose untutor'd mind
> Sees God in clouds, or hears him in the wind:
> His soul, proud Science never taught to stray
> Far as the solar walk, or milky way;
> Yet simple Nature to his hope has giv'n,
> Behind the cloud-topt hill, an humbler heav'n;
> Some safer world in depth of woods embrac'd,
> Some happier island in the wat'ry waste,
> Where slaves once more their native land behold,
> No fiends torment, no Christians thirst for gold.
> To Be, contents his natural desire,
> He asks no Angel's wing, no Seraph's fire;
> But thinks, admitted to that equal sky,
> His faithful dog shall bear him company.[27]

In 1759, the French philosopher François-Marie Arouet Voltaire wrote the satirical *Candide*, about a hapless, idealistic young European who in his travels encounters, among others, the American Indians of Paraguay, who are under the rule of the Jesuit order. Voltaire, whose caustic view of the missionizing aspect of colonization is revealed through a character named Cacambo, describes Paraguay: "*Los Padres* have everything and the people have nothing; 'tis the masterpiece of reason and justice."

Soon Candide visits the Jesuit commandant:

> *Candide was immediately taken to a leafy summerhouse decorated with a very pretty colonnade of green marble and gold, and lattices enclosing parrots, hummingbirds, colibris, guinea hens and many other rare birds. An excellent breakfast stood ready in gold dishes; and while the Paraguayans were eating maize from wooden bowls,*

out of doors and in the heat of the sun, the reverend father Commandant entered the arbor.[28]

Having seen what has happened to missionized Indians, Candide
next encounters "the savages called Oreillons," who are "what the pure
state of nature is." An imaginary American Indian tribe, they dress like
the Brazilian Indians discussed earlier in this chapter. The Oreillons,
who also resemble the medieval wild men, think that Candide is a Jesuit
because he wears the robe of the Jesuit commandant who, in this farce,
he has mistakenly killed shortly after discovering that the Jesuit is his
long lost brother-in-law. Candide and Cacambo

> were surrounded by naked Oreillons, armed with arrows, clubs and
> stone hatchets. Some were boiling a large cauldron, others were
> preparing spits and they were all shouting: "Here's a Jesuit, here's
> a Jesuit! We shall be revenged and have a good dinner; let us eat the
> Jesuit, let us eat the Jesuit!"
> . . . Candide perceived the cauldron and the spits and exclaimed:
> "We are certainly going to be roasted or boiled." Ah! What would
> Dr. Pangloss [his Enlightened teacher] say if he saw what the pure
> state of nature is?[29]

Fortunately, when the Oreillons learn that Candide is not really a Jesuit,

> the Oreillons unbound their two prisoners, overwhelmed them with
> civilities, offered them girls, gave them refreshment, and accom-
> panied them to the frontier of their dominions, shouting joyfully "He
> is not a Jesuit, he is not a Jesuit!"
> Candide could not cease from wondering at the cause of his
> deliverance. "What a nation," said he. "What men! What manners!
> If I had not been so lucky as to stick my sword through the body of
> Mademoiselle Cunegonde's brother I should infallibly have been
> eaten. But after all, there is something good in the pure state of
> nature, since these people, instead of eating me, offered me a thou-
> sand civilities as soon as they knew I was not a Jesuit."[30]

In both fact and fiction, reality and art, the images which Europeans
created or perceived regarding Native Americans came primarily from
European visits to the Americas. Yet, as Montaigne's encounter with the
Brazilian Indians in France reveals, not all the travelers on the Atlantic
went from Europe to America. Occasionally, American Indians would
visit Europe. These visits began in 1493, when Columbus forced at least
six Indians to sail back to Spain with him, but diplomatic visits became
increasingly common.

In 1616, for example, Pocahontas visited England. She was the daughter of Powhatan, the founder of a powerful southern Indian confederacy known by its founder's name. Pocahontas had married Englishman John Rolfe to help seal the diplomatic ties between the two peoples. In addition to her husband and infant son, Pocahontas's delegation included five Powhatan men and five Powhatan women. While in London, Pocahontas met notables such as poet and playwright Ben Jonson, who wrote The Vision of Delight, a Christmas masque in her honor which was performed on Twelfth Night at the royal palace, Whitehall. Unfortunately, the following March Pocahontas fell ill and died before she could return to Virginia.

Perhaps the most famous diplomatic visit by Indians occurred in 1710, when a delegation of four Mohawk Iroquois (including one who was actually an adopted Mahican) visited the court of England's Queen Anne. Called by their hosts the "four kings," they were in fact simply the ambassadors of their people. They brought with them a great purple wampum belt of sacred beads to a monarch they considered to be an ally, a friend, and—most importantly—their equal. Their leader was Te Ye Neen Ho Ga Prow of the Wolf Clan. Known primarily by his English name Hendrick, he would later befriend William Johnson on the frontier of colonial New York and, as an old man (about seventy years old), die in 1755 during a furious battle with the French at Lake George. Equally impressive among the delegates was Saga Yean Qua Prab Ton, known as Brant. Brant was beautifully tattooed upon his face and chest. His grandson, Joseph Brant, Thayendanegea, would visit London in 1775 and later fight during the American Revolution as an ally of the British.

Hendrick and Brant, together with Oh Nee Yeath Ton No Prow (John) and Elow Ob Koam (the Mahican, known as Nicholas) presented the wampum to Queen Anne at St. James Palace on 19 April 1710, and spoke to her through a translator:

> Great Queen, We have undertaken a long and tedious Voyage, which none of our Predecessors [among the Iroquois] could ever be prevail'd upon to undertake. The Motive that induc'd us was, that we might see our Great Queen, and relate to her those Things we thought absolutely necessary for the Good of her, and us her Allies, on the other side of the great Water. We doubt not that our Great Queen has been acquainted with our long and tedious War, in Conjunction with her Children [the English colonists] . . . against her Enemies the French; and that we have been as a strong wall for their Security, even to the Loss of our best Men. . . . And in token of our Friendship, we hung up the Kettle, and took up the Hatchet.[31]

After admonishing the queen to fight the French with more vigor, they noted that if she did not, the Iroquois might have to "stand neuter." The

The Four Indian Kings.

Four Mohawk ambassadors who visited England in 1710: upper left, Te Ye Neen Ho Ga Prow, also known as Hendrick; upper right, Saga Yean Qua Prab Ton, or Brant; lower left, Oh Nee Yeath Ton No Prow, or John; lower right, Elow Ob Koam, or Nicholas. (The Four Indian Kings, engraving by Bernard Lens the Younger, 1710, courtesy of the Huntington Library, San Marino, California.)

queen responded diplomatically, ordering presents to be given to them. Then they began a two-week tour of London. Among the sights they saw were an opera, London Bridge, a Punch and Judy puppet show, a performance of *Macbeth*, a concert, a wrestling match, a cockfight, and bear fights. They dined with the nobility and met with mercantile representatives from New York and New England. They sat for their portraits, commissioned by Queen Anne and painted with remarkable insight by John Verelst. And they visited St. Paul's Cathedral, which was just being finished by its seventy-five-year-old architect, Sir Christopher Wren. Everywhere they went, mobs of admirers followed them. Their tour was, of course, all arranged for them by their English hosts, who also showed them a workhouse for the poor and the insane asylum, Bethlehem Hospital—commonly called Bedlam—where the inmates were exhibited for the amusement and scorn of the British public.

On 4 May 1710, the four Iroquois left their London quarters at the Two Crowns and Cushions near Covent Garden, took a coach to Portsmouth, and boarded the warship *Dragon*, which sailed for Boston. On board were many of the presents Queen Anne had given them (more were to follow). Among these gifts were brass kettles, four hundred pounds of gunpowder, linen shirts, and yards of cotton and wool. Most interesting of all was a "Magick Lathorn with Pictures"—a magic lantern, an early version of today's slide projector. With it pictures on glass were projected through a lens lighted by a bright flame. There is no record of the Iroquois ambassadors gathering their clans together one evening in a village along the Mohawk River and using the magic lantern to show slides of their London holiday, but the magic lantern certainly must have made quite an impression. The four Iroquois are the earliest recorded American tourists to return from Europe with a collection of slides as a record of their trip.

Those Englishmen who could not crowd around the four Mohawks during their visit could read about them in the *Spectator*. Indeed, so popular was the image of the Mohawks that, two years after their departure, a group of young gentlemen formed a club in 1712 called the "Mohocks." They soon became famous for wrecking taverns, rioting in brothels, and in general wreaking havoc around London, with the result that the word *Mohawk* took on a connotation in England of lawlessness.[32] A different mob sixty years later, this one in Boston, took on the disguise of Mohawks again, this time to dump tea into the harbor to protest British taxation. The choice by these Sons of Liberty to dress as Mohawks announced to British authorities that they were American-born, not transplanted Englishmen, and that they were defying authority—just as the gentlemen "Mohocks" in London had done.

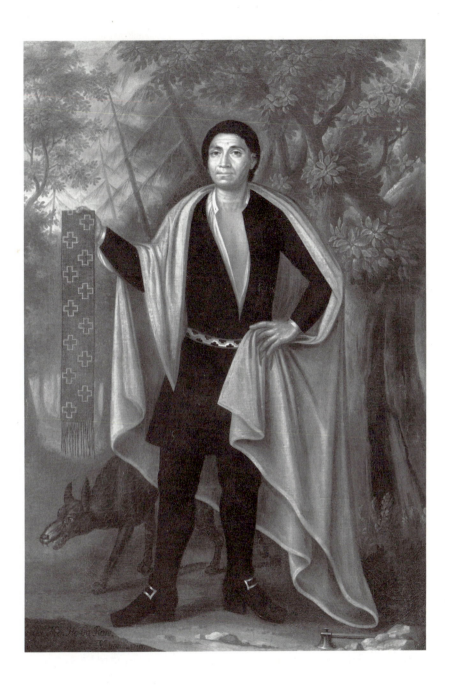

Te Ye Neen Ho Ga Prow, or Hendrick, the chief Mohawk delegate to England in 1710. The delegates presented a wampum belt to Queen Anne, whom they encouraged to more vigorously fight the French. (Portrait by John Verelst, courtesy of the National Archives of Canada/PA-C92414.)

In 1733, a delegation of Creeks from South Carolina led by Tomochichi ("The One Who Causes a Stir") visited London, where their activities were reported by the *London Magazine* and *Gentleman's Magazine*. They had traveled across the Atlantic to enter into an alliance with England and to cement an agreement with the founders of the newly planned Georgia colony, whose leaders made up the Georgia Council. At Kensington Palace, they met King George II. The Creeks, like the Mohawks before them, dressed in English costume for their audience but wore moccasins and put feathers in their hair. They also wore face paint. Tomochichi gave the king a cluster of eagle feathers, explaining through a translator that

> these are the feathers of the eagle which is the swiftest of birds.
> These feathers are a sign of peace in our land and have been carried
> from town to town there and we have brought them over to leave
> with you, O Great King, as a sign of everlasting peace.[33]

Later, Tomochichi allowed that the size of Kensington Palace made it impressive, and that no doubt the English knew many things his own Creek people did not. Nevertheless, he felt that "[t]he English lived worse than the Creeks who were a more innocent people." When Tomochichi and his delegation were presented to the archbishop of Canterbury, it seemed to them that the archbishop should be feared as a conjuror. Then Tomochichi visited Eton, where he spoke to the boys who waited expectantly for the translator to explain precisely what the old man had said. Their reaction was to cheer "Huzza!" Tomochichi had proposed to the headmaster that the boys be given a holiday—perceptive diplomacy in any era.

While Tomochichi and his Creek companions were in England, at least two paintings were executed of them by William Verelst, whose father had painted the four Iroquois in 1710. The entire Creek delegation was portrayed in one painting, together with the Georgia Council, in a work notable for its contrasts: the bewigged Englishmen gathered on the painting's left, with the Creek delegation on the right. The second painting is a three-quarter-length portrait of Tomochichi and his nephew Tooanabey. The tattoos on Tomochichi's chest are striking, as is the live eagle held by the young Tooanabey.

Of all the paintings that included American Indians as subjects, no work is more famous than a dramatic canvas executed in 1770 by Benjamin West, *The Death of General Wolfe*. The British General Wolfe died in 1759 on the Plains of Abraham, even as his troops won a great victory over the French at the siege of Quebec. In the foreground, West placed an Iroquois warrior, accurately portraying the warrior's right shoulder, arm, and leg as marked with stunning tattoos. Although done in the grand European tradition of heroic history paintings, the prominence of the

The Death of General Wolfe, a 1770 painting by Benjamin West based on the British general's death during a battle against the French in 1759. West's paintings often included Iroquois subjects. (Courtesy of the National Gallery of Canada, Ottawa.)

Iroquois warrior marks this scene as distinctly American. West did many other paintings that incorporated Iroquois subjects, including a full-length portrait now in the National Gallery, Washington, D.C., of an Iroquois with a white frontier companion who has been identified either as Sir William Johnson or Guy Johnson.

Important as these paintings are, what Benjamin West *said* about the Iroquois, in a brief exclamation he was later fond of recounting himself, summarizes the concept alluded to earlier in this section: how Europeans and European colonists often attempted to bridge the Atlantic with its European and Indian traditions by seeing Indians not only as noble savages but as sharing a universal common cause. In 1760, Benjamin West traveled to Rome for the first time. There to study the great art, architecture, and sculpture of the ancient world, West was shown the famous Roman sculpture known as the *Apollo Belvedere*, a Roman god portrayed full length as a muscularly graceful nude. The *Apollo Belvedere* had all the hallmarks of what Europeans regarded as classical European sculpture. West's reaction shocked the Italian clergy accompanying him when he remarked: "My God, how like it is to a young Mohawk warrior!"[34]

West's comment is the ultimate embodiment of the noble savage as common cause. The equation of the esthetics of classical sculpture representing the best of European culture with the "natural man" of the American forests was not pluralistic, however. Robert F. Berkhofer, Jr., has written in his book *The White Man's Indian: Images of the American Indian from Columbus to the Present* that European and colonial Enlightenment thinkers

> were not moral relativists either in their judgments upon the ranking of societies or in their belief that historical knowledge proved the superiority of the European. They were absolute and ethnocentric both in their criteria of judgment, or the yardstick to measure progress, and in the proper outcome of mankind's history. They saw cultural diversity, but they did not really approve of it, a view held even among those who espoused primitivism.[35]

Therefore, another work by Benjamin West came as a visual shock that accompanied news of the actual fact. West created a drawing that depicted the return of white women and children captured by various Indian nations during the war known as Pontiac's Rebellion (1763 to 1766). Beginning in 1764, English authorities, making separate peace treaties with each Indian nation, insisted that all white prisoners be returned, but these officials were shocked to find that many of the whites did not want to return. When forced to comply with the treaty conditions, both white "captives" and their adopted Indian relatives wept at

Colonel Guy Johnson, *painted in 1776 by Benjamin West. The Indian in the background has sometimes been identified as the Mohawk leader Joseph Brant, Johnson's aide and colleague. (Courtesy of the National Gallery of Art, Washington, D.C., Andrew W. Mellon Collection.)*

being forcibly separated. In a very real sense, West's work finally human-
ized the European image of the wild man.

Thus by 1775, the start of the American Revolution, Europeans and
their colonial kin had built up a complex impression of American Indians,
a rich tapestry that involved all the arts and literature, intertwined with
nearly every aspect of eighteenth-century life.

The man who most singularly bridged European ideas with the real
life of the English colonist was Benjamin Franklin. Born in 1706, he
was eighty-one when the Philadelphia Convention was convened. During his lifetime, he had seen wars between the French and the English
in which each side had its Indian allies. For the English in the north,
this especially meant their Iroquois allies. In 1783, while in France as
the Patriots' ambassador, Franklin focused many of his previous impressions of the Iroquois into one essay. In the tradition of Montaigne, whom
Franklin admired, Franklin's succinct "Remarks Concerning the Savages
of North-America" remains a classic of both literature and history. Of
all the Enlightenment thinkers on either side of the Atlantic, Franklin
comes the closest to the cultural and moral relativism which Berkhofer
feels was missing in the vast majority of Enlightenment thinkers.
Franklin's major examples are primarily Iroquois, though he also draws
on accounts of the Susquehannas and the Delawares. Franklin's clear
admiration for the Iroquois and the other northeastern Indian peoples
begins with a paragraph in the spirit of Montaigne and moves on in the
spirit of both Rousseau and the newspaper reporter Franklin was:

> Savages we call them, because their manners differ from ours, which
> we think the Perfection of Civility; they think the same of theirs.
>
> Our laborious manner of Life compared with theirs, they esteem
> slavish and base; and the Learning on which we value ourselves,
> they regard as frivolous and useless. An Instance of this occurred
> at the Treaty of Lancaster in Pennsylvania, Anno 1744, between the
> Government of Virginia and the Six Nations. After the principal
> Business was settled, the Commissioners from Virginia acquainted
> the Indians by a speech, that there was at Williamsburg a college
> with a Fund for Educating Indian Youth, and that if the Chiefs of
> the Six Nations would send down half a dozen of their Sons to that
> College, the Government would take Care that they should be well
> provided for, and instructed in all the Learning of the white People.
> It is one of the Indian rules of Politeness not to answer a public
> Proposition the same day that it is made; they think it would be
> treating it as a light Matter; and that they show it Respect by taking
> time to consider it, as a Matter important. They therefore deferred
> their Answer till the day following; when their Speaker began by

expressing their deep Sense of the Kindness of the Virginia Government, in making them that Offer; for we know, says he, that you highly esteem the kind of Learning taught in those Colleges, and that the Maintenance of our Young Men while with you, would be very expensive to you. We are convinced therefore that you mean to do us good by your Proposal, and we thank you heartily. But you who are wise must know, that different Nations have different Conceptions of things; and you will therefore not take it amiss, if our Ideas of this Kind of Education happen not to be the same with yours. We have had some Experience of it: Several of our Young People were formerly brought up at the Colleges of the Northern Provinces; they were instructed in all your Sciences; but when they came back to us, they were bad Runners, ignorant of every means of living in the Woods, unable to bear either Cold or Hunger, knew neither how to build a Cabin, take a Deer, or kill an Enemy, spoke our Language imperfectly; were therefore neither fit for Hunters, Warriors, or Counsellors; they were totally good for nothing. We are however not the less obliged by your kind Offer, tho' we decline accepting it; and to show our grateful Sense of it, if the Gentlemen of Virginia will send us a dozen of their Sons, we will take great Care of their Education, instruct them in all we know, and make Men of them.[36]

Four years after Franklin wrote the following observations on Iroquois Indian government, he would become the sage of the Philadelphia Convention, which would produce the United States Constitution:

The Indian Men, when young, are Hunters and Warriors; when old, Counsellors; for all their Government is by the Counsel or Advice of the Sages; there is no Force, there are no Prisons, no Officers to compel Obedience, or inflict Punishment. Hence they generally study Oratory; the best Speaker having the most influence. The Indian Women till the Ground, dress the Food, nurse and bring up the Children, and preserve and hand down to Posterity the Memory of Public Transactions. . . .

Having frequent Occasions to hold public Councils, they have acquired great Order and Decency in conducting them. The old Men sit in the foremost Ranks, the Warriors in the next, and the Women and Children in the hindmost. The Business of the Women is to take exact notice of what passes, imprint it in their Memories, for they have no Writing, and communicate it to their Children. They are the Records of the Council, and they preserve Tradition of the Stipulations in Treaties a hundred Years back, which when we compare with our Writings we always find exact. He that would speak, rises. The rest observe a profound Silence. When he has finished and sits

*down, they leave him five or six Minutes to recollect, that if he has
omitted any thing he intended to say, or has any thing to add, he
may rise again and deliver it. To interrupt another, even in common
Conversation, is reckoned highly indecent. How different it is from
the Conduct of a polite British House of Commons, where scarce a
Day passes without some Confusion that makes the Speaker hoarse
in calling to order; and how different from the mode of Conversation
in many polite Companies of Europe, where if you do not deliver
your Sentence with great Rapidity, you are cut off in the middle of
it by the impatient Loquacity of those you converse with, & never
suffer'd to finish it.*[37]

The remaining sections of Franklin's essay elaborate on the Indian sense
of courtesy. Despite frequent relapses, courtesy nevertheless became
traditional in both houses of Congress in order to regard the speech of
a political opponent politely. While there were many reasons to pursue
such an ideal, one may have been the example provided by the Iroquois
and other Indians whom Franklin had observed in council.

Another of Franklin's essays centered around the white lynch mob
that murdered innocent Conestoga Indians in 1764. "A Narrative of the
Late Massacres, in Lancaster County, of a Number of Indians, Friends
of this Province, by Persons Unknown," however, also included observations on how the Iroquois scrupulously honored both their treaties and
the free passage of peace delegations:

*[T]he Six Nations, as a Body, have kept Faith with the English ever
since we knew them, now near an Hundred Years; and the governing
Part of those People have had Notions of Honour. . . . As a Proof of
that Honour, I shall only mention one well-known recent Fact. When
six Catawba Deputies, under the Care of Colonel Bull, of Charlestown,
went by Permission into the Mohawks Country, to sue for and treat
of Peace for the Nation, they soon found the Six Nations highly
exasperated, and the Peace at that Time impracticable: They were
therefore in Fear for their own Persons, and apprehended that they
should be killed in their Way back to New York; which being made
known to the Mohawk Chiefs, by Colonel Bull, one of them, by Order
of the Council, made this Speech to the Catawbas:—*

"Strangers and Enemies,

*"While you are in this Country, blow away all Fear out of your
Breasts; change the black Streak of Paint on your Cheek for a red
one, and let your Faces shine with Bear's-Grease; You are safer here
than if you were at home. The Six Nations will not defile their own
Land with Blood of Men that come unarmed to ask for Peace. We
shall send a Guard with you, to see you safe out of our Territories.*

So far you shall have Peace, but no farther. Get home to your own Country, and there take care of yourselves, for there we intend to come and kill you."

The Catawbas came away unhurt accordingly.[38]

In 1766, two of Franklin's essays defended the colonists' ability to boycott English products and live on American products alone. They were entitled "Homespun Celebrates Indian Corn" and "Further Defense of Indian Corn." Both these essays were responses prompted by a challenge that the colonists could not live without England and only on "Indian corn." Franklin, aware, too, that many Europeans actually believed that anything in America was biologically inferior, defends this all-American product:

Indian corn, take it for all in all, is one of the most agreeable and wholesome grains in the world; that its green ears roasted are a delicacy beyond expression; that samp, hominy, succatash, and nokehock, made of it, are so many pleasing varieties; and that a johnny, or hoe-cake, hot from the fire, is better than a Yorkshire muffin.[39]

A far less benign defense of America was threatened by Franklin when he wrote in 1768 that if a war with Britain came, the colonists would defend themselves as "irregulars"—that is, like Indians:

It is well known that America is a Country full of Forests, Mountains, &c. That in such a Country a small irregular Force can give Abundance of Trouble to a regular one that is much greater.[40]

The irregulars Franklin referred to were those who had adapted the Indians' style of fighting by deploying in a line of battle that was shaped by the woods, not by European drill manuals. In fact, the colonists later would do just that. Thus, it would not be an exaggeration to say that American Indians influenced the colonists in peace and in war.

Ironically, the colonists' first battle with the British, at Lexington and Concord on 19 April 1775, would include skirmishes with special troops known as "light infantry," sent into the Massachusetts countryside by their "founder," General Sir Thomas Gage. During the French and Indian War (1754 to 1763), Gage had seen that British survival in frontier fighting depended upon their adapting Indian fighting tactics, just as the colonial "Rangers" had adopted them. Thus in 1757, Gage began the organization of a light infantry regiment,[41] and it would be light infantry, along with grenadiers, that Gage would send to Lexington and Concord.[42]

The most effective irregulars during the colonial era were Major Robert Rogers's Rangers, whose adoption of the Indians' style of forest warfare had inspired Gage's light infantry. That Rogers's Rangers fought so well "Indian style" was due in no small part to the fact that some of them were Christian Stockbridge Indians.[43]

Rogers was also the author of a full-length play, *Ponteach*. Pontiac was an Ottawa leader who had mobilized the Great Lake Indians against the British in 1763, and against whom Rogers had fought. *Ponteach*, published in London in 1766, is a sympathetic if stylized treatment of the northeastern Indians. Rogers had himself seen these Indians cheated by fur traders, army officers, and colonial officials. *Ponteach* was read by the public after its publication, but it was not performed until after Rogers's death in 1795. In the spirit of eighteenth-century farce, Rogers tellingly names the play's three English governors "Sharp," "Gripe," and "Catchum." Rogers gives Ponteach and the other Indians—including a Mohawk—dialogue that combines actual Indian oratory with parts of William Shakespeare and Alexander Pope. Ponteach's address to the three English governors has a strong ring of truth:

> Your Men make Indians drunk, and then they cheat 'em.
> Your Officers, your Colonels, and your Captains
> Are proud, morose, ill-natur'd, churlish Men,
> Treat us with Disrespect, Contempt, and Scorn.
> I tell you plainly this will never do,
> We never thus were treated by the French,
> Them we thought bad enough, but think you worse. . . .
> If you've some good, why don't you send them here?
> These every one are Rogues, and Knaves, and Fools,
> And think no more of Indians than of Dogs.
> Your King had better send his good Men hither,
> And keep his bad ones in some other Country;
> Then you would find that Indians would do well,
> Be peaceable, and honest in their Trade;
> We'd love you, treat you, as our Friends and Brothers,
> And Raise the Hatchet only in your Cause.[44]

While Rogers's dialogue may be more suitable to the eighteenth-century stage than the American forest, the real American language was filled with actual Indian words or expressions drawing upon Indian words or themes. Like the various corn dishes described by Franklin and listed above, Indian words ranged from the smaller details of colonial life, such as *raccoon* (Powhatan Algonquian), to the very words the Founding Fathers so often mentioned while discussing future expansion:[45] *Appalachian*, named after the southern Apalachee Indian Nation; *Ohio* (from the Iroquois meaning "fine west river"); and *Mississippi* (Algonquian for "big river"). And, of course, some of the delegates to the Philadelphia

Convention were from states named after Indian words: *Massachusetts* (Algonquian for "at big hills") and *Connecticut* (Algonquian for "at the long tidal river"). While the first national capital under the new Constitution would be located on the island of *Manhattan* (Algonquian for "hilly island"), the eventual capital would be located on the *Potomac* (from an Indian word, possibly Algonquian, recorded by Captain John Smith, *Poatawomeck*, referring either to an Indian group or perhaps a term associated with trade).

The images and reality of Indians permeated colonial life at nearly every level. Colonial armies could not consider going into battle in the forest without a contingent of Indian scouts. Indeed, because of inter-Indian rivalries, Indian scouts served in colonial armies which were fighting other Indians. Virginians, afraid that Indians living in their midst might rebel, nevertheless needed them to fill their militia quotas. So in 1738, Virginia passed a law requiring Indians who lived among the whites to serve in the militia as unarmed trumpeters or drummers.

During the American Revolution, both Patriot and British armies had Indian contingents. In fact, the Patriots had Indian allies before the British. Christian Stockbridge Indians showed up to help the Patriot army besiege British-held Boston following the battles of Lexington and Concord.

Perhaps the most symbolic visual evidence that has survived from the colonial era to demonstrate the ubiquitousness of American Indians is a painting on a wood panel, circa 1735, of Marten Van Bergen's Hudson Valley farm in Leeds, Greene County, New York. Now in the New York State Historical Association Museum at Cooperstown, New York, the work was originally placed over the fireplace in the home it depicts, and thus it is known as the *Van Bergen* or *Leeds Overmantle*. Painted by an unknown artist, the painting portrays the Van Bergen's fine home and barn, with black slaves, farm animals, and a freight wagon. In the very foreground of this painting of daily life, an Indian man and woman with their child pass by.

In an 1812 letter to Thomas Jefferson, John Adams recalled how he had grown up near an Indian family. The Massachusetts scene he describes below took place at about the same time the *Van Bergen Overmantle* was painted to portray life in the Hudson Valley of New York. What is remarkable about this short account is that it includes the two extremes which in real life faced the colonists, a real life quite apart from the drawing rooms of the European philosophers, where theories could be nurtured safely, aloof from the jarring complexities of real life. This real life, for Adams as well as for all colonists, included Indians who were good neighbors, and whose enterprise included planting orchards, and Indian enemies on the Massachusetts frontier:

I also have felt an Interest in the Indians and a Commiseration for them from my Childhood. Aaron Pomham the Priest and Moses Pomham the King of the Punkapaug and Neponsit Tribes, were frequent Visitors at my Father's house [in Braintree] at least seventy Years ago. I have a distinct rememberance of their Forms and Figures. They were very aged, and the tallest and stoutest Indians I have ever seen. The titles of King and Priest, and the names of Moses and Aaron were given them no doubt by our Massachusetts Divines and Statesmen. There was a numerous Family in this Town, whose Wigwam was within a Mile of this House [in Quincy]. This Family was frequently at my Father's house, and I in my boyish Rambles used to call at their Wigwam, where I never failed to be treated with Whortle Berries, Blackberries, Strawberries or Apples, Plumbs, Peaches, etc., for they had planted a variety of fruit Trees about them. But the Girls went out to Service [i.e., as servants] and the Boys to Sea, till not a Soul is left. We scarcely see an Indian in a year. I remember the Time when Indian Murders, Scalpings, Depredations and conflagrations were as frequent on the Eastern and Northern Frontier of Massachusetts as they are now in Indiana, and spread as much terror. But since the Conquest of Canada [in 1759], all this has ceased; and I believe with you that another Conquest of Canada will quiet the Indians forever and be as great a Blessing to them as to Us.[46]

One of the interesting details mentioned by Adams is that the daughters of the Indians he knew went off to become servants, and that the boys went to sea. Indians had shipped out on New England fishing, whaling, and commercial vessels as early as 1670 (that the tradition continued is indicated in *Moby Dick*, where one of the harpoonists onboard the *Pequod* is an American Indian). The colonial coastal towns, therefore, attracted the first of what in the twentieth century is known as an "urban Indian." The colonial "urban Indian" who is best known today was an Indian of mixed blood. Although he is known primarily for his black heritage, his last name is clearly Indian, and he was referred to in the official records at least once as being an Indian: he is Crispus Attucks, one of the five men killed in Boston by British troops on the night of 5 March 1770, in an incident which became known as "the Boston Massacre."[47]

With Indian words and terms all around the colonists, it was not surprising to find them woven into personal conversation. On 24 January 1776, John Adams wrote to his wife Abigail that he had dined in the style of an Indian feast at the Cambridge, Massachusetts, home of Colonel Thomas Mifflin, where Mifflin was also entertaining some Caughnawaga Mohawks from Canada. Adams was so amused by an analogy made by his white host between the Continental Congress and "the grand Council fire" that he used the term again at the close of his letter:

> *I waited on General Thomas at Roxbury this Morning, and then went to Cambridge where I dined at Col. Mifflins with the General, and Lady, and a vast Collection of other Company, among whom were six or seven Sachems and Warriours, of the French Caganawaga Indians, with several of their Wives and Children. A savage Feast they made of it, yet were polite in the Indian style. One of these sachems is an Englishman a Native of this Colony whose Name was Williams, captivated in his infancy with his Mother, and adopted by some kind Squaw—another I think is half French Blood.*
>
> *Tomorrow We mount for the grand Council Fire—where I shall think often of my little Brood at the Foot of Pens Hill.*[48]

And on 7 September 1787, Alexander Hamilton wrote to a "Mr. Duche" that he knew his friend the Marquis de Lafayette, who was himself fascinated with American Indians, would appreciate the following reference:

> *You can tell the Marquis de la Fayette something which will bring him the greatest pleasure, that is, there is every reason to believe that if the new Constitution is adopted his friend General Washington will be the Chief.*[49]

Although European and colonial cultures absorbed American Indian philosophies, motifs, words, and even foods, it is remarkable that after three centuries of contact little factual information had been gathered and carefully studied by the Europeans about American Indian political systems. This general deficiency existed in spite of a wide literature of published journals and diaries that included observations on Indians, and in spite of more formal efforts to understand Indian political systems by colonists such as the French Jesuits in Canada, Cadwallader Colden, Benjamin Franklin, John Stuart, and Sir William Johnson, as well as English historian William Robertson, who were the exceptions rather than the rule. Often, as in the case with Robertson, even these more thorough investigators exhibited blinding biases that clouded their work. Given this lack of a great body of information on Indian political systems, John Adams, ever the frank realist, wrote in 1787: "To collect together the legislation of the Indians, would take up much room, but would be well worth pains."[50]

Even Jean Jacques Rousseau, writing as late as 1755, formulated his perceptions of the noble savage on the incorrect premise that American Indians had not developed metallurgy and agriculture. While it is true that American Indians north of Mexico were working only in copper,

and not iron, the cultivation of corn was widespread among virtually
all Indians who lived in an environment that was warm enough to grow
it—including Indians in the Southwest, who built irrigation ditches to
supplement the meager precipitation in the arid climate. Furthermore,
agriculture was a primary factor in the overall culture and religion of
Indians such as the Iroquois, a people whose contact with the French
could have been readily studied by Rousseau had he made the effort.
Instead, Rousseau notes of metallurgy and agriculture that "both one
and the other were unknown to the savages of America, who for that
very reason have still remained savages."[51]

Such an interpretation cannot be simply written off as referring to
agriculture on individual plots of land instead of the communal agriculture, because the idea that Indians did not have any agriculture was
common in America as well as in Europe. This idea was expressed
explicitly by defining the Indians as "hunters." It was no small feat for
the colonists to deny the existence of Indian agriculture at the same
time they feasted on a variety of corn dishes. But in fact there are at
least three major reasons why the colonists could overlook Indian agriculture. First, the great cornfields of the Indians were not seen until
they were overrun by settlers or armies, and until that happened, most
whites were totally ignorant of what Indian towns looked like. Second,
the most important economic factor involving Indians was not corn, but
the fur and deerskin trades. The image of the Indians as hunters was
easily reinforced because of this association with the fur and deerskin
trades. Finally, such misperceptions were self-serving. Denying the existence of Indian agriculture had always allowed colonists to believe that
the Indians were nomads and using the lands inefficiently.

Timothy Pickering, a member of the Confederation Congress directly
involved in handling the United States' diplomacies with Indians, could
write to a colleague, Rufus King, on 4 June 1785, that he believed that
Indians were primarily hunters, Rousseau-like. Hence, it would be easier
to acquire their lands whenever the animals they hunted were driven
off by the expanding white settlements:

> Indians having no ideas of wealth, and their numbers always lessen-
> ing in the neighbourhood of our Settlements, their claims for com-
> pensation will likewise be diminished; and besides that, fewer will
> remain to be gratified, the game will be greatly reduced, and lands
> destitute of game will, by hunters, be lightly esteemed.[52]

The hunting image persisted, conveniently, through the Jackson and
Van Buren presidencies, allowing the whites to justify the taking of
Indian lands. Finally, at long last the United States marched west of the

Mississippi, where the agricultural Indian nations such as the Mandans were stricken by smallpox, leaving the United States to deal primarily with some Indians who were indeed what Americans had believed Indians to be all along: real hunters.

The misperception of Indians as lacking agriculture demonstrates how what people believe is often more important in shaping their attitudes than actual fact. It is the Enlightenment attitude, not the Enlightenment's occasional observant scholarship, which most impacted on the white colonists in America.

Both in Europe and in the European colonies in the Americas, the Enlightenment's interest in Native Americans was part of a wide-ranging interest in the peoples and cultures of the entire world, the purpose of which was to sort out, from European perspectives, which ideas from world history should be considered for possible integration into the European perspective and which should be rejected as unworthy.

The English philosopher John Locke recorded that he had spoken with American Indians who visited England.[53] Nevertheless, his impressions of Indians must still be viewed as being based primarily on reports other whites had written. Locke's philosophy, expressed in his *Two Treatises of Government* in 1690, included an idea that would become the basis for many of the Patriots' protests; the Declaration of Independence; part of the Virginia Constitution; the Articles of Confederation; and the Preamble to the United States Constitition: that political power originally and ultimately resided in the people, not in a monarch. Although there were European examples of these ideas, none of them were based scientifically on existing evidence. Ancient and religious examples depended either upon the historical record or upon faith. But in America, what in the European experience had survived only in the historical record or in religion was, from the European perspective, still in existence. The Indians, Europeans declared, were currently demonstrating that power came from "the people." Such an example could be referred to objectively, scientifically, because it did not depend upon historical interpretation or upon religious faith.

Thus, American Indians enabled the Europeans to prove to their own satisfaction that political power rested in "we the people." And this concept justified the American Revolution and ultimately the United States Constitution.

Within that wide-ranging exploration of human potential and alternatives, Native Americans north of Mexico were perceived, wrongly or not, as examples of what all human societies were like in the first stages of social, political, and economic development. John Locke, in his *Two Treatises of Government*, states:

To understand political power aright, and derive it from its original, we must consider what estate all men are naturally in, and that is a state of perfect freedom to order their actions, and dispose of their possessions and persons as they think fit, within the bounds of the law of Nature, without asking leave or depending upon the will of any other man. . . .[54]

Locke theorized that once one human made a compact or contract with another human, they were beginning to add their own laws to the laws of nature and thus evolving from "the state of Nature."[55] In this context, Locke viewed American Indians as having the fewest contractual and governmental controls over them. Locke therefore concluded that Indian leaders, who he called "kings," had power to

command absolutely in war, yet at home, and in time of peace, they exercise very moderate sovereignty, the resolutions of peace and war being ordinarily either in the people or in a council.[56]

It was in this context that Locke concluded that

America . . . is still a pattern of the first ages in Asia and Europe, whilst the inhabitants were too few for the country, and want of people and money gave men no temptation to enlarge their possessions of land or contest for wider extent of ground. . . .[57]

What made the Indians' view of property so very different was that their societies and governments were based on communal landholdings, while the primary goal of white government was the protection of private individual landholdings. The Europeans and their colonists resolved this issue long before the Enlightenment (among the English, as early as 1586) by developing the premise that Indians had become subjects of European empires during the colonial period either by conquest or treaty. Thus, while Indians might locally hold their land in common, the law at the top of the legal pyramid was European and based on private property, not communal property.

The delegates in Philadelphia who wrote the Constitution never resolved another major theme of Enlightenment political philosophy. Locke had said that American Indian societies were closer to an original state of nature because they were not expansionist. Montesquieu affirmed this by pointing out that the republic of Rome became corrupt only after it became imperialistic. Thus, Montesquieu advocated small nations as the best environments in which to protect the full liberties of citizens. Yet, the Constitution was established in part so that the United States could more successfully expand into new colonies called "territories." Philosophically, then, the Constitution was a gamble, a roll of the dice against the philosophical odds that an imperial society would become corrupt when that society became too large to protect individual liberties.

From a practical and obvious point of view, the United States could not expand unless it did so by taking American Indian lands. Under such conditions, American imperialism seems to have been inevitable. Although the white lawmakers within the United States might proclaim philosophically that they would never take Indian lands without the voluntary consent of the Indian peoples involved, the pragmatic side of these very same lawmakers would define the constitutional means to carry out their expansionist goals.

During the debates held in each state on whether or not to ratify the Constitution, two broad interpretations were debated. The so-called Federalists—those who favored the Philadelphia Constitution—maintained that the Constitution was a logical extension of the spirit of the American Revolution and of the Enlightenment. The so-called Anti-Federalists—those who were in favor of continuing the Articles of Confederation—believed that the Constitution betrayed the revolution and the Enlightenment. Subsequent generations have continued the debate. The debate has also raged over the extent to which the authors of the Constitution were ideological and to what degree they were pragmatic.

In terms of Native American history, the Articles of Confederation Congress had, during the American Revolution, offered a glimpse into one alternative. In 1778, the Confederation Congress of the United States made a treaty with the Delaware Indians. Among the terms of that treaty is an offer to work mutually toward the concept of an American Indian state joining the United States:

Article VI.

And it is further agreed on between the contracting parties should it for the future be found conducive for the mutual interest of both parties to invite any other tribes who have been friends to the interest of the United States, to join the present Confederation, and to form a state whereof the Delaware nation shall be the head, and have a representation in Congress. . . .[58]

This treaty clearly implies a willingness to attempt to integrate an American Indian political and social system into the United States. Ironically, such an offer was also an attempt to attract the Delawares into secession from the allegiance they had to the Six Nations. The treaty failed for many reasons, among which was the inability of the white government to prevent its citizens from continuing their encroachments and harrassments of the Delawares. Nevertheless, philosophically the treaty remains one of the outstanding "might have beens" during the era of the American Revolution.

The advocates of the established Articles of Confederation who stood against a ratification of the United States Constitution saw local state sovereignty offering better protection for individual liberty. They feared the centralized federal government proposed in the Constitution. Montesquieu's contention that small states and societies best protected liberty tied in with his view of Native American societies. Montesquieu reviewed the history of world governments according to the main purpose he felt each served:

> Though all governments have the same general end, which is that of preservation, yet each has another particular object. Increase of dominion was the object of Rome; war, that of Sparta; religion, that of the Jewish laws; commerce, that of Marseilles; public tranquility, that of the laws of China; navigation, that of the law of Rhodes; natural liberty, that of the policy of the Savages.[59]

During the Philadelphia Convention, Gouverneur Morris embodied Montesquieu's observation that "savages" best represented the concept of liberty when he stated on July 5 that "[t]he savage State was more favorable to liberty than the Civilized; and sufficiently so to life."[60]

By admitting that "liberty" and "life" were more favorably encouraged in the savage state, Morris was not only affirming Montesquieu's position, he was reiterating a source that had inspired Montesquieu: the works of John Locke. Locke had stated in his *Second Treatise of Government* that there were three basic elements in human experience which related to government: life, liberty, and property.[61] Indeed, Thomas Jefferson had written in the Declaration of Independence that "all men are created equal, that they are endowed by their Creator with certain unalienable rights, that among these are life, liberty, and the pursuit of happiness"— the pursuit of happiness being Jefferson's wily propaganda ploy to broaden the concept of "property" to include a goal that people currently without property could aspire to.

But herein lay the dilemma for the Founding Fathers. The American Revolution had ended successfully in the affirmation and protection of the revolutionaries' lives and liberties. But in the 1780s, their property— their farms, their commerce, and their general financial circumstances— were at best only holding their own and at worst imperiled. The delegates who went to Philadelphia were determined to find a balance that would combine the protection of life and liberty affirmed in the philosophy of the American Revolution, with the protection of property, which while now separate and independent from Britain had not yet been secured. Locke had noted that people

unite *for the mutual* Preservation *of their Lives, Liberties and Estates,*
which I call by the general Name, Property. *The great and chief end*
. . . *of Mens [sic] uniting into Commonwealths, and putting them-*
selves under Government, is the Preservation of their Property. . . .
But though Men when they enter into Society, give up the Equality,
Liberty, and Executive Power they had in the State of Nature, into
the hands of the Society . . . *it being only with an intention in every*
one the better to preserve himself his Liberty and Property.[62]

The essence and nature of liberty is the subject of the Preamble of
the Constitution, a preamble that, as has already been noted, was inspired
in part by John Rutledge's reference to the founding of the Iroquois
Confederacy. The rest of the Constitution written at Philadelphia, however, is simply a structure to ensure the survival of life, liberty, and
property. The Bill of Rights—the first ten amendments—were added to
the Constitution as a result of the pressures brought upon the government during and after the state ratifying conventions. They represent a
return to a strong concern for liberty.

The philosophies of the Enlightenment encouraged white Americans
to consider and evaluate all possible examples of human societies
throughout the world, not the least of which were those of the American
Indians and the Iroquois in particular.

As well as providing one of the inspirations for the eloquence of the
Premable of the Constitution, the very existence of the Iroquois political
system also provided one of many motivations for the whites to achieve
a centralized unity under the Constitution. As a separate political order
capable of allying either with the Indian nations directly to the west of
them, or working with the British who still held forts at Oswego, Niagara,
and Detroit, the Iroquois posed a very real political challenge to the
United States.

Since the American Revolution secured life and liberty more successfully than it secured property, it is logical that the government
created during that revolution, the Articles of Confederation, was also
more successful in protecting life and liberty than in protecting property,
and that the Constitution attempted to redress the deficiency of the
articles in protecting property. In structure, the Articles of Confederation much more resembled the Iroquois Confederacy than did the
Constitution. The articles were intended as a "league of friendship"
among sovereign states, as the second and third articles so clearly convey:

> II. *Each state retains its sovereignty, freedom, and independence,*
> *and every power, jurisdiction, and right, which is not by this Con-*
> *federation expressly delegated to the United States, in Congress*
> *assembled.*

III. The said states hereby severally enter into a firm league of friendship with each other, for their common defence, the security of their liberties, and their mutual and general welfare, binding themselves to assist each other, against all force offered to, or attacks made upon them, or any of them, on account of religion, sovereignty, trade, or any other pretence whatever.[63]

In the trilogy of life, liberty, and property, the first two were conceded by European philosophers, and at the Philadelphia Convention, as existing in "the savage state." But the Founding Fathers rejected the Indians' concept of property, based as it was on a communal ethic. Thus, when the delegates at the Philadelphia Convention set out to create a new government to shore up the protection of property, specific political, economic, and philosophical models of the American Indian were rejected.

The choice of the Founding Fathers was to turn away from American Indian models of local sovereignty represented by the Six Nations. They turned away from the Iroquois model of government by persuasion rather than by centralized cohesion. And they rejected their own Articles of Confederation, the closest white Americans had ever come to reflecting even a part of the decentralized premises of Iroquois government.

On the other hand, the Bill of Rights, amended to the Constitution in 1791—especially the First Amendment—are a reaffirmation of the spirit of "life" and "liberty" which the Enlightenment so admired among American Indians.

At many levels, the Constitution composed at Philadelphia—that is, prior to two centuries of amendments—was a betrayal of values held in esteem by the Iroquois. Women were originally omitted from the United States' political system. Black human life was valued at three-fifths the value of white human life. The Constitution separated government into branches intended more to check than to balance each other, because the checks and balances were achieved through tension. Moreover, the Constitution specifically rejected the Iroquois idea that government is by consensus. Instead, the Constitution mandates the rule of the majority. And under the Constitution, church and state are separate, whereas the Iroquois integrate religion and politics. Finally, the Constitution was defined in terms of private, individual property rights, not communal property rights.

Despite these differences, it must be emphasized that replication should not be the only standard by which the twentieth century should seek to understand how the Iroquois and other Indian people influenced the Founding Fathers and the Constitution. This is seen in a reference by John Adams, who in refuting a similarity to Indians in one instance, admitted another similarity—the similarity being that the United States derived its power just as Indian nations did: from "we the people."

The context of Adams's statement evolves from his acute intent to distance the United States from any appearance that it condoned any hereditary political office. Within the Iroquois and many other Indian political systems, political units, voting rights, and office-holding are defined within the context of separate clans, clans based on heredity. On the other hand, the political units of the United States are based on place of residence. For example, an Iroquois is a member of the same clan wherever that Iroquois resides, whereas a United States citizen legitimately switches state and local political allegiance whenever that citizen moves to another state.

Yet, John Adams admitted that both Indians and the United States based their power on the "people." In the eighteenth century, the concept of the "people" was frequently expressed by the word *nation*, since the words *people* and *nation* were regarded as synonymous. It is this sense that Adams reflects in the following:

> [Regarding] the legislation of the Indians. . . . The sovereignty is in the nation [i.e., the people], it is true, but . . . their royal and aristocratical dignities [i.e., their leaders] are much more generally hereditary, from the popular partiality to particular families.[64]

In addition to the fact that the text of the Constitution created at Philadelphia in 1787 was primarily concerned with the preservation of property—life and liberty having been secured by the revolution—there are other reasons the Founding Fathers rejected certain Native American values in composing the original (pre-amendment) text of the Constitution. Instead, the Founding Fathers did choose to imitate a model much admired by the Enlightenment: that of Rome. They saw that their own tribal ancestors had been conquered by the power of Rome, and thus they rejected Native American examples from the perspective of their own northern European tribal histories. In this sense, the Founding Fathers saw a real and direct connection between the Indian societies on their frontiers and their own national histories, a practical lesson that was at least as important as the theoretical appreciation of Native American cultures that pervaded the Enlightenment.

Quite clearly the Founding Fathers intended to do to the American Indians what Rome had done to the Britons, Germans, and other northern European tribes in their imperialist expansion. One of the major reasons the Anti-Federalists feared the Constitution was its provision for a professional army controlled by a central government rather than by the individual states. The first professional army formed by the new government under the United States Constitution was not raised to fight a European power. In 1792, President George Washington requested and received from Congress a new army whose sole purpose was to defeat the Indian confederacy blocking United States occupation of the Ohio country. The name of this army was "the Legion of the United States"—a legion that could do for America what ancient legions had done for Rome.

As an imperial power, the United States government was following the pattern of logic set forth by another Enlightenment thinker, the Scottish philosopher David Hume. Hume wrote in 1752 that so-called savages did not have "a state of civil government" because

> the chieftain, who had probably acquired his influence during the continuance of war, ruled more by persuasion than command; and till he could employ force to reduce the refractory and disobedient, the society could scarcely be said to have attained a state of civil government. No compact or agreement, it is evident, was expressly formed for general submission, an idea far beyond the comprehension of savages.[65]

Having thus written off the "savages" as not having governments worthy of the name, Hume noted that while original contracts (a la John Locke) may have been "founded on consent and a voluntary impact" even among Europeans, the governments that ruled in his own era had evolved through "a thousand changes." Hume then made telling and revealing points which challenged Locke and any pretense of attempting to protect liberty by reestablishing the simpler governments of the past:

> Almost all the governments which exist at present, or of which there remains any record in history, have been founded originally either on usurpation or conquest or both, without any pretense of a fair consent of voluntary subjection of people. . . .
>
> The face of the earth is continually changing by the increase of small kingdoms into great empires, by the dissolution of great empires into smaller kingdoms, by the planting of colonies, by the migration of tribes. Is there anything discoverable in all these events but force and violence. . . .
>
> It is vain to say that all governments are or should be at first founded on popular consent . . . conquest or usurpation—that is, in plain terms, force—by dissolving the ancient governments, is the origin of almost all the new ones which were ever established in the world. . . .
>
> My intention here is not to exclude the consent of the people from being of just foundation of government. Where it has place, it is surely the best and most sacred of any.[66]

The Founding Fathers at Philadelphia were very much in favor of defining what "place" the consent of the governed would have in the new government. Their opponents, the Anti-Federalists, saw this place for liberty as dangerously constricted. But the Founding Fathers and their supporters, who eventually won ratification for the Constitution, believed that their society was faced with internal chaos such as that of Shay's Rebellion in 1786, and what to them appeared to be a confusing and contradictory array of state governments and their definitions of liberty. Centralized control would, they hoped, provide a remedy.

Thus, the Founding Fathers turned toward a more realistic (or pessimistic) view of human nature, away from Locke's admiration of the original liberties of the so-called savage state. In doing so, they increasingly embraced Rome and not the European tribes of northern Europe. This last point is significant. Not only were the Founding Fathers rejecting the political heritage of the indigenous Native Americans, they were consciously choosing to learn a sobering lesson from their own European past: their own northern European ancestral tribes had all been conquered by armies from a more centralized government, Rome. Furthermore, Saxon England, also very much admired by the Founding Fathers, had been conquered in 1066 by the more centralized power of the Normans.

The analogy was more complex than a direct comparison. John Adams admired the Saxons, but he felt that the history of the German tribes had, after the fall of Rome, culminated in the rise of turbulent monarchies. Thus, Adams reasoned that tribal institutions might over time degenerate into the worse tyranny of monarchies. In 1787, Adams wrote a three-volume treatise while in London as the first United States ambassador to Great Britain. The work, *A Defence of the Constitutions of Government of the United States of America*, explained American politics to the British and justified both the state constitutions and the just completed United States Constitution. In this work, he specifically compares the Germans with the American Indians and rejects both as political models, even though these models were recommended by Enlightenment philosophers. Adams does so at the beginning of the first volume in a passage that depicts what might happen if the Romans Cicero and Tacitus returned to earth in 1787. The two Romans are then told that if Adams and his fellow Americans

> *were advised by some of the greatest philosophers and politicians of the age to . . . set up the governments of ancient Goths and modern Indians—what would they say? That the Americans would be . . . reprehensible if they should listen to such advice.*[67]

In a fascinating psychological choice, the Founding Fathers rejected their own tribal histories for the methods of their conquerors, the Romans and Normans. For them, the ultimate lesson was that societies like Rome won, and that less-centralized peoples, be they Germans, Saxons, or American Indians, lost.

The analogy between the Roman conquest of northern Europe and the white conquest of America was, however, older than the Enlightenment and lay at the very roots of English colonization. Captain John Smith, describing colonial Virginia's 1622 war with the Powhatan Confederacy, observed: "What growing state was there ever in the world which had not the like? Rome grew by oppression, and rose upon the back of her enemies." [68]

In part because of their ancestors' own tribal past, the Founding Fathers could admire individual Indians—for example, in praising their wisdom at councils or their oratory—and at the same time reject the Native American forms of governments. Indeed, since the tribal ancestors of the Founding Fathers had eventually adapted Roman culture, many of the Founding Fathers assumed that American Indians would eventually adapt to the culture of the United States. [69]

On 28 June 1787, during the actual debates in Philadelphia over the nature of the Constitution, James Madison made a lengthy speech on how a greater unity in the United States was necessary because history demonstrated how the lack of unity had ruined past civilizations. [70] He noted how "Carthage & Rome tore one another to pieces instead of uniting their forces to devour the weaker nations of the Earth." Madison continued by citing the conflicts between Austria and France, between England and France, among the ancient Greek states of Sparta, Athens, and Thebes, and between Prussia and Austria. Even as Madison was speaking, the American Indians north of the Ohio were attempting to unify under their new confederacy, the United Indian Nations—a subject referred to at the beginning of this chapter. This new confederacy was unable to convince the oldest confederacy, that of the Iroquois, to join.

Rival Confederacies

Following the American Revolution, American Indians called the thirteen fiercely independent states their "Brothers of the Thirteen Fires." To confront these "brothers," Indian people, including the Iroquois, realized that they would have to initiate countermeasures. The former colonists, now independent, also realized that further measures were necessary. Yet, in the midst of debates within both the white and red societies, new measures were diluted or avoided. Both races fell back on colonial precedents. The whites invented a Constitution which centralized the government of the East Coast and the future colonies—called "territories." The Constitution followed the very pattern of British centralization they had rebelled against. The supreme laws of the whites' new Constitution rested in the central government, not in a confederation of state sovereignties. But Indian nations also failed to create new political answers, and they, too, fell back upon precedent. The difference was that the whites had the economic and demographic strengths to succeed despite their repetition of the past, while the Indian nations simply did not.

Specifically, the dilemma of the 1780s for the white Americans was to create a new unity, while the dilemma for the Iroquois was whether to perpetuate their old confederacy or participate in a new, broader Indian confederacy that would dramatically alter the Iroquois "establishment." While definitions of unity among both red and white were old problems from the past, they took on a desperate sense of emergency during the period from 1783 to 1789.

In September 1783, representatives of most of the British-allied Indian nations north of the Ohio, plus the Cherokees from the south, met at Sandusky, Ohio. They were encouraged by the British, whose agents acted among the Indians in a manner not unlike those French agents acting among the newly independent white colonists. The Mohawk Iroquois leader Joseph Brant attempted to direct the conference toward the creation of a strong confederacy to balance the power of the newly created United States, itself a confederacy under its Articles of Confederation. For the Iroquois, the question was whether to continue their old confederacy, with its capital at Onondaga, or willingly see the axis of Indian power move west to Ohio. The Shawnees had proposed such a confederacy as early as 1746, and in the intervening years the Seneca Iroquois had been the most interested in reconstituting the Indian politics of the north.

But after 1783, the Mohawk Iroquois under Joseph Brant fostered the major thrust of Iroquois participation, and most of these people were refugees from their homeland on the Mohawk River. Joseph Brant was as well known among Indians as George Washington was among the whites. But the "loyalist" conservative faction among the Iroquois was far stronger than the conservative, loyalist faction had been among the colonists during the revolution.

The traditional Iroquois balked at Brant's claims to lead Indian people into a new confederacy. After all, these Mohawks and other Iroquois had moved to Canada, and had taken up homes on the old trading path between Lake Ontario and the key to the West, Detroit. It was easier for them to propose an end to the old Iroquois Confederacy. But those Iroquois still on their original homelands were not convinced that a new confederacy would succeed. The British sponsors behind Joseph Brant had just betrayed Indian people, and they might do so again.

In 1784, the United States and the state of New York imposed the Treaty of Fort Stanwix upon what can only be viewed as a "rump parliament" of Iroquois delegates. How the Iroquois Confederacy would react to this treaty had yet to be determined. Moreover, the clan mothers, who had kept the Iroquois in the American Revolution when many of the warriors wanted to make peace, were evidently persuading the chiefs that the Iroqouis could not survive the devastations of yet another frontier war as they had during the revolution. They could not risk bearing the brunt of white American counterattacks as the buffer between the Americans and the Indians along the Ohio. In 1786, wars sparked from Georgia to the Great Lakes, and the Iroquois Confederacy, meeting at Buffalo Creek in what is now western New York, rejected the 1784 Treaty of Fort Stanwix.

In the midst of this wide-ranging crisis for Indian nations, a meeting was held in Hurontown. In attendance were representatives of the Hurons, Delawares, Shawnees, Ottawas, Ojibwas (Chippewas), Potawatomies, Miamis, and Cherokees. The Six Nations also sent a delegation. An Indian confederacy, based on the concept proposed at Sandusky in 1783, was proposed to block the anticipated expansion of the various states of the United States. The Iroquois remained reluctant to join. Membership would mean an alteration of the autonomy of their own confederacy and participation in a new confederacy made up in part by old enemies and some nations long regarded by the Iroquois as under the laws of their confederacy.

The Iroquois made the decision to remain aloof because by joining the new confederacy, they would have taken on the brunt of the fighting if war broke out since they were on the front line of white expansion. The Iroquois chose to wait and see if the new confederacy might emerge victorious. Even if they did not, white expansion in the past had been diverted from the Iroquois homelands towards some of the very Indian nations now proposing the new confederacy. The strategy might work again.

The new Indian confederacy called itself the United Indian Nations. But which Indian nation would lead? The Mohawk Iroquois Joseph Brant, acting as a pan-Indian leader and not as a representative of the Iroquois, believed that the British in Canada would support the new confederacy. Brant attempted once again to exert leadership while seeking a compromise with the Shawnees, who felt they should lead. The confederacy which emerged actually resembled the old confederacy that had rallied behind Pontiac from 1763 to 1766, with the addition of British-sponsored Iroquois refugees who now lived in Canada, such as Joseph Brant, and a number of those Iroquois, especially Senecas, who lived in Ohio.

The United Indian Nations confederacy was rife with factions. They could not even agree on how and when their messages should be conveyed to the white Americans. Finally, in 1787 their diplomatic appeal

Joseph Brant, or Thayendanegea, the Mohawk warrior and leader who helped form the United Indian Nations confederacy in the mid-1780s. (Portrait by George Catlin after Ezra Ames, 1806, from Life of Joseph Brant by William L. Stone, published in 1865.)

reached the United States. The United Indian Nations asked for peace but threatened war. The white Americans saw it as a bluff. They chose to delay their answer to the appeal. The Congress, at that time under the Articles of Confederation, knew that at Philadelphia a convention was meeting to reform their own society into a stronger confederacy. The rhetoric of the proclamation of the United Indian Nations awaited the test of arms.

The United Indian Nations restructured itself almost annually, but won victories in Ohio until 1794. Among these victories was the most devastating defeat an American army would ever suffer at the hands of any Indian army, and in proportion to the number of soldiers engaged, the most catastrophic defeat of an American army in any war. On 4 November 1791, near the Wabash River, General Arthur St. Clair lost 630 men in an army of 1,400 men (by contrast, George Armstrong Custer lost 216).[71] But by 1794, the United States, centralized under its new Constitution, was ready to move in force. More importantly, the United States had secured the neutrality of the Iroquois Confederacy by conceding major political issues of sovereignty to the Iroquois in negotiations which culminated at the 1794 Treaty of Canadaigua.

The Iroquois did not choose a political reformation or reorganization. Eventually, after 1799, they undertook a renaissance driven by a synthesis of old and new religious beliefs as related by the teacher Handsome Lake. In this way the Iroquois perpetuated their old political system.

Overall, however, in the race to define a new unity among confederated nations, the United States had won. The Thirteen Fires were now one. That single federal flame burned more brightly than the thirteen separate ones, and in a little over a century it would consume the continent.

4.
Perspectives on American Indian Sovereignty and International Law, 1600 to 1776

Howard R. Berman

In August 1987, in the midst of the celebration of two hundred years of constitutional government in the United States, representatives of American Indian nations traveled to Geneva, Switzerland, to join other indigenous peoples seeking United Nations recognition of their right to self-determination.[1] To those unfamiliar with the deep and continuous roots of these aspirations, such claims to nationhood frequently appear abstract and ahistorical. Indeed, most historical writing in the United States, including legal history, has been strikingly silent on this question, emphasizing instead the evolution of federal power in the arena of Indian relations.

This conjuncture of events, constitutional bicentennial with United Nations action, however, invites reconsideration of the fundamental nature of those relations. The silent spaces of history raise the most profound questions, not only for historiography but for law, where the continuity of Indian nationhood remains vulnerable to the exercise of power. What was the nature of indigenous nationhood from first European contact well into the nineteenth century? What role did American Indian nations play in international relations in North America? How did relations with Indian nations affect the United States' own struggle for definition and consolidation in its formative era? To what degree do treaties between Indian nations and European states, and the United States, evidence the international personality of the Indian parties? To what degree do the treaties continue to form a legal basis for consensual, self-determined relationships with the United States?

Each of these questions reflects the fact that the original relationships between Indian nations and other sovereigns were of a decidedly international character.[2] War, peace, intersocietal friendship, and commerce together formed the dynamics of international relations in North America as elsewhere. Before European contact, Indian nations and confederacies were fully independent and self-determined societies. Some Indian nations such as the Six Nations Iroquois Confederacy (Haudenosaunee) had lengthy diplomatic histories with European states by 1776; others had their first sustained encounter with the United States in the nineteenth century during a period in which the American government increasingly was able to dictate the terms of the relationship. In either case, however, the specific relationship that each nation initially established with the United States was born of the principles and practices of international law, and was typically defined through the treaty process.

Obviously then, the links between past and present are of central importance to any analysis of indigenous rights. In both United States law and international law, however, the connections between pre-colonial indigenous self-determination and contemporary status and rights have been clouded by racial and legal concepts of the colonial era. The Eurocentric arrogance and social Darwinism of the late nineteenth and early twentieth centuries effectively erased the memory of a centuries-old historical record of indigenous peoples functioning on the inter-national plane, and of a definite if grudging recognition of indigenous rights in principle and state practice.[3] Although these colonial categories have long been repudiated in virtually every other context, they have continued to exert a curious degree of influence on the debate on indigenous rights in the United States, other countries, and at the international level.

The purpose of this chapter is to begin a reexamination of these historical linkages by exploring the international legal personality and treaty process of American Indian nations in North America from the first significant establishment of relations with European nations to the American Revolution—a period of over one hundred fifty years. This undertaking is necessarily preliminary and limited in geographical scope. Accordingly, it will focus on international relationships in the region encompassing much of the northeastern quadrant of the United States extending into that part of contemporary Canada immediately north of the St. Lawrence River and Great Lakes. This area has been chosen because it was the scene of the most widespread and intense diplomatic activity on the continent, involving four European and numerous Indian nations.

My approach follows the process of analysis employed by the International Court of Justice (World Court) in its 1975 *Advisory Opinion on Western Sahara*.[4] In that opinion, the Court applied the doctrine of "intertemporal law" in determining the international status of the indigenous peoples of the Western Sahara at certain relevant points in history. In international legal analysis, the doctrine of intertemporal law requires that the legal status of an entity or event in the past must be interpreted according to the law of the period in question.[5] It thus provides a counter-weight to the tendency of twentieth-century literature to read nineteenth-century legal concepts back into history. The doctrine is particularly significant for the question of the status of indigenous treaty-making, where the legal discourse has been heavily influenced by the nature of North American power relations in the late nineteenth century. Moreover, in analyzing the legal relations of the Saharan peoples in the late nineteenth century, the Court set aside the conceptual structures of

European colonial jurisprudence to directly scrutinize the actual state practice in the region.[6] Similarly, this article examines the actual practice of the era in question in North America as it reflected and established international law.

The International Legal Context

At the onset of the American War of Independence, Indian sovereignty was fully reflected in the practice of European states. Despite the religious intolerance and cultural antagonisms that had permeated European attitudes toward other peoples for centuries,[7] European states were compelled to recognize and engage Indian nations as political actors in their diplomatic activities on the continent. Each successive European state seeking to establish commercial or settler colonies necessarily as a matter of course entered into treaty relations with indigenous nations concerning territorial cessions, peace and non-aggression, military alliance, and the course of trade.[8] In North America as elsewhere, the treaty-making process was based on a recognition of the mutuality of legal capacity and specific interests of the parties to the agreement.

In the early stages of colonization, these agreements and the continuing relationships they created were frequently decisive to the survival as well as the success of the European project. For Britain and France in particular, political alliances with Indian nations determined the balance of power between their North American enterprises and formed the major part of their economic interests. With the exception of coastal and riverine areas where European populations and military forces were concentrated and European power was gradually imposed, Indian relations required skillful and continuous diplomacy.

Unfortunately, we are left with an asymmetrical record of these transactions. Documentary sources are limited to the state papers of the European parties and occasional memoirs of European participants. As a result, one must be cautious in interpreting a fundamentally bilateral relationship or history of relations solely from the quite interested internal memoranda of one side. Nevertheless, if we cannot always be certain about the accuracy of what was said, we can see with considerably more clarity what was done. For purposes of international legal analysis, the conduct of the parties and the relationship of that conduct to contemporary international life are of primary relevance. From that vantage point, the documents show a remarkably consistent pattern for nearly two hundred years.

In the first instance, the records are *treaty* records. Peaceful relations were established and maintained by mutual consent throughout the period. Structurally, treaty-making included the same elements as in Europe—two or more territorially defined independent political entities bargained the terms of a relationship. Negotiations were at arms length and were conducted on behalf of distinct peoples. Although the power equation between the parties varied according to time and place, it was by no means always in favor of the European side. In many treaty conferences, the European entity gave "presents" that if not forms of tribute were at least inducements to preserve peace. In the absence of peaceful relations, Indian and European nations confronted each other in conditions of active or inactive hostility. In either case, in peace or war, these relationships were of an international rather than internal character. Expressly or de facto, wars and treaties evidenced European recognition of the political personality and territorial sovereignty of Indian nations.

Indian-European alliances were gradually integrated into the fabric of North American affairs. Indian allies protected European colonies from rival European forces and hostile Indian nations.[9] European arms and other assistance were similarly utilized by Indian allies against their own enemies, European or indigenous. European vulnerability was not limited to warfare, however. Particularly in the early period, the major European motivation for being in much of North America was the fur trade, not colonial expansion per se. Trade required agreements relating to access to (or monopoly of) indigenous markets, continuous sources of furs, relative valuation of goods, networks of supply and distribution, and defense of trade routes. Treaty-making and stable relations were essential for all of these purposes.

International Legal Personality

Some preliminary consideration of the international legal personality of Indian nations is in order before beginning an assessment of state practice in North America during these centuries. In the first instance, the most cursory examination of the primary source material of period diplomacy reveals that treaty-making and other elements of international relations were interactive in nature. Rather than a unilateral exercise of European prerogative, intersocietal relations were conducted on a bilateral and multilateral basis between and among distinct peoples over a lengthy span of time. Agreements between European and Indian nations, including those negotiated under the pressure of events, were consensual in an international law sense, representing a mutual accommodation of individual definitions and interests. Looking at the diversity of these relationships over time, from a structural perspective it is clear that Indian nations were territorially defined political entities functioning on the international plane. The methodological imperative of this conclusion is that state practice must be examined in light of the positions and political context of parties on all sides of these transactions, including necessarily the Indian parties.

The use of the term "state practice," however, begs a controversial question—were American Indian nations "states"? If our notion of statehood is limited to the modern configuration of the European nation-state that dominates contemporary political life, the answer would be negative. Indian societies were not organized around the centralization of political power, development of administrative bureaucracies, permanent police and military structures, or codes and courts that social scientists regard as descriptive criteria of contemporary statehood.[10] Indeed, similar Eurocentric perspectives on the nature of statehood were a central theme in the circular reasoning of late nineteenth-century colonial jurisprudence, denying international legal status to indigenous peoples and their territories and legitimizing the colonial process.[11]

International law, however, has never confined international legal personality to a single political structure, nor has any clear definition of statehood ever been broadly accepted.[12] On the contrary, a vast array of political entities have in practice been embraced within that concept. One has only to look to the description of then existing European sovereignties by the early positivist writer G. F. von Martens, writing at the end of the historical era which forms the focus of the present study (1788), to perceive the substantial diversity in size, political organization, and mode of practice of political entities engaged in international relations recognized in that period.[13] For Martens, the key to sovereign status was a condition of independence, which was not required to be absolute in order to be considered effective.[14]

Moreover, for centuries before the modern colonial era, extensive diplomatic relations were maintained between Europe and non-Western peoples in Asia, Africa, North and South America, and the Pacific.[15] Although the historical record of those relations was largely shaped by European conceptions, European overseas activities and the intersocietal accommodations made necessary as a result, transformed and internationalized the parochial "law of nations" of Europe and other regions by diminishing degrees until the consolidation of European domination in the nineteenth century.[16] Influenced by state practice as well as natural law doctrines, early international jurists conceptualized the international community as a universal family of nations that embraced peoples of different cultures and religions.[17]

It is often overlooked in this context that the European societies that first encountered indigenous nations were themselves only in the early stages of evolving forms of statehood in the contemporary sense.[18] European nations that met indigenous nations in North America in the seventeenth century, although different in culture and forms of internal governance, were not so different as political entities that they could not recognize or relate to each other in ways familiar to international relations. The Haudenosaunee or Six Nations Iroquois Confederacy that has an important role in this study was structurally similar in many respects to the States-General formed in the Netherlands following Dutch independence.[19] These two peoples entered into some of the earliest diplomatic relations on the North American continent. Baron Lahontan, who became familiar with the Haudenosaunee from his activities as a soldier in New France in the late seventeenth century, compared them to the Swiss Cantons and observed, "They laugh at the menaces of our Kings and Governors, for they have no notion of dependence, nay the very word to them is insupportable. They look upon themselves as Sovereigns, accountable to none but God alone. . . ."[20]

When viewed according to the doctrine of intertemporal law, the issue of indigenous international legal personality at the time in question does not depend on conformity with late twentieth-century social science definitions of statehood. Numerous Indian nations fulfilled the fundamental criteria of permanent population, territory, government, and capacity for international relations as they were understood in the period, and were sufficiently independent to determine their own affairs without outside rule.[21] The pervasive application of treaty-making over time in North America gives clear evidence of broad European recognition of the international personality of the indigenous peoples of that time and place. Treaty-making, however, was not the source of that international legal personality, nor was it the source of Indian sovereign and territorial rights. As political communities created by the original inhabitants, Indian societies possessed inherent, preexisting sovereign rights and conducted political relations in their own interests on the international plane. For European nations the situation was quite different. As emigrant settler societies, their rights in North America were largely derivative rather than original. Consequently, the content of specific treaties, especially territorial cessions, was a primary source of European right.

Modes of European Legitimation

By the mid-seventeenth century, treaties with indigenous nations had a dual purpose for European states. In North America, they provided the formal intersocietal mechanisms for establishing and regulating evolving relationships consistent with the specific realities of international life on that continent. Additionally, in the European context Indian treaties were increasingly employed by states to legitimize territorial claims in the Western Hemisphere against each other.[22] Although the colonial states had but small footholds in North America, each sought

to maximize its capacity to consolidate and expand its interests by gaining acknowledgment from its competitors of its exclusive right against
other states to act within the region of its claims. England, France,
Holland, Sweden, Spain, and Portugal all desired respect for what might
be termed a "sphere of influence" within which it alone might acquire
allies and negotiate for trade relations or land cessions among the Indian
nations.

That European states would attempt to solidify their claims through
treaties with the indigenous inhabitants is not surprising. For the most
part, these claims had only the most tenuous connections to reality. Based
on various voyages of "discovery" and a complete ignorance of actual
geography, they amounted to little more than imperious assertions
drawn on fanciful and self-serving maps.[23] To complicate matters, most
of the claims substantially overlapped, creating conditions for intense
rivalry and military conflict should any state attempt to transform legal
fiction into colonial expansion. Little movement occurred in that direction before 1600. Most European states had neither the interest nor the
ability to maintain permanent settler colonies across the Atlantic. As the
wealth that Spain extracted from its colonies became apparent, however,
other states began to develop maritime capabilities and dust off old
maps and logbooks. Grandiose claims were issued on the basis of a handful
of casual coastal contacts in an effort to establish incipient legal connections to huge swaths of unknown and thoroughly inhabited territories.

Initially, none of these assertions were intended to define the specific
or potential relationships between European and indigenous nations in
the claimed regions. They were inward-looking claims, confined within
the political geography of Europe and directed to intramural competition. As such, their validity depended on the public law of Europe, and
on the ability of individual states to effectuate them in practice. As early
as the mid-fifteenth century, European princes venturing beyond the
Mediterranean sought legitimation and a *right of exclusivity* for their
relations with non-European peoples by reference to doctrines of international law. Within a few decades of the voyages of Columbus, claims
to rights in newly encountered regions of the globe coalesced around four
medieval legal concepts that long predated European contact with the
Western Hemisphere: conquest, agreement or cession, papal "donation,"
and original occupation (discovery).[24] As originally formulated, these
concepts had a profound medieval cast, as Europeans sought to locate
rights in new situations within familiar categories of socio-political
thought.[25]

Measured against the magnitude of claims, none of these principles
could lead to automatic acceptance. They were more in the nature of
arguments for the recognition of rights of exclusivity, and as such, their

successful application was dependent on the acquiescence of rival states in particular situations. Although the four principles were accorded substantially different weight as sources of right, states tended to advance them, singly or in combination, as interests dictated and as circumstances would provide. No matter which legal arguments were employed, however, by the sixteenth century, states were only willing to exclude themselves from opportunities for trade or colonization, if at all, on the basis of actual settlement and territorial control, or firm relationships established by competitors with indigenous societies.[26]

These four concepts or arguments for legitimation can be readily divided into two categories on the basis of their solidity and effectiveness. Papal "donation"[27] and "discovery" provided the weakest and most tenuous claims, in large measure because they were abstract and unilateral. They amounted to little more than a naked declaration on the part of the asserting European state that its rivals should desist.[28] Both conquest and relationships established by agreement, on the other hand, manifested actual and effective state practice. They were confirmed by the degree to which they created continuing relations between Europeans and indigenous peoples or their lands.[29]

International law has always recognized the effectiveness of rights acquired by cession. Cession is the formal means for the consensual transfer of sovereign and territorial rights.[30] Because the rights so acquired are derived from the ceding state, the criteria for determining the validity of this mode of transfer in a specific situation are first, that the ceding entity possesses the legal capacity to cede and second, that it is transferring rights that it legitimately and actually holds.[31] Indian nations in North America were unquestionably regarded as having requisite international personality to cede rights to other sovereign entities that then formed the root of European titles in international law. The treaty process that produced a cession merely memorialized the sovereign status of all involved parties.

Territorial cessions and the rare conquests were readily mapped. In North America, however, cessions and conquest accounted for only a small portion of the geographical areas over which Europeans contested for influence. Difficulties arose when cession agreements to defined areas were employed in attempts to claim additional zones of exclusive rights to trade or obtain further cessions vis-a-vis competitor states in contiguous regions remaining under Indian sovereignty. For the most part, these claims related to a quest for participation and eventual monopolies in intersocietal trade. As the European presence spread into interior regions, indigenous trade remained the principal economic preoccupation along the territorial and societal frontiers during the seventeenth and eighteenth centuries.

European states were not prepared to accept limitations on trade based on each other's contiguity or hinterland arguments whether based on cession or conquest.[32] The principal means open to them for gaining recognition for claims of this nature became the consent and alliance of the Indian nations affected by European aspirations. Indian nations were not passive fields on which Europeans played out their political conflicts; they were active players whose self-defined interests determined the direction of their favors and the contours of their alliances. Europeans had to obtain friendship and commercial rights from these nations, rights which were then jointly exercised over time to create enduring networks of mutual interest. European diplomacy was exercised more frequently and more vigorously for these purposes in this period than for the more historically visible cession agreements. Indeed, military and commercial connections of this kind in large areas of eastern North America formed the actual basis for British and French sphere of influence claims against each other for a century.

Rights established by consensual agreements, formal cession, or subjugation in North America fell within broadly accepted parameters of international law. These legal principles were applied to the relations between European and indigenous nations just as they were to purely European affairs.

State Practice in North America in the Seventeenth and Eighteenth Centuries

The selection of the geographical region comprising the northeastern quadrant of the United States and adjacent Canada as the focus of this study was almost inevitable. In this area four European nations, the Netherlands, France, Britain, and Sweden, conducted extensive international relations among themselves and with numerous independent indigenous nations having prior sovereign rights on the continent. As a consequence, Indian-European relations are more extensively documented in this part of North America than any other. Of additional importance, however, is the fact that the geography and diplomacy in the region prominently involved the relations of a people known to history as the Six Nations or Iroquois Confederacy and to themselves as the Haudenosaunee, the People of the Longhouse.[33] For nearly two centuries, Haudenosaunee-European relations and Haudenosaunee relations with other Indian nations in the context of European relations dominated North American diplomacy.

The Haudenosaunee were and remain a true confederation, composed originally of five distinct nations, Mohawk, Oneida, Onondaga, Cayuga, and Seneca, and later joined by a sixth, the Tuscarora.[34] From ancient times, these nations have been united under the *Kaianerakoa,* or Great Law of Peace.[35] The Confederacy as a whole, and those communities still governed by traditional laws and institutions, form one of the oldest governments in the world functioning under a continuous set of laws. At a time when Europe was engulfed in incessant warfare and experiencing increasing political fragmentation, the Haudenosaunee consciously created a "United Nations" with a sophisticated structure and explicit ideology. Within that structure, confederate nations enjoy internal sovereignty, with the jurisdiction of the Grand Council of the whole centered primarily around matters concerning inter-nation and external relations.[36]

From the earliest peaceful encounter, Haudenosaunee relations with European nations were defined by principles memorialized in the Guswenta, or Two-Row Wampum, said to record the original treaty with the Dutch. Guswenta is a long beaded belt of white wampum with two parallel lines of purple along its length. The lines symbolize the distinct identity of the two peoples and a mutual engagement to coexist in peace without interference in the affairs of the other.[37]

Bilateral Relations in the Formative Period

Diplomatic Practice of the Netherlands in North America

The Dutch tenure in North America was relatively brief, extending from Hudson's exploratory voyage in 1609[38] to the English conquest of New Netherland in 1664,[39] and again from the Dutch reconquest of 1673 to the Treaty of Westminster in 1674.[40] From the beginning, the primary purpose of Dutch colonization was the fur trade. Although a temporary trade monopoly had been granted by the States-General to the United New Netherland Company in 1614,[41] it was not until the formation of the Dutch West India Company in 1621 that a sustained, systematic commercial and colonial effort was launched. The West India Company was created as an extension of Dutch power into Africa and the Western Hemisphere on the model of the earlier East India Company in Asia. Under its charter, the company was empowered to enter into treaties and alliances "with the princes and natives of the country" (subject to review by the States-General), establish and govern colonies, engage in trade, and direct Dutch military forces within the geographical scope of its mandate.[42]

Dutch actions with respect to relations with Indian nations were consistent with contemporary principles and practices of international law. Indian nations were approached as rightful sovereigns of the territory. The States-General claimed no original title in New Netherland, nor did it purport to grant territorial title in the company's charter. Allen

Trelease points out that Dutch patents conferred ownership only after the extinguishment of Indian title by fair means.[43] Consequently, land acquisition was a two-step process, with the most important step being an international transaction between an Indian nation and the West India Company. Whether the issuing of patents within Dutch society preceded or followed an international cession, it was the cession, not the Dutch grant, that determined the possibility of effective acquisition.

The reasons for this state of affairs are obvious when viewed from an international perspective. The company, with delegated sovereign powers, and the Indian nation concerned existed as two distinct governmental and jurisdictional entities. Each functioned as an independent society and exercised authority within its own territorial domain. Neither purported to exercise political or legislative jurisdiction over the territory or social order of the other. Extraterritorial Dutch patents constituted reserved rights under Dutch law granted (or sold) by the company in expectation of a future cession. Although lands encompassed by the patents may have been extraterritorial, rights of ownership and possession were not. They remained confined to Dutch political society and therefore inchoate until political jurisdiction and dominion were extended to the territory by consensual transfer. Each legal regime, Indian and Dutch, was isolated within its own territorial zone of political operation. Territorial rights could only be legally transferred at the intergovernmental level, even if the agents of purchase and sources of funds were Dutch individuals acting in their own interest. Prior patents thus represented inchoate titles regulating distributional rights among subjects of Dutch jurisdiction, titles that could only vest substantive rights to the lands in question after they had been assimilated to Dutch sovereignty. With some variation, European states and their American successors continued this practice into the nineteenth century.[44]

The States-General never purported to exercise general sovereign or territorial rights within the geography of its claims, or to possess jurisdictional rights against the Indian nations of the region. Of the powers delegated to the West India Company, only the authority to conduct external relations and the responsibility to defend the colony—war, peace, and trade—related to neighboring Indian sovereigns.[45]

External relations with Indian nations were of immediate concern to the New Netherland colony. From 1624 to 1625, the West India Company issued regulations specifically authorizing the governor to enter into treaties and alliances with Indian nations and requiring neutrality in Indian disputes.[46] The Dutch recorded history of these transactions is sporadic—obscure in the important area of commercial relations, but somewhat more evident concerning issues of war and peace.

Haudenosaunee tradition recalls a Mohawk treaty with the Dutch circa 1613. The occurrence of this treaty is a matter of controversy among historians of the period,[47] but certainly by 1642, following Mohawk success against Mahican and other rivals in the beaver wars, Haudenosaunee-Dutch treaty and economic relations were central to intersocietal trade in the region.[48] For the Haudenosaunee, New Netherland was the primary source of European weapons used to extend the Confederacy's hegemony over the fur trade to the north and west against French interests, as well as for "quality of life" trade goods.[49] In turn, the Dutch became increasingly dependent on the Mohawk and western nations of the Confederacy as a source of profitable furs and, in the case of the Mohawks specifically, as a military ally applying pressure to Indian enemies of the settlement at New Amsterdam (New York).[50] Mohawk strength and enmity toward the French also provided a formidable protective buffer to discourage French expansion into Dutch networks of trade.

The sparse historical record makes it difficult to develop a detailed picture of the Indian-Dutch treaty process, but existing documents indicate a practice structurally consistent with European diplomacy of the period. Thematically, agreements were as comprehensive as necessity required for two small European enclaves surrounded by numerous independent Indian societies. Each relationship had to be separately negotiated, confirmed, and maintained.

Diplomatic events in 1645 shed light on the actual political relationships of the period. Dutch aggressiveness and atrocities in the vicinity of New Amsterdam in 1640 placed that colony at war with numerous neighboring Algonquian-speaking peoples. During the years of warfare, New Amsterdam deteriorated badly in physical condition and population, contributing to the near bankruptcy of the West India Company as a whole. In 1644, the company launched a comprehensive review of conditions in New Netherland, including the causes of the Indian wars.[51] Seeking to restore the economic viability of the settlement, the owners determined to forge a general peace with the aggrieved Indian nations.[52] The actual peace occurred in several stages. The key agreement was a treaty of friendship between the Dutch and the Mohawk Nation and their Mahican dependencies. The Mohawks (reported to be receiving "tribute" from the warring nations) were then employed as mediators during the Dutch treaty conference with the combatant "River Indians."[53]

The Articles of Peace which concluded the war contained additional provisions for the amelioration of future conflict. The Indian representatives agreed that their people would not enter Manhattan with arms, and the Dutch in turn agreed not to enter Indian territory with weapons unless escorted by members of that society. Additionally, in an article that formed a virtual archetype for European-Indian treaty-making, each side agreed not to engage in war in the event of an injury, "but they shall come to our Governor and we to their Sachems with the complaint and if any one should have been killed or murdered, the slayer shall promptly be brought to justice."[54]

The war, the treaty process, and the specific content of the treaty all underscore the international character of the several Dutch-Indian relationships. According to the West India Company report ordering the peace process, the attempt of the governor to extract a "contribution" of maize from some of the contiguous nations under the pretense of compensating the Dutch for protecting them against enemies was one of the primary factors initiating the war.[55] More a demand for tribute than a tax, the Dutch attempt nevertheless implied the existence of a protectorate that the affected nations not only rejected but saw as grounds for war. In order to terminate five years of warfare, the Dutch were compelled to seek the "good offices" of the Mohawk Nation, which actually exercised hegemonic influence over the other peoples in question.[56]

The Articles of Peace, drafted in written form by the Dutch, reflected Dutch recognition of the independent nationhood and jurisdictional distinctiveness of their former enemies. The complaint procedure quoted above was not merely a mechanism for dispute resolution short of war, but also constituted a commitment on the part of the Dutch to respect the internal procedures of Indian societies without interference. The complaint procedure as well as the peace pledge could have graced any European treaty of that era.

In negotiating and drafting this treaty, the Dutch extended common European mechanisms for regulating interstate conflicts to its North American relations. Beginning in the ninth century, independent European political entities utilized the treaty process to regulate the practice of state or state-sanctioned private reprisals in the event of an injury to a national in the territory of another state.[57] Virtually from its inception, international law regarded such injuries as the collective responsibility of a state. Rather than allow random retaliations to provoke continuous warfare, Europeans evolved the practice of negotiating procedures designed to forestall conflict, procedures which included a prior demand for justice from the institutions of the offending state.[58]

Similar provisions were incorporated in treaties with the Esopus Indians, a Munsee-speaking society at war with the Dutch during the last years of the New Netherland enterprise.[59] The first peace, negotiated in 1660, followed a measure of Dutch diplomatic success in isolating the Esopus from surrounding nations. In fact, representatives of the Mohawk, Mahican, Catskill, Minquas, and other nations agreed to "remain bondsmen and engage themselves to have this treaty kept inviolate" and to assist the Dutch in the event of breach. The Esopus agreed to indemnify the Dutch with a small cession of territory and to pay a reparation for ransoms previously received for captured Europeans. The peace further involved an exchange of prisoners and a commitment on both sides to avoid war through a complaint process in the case of intersocietal murder.[60] War resumed in 1662, however, and continued sporadically until Dutch scorched earth practices caused the Esopus to seek peace in 1664. The final treaty followed an exchange of prisoners and largely recapitulated the terms of the earlier agreement, adding, however, provisions requiring a rigorous limitation of intersocietal contact, formal ratification by the Esopus council, and an annual ceremony of renewal at a Dutch fort.[61]

In exercising its delegated governmental powers in New Netherland, the West India Company entered into treaties with numerous Indian nations and with British authorities in New England and Virginia,[62] made war with numerous Indian nations and the Swedish colony on the Delaware River, sold munitions to the Mohawks in their conflicts with the French and allied Indian nations,[63] mediated Mohawk-French relations and Mohawk treaties with other nations,[64] sought and received Mohawk mediation and conciliation assistance in Indian-Dutch wars, formed several alliances with Indian nations, and conducted intersocietal trade to the fullest extent possible. Established primarily to conduct that trade, New Netherland was required to use commercial acumen and diplomatic skill rather than power to survive. But here necessity matched intention as the Dutch enterprise was designed to function within the parameters of Indian sovereignty and the rules of international intercourse in its practice of Indian relations. By the end of the fifty-five years of Dutch presence in North America, Indian-Dutch bilateral relations constituted an important element in a complex multidimensional diplomatic environment that involved numerous Indian nations, French, English, and Swedish colonies, and an increasingly important European theater as the seventeenth century unfolded.

Sweden in America, 1638 to 1655

Swedish colonial activity in North America was initiated by King Gustavus Adolphus during Sweden's seventeenth-century rise to great power status in Europe.[65] In typical fashion for that era, a colonizing company, the Swedish South Company, was chartered in 1626 with delegated powers, including authority "to make agreements with Kings, Princes, and Republics, people and inhabitants" of Africa and the Americas.[66] Consistent with the peaceful commercial intent of the enterprise, the company was expressly restricted in the use of force. The charter granted the right to engage in military action for defensive purposes only and required the directors to find "a just cause" for the commencement of war. The company never exercised this mandate, however. The death of the king and other circumstances forestalled the effort, but in late 1637 a successor, the Swedish West India Company, commissioned a colonizing expedition to Delaware Bay led by the expatriate former governor of New Netherland, Peter Minuit.[67]

From the outset, Sweden conducted relations with Indian peoples through the treaty process. The first formal public act of New Sweden was the negotiation of a territorial cession from the indigenous nations of the region. A brief record of the treaty, contained in an "Affidavit of Four Kalmar Nyckel Men," describes a formal procedure in which the representatives of the several nations "declared in what manner they transported, ceded, and transferred the said land with all its jurisdiction, sovereignty, and rights" to the company in exchange for Swedish merchandise.[68] The actual understanding of the Indian leaders as to the nature of this exchange is unknown, but they seem to have regarded the transaction as a foundation for a continuing supply of trade goods.

On several occasions, the cessions had to be reconfirmed by the Swedes with substantial "presents." Sweden was quite concerned to uphold the validity of the cessions. Both England and the Netherlands asserted abstract claims to the same region based on earlier voyages of discovery. New Sweden's title to the territory was derived entirely from the consensual transfer by the indigenous nations. Consequently, colonial authorities scrupulously respected boundaries established by these agreements.[69]

Treaty-making was also employed by Sweden to regulate intersocietal relations. In 1643, minor hostilities were resolved in a treaty of peace.[70] Eleven years later, shortly before the surrender of New Sweden to the Dutch, another treaty was negotiated providing for punishment of individual intersocietal injuries and for a measure of military cooperation in the form of a "defensive league."[71] Throughout the brief history of the Swedish colony, relations between Sweden and contiguous Indian nations were conducted on a consensual basis.[72]

The Formation of French-Haudenosaunee Relations

Although the Haudenosaunee are best known for their influence on the balance of power between English and French aspirations for empire in North America after 1664, the Confederacy had an important and usually hostile relationship with New France going back to the beginning of the seventeenth century. By 1615, France, through the agency of Samuel de Champlain, had established a fur trading network and series of alliances with Indian nations across the northern edge of the St. Lawrence River and lower Great Lakes. French activities in this regard included the use of European weapons against Mohawk warriors in 1609 and 1610, and a brief foray against the Oneida Nation in 1615, leading to decades of intermittent warfare.[73] Trelease refers to a briefly respected peace arrangement in 1624 as the first treaty between the Confederacy and a European nation.[74] Be that as it may, the Haudenosaunee were a principal focus of French military and diplomatic activity in North America for the century preceding the Peace of Utrecht.[75]

The degree of pain administered to New France by the Haudenosaunee in these conflicts can be measured by another temporary peace negotiated between the French and the Mohawk Nation in 1645. In the accord, Governor Montmagny expressly abandoned Indian nations allied with the French to work out their own arrangement with the Mohawks, reserving French protection solely for converted Indians living in communities assimilated to French settlements and regarded as French subjects.[76] The distinction is important. Although France was obligated to these allied Indian nations, they were regarded as independent actors on the diplomatic plane. When forced by necessity, the French were as prepared to reshuffle their international relationships in North America as they were in Europe. The Mohawks did make separate treaties with French trading partners, but the peace was merely a prelude to the Seneca-Mohawk conquest of the Huron Nation. The destruction of the extensive Huron trade network by the end of the decade left the Haudenosaunee the central Indian power in the region of Dutch, French, English, and Swedish settlements.[77]

By 1651, French consternation over the Haudenosaunee was such that the Council of Quebec appealed without success to the commissioners of New England for an alliance against them.[78] Yet another short-lived peace with the Confederacy was negotiated in 1653 at the initiative of the Seneca, Onondaga, Cayuga, and Oneida nations, and later joined by the Mohawks, only to be followed by the resumption of war in 1658.[79]

In 1665, cumulative French losses convinced Louis XIV to launch a major military operation against the Confederacy. The king's instructions to M. Talon, intendant of New France, referred to the Haudenosaunee as "perpetual and irreconcilable enemies of the Colony." Blaming Haudenosaunee warfare for the low population and constant chaos in New France, Louis resolved to "carry war even to their firesides in order totally to exterminate them. . . ."[80] To effectuate these goals, the French government sent four companies of regular infantry, one thousand additional troops, and large stores of munitions across the Atlantic.

Although the French mobilization produced no significant military result, it did precipitate a significant treaty with the Haudenosaunee. The treaty signaled the approaching end of the period in which the French relationship with the Confederacy was strictly bilateral. Henceforward Iroquois-European relations would increasingly occur within a triangular context, with Franco-British rivalry forming the backdrop to

Haudenosaunee relations with each, and with the Confederacy using that rivalry for its own purposes.

In that vein, the Haudenosaunee-French treaty of 1665 marked the beginning of a new era in treaty language as France and England began to seek documents legitimizing their mutually antagonistic imperial claims. That these treaties were drafted with an eye to Europe is baldly evident in the 1665 record of negotiations.[81] The preamble of the agreement began with a lengthy bombastic and self-congratulatory paean to the sacred (and on paper declared to be successful) mission of Louis XIV to achieve dominion over the Iroquois, and continued with the assertion that the present conference was merely a renewal of an earlier Confederacy submission to French sovereignty: "[T]he above named Ambassadors [Iroquois] are not come to demand a new peace, not pretending that the first union of the Iroquois with the French is broken or interrupted, but only to supplicate the confirmation of the former by granting them the continuance of the same protection that they formerly received from His Majesty's Arms. . . ."[82]

In light of the previous history of warfare between these nations, French rhetoric would be simply absurd were it not for the obvious political intent of the treaty. By memorializing a fictional earlier acceptance of French sovereignty, the treaty was designed to bolster French sphere of influence claims concerning Iroquoia antecedent to the English conquest of New Netherland and any subsequent English treaties with the Haudenosaunee. Louis XIV was well aware of the potential uses of this terminology. Although he had ordered the extermination of the Confederacy, he approved the treaty sent from New France, "remarking that you [the governor] had principally in view to acquire a possession adverse to the actual or future pretensions of the European nations."[83]

The political relationship between the two peoples was described in the document as "protection" and "vassalage," the latter a feudal concept continued in the relations of states into the twentieth century. Under these concepts, the protected or vassal state retained its national identity and internal independence, but symbolically recognized the suzerainty of another state on the international level.[84] Had this terminology reflected the reality of the relationship or had the French possessed the power to transform rhetoric to reality, Haudenosaunee vassalage under the law of nations would have eliminated any countervailing English claims to a Confederacy alliance or protectorate.

In bilateral terms, the transparency of the French "protectorate" was evident at the outset. France had no power to prevent the nations of the Confederacy from forming commercial agreements, military alliances, or other agreements of an international character with the British; nor could they control Haudenosaunee activities affecting French interests among Indian nations of the north and west. Moreover, period records attest to a continuation of French hostility toward the Confederacy despite the treaty. French officials debated the desirability of ever coming to a peace with the Mohawk Nation and subsequently launched a large-scale invasion of Mohawk territory within months of the treaty.[85] In the next year, correspondence between New France and the French Court discussed a second invasion of the Mohawk Nation "notwithstanding the treaty concluded with them."[86] At the same time, the Confederacy continued to conduct international relations according to its own definitions and interests.

Imperial pronouncements aside, the treaty provided for peace between the French, the Indian nations allied with New France, and four of the five nations of the Confederacy, excepting the absent Mohawk Nation. Prisoners were formally exchanged, and the Haudenosaunee negotiators agreed to accept a few French families and Jesuit priests into their communities. The express purpose of the French sojourners was to "cement" the peace and facilitate "correspondence." Reciprocally, the Haudenosaunee were to send two principal families from each nation to reside in French settlements. The parties further agreed that hostilities would be suspended pending ratification by the Indian nations within a four-month period and, in the interim, French or allied fighting involving Mohawk or Oneida war parties then in the field would not constitute an infraction of the treaty.[87]

The French-Haudenosaunee treaty was considered to be of sufficient significance for the serial ratifications of the Onondaga, Seneca, and Oneida nations to be printed in Dumont's majesterial compendium, *Corps Universel Diplomatique du Droit des Gens,* published in Amsterdam in 1726 to 1731. Included among the European treaties for the year 1666, each of the ratifications was titled, "Paix accordi' par l' Empereur de FRANCE aux IROQUOIS de la Nation [Seneca], [Onondaga], [Oneida]."[88] Although the title as well as much of the text reflects French arrogance, concealing the Haudenosaunee lobe of the intent of the parties, French acceptance of the international legal status of the Confederacy is clear. Relations with the Confederacy were smoothly integrated into French diplomatic practice of the era, with modifications for cultural differences only evident in the rituals of negotiation. Moreover, open warfare was the more typical condition of a relationship only occasionally punctuated by relatively short-lived treaties of peace. Intervals of peace were fashioned out of necessity as the French found themselves unable to impose a more favorable result on the Haudenosaunee, and the Confederacy on its part periodically responded to short-term and expensive mobilizations of French military forces from the European metropolis.

In assessing Haudenosaunee-French relations, an understanding of the nature of North American warfare and of the ebb and flow of power in each of these societies over time is essential to comprehending the treaty process. Until the 1670s, the population of New France amounted to approximately 2,000 Europeans.[89] Although firearms and cannon, European military techniques, and defensible location made concentrated European settlements largely impregnable to Indian attack, any activities outside of the walls, particularly those relating to the economic lifeblood of intersocietal relations in North America—the fur trade—were exceedingly vulnerable. Under these circumstances, New France, like other small European enclaves, was dependent on allied Indian nations for its physical survival and economic reality. If the French could not be forcibly dislodged from their strongholds by a few Indian nations acting alone, neither could New France function economically without large-scale Indian cooperation and at least relative peace. Population growth obviously strengthened the French position over time and allowed for a measure of expansion in the number of fortified areas, but did not appreciably alter the logic of that position.

Militarily, New France was able to vary its power by periodically importing large numbers of soldiers from Europe. The offensive potential of these forces was quite limited, however. European soldiers were poorly adapted to forest warfare. In the dense forest environment and harsh winters of the area, campaigns could only be of brief duration. Because supply lines were impossible in ventures of any distance and roads were nonexistent, food and ammunition had to be carried by the troops overland. By the time an army reached Indian towns several hundred miles away or more, the soldiers were usually sick, exhausted, and hungry. Moreover, Indian warriors wisely declined to directly engage such armies. Towns were evacuated in front of the French march, and guerilla skirmishes were launched at the French at their most vulnerable point—on the march home. With neither the opportunity to fight a decisive battle nor the capacity to occupy temporarily evacuated territory, the invading army could do nothing more than burn towns, cornfields, stores of corn, and other staples of the enemy (classic scorched earth tactics), perhaps leave behind symbols of "conquest," and retreat before food ran out and counterattacking Indian forces had time to mobilize in numbers.

Both sides had economic vulnerabilities and economic limitations in their ability to carry out war. The Haudenosaunee, as an agricultural people, experienced hardship when their food stores were destroyed. After such attacks, they were particularly disposed toward peace, at least until an agricultural infrastructure was restored. The offensive ability of the Confederacy was also circumscribed. Effective warfare required access to European munitions that could only be obtained through the fur trade. Large numbers of Indian men were thus diverted on a seasonal basis for hunting and trade. For the French during the seventeenth century, maintaining and increasing the fur trade was everything; the viability of New France in the period was largely an economic calculation. Military campaigns against the Haudenosaunee were prohibitively expensive, minimally effective, and were undertaken only when the pain of Confederacy attacks on the sources of furs and on the French themselves became unbearable. French-Haudenosaunee peace treaties were generally made at times of mutual exhaustion and frustration, and represent careful assessments of the consequences of extended war by both parties.

Great Britain and the Haudenosaunee

During the life of New Netherland, inter-European international relations were largely peripheral to the dynamics of Indian-European conduct in North America. However, with the English conquest of the Dutch colony, the growing interest of Louis XIV in American affairs, and the rise of France and England as world powers, North America became a prominent venue of European conflict for the following century. Within this context, the Haudenosaunee and other Indian nations became important actors on the international plane.

One of the first actions taken by the new English authorities in the renamed Colony of New York was the establishment of a formal relationship with the nations of the Confederacy sufficient to prevent intersocietal conflict. The 1664 treaty between the English and the Mohawk and Seneca nations provided for an agreed mechanism for peaceful dispute settlement along the lines of previous Dutch practice:

> That if any English, Dutch, or Indian (under the proteccon of the English) do any wrong injury or violence to any of ye said Princes or their subjects in any sort whatever, if they complaine to the Governor at New Yorke, or to the Officer in Cheife at Albany, if the person so offending can be discovered, that person shall receive condigne punishment and all due satisfaccon shall be given; and the like shall be done for all other English Plantations.
>
> That if any Indian belonging to any of the Sachims aforesaid do any wrong injury or damage to the English, Dutch, or Indians under the protection of the English, if complaint be made to ye Sachims and the person be discovered who did the injury, then the person so offending shall be punished and all just satisfaccon shall be given to any of His Maties [Majesty's] subjects in any Colony or other English Plantacon in America.[90] (Emphasis added.)

The terminology of the treaty is significant in a number of respects. Quite obviously, it is an international agreement. The governmental institutions of the Indian nations are termed "princes," and the population "their subjects." The subject matter of the treaty was trade, peace, and dispute resolution, anticipating a continuing relationship. Each society pledged itself to punish its own violators of international peace within its own jurisdictional structures and to give "just satisfaction" or reparations to the injured party across national lines. As in modern international relations, the responsibility for making an injury whole resided in the nation whose member committed the grievance, as each side agreed to be collectively responsible for such acts. Moreover, the mutual recognition of independent political realms and implicit promise of noninterference was entirely consistent with both European state practice under the law of nations and Haudenosaunee principle and practice memorialized in the Two-Row Wampum.

An interesting facet of the treaty in this regard is the distinction in political status made between the Haudenosaunee nations as independent actors, parties to the agreement, and the small Algonquian nations "under the protection of the English" for whose conduct the English agreed to bear state responsibility and whose interest the English claimed to represent. As protectorates, these latter nations would continue to maintain their distinct political personality, but under the law of nations and English intentions, their external relations would be managed by the protecting state. The record is unclear as to the specific substance or duration of these protectorates, if they existed at all, but the treatment of these peoples as politically distinct though protected entities stands in sharp contrast with the parallel practice of the English to directly incorporate the conquered Swedish and Dutch inhabitants on the Delaware River and in New Amsterdam (New York) and Fort Orange (Albany) proper into the English realm.[91] So long as Indian political institutions and social cohesion remained viable, the English related to them on a political level.

The conquest of New Netherland opened a new era in North American international relations. The active British presence in the fur trade brought that nation into direct competition with New France, a competition that eventually would be heavily influenced by Franco-British conflict in Europe. The establishment of the Colony of New York in the hands of the royal family also brought the British Crown more directly into the diplomacy of Indian relations. Although individual colonies exercising delegated governmental powers under their charters autonomously made war and entered into treaties and alliances with neighboring Indian nations, British authorities in New York rapidly assumed control of Indian relations in the primary theater of multilateral conflict and diplomacy in North America. In their initial exercise of the diplomatic mandate, Crown representatives adhered closely to the principles and practices of international law.

For example, the instructions given by Charles II to Richard Nicholls and others in 1664 authorizing the subjugation of New Netherland included a fact-finding and diplomatic mission to the New England colonies on the matter of Indian relations. In Massachusetts, Nicholls was specifically ordered to inquire into the situation regarding treaties made with "neighbor Kings and Princes or the other Natives" adjoining the colony to determine whether they have been "observed and performed" on the part of the British. If not, the commissioners were to ensure proper implementation and arrange reparations for past breaches in the name of the Crown. The commissioners were further instructed to use all means, including direct meetings, to reassure Indian leaders of the good faith of the British government and to "enter into such further treaties with them as you shall judge convenient" as the representatives of the king.[92]

Additionally, during a mission to Connecticut, the commissioners were to investigate the validity of a reported 1644 grant "from the Chiefe Sachim and other the Princes [*sic*] of a large tract of ground about the Narragansett Bay, who as we are informed did . . . by a formall instrument under their hands and seales, transferre that their Countrey to our Royall Father, for his protection, and become his subjects. . . ." If found valid, the document was to be treated as a cession, and the territory taken in the name of the king. Existing property holders were to be issued new titles to their existing estates, with the requirement of annual payments from "our tennants." Complaints from the ceding Indian nation were to be examined and repaired, and assurances given of royal protection against oppression.[93] These instructions regarding New England and the 1664 treaty with the Haudenosaunee negotiated by these same commissioners after the capitulation of the Dutch give fair indication of the practice of the British state toward international relations with Indian nations in this formative period of Crown involvement.

Although the British stepped readily into the shoes of the Dutch in Albany, administering a center of trade and providing weapons to the Haudenosaunee, no further record of significant diplomatic activity in this region is evident until after the second conquest of a briefly revived New Netherland. Renewed treaty-making was apparently prompted by conflicts between the Haudenosaunee and other British colonies, and by increasingly difficult relations between Britain and France. In a sparsely documented series of treaties brokered by the governor of New York, the Haudenosaunee agreed to peaceful relations and friendship with Massachusetts and Connecticut (1677), Maryland and Virginia (1677),[94] and reconfirmed the agreement with Virginia in 1679.[95]

Jennings regards these three treaties in the aggregate as forming the Covenant Chain, a British-Haudenosaunee metaphor for the extensive general friendship and occasional alliance between the Confederacy, together with its allied and tributary Indian nations, and the British in North America.[96] The Covenant Chain is indeed a compelling image, symbolizing a lengthy relationship in historical terms, but revealing little of its varying substance. From the perspective of international legal relations, it is perhaps more useful to describe the Haudenosaunee-British relationship apart from the symbolism as a complex, nuanced, and evolving friendship and intermittent alliance that, until 1760, can best be understood in the cauldron of British-Haudenosaunee-French conflict.

Interindigenous International Relations

By the time Britain established itself at Albany, contiguous to Confederacy territory, the Haudenosaunee had risen to the height of their military and political power. Confederacy influence ranged from the upper Great Lakes through the Ohio Valley and Pennsylvania to the limits of Cherokee territory in the Carolinas. Throughout this vast region, the Haudenosaunee enjoyed a persuasive political and commercial hegemony that, despite erosion during the eighteenth century, placed the Confederacy in a position of influence with other Indian nations into the wars of the 1790s.

In his recent book *The Ambiguous Iroquois Empire*, Francis Jennings has made an admirable attempt to reconstruct aspects of inter-Indian international relations as seen through European documents of that era.[97] Jennings has succeeded in destroying the European generated myth of a "forest empire" and has revealed the tantalizing outlines of a considerably more complex series of interrelationships among indigenous nations in North America. The notion of empire, like the term "princes" often used to describe indigenous leaders, was a projection of European ethnocentrism onto significantly different North American cultures and political relations.

In reality, Haudenosaunee political hegemony can best be described as a network of indigenous alliances in which the Confederacy played a dominant and principal role in the control of trade routes, the allocation of rights in large but relatively unpopulated hunting territories, and the process of international relations with the Dutch, French, and English. Although warfare among Indian nations in certain periods could be frequent and catastrophic as in Europe, Confederacy hegemony once established was maintained less by force than by the skillful manipulation of a geographical position adjacent to New York and New France, friendship with the British, and superb diplomacy. In turn, the extensive network of Haudenosaunee indigenous alliances made the Confederacy a significant commercial and military friend or formidable foe for the Europeans.

Despite efforts such as Jennings's study, it is unlikely that European documents can provide anything more than a shadow play of inter-indigenous international relations. In addition to the cultural and linguistic gulf that Europeans of the period were so poorly able to bridge, European authorities and private memorialists could only have been aware of occasional fragments of indigenous diplomatic intercourse. Of equal importance, historians have rarely attempted to understand the cosmological and ideological imperatives that guided indigenous nations in analyzing and formulating their external relations. In the case of the Haudenosaunee, the *Kaianerakoa* or Great Law of Peace under which the Confederacy was formed out of five individual nations undoubtedly shaped Confederacy practice in dealing with other peoples. Until histories can be written from the perspective of indigenous participants, or at least from a more symmetrical position incorporating an indigenous composition of reality, our sense of North American relations, particularly in the seventeenth century will remain one-dimensional.[98]

A few visible elements of indigenous North American international perspectives do appear in the historical record of intersocietal relations, however. The superb skill of Haudenosaunee diplomatic practice, long noted by historians, did not spring fully formed from European encounters. On the contrary, indigenous diplomatic procedures were highly developed and unique to North America. European diplomats were compelled to adapt to a treaty-making process defined by the indigenous parties, including symbolic expression, just as indigenous nations were bound to adapt to written treaty records and European mapping techniques.[99] More substantively, the principles symbolized in the Two-Row Wampum demonstrate a well-developed indigenous philosophy of respect for what we now call the right of self-determination of peoples as the basis for coexistence already in place at the inception of the Indian-European relationship in this region.

French-Haudenosaunee-British Triangular Relations, 1670 to 1701

The Franco-Haudenosaunee treaties of 1665 and 1666 provided the preface for a two-tiered structure of diplomacy leading to the Peace of Utrecht in 1713.[100] Although the primary practice of treaty-making in North America remained grounded in necessity (as three intensely dynamic societies adjusted their interests and relations), Britain and France increasingly began to duel for mutual recognition of exclusive spheres of influence in regions critical to the fur trade.

One dimension of diplomacy, of course, involved the creation of actual conditions of influence, largely through relations with the Haudenosaunee and other Indian nations. Because of geographical position, trade, warfare, and European and interindigenous diplomacy, the Confederacy continued to hold the key to the balance of power throughout the period. Both Britain and France had to contend with the independent and never entirely predictable strategies and conduct of the Haudenosaunee nations. On a second level, however, France and Britain began to create written records of Haudenosaunee expressions of acceptance of European sphere of influence claims that could be employed in the diplomatic galleries of Europe to legitimize their aspirations against each other. Although this discourse bore no greater connection to reality throughout the period than existed at the time of the 1665 treaty,[101] and although neither Britain nor France ever gave credence to each other's bare legalisms in concluding joint agreements on North American affairs, the language of purported submissions has clouded the historical record and affected the perception of historians on the question of the international legal status of Indian nations.

Period records do contain occasional statements by Haudenosaunee representatives indicating recognition of themselves as "subjects" of a (generally British) king, or placing their lands under the authority of one or the other European rival, but these statements are contradicted by clear assertions of sovereign independence, and more significantly, by manifestly independent action. One must be exceedingly cautious in giving weight to such obviously self-serving expressions in European records. Modern historians of the period have tended to take these statements at face value though very much in the context of the total relationships involved. Trelease interpreted them variously as reflecting the diplomatic purpose, "to conciliate the English and win their support" while continuing "to regard themselves as politically independent of all Europeans, as they were in fact, and to act accordingly."[102] Francis Jennings viewed the texts as representing a concept of relationship that was clearly understood by the British to function on two levels—one real (Haudenosaunee independence and consensual relations) and one symbolic, to be employed against the French.[103]

Confusion, however, persists. Although contributing much to the exposure of the British diplomatic agenda behind statements of Haudenosaunee "submission," Jennings has nonetheless described the Confederacy as "[p]roperly speaking . . . nearer vassals than subjects, closely resembling medieval communities of freemen whose acknowledged lord perforce respected their chartered liberties."[104] Leaving aside the question of vassalage as a political relationship for the moment, Jennings's description of the Confederacy loses sight of the fundamentally inter-national character of the Haudenosaunee-British relationship and the centrality of the treaty process in determining and adjusting the shape of that relationship. It also ignores the fact that the Confederacy con-tinued to maintain an independent relationship with France, a relation-ship with its own dynamics, influenced by a close economic and politi-cal affinity with the British, but not dictated by it.

At no point was the Confederacy incorporated within British imperial control. The Haudenosaunee-British relationship symbolized by the Covenant Chain was at most a consensual alliance of distinct peoples negotiated and maintained in a complex international environment, not a constitutional arrangement. Although the alliance, when it existed, was entirely *sui generis*, by an admittedly imperfect analogy it evolved to resemble many aspects of the NATO arrangement during the cold war with the Soviet bloc. Both alliances featured a principal partner with a larger population, economy, and military capacity. Nevertheless, the principal partner was able to direct the alliance only on the basis of mutual interest, cooperation, positive inducements, persuasion, and oc-casional threats of withdrawal, not compulsion. The glue was security, interdependence, and mutual need. Balance was maintained by the al-ways open possibility that one of the members would seek its own arrangement or declare neutrality in a largely bipolar struggle. Finally, to exhaust the analogy, in both alliances all partners also conducted independent diplomatic relations with members of the opposing bloc and other political entities. In the case of the Haudenosaunee-British relationship, that independence extended to decisions of war and peace.

"Protection" must be understood in that context. In reality, the British were unreliable allies in these decades. During periods of open warfare, British authorities rarely did more than assure a continuing supply of munitions at the usual price. In any event, if the Haudenosaunee were under protection or vassalage, they were a protectorate or vassal as a distinct political and territorial entity.[105] However, the burden remains on those asserting the existence of that relationship to demonstrate either the original and continuing consent of the Confederacy to the arrangement, or the imposition of that status through the exercise of British power. In substance, a legally meaningful protectorate or vassalage relationship would minimally involve some transfer of authority over external relations to the protecting state. The historical record of the period, however, does not support any such notion of European control of Haudenosaunee diplomacy. Neither Britain nor France had the ability to conduct international relations on behalf of the Confederacy nor to uni-laterally bind the Confederacy to any agreements they might make among themselves. As in any complex international environment, relations were influenced to some degree by the policies of other closely allied entities; nevertheless, the Haudenosaunee tenaciously and demonstrably exercised external relations independent of European domination for the duration of the period under study.[106]

The Dynamics of Peace, 1670 to 1683

Independent exercise of external relations is indeed the principal measure of the dimensions of the international legal personality of the Confederacy in each historical phase of its encounter with European nations. During the initial decades of societal interaction, political relations were sporadic and Confederacy independence obvious. The British conquest of New Netherland did not alter this political equation. As Anglo-French conflict in North America intensified, however, Britain began to raise claims in its relations with France that the Haudenosaunee had become assimilated to British authority, claims purportedly based on Confederacy consent. Although similar French statements have not been taken seriously, British assertions (and the nonexistence of contemporaneous Haudenosaunee written records) have cast an element of uncertainty on the political status of the Confederacy in ensuing years. In order to properly evaluate the authenticity and consequences of these claims, the practice of the concerned parties must be examined in terms of the context in which the claims arose, their actual substance, the degree to which they were accepted by the Haudenosaunee or France at any given point, and if valid, the continuity or effective withdrawal of Haudenosaunee consent over time.

French-Haudenosaunee-British triangular relations developed slowly through the 1670s and 1680s. In the first few years after the establishment of the Colony of New York, the English were largely indifferent to the course of Haudenosaunee-French conduct in both peace and war. Initially, the English were content with their own peaceful relations with, and position of supplier to, the Confederacy and were otherwise minimally involved in the affairs of New France. In 1666, for example, when a French punitive expedition mounted an unsuccessful campaign in the Mohawk territory near the British town of Schenectady, the cold, exhausted, and wounded French troops were aided and supplied for the march home by the authorities at Albany. Despite friendly relations with the Mohawk Nation and on-going Anglo-French warfare in Europe, the British did not at that time regard a French invasion of Mohawk territory as an affront to Britain, nor did they perceive an obligation to aid in the defense of Mohawk towns.[107]

Overall peaceful relations in North America were significantly enhanced by European developments in 1670 when the Stuart and Bourbon dynasties signed a secret treaty of alliance against Britain's then current ally, the Dutch.[108] Although Britain and France continued to dispute antagonistic claims in various regions of North America and the Caribbean, the entente held until the fall of James II of Britain in 1688. As a consequence of the political configuration in Europe and the enjoyment of a thriving fur trade in its colonial enclave, the British government had little incentive to encourage confrontations between the Confederacy and France.

In fact, active Anglo-Haudenosaunee relations were formed during a period in which the principal threats to English colonial enclaves came from Indian nations and the Dutch. After the restoration of New York pursuant to the Anglo-Dutch treaty of 1674,[109] British authorities were preoccupied for a number of years with Indian affairs.[110] A great deal of that preoccupation, from Virginia to Massachusetts, concerned the Haudenosaunee.

In 1675, Edmond Andros, governor of New York, traveled to the Mohawk country to renew relations with the Confederacy interrupted by the short Dutch interregnum.[111] The following year, Andros enticed the Mohawk Nation to attack confederated Algonquian-speaking Indian nations at war with the New England colonies.[112] Unwilling to limit themselves to the British agenda, the Mohawks pursued their own war objectives against these ancient enemies, leading Massachusetts and Connecticut to seek a separate treaty with the Haudenosaunee. Similar conflicts between the Haudenosaunee and the Maryland and Virginia colonies produced a series of treaties between 1677 and 1684 concerning relations in those quarters.[113]

These conflicts and the treaties negotiated to resolve them offer some, albeit meager, insights into the international character of the Haudenosaunee relationship. Despite assertions by Andros to his fellow governors that the Confederacy was "under his government," assertions motivated by boundary disputes rooted in overlapping charter claims among the English colonies, he could neither control Confederacy conduct nor negotiate on their behalf. The Haudenosaunee relentlessly determined their own relations with the other colonies and among Indian nations as they had with the French.[114] In matters concerning hegemonic relations, trade, or other networks of influence with other Indian nations, the actual dynamics of diplomacy are rarely displayed in the record, but as Jennings has noted, the Confederacy never accepted the notion that the English colonies had the capacity to treat with them on behalf of Indian allies and clients—insisting always on direct and distinct relations.[115]

The friendly relationship with the British was maintained because of a high degree of economic interdependence and the strategic geopolitical position of the Confederacy. It was managed on the basis of diplomatic and economic persuasion rather than dictation or coercion. In reality, the British were never in a position to coerce the Confederacy. Despite Haudenosaunee warfare against Indian nations allied with the English, and sporadic armed conflicts with English settlers in the southern colonies, disputes were always resolved, no matter how unsatisfactorily from the English perspective, by the treaty process rather than by military force.[116]

Haudenosaunee relations with France in this period were uncharacteristically calm. For the most part, the Franco-Haudenosaunee treaties of 1665 and 1666 began nearly two decades of peace or at least nonbelligerence between the two peoples. Despite the absence of direct conflict, however, Confederacy affairs were accorded great importance by the French government. From 1665 until the end of his reign, Louis XIV was directly involved in shaping French policy in Haudenosaunee relations, either personally or through his highest ministers of state.[117] Louis at times viewed the fur trade in his North American colony as a potential source of revenue to finance his European ambitions. The peace of 1665, although advantageous to France, also freed Haudenosaunee warriors and traders to operate in the territories of western Indian nations whose furs comprised the bulk of the French colonial economy. Confederacy war and diplomacy among those nations created new alliances, trade routes, and dependencies that ultimately benefited British rather than French commerce.

In 1672, with a keen sense of the continuing danger posed by the Confederacy to French interests, Louis dispatched the Count de Frontenac as governor of New France. Frontenac's instructions began with a historical review of the "expeditions and cruelties" of the Haudenosaunee against the inhabitants of the colony in the past, and with a description of the war policy of the king leading to the treaty of peace in 1665. The governor was cautioned to maintain the readiness of the settlers of New France "so as to keep them in a condition not only to repel any insults the Iroquois may commit against them, but even to attack them whenever . . . the peace of the Colony may require it."[118] Once in North America, Frontenac developed a comprehensive diplomatic and commercial strategy to enhance the economic viability of the colony by expanding the geographical scope of the French fur trade. Central elements of the plan involved maintaining peace with the Confederacy while exploring regions to the west beyond Haudenosaunee hegemony in order to establish commercial relations with independent Indian nations in those areas. A key aspect of the strategy involved construction of a fortified trading station at the juncture of Lake Ontario and the St. Lawrence River—on the margins of Haudenosaunee territory.[119]

Frontenac had little choice but to implement this strategy through diplomacy rather than force.[120] The ensuing treaty was directly stimulated by intelligence reports of Haudenosaunee diplomatic activities that seemed to pose two distinct threats to New France, and which illustrated the independent international role of the Confederacy in that period. In the latest edition of the round-robin European wars, the Dutch enemies of the Franco-British entente briefly ousted the English from a subsequently reconstituted New Netherland during 1673 to 1674. Frontenac reported that twenty Dutch ambassadors were sent among the Confederacy to encourage a renewal of Haudenosaunee war against the French.[121] In addition, the French were aware that the Confederacy had been negotiating a commercial treaty with the Ottawa Nation to the north (the principal suppliers of furs to New France), involving a direct exchange of European trade goods for Ottawa furs. Fearing that this commercial alliance if implemented would not only destroy the French fur trade, but also possibly lead to a combined Ottawa-Haudenosaunee military assault against New France, Frontenac, anxious to confirm the peace, invited the Confederacy to a treaty conference in 1673.[122]

During the conference, Frontenac reaffirmed the peace of 1665 and somewhat surprisingly gained Haudenosaunee agreement for the construction of the planned fort.[123] Mutual economic motivation for maintaining the peace was strong. Mutuality of interest for the establishment of Fort Frontenac, however, was more obscure. From the French perspective, the fort gave New France a small military bastion on the frontiers of the Confederacy, and a western location for trade to preempt rival Haudenosaunee commercial incursions to the north. Haudenosaunee motives were far less clear. It is quite likely that the Confederacy was hedging its bets—its English trading partner controlled New York for only nine years before being briefly supplanted by the Dutch. The Haudenosaunee may well have been seeking an alternative European trading connection, located much closer to the western nations of the Confederacy and far from the centers of French power, in case of instability among their chief sources of European trade goods and munitions. In any event, the French post was established on the basis of an express consensual arrangement.[124]

Although commercial rivalries between the two nations continued in the aftermath of the treaty, a state of nonbelligerence was maintained through the decade. Eventually, however, economic interest led to open conflict.[125] As early as 1677, the Confederacy had been at war with the Illinois peoples in the Mississippi watershed. By the end of the decade, the French explorer La Salle was reportedly selling European weapons to the Illinois, while simultaneously negotiating for an Indian alliance in the region to oppose the Haudenosaunee and divert trade to France.[126] In response, Seneca and Onondaga warriors of the Confederacy attacked the Illinois in force during 1680 in order to prevent the consolidation of that alliance.

In 1682, several Indian nations allied with New France appealed to Frontenac for help against the Haudenosaunee warriors.[127] Without forces at his disposal sufficient even to confidently make an appearance in Confederacy country, Frontenac could only request a treaty conference with the Haudenosaunee in Montreal. All he received, however, was a visit from a single Confederacy envoy representing the "Whole House." The ambassador assured the governor that the Haudenosaunee would not attack the allied nations if they themselves kept the peace, but when pressed stated that the war against the Illinois would continue. In response, Frontenac was only able to warn the Confederacy of the hazards of war and propose his own mediation between the warring parties at some future treaty conference.[128] Although the governor achieved a commitment from the Confederacy to forbear unprovoked attacks against New France's closest trading partners, the inability to direct or persuade the Haudenosaunee to break off disruptive warfare in an important region of economic interest to the colony symbolizes the oscillations in strength between these rivals during this period.

As these events unfolded, Louis XIV embarked on a more aggressive strategy against the Haudenosaunee. In his instructions to Frontenac's successor, de La Barre, he directed that a strong expeditionary force be sent to the margins of Confederacy territory to demonstrate French power. The governor was expressly authorized to attack "should they do anything against the French," with the caution, however, that he was not to begin a war unless it could be quickly and thoroughly won with certainty. He was further instructed to maintain peace among the western nations that formed France's principal trading partners and, in particular, to protect them, including the Illinois, from the Confederacy.[129]

By late 1682, New France began to mobilize for war with the Haudenosaunee.[130] As part of the preparations, La Barre proposed to Versailles that the king contact the Duke of York to prevent British colonial assistance to the Confederacy.[131] The specific outcome of the diplomatic initiative is uncertain, but the following year Louis advised his governor that precise orders had been issued by the English king to New York officials "to maintain good correspondence with us, and carefully to avoid whatever may interrupt it."[132]

Despite clear authorization to place the colony on a war footing, the governor received no definitive order to commence an attack on the Confederacy from the French Court. As the issue was debated, La Barre opened a diplomatic channel to the Haudenosaunee. An envoy was instructed to invite Confederacy representatives to a conference at Montreal with the interim proposition "that whatever might occur during the trading season among the Ottawa [in the western war] should not disturb the peace" between the two peoples. According to La Barre's report of the meetings, the Haudenosaunee embassy agreed to recommend to their nations that "friendship" for the Ottawas, Algonquians, and Hurons (the Illinois were not named) be effected. They promised to return with Confederacy warriors in the spring of 1684 to confirm an agreement. Later intelligence, however, convinced La Barre that the Confederacy was pursuing a strategy parallel to his own—engaging in diplomacy to buy time to prepare for war.[133]

The permutations of Franco-Haudenosaunee relations during these two decades of relative peace, and most particularly during the years of disintegration leading to war, underscore the absurdity of the French assertion of vassalage in the 1665 treaty. The Haudenosaunee, not the British, remained the principal threat to the survival and profitability of New France. The two peoples maintained an uneasy coexistence rooted in a mutual desire to avoid direct conflict. Relations were entirely at arms length and had to be periodically adjusted through the treaty process. France acquired no authority, even in a nominal or symbolic sense, over any aspect of Haudenosaunee affairs. Throughout the period, the Confederacy maintained independent relations with the British, Dutch, and Indian nations both allied with and hostile to New France. In reality, the two nations were sharp competitors constantly maneuvering for advantage in the North American theater of international trade.

The Shadow of War, 1684 to 1701

As the intensity of French-Haudenosaunee-British triangular relations increased with the approach and onset of war, clear signposts eventually emerged for sorting reality from rhetoric, substance from symbolism. In early 1684, Haudenosaunee warfare in the west brought the Confederacy on a collision course with France. Seneca warriors intercepted a group of French arms traders, seized cargo, and briefly attacked a fortified outpost on the Illinois River that served as a forward bastion for French influence among the Indian nations of the region. In response, Governor La Barre sought authorization for a counterattack against the Senecas, coupling his request with a renewed effort to neutralize the British in New York.[134] On July 31, Louis XIV reluctantly gave approval for war.[135]

France apparently assumed that the forthcoming conflict against the western nations of the Haudenosaunee would proceed on the same basis as earlier campaigns, with the European trading partners of the Confederacy providing arms for a price but otherwise not interfering in a bilateral situation. Seeking to improve the French position and relying on Anglo-

French treaty commitments and his close relationship with the British Crown, Louis once again ordered his ambassador in London to request a set of instructions from the Duke of York to his governor, this time not only prohibiting assistance to the Haudenosaunee but also ordering "that he act in concert and entire correspondence with the said de La Barre." [136]

To the same end, the French governor opened direct contacts with Thomas Dongan, recently appointed governor of New York. In his initial approach, La Barre politely recited the nature of the *casus belli* with the Seneca Nation. Citing the "close Union and Fraternity" of the two crowns, he formally requested Dongan to forbid the sale of arms and ammunition to the Confederacy either directly or indirectly. [137] La Barre's approach was naive, failing to appreciate the degree to which the English relied on the Haudenosaunee as a barrier against New France and profited from Haudenosaunee western hegemony, but Dongan's response went far beyond anything that he might have anticipated.

In his reply, the New York governor announced that "those Indyans are under this Government" and proceeded to make a territorial claim to their lands to the border of Canada. He advised La Barre not to commit any act of hostility or permit his people to enter the region south of Lake Erie and Lake Ontario, promising on his part to "send for the Indyans and require of them to do what is just in order to [sic] a satisfaction to your pretences." [138] Days later, after hearing an erroneous report that a French attack had already begun, Dongan sent a second communication to La Barre reaffirming his earlier position and recommending that if the dispute with the Confederacy could not be settled peacefully, it be referred to Europe for resolution. "I should be very sorry to hear that you invade the Duke's Territories," he stated, and then with an excellent flourish of symbolism, "to prevent as much as I can all the inconveniencyes that may happen, I have . . . ordered the coates of Armes of His Royal Highnesse, the Duke of York to be put up in the Indyan Castles *which may diswade you from acting* anything that may create a misunderstanding between us." [139] (Emphasis added.)

By initiating these claims in an environment of international conflict, Dongan became the architect of much of the confusion that has attached to Anglo-Haudenosaunee relations. His "protectorate," however, was a political charade. Throughout the series of communications, Dongan was careful to couple his claims with increasingly detailed appeals to La Barre to accept his intervention in gaining reparations from the Haudenosaunee in place of war. Conceding nothing, La Barre chose to interpret Dongan's approach as an offer of mediation and called the bluff: "I pray you, then, . . . if the Senecas and Cayugas wish your services as their intercessor, to take security from them, not in the Indian but in the European fashion, without which, and the honor of hearing from you, I shall attack them towards the 20th of August." [140]

Dongan had no greater success convincing the Haudenosaunee of their submission to his authority. From the beginning of his tenure in New York, the governor set out to extract statements of assent to his proposition that the Confederacy had placed themselves and their lands, ambiguously, under the Duke of York or the Crown of England. [141] Under the shadow of La Barre's imminent invasion of Haudenosaunee territory, Dongan was hard pressed to give substance to his political claims made to the French governor without Confederacy knowledge—substance that could only be gained through Haudenosaunee consent and cooperation. An opportunity to reach such an understanding arose later that summer (1684) through a treaty conference between the governor of Virginia and the Haudenosaunee hosted by Dongan at Albany to resolve conflicts created by Confederacy activities around Virginia settlements.

Faced with war, the Haudenosaunee were reported in the New York records as having accepted Dongan's offer of "protection," which they nevertheless defined in terms of defensive assistance against French attacks. Reviewing the historical relationship of the two peoples, the Onondaga speaker reminded the governor that when the British first established small settlements "we treated you civilly, and gave you Land. We hope, therefore, now that you are Great and we Small, you will protect us from the French." Probing to the core of English self-interest, he pointed out that a Confederacy defeat would mean that "the French will get all the Bever [sic]." It is quite clear that the Haudenosaunee regarded "protection" as a strictly consensual arrangement for a particular purpose. Addressing both governors, the speaker continued, "Let your Friend, the great Sachem that lives on the other side of the great Lake, know this, *that We being a Free People, tho' united to the English, may give our Lands, and be joyn'd to the Sachem we like best.*" [142] (Emphasis added.)

During the course of the treaty conference, a representative from New France arrived in Albany in a further attempt to convince the New York governor of the justice of the French position. The Seneca envoy threw the blame back on New France. Stressing that war in the west was essential to defending Haudenosaunee and English interests in the fur trade, he denounced the French for arming his enemies. The Seneca Nation would offer reparations to La Barre if Dongan insisted, he added, but reminded the governor that it was France, not the Senecas that threatened war. [143] In reality, the Haudenosaunee had already agreed among themselves at a Confederacy Grand Council to offer reparations and a new peace treaty to New France in an effort to forestall the war, an offer immediately communicated to La Barre. [144]

La Barre, however, had already decided on war. In July of 1684 he sent off an expedition of approximately 1,200 men from Montreal to be joined by hundreds of Indian warriors organized by French agents in the west. After an arduous journey up the St. Lawrence River, however, the French soldiers were devastated by sickness. Realizing that his war plans had collapsed, La Barre attempted to salvage something from the enterprise by pursuing the treaty option opened by the Confederacy. He quickly scrambled to conceal his hostile intent, sending surviving troops back to the colony and intercepting and turning back the allied warriors from the western nations.[145]

An agent was dispatched to the Confederacy capital of Onondaga to invite the Haudenosaunee to a conference at the French encampment to the north. At the same time, Dongan sent his personal interpreter to Onondaga with orders to attempt to prevent a treaty with New France.[146] Earlier, during the treaty conference with Virginia, Dongan "advised" the Haudenosaunee representatives that if difficulties arose with the French (!), he would "compose" it, adding, "Make no Covenant or Agreement with the French, or any other Nation, without my Knowledge or Approbation."[147] Dongan's latest message to the Haudenosaunee was cast in stronger terms. They were informed that they must not meet La Barre without his permission and that likewise, if the French governor wished to meet with them he must apply to Dongan for his consent. The answer of the Confederacy was swift and certain: "You say we are Subjects to the King of England and Duke of York, but we say, we are Brethren. We must take care of our selves. Those Arms [coat of arms of the Duke of York] fixed upon the Post . . . cannot defend us against the Arms of La Barre."[148]

If the Haudenosaunee had accommodated to Dongan's theater piece, they would have deprived themselves of an effortless victory over the French. Instead, they continued to exercise their prerogative of independent political action and sent a delegation to treat with New France. His army in shambles, La Barre was ridiculed by the Confederacy ambassadors. He opened the treaty conference with a bombastic address accusing the Haudenosaunee of violating existing treaty commitments and threatening war unless reparations were paid, Illinois and allied prisoners released, and the Confederacy agreed not to guide English traders into the western Great Lakes region. La Barre closed his address with an assurance that the French were "the Brethren and Friends of the five Nations" and would hold to the peace if the Confederacy would observe their treaties.[149]

Despite La Barre's effort to conceal his original military purpose and the scope of his failure, the Haudenosaunee were quite aware of the actual situation. In words dripping with sarcasm, the Onondaga ambassador

Otreouate observed that the governor "raves in a Camp of sick People." He then proceeded to answer La Barre point by point. The Confederacy position that he articulated pointedly illustrates the Haudenosaunee analysis of international relations in North America. Otreouate began by asserting the right to seize French munitions intended for the use of belligerents at war with the Confederacy and emphatically refused reparations. As for the charge that Haudenosaunee warriors escorted English traders into areas of French commercial hegemony, the speaker responded with an affirmation of Haudenosaunee sovereignty:

> We have conducted the English to our Lakes, in order to traffick with the Outaouas, and the Hurons; just as the Algonkins conducted the French to our five Cantons, in order to carry on a Commerce that the English lay claim to as their Right. We are born Freemen, and have no dependence either upon [France] or [England]. We have a power to go where we please, to conduct who we will to the places we resort to, and to buy and sell where we think fit. If your allies are your Slaves or Children, you may e'en treat them as such, and rob 'em of the liberty of entertaining any other Nation but your own.[150] (Emphasis added.)

The war against the Illinois and allied nations was justified without apology in terms redolent of European "just war" concepts. The war began, he explained, because those nations entered areas claimed by the Confederacy, hunted fur-bearing animals there to extinction, and further conspired against Haudenosaunee interests. "We have done less than the English and the French," he continued, "*who without any right*, have usurp'd the Grounds they are now possess'd of; and of which they have dislodg'd several Nations, in order to make way for their building of Cities, Villages, and Forts."[151] (Emphasis added.) Warning La Barre not to militarize Fort Frontenac near Haudenosaunee territory, Otreouate emphasized the desire of the Confederacy to maintain peaceful relations with France. He made the limits of Haudenosaunee forbearance clear, however; peace would be kept "till such time as [France] and [England], do either joyntly or separately offer to invade the Country, that the great Spirit has dispos'd of in the favour of our Ancestors."[152]

The treaty represented the complete failure of French and British efforts to achieve dominance over the Haudenosaunee. France failed to achieve its goal of suppressing the Confederacy as an economic competitor. Worse, in accepting Haudenosaunee terms for renewing the peace, New France proved itself visibly incapable of protecting key allies from warfare and destruction. The Confederacy continued to pursue the western war according to its own discretion, having made no commitment to do otherwise. Similarly, Dongan's attempt to gain Haudenosaunee and

French recognition of a British protectorate came to nothing. The Confederacy emphatically repudiated the notion that they were subjects of the British Crown and that Dongan had any authority whatever to manage or arrange their international relations. In treating directly with the French, they continued on a well-worn path of independence, oblivious to the legal theories of others.

The French, however, were keenly aware of the political implications of Dongan's legalisms to their interests. In a report to the French minister of the marine and colonies shortly after the debacle, the New York governor's symbolic action of raising the Duke's arms was characterized as an act "to take first possession of the country."[153] Taken as such, it perfectly mirrored Louis XIV's earlier stratagem to preempt British influence by declaring (in a consensual treaty format) that the Haudenosaunee nations were vassals of France.[154] Thus, although neither European state could accomplish actual suzerainty over Confederacy affairs, a symbolic contest was joined to establish European recognition of an exclusive sphere of influence in Haudenosaunee country for one or the other.

Louis XIV doggedly pursued the matter at both North American and European levels. "Displeased" with the abandonment of the Illinois, he moved early in 1685 to replace La Barre with the Marquis de Denonville as governor. Determined to achieve a peace in accord with French interests, namely firm control of the fur trade, the French monarch instructed his new governor to "humble" the Haudenosaunee and "sustain" the Illinois and other allies. Although Louis did not wish to disrupt his friendly relations with Britain, he was not prepared to tolerate Dongan's erstwhile expansionism. In an extraordinary measure considering the rare state of goodwill between the two traditional European rivals, the French king declared to his governor that if the English "excite and aid the Indians, they must be treated as enemies when found on Indian territory, without, at the same time, attempting anything on territory under the obedience of the King of England."[155] Quite obviously, the French territorial definition of the British North American realm did not include the territory of the Haudenosaunee.

In a companion communication addressed to the French ambassador in London, the minister of the marine and colonies complained that Dongan tried to prevent the Haudenosaunee from treating with France, offered them military support, and raised his flags in their villages "notwithstanding those Nations have always been subject to France, since their country was discovered by the French, without any objection on the part of the English." The ambassador was instructed to demand "precise orders obliging that governor to confine himself within the limits of his government."[156] Although the territorial distinction made by the French accurately reflected the actual political situation in North

America, the claim of an exclusive French sphere of influence was a fantasy of the diplomatic game. Nevertheless, in raising the claim at the highest level of European diplomacy, Louis gave notice that France was prepared to stake out a negotiating position of its own on the question of exclusive influence over Haudenosaunee relations.

During that period, however, relations with the Confederacy were but one item in a rapidly escalating series of disputes between France and Britain over economic and colonial interests in the Western Hemisphere that, together with contemporaneous European intrigues, threatened to disrupt the Stuart-Bourbon entente. The two states argued repeatedly over colonial rights in the West Indies, Acadia, and also in the Hudson Bay region, where armed assaults against trading posts had already occurred. Seeking to prevent war in the hemisphere and preserve their mutual alliance, Britain and France began negotiations to adjust their differences in 1686.[157] Unable to reach specific agreement, particularly in relation to Hudson Bay, the parties nevertheless entered into a treaty requiring strict neutrality between the two states in their American possessions, even if war should break out between them in Europe.[158]

The third article of the 1686 treaty completed a project that Louis XIV had pursued since 1682—a commitment of British neutrality in the event of war with the Haudenosaunee. In the article, both parties agreed to refrain from bringing "any aid or supplies of men or provisions to barbarians with whom [either monarch] is carrying on war." Although stated in general terms, the "barbarians" in question certainly included the Haudenosaunee. Thus, with the stroke of a pen, James II destroyed whatever remained of the symbolic architecture of Dongan's British protectorate over the Confederacy. James's putative "subjects" were left to their own devices in any armed conflict with New France.[159]

To the authorities of New France, the most dangerous Haudenosaunee activity was the escorting of English trading expeditions to the western nations. Perceiving a direct threat to the commercial viability of the French colony, Denonville attempted to respond in both military and political terms. In a report to Versailles the governor informed the ministry of his plans for war, despite fatalistic doubts as to the capacity of New France to defend against Haudenosaunee counterattacks.[160] Appended to the report was a "Memoir in proof of the Right of the French to the Iroquois country and to Hudson's Bay" intended to provide a factual basis for French legal claims against the British.[161] In March of 1687, Louis XIV approved the war plans and commended Denonville for his memoir on French rights. He informed the governor that Britain and France had agreed to appoint commissioners to resolve disputes in the Americas left pending by the treaty of neutrality.[162]

By the time permission for war was received, Denonville was well advanced in preparations against the Seneca Nation. In late June, a force of 3,000 Frenchmen and Indian allies converged on Seneca territory. After a fierce but indecisive battle at a Seneca ambush site, the elusive warriors withdrew, having previously evacuated and burned their own villages. As in previous campaigns, the French found no other enemies to engage and had to content themselves with destroying food stocks. Denonville confirmed his "conquest" with a ceremonial, taking possession of the country in the name of the king.[163] On the basis of previous French experience, however, the governor realized that without some more tangible effort to dominate the territory, his invasion and ceremony would accomplish nothing more than a winter of hardship for the Seneca Nation. Consequently, he decided to station large garrisons in two strategic locations, a new fort constructed at Niagara and the fortified trading post built by Frontenac in 1675 near the juncture of Lake Ontario and the St. Lawrence River.[164]

Learning of the French attack, Dongan resumed his efforts to entice the Confederacy into accepting British suzerainty. In the first of two messages to the assembled nations at Onondaga, he offered his services as their agent: "Lett me know by ye first Post whether the Breth[ren] of ye 5 nations are of opinion that I should send to ye french to see if they be inclined for Peace or nott . . . and if ye french be willing I shal make a Better Peace for yu than you can doe yr Selfs."[165] A few days later he repeated the offer, expressing alarm that as "subjects" the Confederacy might negotiate their own peace without his "consent." If the Confederacy ignored his advice, he threatened, "I will not trouble my Self any longer wth ye Brethren but goe doune to N: Yorke, for wee can live without ye Brethren but can Scarcely believe they can live without us; having Everything thrice as cheep here as Elsewhere."[166] Dongan's second message revealed quite clearly that the basis for the Anglo-Haudenosaunee relationship was economic. In light of the high degree of economic interdependence between the two peoples, however, the offer of withdrawal from active relations was hardly a credible threat.

Because of the Anglo-French neutrality treaty, Dongan was incapable of holding up his end of what the Haudenosaunee considered to be a British alliance. In place of military assistance, he offered legal theory. At a conference with the Confederacy soon after the French incursion, he assured the Haudenosaunee that they brought the trouble on themselves by independently treating with La Barre in 1684. If they would only act as the king's subjects by making no treaties without his consent, he maintained, they would receive the benefit of the recent treaty between Britain and France. Dongan assured them that the French king would not dare to enter the king of England's territories "if he thought the Brethren were the King of England's subjects." [167] In response, Dongan was informed that the Confederacy was intent on carrying the war to the French. Hoping for further assistance from the king's subjects, the Haudenosaunee spokesman promised not to make peace without the governor's "commands." [168]

Unlike the years 1664 to 1666 when a French invasion brought about the end of a war with the Haudenosaunee, Denonville's raid marked the beginning of a deadly conflict. Upon returning to the colony, Denonville expressed renewed concerns over the vulnerability of New France. [169] His fears immediately proved to be prophetic when, within weeks, Confederacy warriors launched raids against indefensible settlements outside Montreal. Warfare that began as a minimally contested invasion of Haudenosaunee territory was rapidly transformed into a startling French defeat. A combination of winter weather and Haudenosaunee warriors completely cut off the two garrisons left to represent French power in Seneca country. By spring, disease and starvation decimated both forward posts, resulting in the abandonment of the fort at Niagara. Moreover, the colony experienced economic as well as military decline; for two years no shipment of furs arrived from the most important western trading station. [170] Although the Haudenosaunee received some munitions from New York, the war was waged without direct involvement of the British ally.

Ironically, as guerilla war swept through New France, commissioners appointed by Louis XIV and James II to define the territorial limits of their sphere of influence claims debated Haudenosaunee affairs in London. After six months of negotiations, a new British claim concerning the Haudenosaunee was apparently tabled. Following a complaint by the French commissioners that Governor Dongan was supplying arms to the Haudenosaunee in violation of the 1686 treaty of neutrality, the British commissioners advised James II that in order to secure the fur trade and protect the security of his dominions, the Confederacy should be supported and protected. Resurrecting Dongan's correspondence, they further advised him to inform the French that the Haudenosaunee were his "subjects as appears by their submissions and acknowledgments made by them from the first settlements in these parts, and more lately by the voluntary submission made and confirmed by them in writing to the Crown of England, the 30th day of July 1684." [171]

Returning to the bargaining table, the British commissioners communicated a claim to suzerainty over the Haudenosaunee based on a putatively consensual subjection by the Confederacy to the Crown. In response, the French ambassadors denied the "novel" contention and reiterated their own claim based on acts of Champlain taking possession of the country in the name of France in the early seventeenth century and on treaties concluded with the Confederacy in 1665 and 1666 "whereby they placed themselves under His Majesty's protection, and declared themselves his subjects." They further asserted that since 1666 the Haudenosaunee had recognized French dominion "without any interruption."[172]

Although both governments claimed suzerainty entirely on the basis of voluntary subjection by treaty consistent with the principles of international law, in light of the actual situation in North America these contentions were surreal. In any event, the claims were sufficiently abstract to be irreconcilable, and the commissioners could only agree to retain the status quo under the neutrality treaty pending future negotiations scheduled for 1689.[173]

The interim agreement negotiated by the commissioners stimulated a flurry of peace efforts by the two governors in North America. The Haudenosaunee, however, continued to reserve decisions to themselves. During the summer of 1688, while Seneca and Mohawk warriors continued to attack Canada, Onondaga, Cayuga, and Oneida representatives met Denonville to discuss Haudenosaunee neutrality between Britain and France. Although the discussions were preliminary and never resumed, the Confederacy representatives were reported to have clearly stated their independence from both countries.[174] Eventually, a cease-fire without a formal treaty of peace was brokered by Edmond Andros, who replaced Dongan in New York. Conditions in New France were sufficiently dire by late 1688, however, for Denonville in correspondence with his ministry to raise the possibility of ceding French claims over the Confederacy to the British in return for a British commitment to restrain Haudenosaunee warfare and a pledge not to establish any British presence within their country.[175] The British also began to feel the bite of war. Warriors of the Abenaki Nation allied with France attacked border settlements in New England, capturing a fort in Pemaquid (Maine).

The Politics of War, 1689 to 1701

Soon thereafter, events in Europe took a dramatic turn that made comprehensive warfare in North America inevitable. In February 1689, following the overthrow of the Stuart dynasty, William of Orange assumed the British throne. The new king moved swiftly to bring Britain into the League of Augsburg, organized in Europe to challenge French power, and formally declared war the following May. Although European affairs provided the primary cause for war, Britain also listed among its grievances French encroachments in Hudson Bay, Newfoundland, New England, and the West Indies.[176]

News of the "War of the League of Augsburg" (King William's War) filtered slowly into British North America during the summer and fall of 1689. Actual warfare, however, was not initiated by the British but by the Haudenosaunee, independently rekindling their smoldering conflict with New France. In late July of that year, the Confederacy launched a large-scale attack against the settlement of La Chine, near Montreal.[177] Faced with continuing Haudenosaunee attacks and the loss of support from Indian allies disenchanted with French impotence, the Count de Frontenac, Denonville's successor, unsuccessfully sought peace with the Confederacy. For the Haudenosaunee, the advent of the British declaration of war meant that for the first time a martial alliance against their old enemy was at hand. Under the circumstances, they had no desire for negotiating a peace.[178]

The war provides a vantage point for both retrospective and prospective analyses of the international legal personality of the Confederacy. Retrospectively, the Confederacy had unilaterally exercised the powers of war and peace. For at least thirteen years the Haudenosaunee had conducted an entirely independent war against Indian nations politically and commercially aligned with France. From the time of Denonville's 1687 campaign against the Seneca Nation, the Confederacy also maintained an independent war directly against New France. Though a succession of New York governors attempted to entice the Confederacy into ceding negotiating authority to the Crown in the 1670s and 1680s, the Haudenosaunee consistently and aggressively conducted their own foreign relations with France in peace and war as they had for decades.

For most of the period, Haudenosaunee definitions were paralleled by European conduct. Although James II (in the midst of negotiations over sphere of influence claims in North America in 1687) had instructed the governor of New York to assist the Confederacy nations in defending against French invasions, he did so only to produce a tangible manifestation of British assertions of authority in the region. That same monarch had previously obligated Britain to stand neutral in the Franco-Haudenosaunee war. On his part, Louis XIV viewed the Confederacy as an independent territorial and political entity rather than an extension of British dominion. France never regarded Haudenosaunee warfare as a violation of its own treaties of peace with Britain, demanding rather neutrality, prohibition of arms sales, and at one stage active assistance against the Confederacy as the measure of British obligation to that relationship.

Looking back over the Anglo-Haudenosaunee bond from the perspective of 1690, it is difficult to characterize it even as an alliance in any real sense. From 1664, the Confederacy maintained a relationship of close amity and economic interdependence with the English in New York as they had with Dutch predecessors in New Netherland. From 1677 to 1684 formal relations were also established with English colonial enclaves in New England, Maryland, and Virginia. In the case of the southern entities, the Confederacy freely attacked and formed its own hegemonic relations with Indian nations allied to those colonies with little regard to English interests.

Relations with New York were obviously much closer, but that colony never rendered active assistance in Haudenosaunee conflicts with New France. When faced with the clear prospect of French attacks against Haudenosaunee communities, the New York governors acted only on a diplomatic level in an attempt to persuade French forbearance by argument or threat. Although the British did supply the Confederacy with arms, without which the Haudenosaunee would have been unable to wage war effectively, they acted primarily as arms merchants rather than allies in these transactions. Moreover, in the waning days of the Stuart dynasty when Britain and France were attempting to avoid war by negotiating their North American disputes, the British had a difficult time persuading Haudenosaunee allies to refrain from attacking New France, accomplishing only a brief cease-fire broken by renewed Confederacy warfare in 1689. Despite British machinations, the Haudenosaunee had retained their independence by any standard.

When the War of the League of Augsburg spread to North America, it was superimposed on an ongoing Confederacy war that had been in process for nearly a decade. The question raised by the European dimension of warfare then, is whether the conflict situation as a whole, in 1690 or after, created or revealed some change in the Haudenosaunee-British relationship that materially affected Haudenosaunee independence or international personality. Since Britain at no time maintained sufficient force in the region to compel Haudenosaunee submission, some consensual arrangement would have to be identified to support an alteration. As in earlier periods, contemporary treaty records do not contain any clear and express agreements by the Confederacy to accept either British sovereignty or a British protectorate involving any diminution in the scope of Haudenosaunee freedom in conducting external relations. If the Confederacy had consented to one of these arrangements in some form, British governors and their scribes were sufficiently sophisticated to memorialize agreement in the most formal and legally effective terms. Conference records do contain various expressions of Haudenosaunee acceptance of subject status and protection, however. Although these minutes are too self-serving of British interests to be credible of themselves, they continued to raise a fundamental ambiguity that can only be resolved by examining actual conduct.

The claim of subject status can be disposed of rather easily. At no time was the Confederacy territory or polity ever incorporated into the British domain. Neither the Parliament nor the monarch ruling by decree (representing different constitutional aspects of the British realm) ever possessed or attempted to exercise any legislative authority in Haudeno-saunee country. Haudenosaunee individuals owed no fealty to the Crown, nor were they regarded as treasonous if they attacked British settlements or allied Indian nations. In terms of the war effort, Britain assumed no authority to conscript Haudenosaunee persons or to enter Haudenosaunee territory with an army without specific Confederacy consent. In sum, the Confederacy remained a distinct political entity with complete internal sovereign independence.

The question of external status requires closer analysis. Did Britain have responsibility for and authority over the defense of Haudenosaunee territory in this period? Did Britain acquire authority over Haudenosaunee decisions to initiate warfare against France or Indian nations? Did Britain acquire control over the conduct of external relations, including the right to treat on behalf of the Confederacy and consequently to bind the Confederacy to British agreements? In the absence of this authority, did the Confederacy nevertheless agree to restrict its own foreign affairs practice so as to achieve consistency with British policy or agree to bind itself to the requirement of British consent? Finally, if the Haudenosaunee did agree to cede some authority over external relations to Britain, did the Confederacy so completely divest its external identity, despite retaining internal sovereignty, that it lost or seriously compromised its international legal personality? The history of the war, or more accurately, of the wars does not support any such notions of British control.

The War of the League of Augsburg never subsumed the preexisting Franco-Haudenosaunee war, but it provided the possibility of a new dimension for Anglo-Haudenosaunee relations. In 1690, for the first time in the twenty-six years since their initial treaty of friendship, the two peoples were engaged in fighting against France as a common enemy. Once again, however, prospects for a military component to the Anglo-Haudenosaunee Covenant Chain alliance were more apparent than real.

The European war in North America was an affair of brief duration in terms of actual combat between the colonies. In 1690, French forces invaded New York and ravaged the town of Schenectady. Despite Mohawk exhortations to stay and fight, many residents of nearby Albany left their homes and fled to Manhattan. Later that year, a joint Mohawk-intercolonial invasion of Canada was negotiated, but ended with a small raid on Montreal when a smallpox epidemic reduced the Mohawk and British forces. Warfare was also hampered by political chaos in New York. From the fall of James II until 1691, the colony was governed on an ad hoc basis with a great deal of local strife. Indian relations were also conducted ad hoc until the arrival of Henry Sloughter as Crown representative in that year.

By 1691, the Confederacy had received and rejected several peace initiatives from New France. Despite a firm policy to pursue the war, however, the Haudenosaunee were increasingly distressed by the lack of participation of the British "brethren." Perceiving Confederacy dissatisfaction and fearing repeated French efforts to gain a treaty of neutrality, Governor Sloughter met with the Haudenosaunee within months of his arrival to confirm an alliance.[179] Discussions at this conference are particularly illuminating because they present in clear fashion the definition of the alliance held by each party to the relationship at that time.

In previous conference records the Confederacy had at times paid lip service to British assertions of suzerainty while continuing to make independent decisions in their international relations. Now that the alliance had acquired a tangible character in the midst of war the Haudenosaunee had no patience with symbolism. Clearly angry, the ambassadors demanded reciprocity in all aspects of the alliance. When Sloughter reminded the Confederacy that previous governors had "stricktly charged" them not to treat with the French enemy "without particular orders," they replied that they had no intention of making peace without "common" consent, requiring on their part "that our Brethren the Christians keep no correspondence with [the French] by letters or otherwise." Mixing encouragement with thinly-veiled criticism, the ambassadors pointedly told the governor "as you encouraged us yesterday to prosecute the warr we say the same to you today."[180] The Confederacy was speaking as an independent people seeking greater commitment from a reluctant ally, not as a besieged people petitioning for the protection of a patron state. Haudenosaunee desires for military assistance went unfulfilled, however, and the Indian nations continued to bear the brunt of the war effort. With the exception of a second British-led joint expedition against Montreal in 1691 and one comic-opera British naval venture at Quebec in the same period, the war remained a Franco-Haudenosaunee conflict for the duration.

As the British implemented a purely defensive strategy in New York and the alliance increasingly became insubstantial, retaining the loyalty of the Haudenosaunee buffer nations became an obsession of British North American diplomacy. Every report of a peace-feeler from New France was followed by a British treaty conference with the Haudenosaunee to cement the alliance.[181] Political assertions of protection aside, in actuality the British relied heavily on Haudenosaunee enmity and active warfare with New France to form a preemptive and protective barrier against French attacks in New York and elsewhere during the course of the Anglo-French conflict. As a pragmatic defensive measure, the British had every interest in preventing a premature termination of Franco-Haudenosaunee hostilities.

Throughout the long war, however, the Confederacy maintained open diplomatic channels to New France. Peace sentiments were largely a function of Haudenosaunee assessments of the fortunes of war in any given period. Discussions were particularly intense following French incursions in the Mohawk territory in 1693 and Onondaga-Oneida territories in 1696, but the alliance held.[182] Apart from British blandishments and increasing amounts of "presents," the Confederacy had its own motivations for continuing the struggle. In reality, the Franco-Haudenosaunee and Anglo-French wars were parallel conflicts that only occasionally intersected in an active sense. So long as grievances against New France accumulated, the war effort was reasonably successful, and the possibility of more extensive British involvement existed, the Confederacy was prepared to carry on.[183]

The active link was shattered by the British, not the Haudenosaunee. After years of negotiation, the War of the League of Augsburg ended in a stalemate with the signing of the Treaty of Ryswyk in 1697. Anglo-French disputes in North America continued unadjusted, however. The two sides could only agree to restore the *status quo ante-bellum* with, once again, commissioners appointed to negotiate a mutually recognized territorial definition of sphere of influence claims.[184] Neither party purported to treat on behalf of its Indian allies, however, and the Indian wars predating the European conflict continued for several years.[185] The Anglo-Haudenosaunee alliance had always been hollow from a military perspective, but despite repeated pleas to the Confederacy not to negotiate a separate peace, Britain had done precisely that—forged a treaty without warning, much less consulting the allies.

Notwithstanding these events, British diplomacy continued to focus on preventing the Haudenosaunee from negotiating independently for peace with France. As in 1687 and 1688, when British and French commissioners last had met to debate their respective North American claims, the British argument for hegemony over the Confederacy remained a purported consensual subjection to a British protectorate. An independent Franco-Haudenosaunee peace treaty would have too thoroughly contradicted any basis for British suzerainty, even considering the rarified symbology of European diplomatic discourse on North American questions. As a result, Britain had a self-defined stake in the endgame of the Haudenosaunee war while France, because of the British interest, also concerned itself with the form as well as the substance of peace with the Confederacy.

As previously noted, sphere of influence and other colonial disputes between Britain and France involved Hudson Bay, Acadia, and islands of the West Indies as well as Iroquoia, the territory of the Confederacy. Among these issues, because of its position in the fur trade and as a protective buffer against New France, Haudenosaunee relations were extremely important to Britain. The French posture toward the Confederacy seemed more ambiguous, however. Despite rather fanciful counterclaims of Haudenosaunee vassalage to France, the close friendship between the Confederacy and the British was undeniable. Moreover, the French government gave indication that it desired to leave the situation sufficiently open so as not to prejudge the outcome of the commissioners' negotiations on the broad range of differences.[186]

Stripped of its most grandiose assertions, the French position denied British suzerainty on the basis of decades of independent French treaty relations with the Confederacy long predating and also postdating the British entry into New York. The primary project of French diplomacy, however, was to finally end sixty years of painful and costly warfare with the Haudenosaunee that had severely diminished the economic output of New France. Otherwise, sphere of influence claims in Iroquoia might be negotiated away in adjusting other French interests in the hemisphere and in Europe.

Despite hopes for further agreement in Europe, so long as war conditions continued, actual peace had to be negotiated between the combatants in North America. A new avenue had been opened by a Haudenosaunee embassy to New France shortly before news of the Treaty of Ryswyk reached the colonies. Although the approach was tentative and the overture clearly did not include terms for an end to the war against French-allied Indian nations that had begun the current Franco-Haudenosaunee conflict twenty years before, both sides were sufficiently interested to continue discussions.[187]

The British moved quickly in an effort to abort the process. Governor Bellomont of New York "informed" the governor of New France that as subjects of the Crown the Haudenosaunee were already included in the peace of Ryswyk. As the status of the Confederacy was a central element in the sphere of influence disputes between the two countries, Bellomont's contention was rejected out of hand. France would continue to maintain its own distinct relationship with its Indian enemies.[188] Without French acquiescence to his claims of suzerainty, Bellomont found himself in the same situation as his predecessor, Dongan, years before. The only way that Britain could acquire actual authority in the situation was through genuine Haudenosaunee consent to a protectorate in the European mode. When that consent was not forthcoming, the governor could do little more than attempt to persuade the Confederacy not to treat for peace.[189] Although Bellomont succeeded in forestalling a treaty for nearly two years, Confederacy interests required a peace that Britain had no power to provide.

France had more leverage on questions of war and peace at that stage in the conflict than the British could hope to mobilize. The peace of Ryswyk between Britain and France eventually resulted in a de facto cease-fire in the Franco-Haudenosaunee war, since neither European power wished to risk destabilizing a delicate peace in Europe because of North American strife. Indeed, by 1699 the two countries had agreed to take measures to avoid an outbreak of active Franco-Haudenosaunee hostilities during the pendency of diplomatic negotiations on sphere of influence claims. As an interim measure, Louis XIV expressly instructed his governor to extend the peace of Ryswyk to the Haudenosaunee, including an exchange of prisoners and hostages.[190] Because of the political détente in Europe, the British were able to assert during their own negotiations with the Haudenosaunee that the Confederacy had been included in the peace treaty as British "subjects" and promise future protection without fear of immediate contradiction by French military action. British strategies were based on the hope that the Confederacy could be persuaded that it had in fact been protected and would consequently maintain a passive posture while Britain attempted to convince France that peace with the Haudenosaunee could only be achieved under British suzerainty.

The Advent of Haudenosaunee Neutrality

The illusion of an existing Pax Britannica for the Haudenosaunee could not be sustained for long, however. Although hostilities with France were suspended, the tertiary war with French allied Indian nations initiated by the Confederacy in the 1670s continued unabated. By the conclusion of the Treaty of Ryswyk, a twenty-year-long, two-front war and at least one smallpox epidemic had weakened the Haudenosaunee nations to the point that they were increasingly vulnerable to Indian attacks from the west. As those attacks increased in number and fury, the Confederacy did approach the British to negotiate an end to the fighting.[191] Britain, of course, had no capacity to intervene at any level. New France remained the sole force that could influence the actions of the western nations and had already emphatically rejected British efforts to make or mediate a Franco-Haudenosaunee peace. The French insisted that the Haudenosaunee address them directly with commitments for a comprehensive peace with New France and its allies.[192]

Final negotiations involving the Confederacy, France, and the western Indian nations began at Montreal during the summer of 1700, three years after the Treaty of Ryswyk.[193] The eventual treaty was a stunning defeat for British North American diplomacy. In addition to mutual declarations of peace and final arrangements for a prisoner exchange, France insisted and the Haudenosaunee agreed that the Confederacy would maintain a position of strict neutrality in any future Anglo-French conflict. All parties also agreed that France would be responsible for enforcing the peace among Indian nations by allying with the victim against any aggressor nation initiating conflict. The terms were to be ratified at a grand conference of the nations in Montreal the following year.[194]

At the same time, other Confederacy negotiators were in Albany to meet with Governor Bellomont. Unaware of the treaty conference in Montreal, Bellomont again warned the Haudenosaunee against relations with France. With rather obvious sarcasm, the Confederacy ambassador responded:

> *You say you will support us against all our King's and our ennemies; wee will then forebear keeping any more correspondence with the French of Canada, if the Great King of England will defend our people from the [Indian nations] . . . over whom the French have an influence, and who have been encourag'd by the French to destroy aboundance of our people even since the peace between the two Crowns. . . .*

The governor had no greater success in his other aspirations for the conference. The Haudenosaunee would not agree to expel French Jesuits (who were in effect playing an ambassadorial role) from their communities and only reluctantly and disingenuously agreed to plans for a joint British-Haudenosaunee fort at Onondaga. The only unqualified British success at the meeting was a Confederacy agreement to allow traders from other Indian nations to pass through Haudenosaunee territory to Albany.[195]

The conference too readily exposed the illusion of British control—Haudenosaunee independence was palpable. After nearly twenty years of asserting suzerainty, the British in 1700 constantly had to negotiate all aspects of the relationship with the Confederacy. Without specific consent, Britain had no power to limit Haudenosaunee diplomacy, to expel French diplomatic and ideological agents, to enter and fortify Confederacy territory, or to conduct trade in or across the confederate nations. Moreover, the Haudenosaunee were simultaneously and secretly negotiating a separate peace with France. Governor Bellomont regarded the conference as "the greatest fatigue I ever underwent in my whole life."[196] The lords of trade had a more political reaction. Learning of the Franco-Haudenosaunee preliminary treaty, and realizing that the substantive negotiations at Albany further undercut British pretensions, they cautioned Bellomont to keep the Albany treaty records in strict secrecy.[197]

The Franco-Haudenosaunee neutrality treaty was duly ratified in 1701 at a conference involving all of the principal nations allied to New France.[198] As in the previous year, the Confederacy simultaneously sent ambassadors to treat at Albany. The Covenant Chain relationship was solemnly renewed on both sides, and the British were reassured that the Confederacy regarded continued friendship with their "brethren" as unaffected by the French treaty.[199]

French-Haudenosaunee-British Triangular Relations, 1702 to 1760

The 1701 treaty of neutrality created a paradigm for triangular relations for the duration of the French tenure in eastern North America. To a large degree the structure of the peace merely reaffirmed the independent diplomatic posture of the Confederacy between the European states; however, the specific character of Haudenosaunee relations with both countries was transformed by the commitment to neutrality. From that point, the Haudenosaunee formed a geographical and political barrier for both colonial entities. Confederacy diplomatic strategies were also transformed. As the main element in the balance of power, Haudenosaunee nations were positioned to extract maximum advantage from European ambition, rivalry, and insecurity.

For both the Haudenosaunee and France, neutrality became the cornerstone principle of their mutual relations. France continued to regard the Confederacy, rather than the populous British colonies, as the most dangerous threat to Canada.[200] The Haudenosaunee, weakened by disease and war, adopted neutrality as a policy imperative as well as a treaty obligation to France. Neutrality was immediately tested, however. In 1702, within a year of the Franco-Haudenosaunee peace, Britain and France were again at war, this time over dynastic succession to the Spanish throne.[201]

Despite numerous efforts by Britain to suborn the 1701 treaty, the Confederacy maintained independent peaceful relations with both combatants during the decade of war. Indeed, in the early stages of the conflict, the Haudenosaunee unsuccessfully attempted to promote a comprehensive North American neutrality agreement involving all parties in an effort to preempt the possibility that Iroquoia would be dragged into the European struggle. In 1703, a Haudenosaunee embassy to Quebec confirmed the peace and offered Confederacy mediation for the negotiation of a neutrality agreement between New France and the British colonies during the pendency of the war in Europe. In reply, Governor Vaudreuil agreed to seek instructions from the king.[202] The ministry responded in positive terms to the notion of intercolonial neutrality, but "for the King's glory" rejected the offer of direct Haudenosaunee mediation. Instead, Ponchartrain suggested that French authorities should hint to Confederacy representatives that if the British wished to end hostilities, New France could be persuaded to reciprocate.[203]

The only serious threat to Haudenosaunee neutrality occurred in 1709 during the later stages of the war. British diplomacy succeeded in attracting large numbers of Confederacy warriors for a planned invasion of Canada to oust the French by land and sea. Although no formal Confederacy position was taken to ally with Britain,[204] over 400 Mohawk, Oneida, Onondaga, and Cayuga men assembled with British forces from New York and New England. Sickness and the failure of the British government to supply promised warships aborted the invasion, however, and Confederacy relations with France were sustained.[205]

Haudenosaunee neutrality occurred in a period in which international practice with respect to the rights and duties of neutral states had not yet crystallized into anything resembling the modern form. From the Middle Ages to the late eighteenth century, neutrality did not require impartiality between belligerents or even complete noninvolvement in armed conflict. For example, a neutral state might legitimately assist a belligerent to the extent required by previous treaty commitment, including furnishing troops, conferring a right of passage through neutral territory, and supplying resources. In general, neutral states could allow one or more of the belligerents access to resources or the right to levy troops within its territory, and were under no duty to prevent their people from joining the military of, or selling munitions to, any party to the conflict.[206]

Although strict neutrality might be required on the basis of express treaty obligations, "qualified neutrality" was the accepted practice of the era. In the case of Franco-Haudenosaunee relations, France was prepared to tolerate substantial deviations from strict neutrality so long as an outbreak of war with the Confederacy was foreclosed. Moreover, France had few policy options in terms of Haudenosaunee behavior; it was manifestly not in the French interest to drive the Confederacy into an active alliance with Britain.

In turn, Britain proved unable to persuade the Confederacy that a military alliance against France was in its interest.[207] In fact, the revised political climate caused the British considerable anxiety over the prospects for continued friendship. Despite claims to suzerainty, Britain was always acutely aware of the strategic importance of actively maintaining harmony in Haudenosaunee relations. From the early stages of the previous Anglo-French war in 1691, the Crown began the practice of giving substantial presents to the Haudenosaunee allies to lubricate renewals of the Covenant Chain and thus preserve a military barrier to French expansion. In the more flexible and less predictable diplomatic environment of Franco-Haudenosaunee peace, British presents became a regular part of the diplomatic process.[208]

The Peace of Utrecht (1713)

Although the neutrality treaty had a profound effect on political realities in North America, it had little visible impact on the symbolic duel between Britain and France over respective sphere of influence claims in Iroquoia. Britain in particular continued to press its claims to suzerainty within European diplomacy.[209] Although the European rivals had never been able to resolve their North American disputes on the basis of "legal" persuasion, the advent of war in Europe opened other possible avenues of settlement. As the war progressed, Britain and its European allies achieved a clearly dominant position in the European theater. Seeking to cut his losses in Spain, Louis XIV prepared to use his North American possessions and claims as bargaining chips for an acceptable peace.

Negotiations leading to the Peace of Utrecht occurred in several stages over a period of years. Although European affairs were the primary concern of the negotiators, as time passed North American issues became important points of contention between Britain and France, the principal adversaries in the war. Initially, discussions on North America were limited to Newfoundland, Hudson Bay, and Acadia, all regions in which either France or Britain had established actual territorial possession to some extent.[210]

The issue of relations with the Haudenosaunee and other Indian nations was first raised by British plenipotentiaries prior to the peace congress at Utrecht during negotiations for the suspension of hostilities. Coupled with demands for cessions of Newfoundland and Acadia and the "restoration" of Hudson Bay, British negotiators inserted a proposed clause requiring the French to refrain from hindering reciprocal negotiations between the British and Indian nations and from disturbing the Five Nations (Haudenosaunee) and others in amity with Great Britain.[211] The clause referred collectively to the "Five Nations . . . and others," giving no specific indication of the British definition of the legal or political relationship of any particular Indian nations to the Crown. Without differentiation, they were all described as either "under submission" to (*sous l'obeissance*) or "in amity" with (*dans l'amitié*) the British state. These phrases encompass a broad range of possible political relations from mere friendship to alliance to protection or vassalage.

Following later negotiations in which the French expressed a willingness with some reservations to consider the demanded territorial cessions, British representatives brought forth *a projet* for the final treaty containing five proposed articles related to North America. The thirteenth paragraph, which required France not to "molest" Indian nations in the British orbit, distinctly referred to the Confederacy as "subject to" Great Britain (*imperio subjectas*). It also specified the types of Anglo-

Indian relations that France would not be allowed to hinder—the proposed text granted to Britain full liberty of travel and trade in the region of the Great Lakes, and recognized a reciprocal right of the Indian nations of those territories to trade with the British.[212]

Louis XIV strenuously objected to these provisions. Although he agreed that the boundaries between New France and the British colonies should be precisely fixed by commissioners, he noted that under the law of nations, if Indian nations were truly subject to either state, no special articles were needed and if they were independent, no proposals could be made on their behalf. Moreover, he asserted that Indian trade within the fixed boundaries should be limited to the state concerned and should not cross colonial frontiers.[213]

The final treaty text (Article 15) represented a compromise formula on the issue of European relations with Indian nations that again left the situation ambiguous. Both parties reciprocally agreed not to molest Indian nations subject to, or in amity with, the other and to accord each other full freedom to trade with those nations. Equally, both parties were required to allow Indian nations to travel to either colony for purposes of trade without any molestation or hindrance. Finally, commissioners were to be appointed to determine "exactly" which Indian nations were the subjects or friends of the European states—in other words to define the respective spheres of influence.[214] The only Indian nations expressly recognized in the treaty as politically related to either side were the "Five Nations or cantons," the Haudenosaunee.

British sources and some commentators have cited Article 15 of the Treaty of Utrecht as expressing French recognition of the British claim of subject status for the Haudenosaunee.[215] That notion, however, is not supported in the text. Subjects of each country were clearly identified as such (*Galliae subditi, Britaniae subditi*). The Confederacy, however, was described in the original Latin text as subjected *to* the imperium of Great Britain (*Magnae Britanniae Imperio Subjectas*). Other unnamed Indian nations were described as subject to or friends of either Britain or France. The distinction is important. Subjects *of* a state are entirely within its sovereign authority; they are nationals of the state. Peoples or states subject *to* another state, however, are legally and politically linked with the more powerful state in a corporate sense as a vassal or protectorate. In other words they retain their distinct political identity. Subject *of* is the language of incorporation; subject *to* is the language of a political relationship established in international law by consent or force.

Overall, Article 15 represented a clear gain for Britain only on the issue of the fur trade. The British acquired at least the possibility of more extensive trade relations with Indian nations in the far west that formed the major source of supply. On the issue of Haudenosaunee relations, however, France conceded little of substance. Aside from nominal recognition of British influence, the French agreed only to refrain from molesting the Confederacy. Nothing in the treaty required France to abstain from continuing diplomatic or commercial relations. On the contrary, trading rights were expressly reserved for both European states. Since most Confederacy trade historically went to the British, the reservation of commercial rights in this instance was primarily important for assuring French access to Haudenosaunee territory without British interference.

Moreover, the fact that Haudenosaunee neutrality successfully had survived a decade of Anglo-French warfare made French recognition of British influence considerably less threatening. In practical terms, the close relationship between the Haudenosaunee and the British was undeniable and effective whether formally recognized or not. As early as 1698, Louis XIV had been willing to concede a British sphere of influence if it would guarantee an end to Confederacy threats to New France.[216] Unlike the situation with Newfoundland, Hudson Bay, and Acadia, where France actually ceded territorial rights and claims, the agreement concerning the Confederacy merely required a minimal level of abstention that was objectively in the French interest. As long as the Haudenosaunee kept the peace, France had no motivation to "molest" them.[217]

Of course, neither France nor Britain had anything to cede with respect to the Haudenosaunee beyond their abstract claims. The legal effect of the treaty could only extend to the bilateral allocation of rights as between the parties. The treaty could not create a relationship between Britain and the Confederacy; it could only memorialize French recognition of such a relationship where it existed. One of the most fundamental principles of international law from its inception is that treaties can only bind the parties—third parties may not be bound without their express consent. To the extent that the Confederacy retained its political independence and international personality, therefore, its particular status could not have been affected by Anglo-French agreement.[218]

Had the French totally abstained from relations with the Confederacy, the scope of Confederacy international relations de facto would have been limited to Britain and other Indian nations, but de facto and de jure, France did not agree to leave the field. Triangular diplomatic relations continued for an additional fifty years. As a result, the British gained nothing from the Treaty of Utrecht in Confederacy relations that they did not already possess on the basis of mutual friendship, economic interdependence, and intermittent consensual alliance.

The Practice of Neutrality

The Treaty of Utrecht did nothing to change the structural relationships between the Confederacy and Britain and France respectively. The Haudenosaunee continued to maintain independent treaty and commercial relations with the rival European states and a large network of Indian nations. As in the past, the treaty process continued to regulate all aspects of international relations from general questions of the nature of relationships to such important specific issues as terms of trade, rights of passage, military assistance, establishment of permanent outposts, and so forth. If anything, the Peace of Utrecht, combined with the pre-existing Franco-Haudenosaunee neutrality treaty, increased the space for independent Confederacy diplomacy. With its geopolitical importance intact, the Confederacy was well positioned to use diplomatic skill to avoid European domination and expand influence among the Indian nations.

French acknowledgment of a British sphere of influence proved illusory as well. In the absence of voluntary Haudenosaunee abstention from relations with France, Britain had no means to impede much less suppress independent Franco-Haudenosaunee diplomacy. Throughout the ensuing thirty years of peace, France took full advantage of every opening to increase political influence among the Haudenosaunee nations, while British authorities grumbled on the sidelines during Confederacy embassies to Montreal and French embassies to Onondaga. The Covenant Chain arrangement between Britain and the Haudenosaunee remained the principal Haudenosaunee international relationship, but active French diplomacy underscored the fact that this relationship was based on mutual need and a tradition of friendship rather than political authority.[219] The always open possibility that the balance of power could be altered by a Confederacy decision to transform neutrality with France into an active alliance meant that Britain was required to use diplomacy quite persistently to maintain Haudenosaunee contentment.[220]

In all matters, Britain could simply negotiate and hope to persuade. For example, the Confederacy insisted on maintaining independent relations with other Indian nations, even if those nations were allied with or protectorates of Britain. In 1717, the governor of Virginia complained that the Haudenosaunee had attacked a group of Catawba emissaries confirming a treaty of peace under the walls of a British fort. Confederacy representatives apologized for the action during a treaty conference at Albany, but invited Virginia to bring the Catawbas north to directly negotiate peace.[221] The Haudenosaunee were willing to accept British mediation but not control of their inter-Indian relations.

The Haudenosaunee also reserved the right to determine whether and when the relationship required them to assist Britain against enemy Indian nations. Although agreeing with the definition of the Covenant Chain alliance presented by the New York governor during the same treaty conference, Confederacy representatives nevertheless stated that "if ye English should be molested by their Indian neighbours we will be Ready & willing to doe to ye utmost of our Power but if ye English act of Pride or malice should be ye aggressors & fall upon their Indian neighbours without a Cause we must first Consider of it before we offerd any assistance against those Indians." [222] (Emphasis added.)

Britain was also required to negotiate rights of "free passage" across Confederacy territory for distant Indian nations seeking to trade directly with the British and for British merchants traveling to the west. [223] British negotiators had very uneven substantive success on this question because the issue of direct trade with the western nations at times brought Britain into economic and political competition with Haudenosaunee interests. Territorial sovereignty also required Britain and France to negotiate specific consent for the construction of trading houses or forts within Confederacy jurisdiction. Both Fort Niagara, built by the French, and the fortified British trading post at Oswego were erected with the colorable consent of the Haudenosaunee, British and French mutual recriminations about violations of the Treaty of Utrecht notwithstanding. [224] The Confederacy maintained tight control over European activities within its territory, permitting just enough to serve its own trading interests while maintaining a low level balance of power between the Europeans in strategic areas. [225]

The absence of British authority over Haudenosaunee external relations is most evident, however, during periods of Anglo-French war. The era of general peace in North America brought about by the Treaty of Utrecht ended in the War of Austrian Succession (King George's War) in 1744. At a treaty conference shortly after the outbreak of hostilities, British authorities pointedly voiced their expectation that the Confederacy would assist the colonies in the "vigorous prosecution" of the war "offensively and defensively," and would in addition either expel or turn over any Frenchmen entering Iroquoia. Haudenosaunee representatives directly refused to expel the French, explaining that they were "inclined to peace" and would not act as "aggressors." On the issue of war, they would only agree to a defensive alliance if one of the parties were attacked. [226]

The following year, the British again unsuccessfully attempted to press the Confederacy into an active role in the war. Governor Clinton of New York reminded the Haudenosaunee ambassadors that they had promised in the treaty of the previous year to assist the British when attacked. He then presented instances of French-inspired Indian attacks against New England settlers.[227] The ambassadors dissembled. In place of a direct commitment, they offered to mediate and demand "satisfaction" from the French and their Indian allies. Only if offers for a peaceful settlement were refused would the Confederacy be prepared to fight. Unknown to the British, the Haudenosaunee had already undertaken a diplomatic initiative to convince the traditional Indian allies of New France in the west to remain neutral in the conflict, thus minimizing the possibility that the Confederacy would be dragged into an unwelcome war. Moreover, two months before the conference with Clinton, Haudenosaunee ambassadors formally had renewed the neutrality treaty with France, requesting that the war with Britain not be carried into their territories.[228] Through skillful diplomacy, the Confederacy was able to preserve neutrality and insulate its territory from warfare without alienating its British friends.

As the war came to a close, however, British authorities again renewed their claim to the French that the Crown was suzerain to Haudenosaunee vassals. The issue arose in the context of a French demand that the Confederacy independently treat for the release of Mohawk prisoners of war who had fought with the British, in exchange for French prisoners taken by the Mohawks.[229] The brief debate was argued on the basis of principles of international law. Maintaining that the Treaty of Utrecht had acknowledged that the Confederacy was "under His Majesty's Protection," the New York governor claimed that these "vassals" were engaged in the king's war. Consequently,

> it belongs to him to treat for their release and . . . it is contrary to the Custom of Nations for one Prince to require the Subjects and Vassalls of another Prince to come into his Territories to treat for the Redemption of their Brethren taken Prisoners in Warr, and that such an innovation is an Infraction of the Right that every Prince has over his own Subjects and Vassalls. . . .[230]

Britain was directly claiming the right to assert international responsibility for the actions of Mohawk belligerents. The British position would have had legal weight had the governor characterized the Mohawks as merely individuals recruited into the war effort. Instead, Governor Shirley invoked the shopworn notion of Haudenosaunee subjection to the Crown.

After resolving some confusion over the language of the Treaty of Utrecht, the French governor responded with his own views of the applicability of international law to the situation:

That neither the Treaty of Utrecht nor any other similar one can make the Iroquois subjects of Great Britain. They claim to be free, as they have declared an infinite number of times, and as their conduct, and yours towards them proves, inasmuch as for one hundred and fifty years they have concluded peace and made war independent of you, and often in opposition to you, without your having ever attempted to force them to obey you. The Plenipotentiaries of Utrecht could not, then, legitimately subject them to you. The English are too well read in the Law of Nations not to appreciate this truth.[231]

The French reply was based on direct consultation as well as legal analysis. During a treaty conference at Quebec in November 1748, Governor Galissonière read the British communications to Confederacy envoys.[232] The ambassadors responded, as they had sixty years earlier, that they had never ceded their territories "which they hold only of Heaven." Speaking for the entire Confederacy, the Cayuga Chief Toniohae emphatically noted "that in this and the preceeding wars, the English had continually solicited them to take up the hatchet [declare war] against the French, which they constantly refused to do . . ." as proof that the Haudenosaunee nations were not subjects or vassals of the British Crown.[233]

The scene was highly ironic. The Haudenosaunee statements were uttered during an independent diplomatic mission to a treaty conference with France intended to resolve a prisoner exchange and reaffirm neutrality. It is hard to imagine a more substantive repudiation of the British position. In addressing the issue, the Confederacy representatives touched on the essential basis for the continuity of their international legal personality—they had never ceded sovereign authority in the international realm. Indeed, despite the persistent evocation of European claims, Indian nations had remained sovereign in the interior reaches of North America.[234]

Britain again became painfully aware of Haudenosaunee independence in 1753 during a period of aggressive French expansion into the Ohio Valley. Following years of inaction in response to Mohawk appeals against British territorial encroachments, Mohawk Nation representatives declared the Covenant Chain relationship broken.[235] Fearing the potential consequences of Haudenosaunee estrangement, the Board of Trade ordered all of the colonial governors to jointly negotiate a renewal of the Covenant Chain.[236] In a contemporaneous communication to the governor of New York, the lords of trade emphasized the British government's view of the nature of the relationship. Referring to the "great consequence that the friendship and alliance of the Six Nations [Haudenosaunee] is to all His Majesty's Colonies and Plantations in America," the lords of trade observed that "we consider that this friendship and alliance is only to be gain'd and preserved by making presents to them at proper times and upon proper occasions and *by an inviolable observance of all our engagements with them.*"[237] (Emphasis added.)

Aftermath

French-Haudenosaunee-British triangular relations ended only with the cession to Britain of the French colony of Canada in the 1763 Treaty of Paris at the close of the Seven Years' War.[238] The withdrawal of France from the geographical region of Haudenosaunee international relations had inevitable consequences for the bilateral relationship between the Confederacy and Britain, but did not transform the international character of that relationship. Great Britain and the Haudenosaunee continued to organize their mutual affairs through the treaty process.[239] Rather than purport to incorporate Indian nations, Britain continued to establish and maintain relations through treaty-making.

Indeed, the transition from French to British influence in the western country was by no means effected by the conquest of New France or by the Treaty of Paris. Indian nations allied with France and led by the Ottawa chief, Pontiac, continued hostilities against British forces attempting to place themselves in frontier forts and trading houses formerly controlled by the French. The Indian war, which peaked in intensity during 1763 and 1764, ended in stages as Britain successfully negotiated for peace and trading rights in a series of treaties culminating with an agreement with Pontiac in 1766.[240] Consistent with the French experience in those regions, Britain was able to ensure its presence only through a consensual process shaped by a combination of diplomacy, military action, and inducements of trade.

Almost simultaneously, Britain began to respond to the new international situation in North America by negotiating boundary treaties with Indian nations and confederacies contiguous to British colonies from Florida to Canada, including the Haudenosaunee.[241] Unquestionably, the end of balance of power considerations in British North American diplomacy produced a shift of strength to the advantage of Britain. Each of the boundary treaties, for example, involved territorial cessions. Nevertheless, these treaties resulted from an imperative to clarify the distribution of recognized territorial sovereignty between Indian nations and the settler colonies, and reflected the continuity of the British practice of maintaining relations with those nations through the treaty process.

Despite the defeat and expulsion of France, Britain remained acutely sensitive to the possibility of a large-scale alliance of the Indian nations much greater than "Pontiac's War" against Crown possessions. In 1763,

Johnson Hall, a mansion built by Sir William Johnson near Fort Johnson, New York, that served as the meeting place for councils between Iroquois and English delegations. (Painting by E. L. Henry, 1903, owned by John B. Knox; courtesy of the Albany Institute of History and Art.)

Sir William Johnson, superintendent of Indian relations in the northern colonies, gave perhaps the most candid and accurate British description of the reality of the status of the Haudenosaunee and other nations in nearly a century:

> The Indians of the Ottawa Confederacy . . . and also the Six Nations, however their sentiments may have been misrepresented, all along considered the Northern parts of North America, as their sole property from the beginning; and although the conveniences of Trade (with fair speaches and promises) induced them to afford both, us and the French settlements in their Country, yet they have never understood such settlement as a Dominion, especially as neither we, nor the French ever made a conquest of them; they have even repeatedly said at several conferences in my presence, that "they were amused by both parties with stories of their upright intentions, and that they made War for the protection of the Indians' Rights," but that they plainly found, it was carried on, to see who would become masters of what was the property of neither one nor the other. . . .[242]

The ultimate accuracy of that description was underscored in 1775 when the Confederacy entered into treaty relations with the "Twelve United Colonies" (before they had acquired broadly recognized international legal personality), promising neutrality in the coming conflagration with the old ally.[243]

Although Anglo-Haudenosaunee relations varied over time according to needs, interests, and historical circumstances, Britain's diplomatic claims that the Confederacy was subject, vassal, or protectorate were transparent fictions. Evidence does not even support the existence of a consistent alliance in any full sense during the century of relations prior to the French defeat. The Haudenosaunee and the British were active military allies only during periods of the 1680s and 1690s—at most one and a half decades of qualified coordination.

Despite the frequent quest for a more substantive alliance, Britain was content to live with the Haudenosaunee as a strategic buffer, potential military ally, and important contributor to the economic well-being of New York and the imperial center. Indeed, the strongest case can be made for an economic alliance as the root of the relationship—a fact frequently brought home by Confederacy envoys during negotiations with the British. From this perspective, the Covenant Chain emerges as a regional order of close international cooperation, promoting peace and stability in intersocietal economic and political relations among its participants.

Conclusion

During the nearly two centuries of European presence in North America preceding the American War of Independence, a public order of a decidedly international character evolved among Indian and European nations. The nature of that order was determined by the cooperation and conflict of distinct nations seeking to adjust their relations and defend their respective interests—the essence of an international legal regime. Situations, of course, varied according to time and place. At times, European imperial actions produced conquest, forcible dispossession, or voluntary migration of indigenous societies. With the more populous and powerful Indian nations and confederacies in interior regions, however, European states were obliged to respect Indian sovereignty and utilize the practice of diplomacy to form consensual relations. The hallmark of the epoch was the treaty process.[244] Seventeenth- and eighteenth-century treaties, in the aggregate, bear compelling witness to the presence of Indian nations as independent actors on the international plane.

When the United States came into being, it joined a political reality and a received tradition that determined the practice of its relations with Indian nations. In seeking to consolidate its own political existence, one of the first imperatives for the United States was the negotiation of treaties of peace with many of the same Indian nations that had been actively involved in European diplomacy and whose hostility posed a serious threat to the stability of the new state.[245] Indeed, many of those same Indian nations continued to maintain independent relations with European powers until the end of the Napoleonic era, despite United States claims to territorial sovereignty.[246]

The internal structural reorganization of the United States from a confederation to a federal state, brought about by the adoption of the Constitution in 1789, did not alter the fundamental dynamics of international relations with Indian nations. Under the Constitution, the new federal government continued to negotiate treaties through the foreign affairs process of the state. From 1789 until 1795, with the exception of one consular agreement with France, all of the treaties receiving the consent of the Senate for ratification were made with Indian nations.[247]

Writing in 1832, four decades after the advent of constitutional government in the United States, Chief Justice John Marshall had this to say about the status of Indian nations:

> *The Indian nations had always been considered as distinct, independent, political communities, retaining their original natural rights, as*

the undisputed possessors of the soil, from time immemorial, with the single exception of that imposed by irresistible power, which excluded them from intercourse with any other European potentate than the first discoverer of the coast of the particular region claimed; and this was a restriction which those European potentates imposed on themselves, as well as on the Indians. The very term "nation," so generally applied to them, means "a people distinct from others." The constitution, by declaring treaties already made, as well as those to be made, to be the supreme law of the land, has adopted and sanctioned the previous treaties with the Indian nations, and consequently, admits their rank among those powers who are capable of making treaties. The words "treaty" and "nation" are words of our own language, selected in our diplomatic and legislative proceedings, by ourselves, having each a definite and well-understood meaning. We have applied them to Indians, as we have applied them to the other nations of the earth; they are applied to all in the same sense.[248]

Despite the reference to his "doctrine of discovery," Marshall's words remain a powerful expression of the inherent rights of the original nations of the continent.

5.
United States–
Indian Relations:
The Constitutional Basis

Curtis G. Berkey

The recent two-hundredth anniversary of the United States Constitution and Bill of Rights presents an opportunity to take a fresh look at the legal and political relationship between Indian nations and the United States. The history of Indian–United States relations for the past one hundred and fifty years has been marked by oppressive laws and policies often designed to undermine the autonomy of Indian nations and to weaken their cultures. At one time or another, almost every aspect of the internal and external relations of Indian nations has been subjected to the unrestrained authority of the United States. Two examples illuminate the point. Much Indian land is not constitutionally protected against expropriation by the federal government because the courts of the United States do not regard such land as property in the constitutional sense. Further, existing legal principles permit Indian governments and their sovereign powers to be dissolved by Congress or by the courts without constitutional or other legal restraints.

The federal government's assertion of unrestricted authority over Indian nations, particularly their land and governments, rests on a flimsy legal foundation. It is said to arise, almost mythically, from an amalgamation of judicial decisions, federal statutes, and administrative rulings. Although the juridical basis for this so-called plenary authority has not been persuasively established, most courts and many lawyers accept uncritically such power.

To be sure, the scope of federal power over Indian nations has been justly subject to a barrage of scholarly criticism in recent years.[1] This debate, however, has not adequately heeded the relevance of history and the ideas of the framers of the Constitution with regard to the nature and scope of the federal government's powers in Indian relations. The historical record is a critical part of this discussion because it shows that the original relationship between the United States and Indian nations was based on equality and the mutual respect accorded sovereign nations under international law and practice. Moreover, the record shows quite plainly that the scope of the powers the federal government asserts today is inconsistent with the ideas of the framers.

The central Indian affairs issues facing the delegates to the Constitutional Convention of 1787 were whether the management of external relations with Indian nations should be the exclusive responsibility of the federal government, and what role, if any, the separate states should play. The idea that the authority of the federal government would include the power to violate the sovereignty of Indian nations by exercising powers over them would have been preposterous to most of the delegates. That issue was not even marginally part of the debate. Rather, the exclusive authority of Congress and the president was understood to extend only to those matters necessary to conduct foreign, or external, relations with Indian tribes.

This chapter tells the story of how and why the federal government acquired authority over Indian affairs in the Constitution. Our goal is to answer this basic question: what was the nature and scope of the constitutional authority that the framers intended to confer regarding the management of relations with Indian nations?

From the standpoint of history, a number of important related questions naturally arise. How did the framers and other statesmen view the status of Indian nations in relation to the United States, and how did they envision the relationship of Indian nations to the new government established by the Constitution; what considerations and concerns lay behind the Constitutional Convention's decision to give Congress and the president exclusive responsibility for the management of Indian affairs; and what did the framers and others think about the scope of Congress' powers in managing Indian affairs?

Answers to these questions require analysis of the records of the Constitutional Convention of 1787 and the state ratifying conventions that followed, as well as the writings and correspondence of the leading statesmen.

Because the experience of the United States in dealing with Indian nations during the Articles of Confederation period presumably shaped much of the thinking about Indian affairs, the policies and practices of the Continental Congress toward Indians must also be examined. Likewise, the British experience with Indian relations must be reviewed briefly, because it influenced the ideas of the framers as well.

The British Experience

The British government faced two alarming problems in its dealings with Indian nations. The first problem was avoiding a major war with powerful Indian nations capable of destroying the infant colonies. A second, related problem was preventing an Indian alliance with the French in Britain's continuing competition with France for the right to acquire Indian land and for fur trading privileges with Indians. The British responded to both problems by adopting a centralized Indian policy that was based on the premise that Indian tribes had inherent rights to independent nationhood. This policy foreshadowed the policies adopted by the American government after independence in 1776.

The Indian nations, particularly the Six Nations Iroquois Confederacy, represented a real threat to the peace and security of the struggling American colonies in the eighteenth century. Land was the most frequent source of conflict; unscrupulous land speculators bought and sold Indian lands as if no one owned them, and colonial governments frequently encroached on Indian territories. Predictably, Indian nations often retaliated with violence to avenge the violation of their land rights. The colonial governments were either unwilling or unable to control the wrongful conduct of the land speculators. Although the British government initially left the management of Indian affairs to the colonies separately, the Crown soon realized that colonial mismanagement jeopardized the safety of all the colonies. It soon became apparent that the actions of a single colony, or of an individual land speculator for that matter, could easily precipitate a major Indian war. British officials gradually grasped the need for more centralized control over relations with Indian nations.

The British policy of centralization is rooted in a 1753 directive from the British lords of trade to Sir Davers Osborne, the governor of the Colony of New York, that ". . . when the Indians are disposed to sell any of their lands the purchase ought to be made in His Majesty's name and at the publick charge."[2] The need for central governmental control over relations with Indian nations also underlies the 1761 draft of instructions from the Crown to the governors of all the colonies. Because of "great complaints that Settlements have been made and possession taken of [Indian] Lands" that were reserved by treaty with Great Britain, and the "fatal Effects which would attend a discontent amongst the Indians in the present situation of affairs," the Crown ordered the royal governors not to approve any grant of or settlements on Indian lands. The instruction also authorized prosecution of any person purchasing Indian lands without a license obtained from the Crown.[3]

The trend toward the Crown's control of Indian land purchases culminated in 1763 with the issuance of a royal proclamation that established a general boundary line at the crest of the Appalachian Mountains between white settlements and Indian territories. The proclamation also prohibited the issuance of "warrants of survey" on patents for lands lying west of the boundary line. As to lands east of the line, lying within the colonial boundaries, purchases of Indian land were valid only if conducted under the authority of the Crown "at some public meeting or assembly of the said Indians. . . ."[4]

The British also made efforts to establish uniform regulations for trading with Indian nations, and they sought to regularize relations by appointing Indian superintendents with authority to act in the name of the

Crown. None of these efforts to centralize Indian policy was completely successful. The British experience, however, taught a valuable lesson about the administration of Indian affairs: relations with powerful Indian nations implicated the interests of the colonies as a whole and could not, therefore, be left to the colonial authorities separately.

The colonies themselves recognized that Indian affairs were too important to the security of the colonies to be left to the colonial governments. In Benjamin Franklin's Albany Plan of Union, drafted in 1754, special provision was made for relations with Indian nations. The plan recommended the creation of a single "General Government," consisting of a president general and grand council, with authority to govern in matters of concern to the colonies as a whole. Maintaining peace with Indian nations was prominent among the concerns reflected in Franklin's plan. The Albany Plan gave the president authority, with the advice of the grand council, to conduct relations with Indian nations by making treaties, engaging in war and peace, and regulating trade.[5] Although the Albany Plan was not adopted, its premise that the management of Indian relations should be placed under the exclusive control of a central government was followed in structuring the Indian affairs power under the Articles of Confederation and the Constitution over thirty years later.

Another prominent feature of British policy that would influence Indian-white relations years later was the Crown's treatment of Indian tribes as independent nations. By recognizing the inherent sovereignty of Indian nations, Britain placed its conduct of Indian affairs within the realm of international diplomatic negotiations. This does not mean, however, that the sovereignty of Indian nations depended on European recognition for its legitimacy. On the contrary, Indian sovereignty was inherent in the status of Indian tribes as separate peoples possessing lands and governments.

Britain continued the European tradition of conducting relations with Indian nations by treaty. For example, Britain made treaties with the Five Nations Iroquois Confederacy in 1701 and 1726. Again in 1768, the British treated with the Six Nations Confederacy to establish the precise location of the boundary line between the Indian territory and the colonies, as required by the 1763 Royal Proclamation.[6]

In the eighteenth century, the British competed with France for the right to acquire Indian land and control the fur trade. In this conflict, the Crown necessarily respected Indian nations as major participants in the geopolitical relationships of the day. Britain's interest lay in establishing a plausible basis for a right to acquire Indian lands in the Ohio Valley and Great Lakes regions. Lacking any rights based on discovery or possession of that area, the Crown sought to bolster its claims under a political theory that Britain's sovereignty over the lands derived from the supposed sovereignty of the Five Nations Iroquois Confederacy over the area.

To make the theory feasible, Britain advocated the political fiction that the Iroquois Confederacy was a dependent subject of the Colony of New York, so that the Confederacy's claims devolved upon Britain. This assertion most definitely did not reflect the actual relationship between the Iroquois and New York.[7] Even William Johnson, the British Indian agent with responsibility for relations with the Six Nations, admitted that in reality, the Five Nations were not subjects: ". . . the Indians, who tho[ugh] called subjects, are a foreign people, and are to be treated with as immediately from the King, by His Majesty's Governor. . . ."[8] As might be expected, France, as Britain's competitor, firmly maintained that Indian nations were independent and not subject to British sovereignty. For example, in 1748, the Marquis de la Gulissoniera observed in a letter to New York colonial governor Clinton that the independence of the Mohawk Nation "is so well established, that assuredly no educated Englishman can gainsay it."[9]

Scholars generally agree that the British theory of sovereignty over the Six Nations did not match the reality of that relationship. For example, in Francis Jennings's study of the Covenant Chain, which comprised shifting alliances among the Crown, its colonies, and Indian nations in the early part of the eighteenth century, he concludes that Britain gave de facto recognition to the independence of Indian nations while maintaining official pretensions to sovereignty over them in order to support English claims against the French.[10]

The British had a long history of dealing with Indian nations as equal members of the international community of nations. This tradition had important implications for relations between Indian nations and the new American government established in 1774. For one thing, it meant that the United States could not validly claim a right of sovereignty over Indian nations under a theory of successorship, that is, by claiming to assume all rights the British claimed or exercised. The British had no recognized authority over the Indian nations, and the United States could have no greater rights in this regard without Indian consent to the exercise of such authority.

It also meant that many Indian nations legitimately expected to be accorded the respect due sovereign nations under international law. The failure of the newly created state governments to respect Indian sovereignty and land rights would become a major cause of the Indian troubles the Continental Congress faced in the early years of the new republic.

Indian Affairs during the Early Years of the Articles of Confederation Period, 1774 to 1782

The experience of American political and military leaders in establishing and administering a new government during the period 1774 to 1782 is relevant to discerning the intent of the framers regarding the constitutional power to control Indian relations. Although political theory played a part in influencing the framers' concepts, the practical experience of the Continental Congress with Indian nations was more influential in shaping ideas about how to manage Indian relations.

Indian affairs were among the foremost concerns of the American revolutionary leaders and government officials. From the first Continental Congress formed in 1774, through the American Revolution, and to the years under the confederated national government created by the ratification of the Articles of Confederation in 1781, American political leaders wrestled with the problem of maintaining harmonious relations with the Indian nations that surrounded the new nation. The American goal was first to ensure the neutrality of the Indian nations, especially the Six Nations Iroquois Confederacy, in the War of Independence. After the Peace of Paris ended the war in 1783, Congress' goal was to prevent war with Indian nations by protecting their land against state encroachment and by centralizing the control of Indian trade.

In trying to nationalize the management of Indian affairs, the Continental Congress encountered much the same difficulty the British had. Just as British efforts were hampered by disobedient colonies intent on pursuing their own selfish ends, so, too, the directives of the Continental Congress were often hindered by recalcitrant state governments seeking to enrich themselves at the expense of the union. Not unexpectedly, the mistreatment of Indian nations by the states during this period endangered the safety of the union as a whole. Congressional policy, therefore, focused on securing the supremacy of confederal authority over Indian affairs to the complete exclusion of the states. As we shall see, this effort was not entirely successful. The inability of Congress to enforce its will in Indian affairs and to prevent state encroachments on confederal authority was one of the leading reasons many statesmen came to believe in 1787 that a stronger national government was needed.

Even before it was constitutionally established under the Articles of Confederation, the Continental Congress exercised a variety of important powers in managing Indian affairs. By informal acquiescence of the states, Congress asserted authority over Indian matters involving war and peace, treaty-making, land boundaries, and trade. When the American Revolution broke out in 1775, Indian nations, particularly the

Six Nations Iroquois Confederacy and its western allies, occupied a strategically important place in the balance of power. Given the close historical relationship between the Six Nations and the British, Congress took very seriously the possibility of a military alliance against the Americans. It does not overstate the gravity of the situation to say that the Six Nations quite possibly could have prevented an American victory by siding with the British. As a result, obtaining a pledge of neutrality from the Six Nations was a paramount concern of the American government.

On 16 June 1775, the First Continental Congress appointed a committee to develop an Indian affairs policy.[11] Two members of this committee, Benjamin Franklin and James Wilson, later represented the state of Pennsylvania as delegates to the Constitutional Convention of 1787. On 12 July 1775, the committee recommended a policy of pacification, noting that "securing and preserving the friendship of the Indian Nations, appears to be a subject of utmost moment to these colonies."[12] Based on these recommendations, Congress adopted an official policy of seeking alliances of friendship through formal treaty-making. Three departments covering the northern, middle, and southern sections of the country were set up, with commissioners to be appointed with authority to carry on diplomatic relations with Indian tribes through treaties.[13] Benjamin Franklin and James Wilson were appointed commissioners for the middle department.[14] To guard against British instigation of Indian hostilities, Congress also authorized its Indian commissioners to take into custody any person inciting the Indian nations.

The next day, Congress put its new policy into effect by authorizing a speech to be delivered to the Six Nations Iroquois Confederacy calling for treaty proceedings to negotiate the neutrality issue. Addressing the Six Nations as "brothers," a term of equality and respect in the diplomatic parlance of the day, the speech recounted the troubles the colonies were having with the British king and urged the Six Nations to "remain at home and not join on either side, but keep the hatchet buried deep."[15]

On 25 August 1775, four commissioners appointed by Congress met with the Six Nations at German Flats near Albany, New York. The speech Congress had approved was delivered and, after some discussion, the Six Nations Confederacy pledged its official neutrality. In exchange, Congress promised to seek ways to improve trade relations between Indians and whites. Several months later, Congress resolved to "exert . . . strenuous endeavours to procure the goods the Indians may want, and put the trade under such wise regulations, as that mutual justice may be effected. . . ."[16] Although some military forces of the Six Nations eventually fought on the side of the British, the Iroquois Confederacy as a whole remained officially neutral. The German Flats Treaty is an early example of congressional exercise of the treaty-making power.

Congress assumed the power of making treaties with Indian nations because Indian relations were necessarily national in scope. Congress jealously guarded its authority in this area. In early 1776, it was reported to Congress that the governor of Pennsylvania, William Penn, had invited the Six Nations to come to Philadelphia to make a treaty with the state. Congress reacted with alarm, and with uncharacteristic speed, appointed a committee to investigate the matter.[17] The committee reported that the rumor was without foundation, but Congress thought the matter so serious that it ordered General Philip Schuyler, the Indian commissioner for the northern department, to arrest the person who "pretended to have carried such an invitation to the Indians."[18]

There is abundant evidence that Congress, both before as well as after the Articles of Confederation, recognized that Indian tribes were inherently sovereign nations. Consider the treaty with the Delaware Nation in 1778. Article II declares that "perpetual peace and friendship shall henceforth take place, and subsist between the contracting parties"; and it further establishes a mutual defense pact to operate whenever either party is involved in a "just and necessary war with any other nation or nations."[19]

The treaty also shows the respect for Indian territorial rights and boundaries that was typical of congressional policy in this era. Article III contains the agreement of the Delaware Nation to permit United States troops to pass through "the country of the Delaware Nation" on their way to the posts and forts still held by the British. In Article VI, the United States admits that the separate state governments are a threat to the land rights of the Delaware Nation, and to remedy this problem the United States agrees to "guarantee to the aforesaid nation of Delawares, and their heirs, all their territorial rights in the fullest and most ample manner. . . ."[20]

Article IV provides that both the United States and the Delaware Nation shall have jurisdiction over offenses against the peace established by the treaty. It provides that persons who violate the peace shall be imprisoned by either party until "a fair and impartial trial can be had by judges or juries of both parties, as near can be to the laws, customs and usages of the contracting parties and natural justice."[21]

The 1778 Delaware Nation Treaty has all the markings of a treaty with a foreign nation arrived at through the usual diplomatic negotiations. The treaty is made between the United States and the "Delaware Nation," explicitly recognizing the international status of Indian tribes at that time. The treaty addresses matters typically the subject of international agreements: war and peace, territorial rights and jurisdiction. United States Supreme Court Chief Justice John Marshall observed many years later that "[t]his treaty, in its language, and in its provisions, is formed, as near as may be, on the model of treaties between the crowned heads of Europe."[22]

Particularly in matters of war and peace, Congress regarded Indian tribes as nations responsible for the belligerent acts of their citizens. For example, on 19 August 1776, Congress instructed the Indian commissioners in the northern department to investigate the murder of a non-Indian near Pittsburgh, which was believed to have been committed by an Indian. The resolution provided that if the Indian nation responsible punishes the offender, "this Congress will not consider the same as a national act."[23] Similarly, Congress consistently demanded, pursuant to established rules of international law, that Indian nations be held responsible for depredations committed by their citizens. On 19 June 1779, Congress resolved that the Six Nations Confederacy should provide satisfaction for past and future "injuries and depredations."[24]

There is no hint during the early national period that Congress believed it had authority over the internal affairs of Indian nations. Much of the available evidence points in the other direction. Congress showed respect for the sovereignty of Indian nations in 1776 when it recommended that "disputes which shall arise between any of the white people and the Indians in their dealings, if the latter will consent, be determined by arbitrators, chosen, one by each of the parties, and another by the commissioners for Indian affairs. . . ."[25]

Congress' powers grew as the demands of the American Revolution created a greater need for coordination of policy and actions by a central government. Many revolutionary leaders came to believe that a formal union of the colonies was needed to strengthen the resistance against Britain. To respond to this need, Congress adopted Articles of Confederation in 1777, and the states ratified them in 1781. The articles gave a constitutional basis to all the powers Congress had been exercising from 1774, including war powers, the management of Indian affairs, and the regulation of trade and commerce. The articles, moreover, sought to define the political and legal relationship between the states and Congress. Simply described, the articles divided authority into two spheres: Congress as the national sovereign exercised authority over those areas of national concern, and the states retained authority over those matters exclusively local in character.

The attempt to divide sovereignty in this fashion, of course, worked better in theory than it did in practice, as Congress and the states vied for control of various aspects of governmental affairs. Congress' ability to carry out effective national policies, including Indian policy, was seriously undermined by the failure of the articles to grant Congress the power to coerce the states into obeying its laws and directives. Although few doubted that laws enacted by Congress were binding and enforceable against the states, the effectiveness of the national laws too often depended merely on the willingness or the ability of the states to comply voluntarily. Several states, particularly New York in its dealings with the Six Nations Confederacy, consistently placed parochial state interests above the national interest. The articles thus created a system that was in some ways doomed to failure: Congress was given responsibility to conduct the national affairs of the United States without being given the means to govern effectively.

The articles addressed Indian affairs in three sections. In Article IX, clause 4, Congress was given the "sole and exclusive right and power of . . . regulating the trade and managing all affairs with the Indians, not members of any of the States, provided that the legislative right of any State within its own limits be not infringed or violated." This section seems to be broad enough to cover practically all Indian affairs matters which Congress might want to address, but other parts of the articles were also relied on to uphold congressional powers in this regard.

The articles also gave Congress power regarding Indian relations in the section dealing with foreign relations. Article IX, clause 1, gave Congress the "sole and exclusive right and power of determining on peace and war, except in cases mentioned in the sixth article . . . [and] entering into treaties and alliances." Although clause 1 does not mention Indian nations specifically, its reference to Article VI shows that the drafters had Indian nations in mind in giving Congress these powers. Article VI prohibits the states from engaging in war without the consent of Congress "unless such State be actually invaded by enemies, or shall have received certain advice of a resolution being formed by some nation of Indians to invade such State, and the danger is so imminent as not to admit of a delay, till the United States in Congress assembled can be consulted." By giving the states a limited authority to engage in defensive wars against Indians, the articles by implication reserved all other such authority for Congress.

Article VI also sharply curtailed the role of the states in managing the foreign relations of the United States. It reads: "No State without the consent of the United States in Congress assembled, shall send any embassy to, or receive any embassy from, or enter into any conference, agreement, alliance or treaty with any king, prince or state. . . ." Because Congress treated many Indian nations as states capable of making treaties and waging war, presumably the prohibition of Article VI applied with equal force to Indian nations. Article VI is further evidence that Congress' foreign relations power included authority to deal with Indian nations.

The history of the drafting and adoption of the articles sheds additional light on the perceptions and concerns which motivated the drafters to centralize the management of Indian affairs. In 1775, Benjamin Franklin authored the first plan of confederation. Franklin's plan contained the most detailed provisions for governing Indian relations of any draft of a constitution before or after. It gave Congress the authority over war with Indians, except in cases of imminent invasion by "some Nations of Indians." It provided for a "perpetual alliance" with the Six Nations and their neighbors, and for the security of Indian lands. The plan also contained the genesis of the long-standing federal policy of prohibiting Indian land transactions without the approval of Congress. In Article XIV, it prohibited purchases of Indian lands by colonies or private persons before the boundaries of the colonies were set. Thereafter, all purchases of land outside those limits must be made by "[c]ontracts between the United States" and the "great Councils of the Indians."[26] In addition to these specific provisions, the plan granted Congress the general power to regulate trade and manage "all Affairs with the Indians."[27] Although the Franklin Plan was not debated by Congress, its principles served as the basis for the draft of the Articles of Confederation prepared by John Dickinson for the congressional drafting committee that reported in July 1776.

During the congressional debates on the Dickinson Plan, which lasted from July 1776 to October 1777, the specific provisions for controlling Indian land purchases were deleted in favor of a more general congressional power to legislate on all matters touching on relations with Indians. In this debate, the provisions on Indian lands became entangled with the issue of state claims to the so-called western lands. Many states claimed the right to acquire from Indian nations extensive tracts of land beyond the Appalachian Mountains, based on charters from the king granted when the colonies were founded. States with charter claims were reluctant to give Congress the power to limit their boundaries because they feared losing the right to dispose of those lands on terms favorable to the state. A constitutional prohibition against purchases of Indian land was viewed as a threat to the states' western claims.

Most statesmen thought, however, that Congress should have authority over Indian land purchases, in light of the threat to peace that Indian land violations posed. So the committee opted for a simple broad statement of congressional power: "The United States Assembled shall have the sole and exclusive right and power of . . . regulating the trade, and managing the affairs with the Indians not members of the States."[28] After more discussion of Congress' role in the western lands matter, in October 1777, Congress adopted language designed to preserve whatever rights the states had to western lands. Congress' Indian affairs power was qualified: "provided, that the legislative right of any State, within its own limits be not infringed or violated."[29]

The final draft of the articles thus appeared to give Congress unfettered power in matters of war and peace and treaties relating to Indians, but as to matters of Indian trade and other affairs, Congress' authority was limited in two ways. First, its authority extended only to Indians "not members of any of the States." Second, it was restrained from infringing the "legislative right of any State, within its own limits." The war and treaty powers were, practically speaking, broad enough to authorize almost all the actions Congress desired to take. But the ambiguity of the "not members" and "legislative right" provisions, and the uncertainty of whether those qualifications also applied to Congress' war and treaty powers regarding Indians, gave the states a political justification to ignore congressional enactments and treaties.

A few states argued that the "not members" proviso should receive a geographical interpretation, that congressional authority extended only to those Indians located outside the physical boundaries of states or colonies. For example, in 1785, when Georgia made a separate treaty with the Creeks at Galphinton, the state declared in the treaty that the Indians within Georgia's limits "have been, and now are, members of the [state], since the day and date of the constitution of the state."[30]

As a matter of constitutional law, however, the "not members" proviso should not have been a serious obstacle to confederal supremacy in Indian affairs. There was very little support for Georgia's view in either the legislative history of the articles or in the common understanding and practice of the time. In the debate on 26 July 1776, Thomas Jefferson suggested that this phrase applies to those Indians who "live in the colony" in the sense that they are "subject to the laws [of the colony or state] in some degree."[31] Carter Braxton, a delegate from Virginia, agreed that the phrase excepted Indians "as are tributary to any state."[32] James Madison, the primary architect of the Indian relations power in the Constitution, interpreted it this way: "By Indians not members of a State, must be meant those, I conceive, who do not live within the body of the Society, or whose Persons or property form no objects of its laws."[33] Moreover, on 28 October 1777, Congress rejected an amendment to the articles that would have placed a definite territorial restriction on Congress' powers. It was moved to replace the "not members" clause with "not residing within the limits of any of the United States."[34]

A consensus existed, then, that Congress should have authority to manage relations with all Indian nations except those that had lost their independence through assimilation. Under the confederal system, Congress was to be concerned exclusively with matters of national and international moment. As a practical matter, the "not members" limitation on Congress' authority meant very little, since at no time did Congress refuse to take action on the basis of the "not members" clause. It thus can be inferred that the great majority of Indian nations retained their autonomy during this period. This lends additional support to the view that relations with Indians were akin to the relationships Congress maintained with other nation-states.

The "legislative right" proviso of Article IX, clause 4, created more thorny problems for Congress. It was controversial because it pitted Congress against several states that sought to acquire Indian land without authorization from Congress. Throughout this period, Indian land was viewed as a great economic resource for that government that could exploit it. Congress wanted Indian lands in order to create a national domain that could, in turn, be sold to non-Indians to help satisfy the huge national debt incurred during the American Revolution. Congress also knew that it needed the power to regulate or prohibit Indian land deals by the states in order to restrain the greed of the states and maintain peace. The states, on the other hand, coveted Indian lands in order to enlarge their territories and, thereby, to increase their political power in relation to other states. The states also asserted authority over Indian lands because they wanted to invalidate several purchases of Indian land made by land speculators in the western areas the states claimed.

The states' rights advocates took the position that the legislative right proviso of Article IX, clause 4, reserved to the states the right to acquire Indian lands without the authorization or approval of Congress. They drew support by arguing that the legislative right provision was added to the Indian affairs power during the debate over Congress' role in resolving the western lands controversy. This argument, however, was ultimately unsuccessful, as Congress asserted and exercised the paramount right to control Indian land deals with states. The consensus was that the legislative right provision gave the states a right to acquire Indian land, a "right of preemption" in the language of that day, but it was well understood that this right was subject to Congress' supreme regulatory power.

Perhaps the best expression of this understanding is contained in a 1784 letter written by James Madison to James Monroe discussing the lawfulness of New York's attempt to make a separate land cession treaty with the Oneida Nation. Madison wrote: ". . . [a]s far as [New York] may have asserted [the right to purchase] in contravention of the Genl. Treaty, or even unconfidentially with the Commisrs. of Congs., she has violated both duty and decorum."[35] The "Genl. Treaty" to which Madison refers was the Treaty of Fort Stanwix of 1784 with the Six Nations Confederacy, which guaranteed the lands of the Confederacy against seizure by the states.

Congressional Indian Policy under the Articles of Confederation from 1783 to 1787

The events during the period 1783 to 1787 brought into sharp focus the concerns that motivated the framers to give Congress and the president exclusive responsibility under the Constitution for managing relations with Indian nations. This period was filled with turmoil and controversy over Indian affairs. The national Indian policy was dictated by two fears. First, Congress was concerned that encroachments on Indian land rights by the states could cause a major Indian war that Congress was not economically or militarily prepared to fight. Second, Congress was afraid that the Indian forces that had fought on the side of the British would once again unite with the British against the United States. This fear was well founded because the British had not yet abandoned their forts at Niagara and Oswego despite the peace established by the Treaty of Paris in 1783. Although the Articles of Confederation had given Congress the authority necessary to devise policies to meet these goals, congressional efforts were never completely effective, due to the defiance of New York, North Carolina, and Georgia.

Congress moved quickly after the close of the American Revolution to bring about peace with Indian nations. In April 1783, John Dickinson, the president of Pennsylvania, wrote to the Pennsylvania congressional delegates that hostilities between Indians and the inhabitants of the state were continuing on the frontier.[36] At Dickinson's urging, Congress dispatched Ephraim Douglas on a diplomatic mission to inform the Indians in the northern department that peace had been achieved between the United States and Britain, and that only the United States would now be dealing with Indian nations. Douglas found that the Indians would agree to maintain the peace "unless they were compelled to a contrary conduct by the Americans seizing on their Lands which [the Indians] would never quietly submit to."[37]

Congress' fears about the designs of the states were realized in July 1783, when word was received that the state of New York had devised a plan to expel from the state the Seneca, Onondaga, and Cayuga nations.[38] George Washington confidently predicted that "if the Legislature of the State of New York should insist upon expelling the Six Nations from all the Country they inhabited previous to the War, within their territory . . . it will end in another Indian war. . . ."[39] Washington proposed the regulation of Indian land purchases by governmental authority and the establishment of a boundary between Indians and whites.

Congress followed Washington's recommendations by issuing a proclamation forbidding, without the authority of Congress, settlements or purchases of Indian lands outside "the limits or jurisdiction of any particular state."[40] The proclamation's qualifying language hardly limited its reach, however; Congress intended to apply the proclamation to practically all Indians and Indian lands. Congress' intent is evident by its rejection of language that would have limited the reach of the proclamation to Indian nations residing outside the geographic boundaries of the states.[41]

Stronger measures were needed, however, to achieve permanent peace. On 15 October 1783, Congress established a four-pronged Indian policy for the northern and middle departments. This policy committed the United States to seeking peaceful relations, to obtaining land cessions through treaties, to establishing mutually agreed upon boundaries between the Indian territories and white settlements, and to establishing uniform regulations governing Indian trade.[42] A warning of the potential difficulties in implementing this policy is contained in a resolution tacked onto the end of the report: "Resolved, That the preceding measures of Congress relative to Indian affairs, shall not be construed to affect the territorial claims of any of the states, or their legislative rights within their respective limits."[43]

The 1783 policy statement confirms that Congress was dealing with Indian tribes as independent nations. There is no suggestion here that Congress believed it had any authority over the purely internal matters of Indian nations. Except for trade, each of the policy goals required Congress to seek international treaty agreements with Indian nations. The respect accorded the sovereignty of tribes is evident in the boundary provision, in which the United States stated its intention to restrain its citizens from hunting and settling within the Indian territories.[44] Congress also decided to demand that all prisoners taken by Indian nations during the war be released to the United States, a procedure typically found in international agreements ending hostilities.[45]

Regarding land cessions, Congress naively hoped that it could obtain Indian land without giving up anything of value in return. Two arguments were to be advanced in order to induce Indian nations to part with their lands. First, tribes were to be informed that the United States demanded "atonement" for the injuries caused by Indians who fought on the side of the British during the war. Second, tribes were to be informed that Britain had ceded to the United States in the 1783 Treaty of Paris its sovereignty over the territory stretching from the Atlantic Ocean to the Mississippi River, and that this cession made Indian nations somehow dependent on the United States.[46]

As a negotiating tactic, Congress' plan may have made sense, but it was unrealistic to think that Indian land could be obtained without giving up anything in return, as subsequent events proved. On 23 October 1784, in the Treaty of Fort Stanwix, the powerful Six Nations Iroquois Confederacy agreed to peaceful relations with the United States. In exchange for the Six Nations' relinquishment of their claims to all lands in the Ohio Valley region, the United States agreed to protect the territories of the Confederacy against all encroachments, seizure, or other violation.[47] This guarantee put Congress on a collision course with the state of New York, which made no secret of its plans to acquire Indian lands despite congressional resolves and treaties. Beginning in 1782, when the state began granting the lands of the Six Nations as bounty payments to its soldiers who had served during the war, New York aggressively sought Indian lands. Congress was also aware of New York's intention to expel the Six Nations in order to clear the way for white settlement in its western areas.

Congress' ideas about the dependency of Indian nations also took a beating at Fort Stanwix. The Six Nations representatives insisted to the United States commissioners that they were "free and independent" and under the influence of no other sovereign.[48] Noteworthy also is the fact that the United States came to the Six Nations seeking peace out of the realization that the Confederacy continued to represent a real threat in 1784. James Madison, who attended part of the negotiations, understood the precarious position of the United States before negotiations began:

> What the upshot of the Treaty will be is uncertain. The possession of the posts of Niagara &c. by the British is a very inauspicious circumstance. Another is that we are not likely to make a figure otherwise that will impress a high idea of our power or opulence.[49]

Rather than establishing the sovereignty of the United States over the Six Nations, the Treaty of Fort Stanwix recognized and guaranteed the right of the Six Nations to independence.

While Congress sought to strengthen its ability to manage Indian relations, New York attempted at every turn to subvert and frustrate congressional initiatives. Before the Treaty of Fort Stanwix, New York tried to make a separate land cession agreement with certain members of the Oneida Nation. When the United States treaty commissioners learned of New York's plans, they admonished New York officials that the state's business would be "more properly transacted at the same time with and in Subordination to the General Treaty."[50] After the state's effort was aborted, New York officials attempted to undermine Congress' plans to obtain a land cession at Fort Stanwix. The state sent two officials to attend the proceedings with instructions to use their "best endeavours to counteract and frustrate" anything that may prove "detrimental" to the state.[51]

New York State defied Congress again in 1785 when it tricked and pressured several Oneida individuals, who had no authority to act on behalf of the Oneida Nation, into ceding 250,000 acres of Oneida land in return for $11,500 in goods and cash.[52] Although Congress upheld its exclusive constitutional authority over Indian affairs, it was unable to prevent New York's land grab. The state's fraudulent deal was a severe blow to Congress' efforts to keep the peace. As the Oneidas recognized, "this News about selling our Lands will make a great noise in the Six Nations. . . ."[53] The danger extended beyond New York because the United States had not yet made a peace treaty with the western Indian nations, which could have easily formed an alliance with the Six Nations. Even though major warfare did not break out, this episode heightened concerns about state dealings with Indians without congressional control.

Congress was ineffectual in preventing state violations of the Treaty of Fort Stanwix. On 4 October 1785, a congressional committee recommended that an agent be appointed to manage affairs with the Six Nations and that the member nations should be informed that "Congress will preserve inviolate the Treaty of Fort Stanwix . . . and that the Reservations in that treaty in favor of any of the said Tribes will be at all times faithfully regarded by Congress."[54] Despite these feeble moves by Congress, New York was generally able to violate with impunity the Treaty of Fort Stanwix.

Congress faced the same problems with defiant states in the South. For years, Georgia and North Carolina had coveted the vast territories of the Creek Nation and Cherokee Nation. The specter of a major Indian war loomed in the South as well if Congress could not establish its control over Indian affairs. Congress' southern Indian policy closely paralleled its northern policy: subordinate state efforts to acquire Indian land to the federal authorities, obtain cessions of land, establish an Indian-white boundary, and restrain white settlers from trespassing on Indian lands.[55] Congress was even more explicit about its paramount authority over Indian land deals, because the threat of warfare arising from fraudulent state treaties was even greater in the South. The treaty commissioners were specifically instructed to disapprove all prior state land cession treaties with Indians unless those treaties "appear manifestly and perfectly consistent with the design of the Treaties now proposed to be held."[56]

Congress' authority was sharply controverted in the South. Georgia and North Carolina were even more ruthless than New York in their desire to enrich the landholdings of their citizens. Both states had extensive territorial claims based on royal charters. They argued that the "legislative right" proviso of Article IX, clause 4, of the Articles of Confederation preserved their right to deal separately with Indians located within the boundaries of the charter claims. The South, during the period

1785 to 1787, presented perhaps the greatest test of congressional authority to manage Indian relations.

Despite the machinations of the states, Congress made peace treaties with the Cherokee Nation in 1785, with the Choctaw Nation in 1786, and with the Chickasaw Nation in 1786. These treaties went even farther than the Treaty of Fort Stanwix in acknowledging the sovereignty and independence of the signatory Indian nations. For example, common to all three was a provision recognizing the right of the affected Indian nation to punish United States citizens who attempted to settle within the territory reserved to the tribes by the treaties.[57] In a provision aimed at the states, all three treaties stated that "for the prevention of injuries or oppressions on the part of the citizens or Indians, the United States in Congress assembled shall have the sole and exclusive right of regulating the trade with the Indians, and managing all their affairs in the manner as they think proper."[58] The authority to manage "all their affairs" was not meant to confer on Congress the power of managing the internal governmental and political affairs of the Cherokee Nation. In the legal idiom of that day, the phrase almost certainly was understood to encompass the usual objects of Congress' management of Indian relations: land boundaries and land rights guarantees; war and peace; and trade.

In the years following, the states and their citizens largely ignored the guarantees made in these treaties, frequently violating the boundary lines. As in the North, Congress' weak financial condition and lack of military power rendered any enforcement attempts ineffectual.

One other congressional initiative during this period should be noted. Congress restructured its administration of Indian affairs in an ordinance enacted on 7 August 1786. The new law divided responsibility between southern and northern departments, and authorized the appointment of a superintendent for each, to serve for a two-year period. The law also formally placed the management of Indian affairs under the secretary of war, providing that all communications to Congress concerning Indian matters should be made through him. The focus of the law, however, was on commercial intercourse between United States citizens and Indian nations. It created a system for the licensing of Indian traders and, significantly, for the issuance of passports to travel through the territory of Indian nations.[59] Congress' goal evidently was to control, as much as possible, contacts between whites and Indians in order to reduce the chances of conflict.

However, Congress was not completely successful in even this modest attempt to enhance its power. The North Carolina delegates to Congress obtained approval of an amendment to the ordinance requiring the Indian superintendent to act in conjunction with the states "in all cases where transactions with any nation or tribe of Indians ... cannot be done without interfering with the legislative rights of a state." [60] William Few, who later attended the 1787 Constitutional Convention as a delegate from North Carolina, cosponsored this amendment.

To summarize, on the eve of the Constitutional Convention of 1787, the state of Indian affairs looked grave to many American statesmen. The threat of Indian war existed in both the North and South, and fears abounded that powerful Indian nations might form alliances with the British and Spanish. On 24 October 1786, James Madison wrote to Thomas Jefferson that "[w]e hear from Georgia that state is threatened by a dangerous war with the Creek Indians. . . . The idea here is that the Indians derive their motive as well as their means from their Spanish neighbors." [61]

The outbreak of Shay's Rebellion in Massachusetts in 1786 exacerbated fears that the federal government would be toppled unless it was strengthened. There was even panic that Indian hostilities would fuel domestic rebellion. In March 1786, the *Pennsylvania Herald* carried an article by a writer under the name "Americanius," who warned that ". . . Vermont, Canada, the Indian nations, etc. will join their forces to the monster REBELLION and drive you head-long into the pit of POLITICAL DAMNATION." [62] The Connecticut congressional delegation likewise warned of a "great crisis," writing to the governor on 12 April 1786 that "the fickle Indian nations [are] ready to join those who best can supply their wants, and [are] jealous of the approach of the Americans so near their Territories. . . ." [63] Although these writers may have exaggerated the danger, they nevertheless accurately conveyed the sense of alarm many Americans felt during this time.

By 1786, virtually all the efforts of Congress to restrain the avarice of the states had failed. Forced to confront Indian nations that were in many respects foreign to the United States, Congress struggled within the limits of its authority under the Articles of Confederation to devise a national Indian policy that would keep Indian nations pacified, while at the same time acquiring their lands to enlarge the national domain. Its lack of real enforcement authority, the defiance of several large states, and inadequate economic and military resources crippled what modest efforts Congress made to manage relations with Indians. Writing in 1784, George Washington accurately expressed the obstacles Congress faced: ". . . there is a kind of fatality attending all our public measures, inconceivable delays, particular States counteracting the plans of the United States when submitted to them, opposing each other upon all occasions, torn by internal disputes, or supinely negligent and inattentive to everything which is not local. . . ." [64]

The Constitutional Convention of 1787

The proceedings of the Constitutional Convention of 1787 are also relevant in determining the framers' intent with regard to the power to manage relations with Indian nations. Congress responded on 21 February 1787 to growing demands for reform of the national government by calling for a "convention of delegates" to meet in Philadelphia "for the sole and express purpose of revising the Articles of Confederation" so as to "render the federal constitution adequate to the exigencies of Government and the preservation of the Union."[65] The convention met through the summer months of 1787 and finished its work on September 17.

The Constitutional Convention completed the process, begun during the First Continental Congress, of nationalizing the management of relations with Indians. With surprising unanimity, the delegates agreed simply to empower Congress with authority to "regulate commerce . . . with the Indian Tribes."[66] The convention also gave the national government exclusive authority to make treaties with Indian nations and to exercise the powers of war and peace. It eliminated the authority the states had under the Articles of Confederation to engage in defensive wars against Indians.

Under the Constitution, the management of Indian relations became the sole responsibility of the federal government; the states were legally and practically disabled from conducting separate relations as they had done under the Articles of Confederation. It is noteworthy that the framers did not intend to give Congress or the president a general, open-ended power over Indian affairs. Congress, and the president in the case of treaties, was given a very limited authority specifically designed to remedy the kinds of problems that had crippled the federal government under the Articles of Confederation. There were three motivating concerns: the need for a stronger and more effective national defense against Indian military attack or invasion; the need to establish a stronger constitutional basis for preventing state encroachments on Indian lands and for protecting Indian land rights; and the need to centralize authority over Indian trade. The convention delegates chose to address these concerns by giving Congress, along with the president in certain cases, exclusive authority to make treaties, to conduct war and peace, and to regulate commerce with Indian nations. Significantly, none of these powers was qualified by the limitations that had caused such serious strife under the Articles of Confederation.

There is relatively little documentary evidence of the actual debates at the Constitutional Convention. Consequently, the delegates' experience with and knowledge of Indian affairs, as reflected in their writings, also must be examined for insights about the intent of the framers.

The biographical portrait of the convention delegates reveals a wide range of experience in Indian affairs. Thirty-nine of the fifty-five delegates had served at one time or another in the Continental Congress.[67] Several delegates had prominent roles in the formulation of Indian policy under the Articles of Confederation. James Madison of Virginia, Alexander Hamilton of New York, James Wilson of Pennsylvania, and Oliver Ellsworth of Connecticut all served on the congressional committee appointed in 1783 to recommend a national Indian policy after the Treaty of Paris. Benjamin Franklin, representing Pennsylvania, had a hand in drafting the Indian affairs provisions of the Articles of Confederation, as did John Dickinson, who attended the convention as a delegate from Delaware. Both Franklin and Dickinson were strong advocates of a revitalized role for the federal government in Indian affairs.

With the possible exception of Franklin, James Madison was by far the most experienced and knowledgeable about Indian affairs. Madison attended the Treaty of Fort Stanwix negotiations in 1784 and consistently supported the supremacy of Congress in Indian affairs. Madison understood perhaps better than anyone the problems created by the ambiguous provisions of the Articles of Confederation that gave the states a claim to authority in Indian affairs. In April 1787, writing about the vices of the American political system, Madison listed Georgia's wars and treaties with Indian nations as examples of "encroachments by the states on the federal authority."[68] Later in *The Federalist Papers,* Madison characterized the Indian affairs provisions under the articles as "obscure and contradictory," and observed that it was "absolutely incomprehensible" that trade with Indians located within the states could be regulated by Congress without "intruding on the internal rights of legislation" of those states.[69] Madison, in Federalist No. 42, was writing as an advocate for the new constitution, so his characterization of the problems under the articles system was argumentative and somewhat overdrawn, but certainly Madison believed that harmonious relations with Indian nations required a strong central government with a mandate to govern without interference from the states.

George Washington, who headed the Virginia delegation, also exerted considerable influence over the shape of the new government, although he participated very little in the actual debates at the convention.[70] Washington shared Madison's view that a strong national government was necessary to manage relations with Indians, and he was acutely aware of the threat to peace that state land seizures presented. During the Articles of Confederation period, Washington's primary concern was to provide for the peaceful acquisition and settlement of new territories obtained from Indian nations. Washington favored strong national measures establishing boundaries between the Indian country and white settlement. He believed that either Congress or the states should regulate the acquisition of Indian lands by private persons.[71] Congress adopted his recommendation for a federal Indian policy based on treaty agreements in October 1783.

Another influential delegate was James Wilson, who represented Pennsylvania. Wilson's concern about Indian affairs grew out of his interests as a speculator in western lands and his desire to expand the territorial limits of the United States. He was a leading member of the Illinois and Wabash Land Company, which had acquired the right of preemption to vast areas of Indian land. Wilson's financial interests led him to favor congressional control over Indian land transactions because he hoped Congress would validate land company purchases from Indians by extinguishing the Indian title.[72] Wilson's nationalist outlook, however, was also consistent with the views and interests of Pennsylvania. That state did not oppose federal authority over Indian affairs during the Articles of Confederation period and had willingly submitted to federal authority when it purchased certain lands of the Six Nations in 1784.

Wilson's participation in the drafting of the Articles of Confederation in 1776 shows he believed strongly that the powers of the central government did not extend to the internal affairs of Indian nations. In the debate on the Indian affairs power, Wilson noted that "[w]e have no right over the Indians, whether within or without the real or pretended limits of any Colony. They will not allow themselves to be classed according to the bounds of Colonies."[73] Even in 1776, Wilson saw the need for uniform management of Indian affairs: "No lasting peace will be [made] with the Indians unless made by some one body. . . . No power ought to treat with the Indians, but the United States."[74] He argued the same principle should govern trade with Indians. Wilson also pointed out that the Indian nations were acquainted with the benefits of confederation from the example of the Six Nations Iroquois Confederacy.[75]

The state of New York was represented by Alexander Hamilton, an avowed Federalist, and Robert Yates and John Lansing, both strong Anti-Federalists. Yates and Lansing grew so disgruntled with the nationalist direction of the convention that they walked out in July. Like the other nationalists, Hamilton was concerned about the international implications of Indian relations. He favored central governmental control in order to provide for a strong defense in the event of Indian alliances with Britain and Spain. Hamilton argued:

> *The territories of Britain, Spain and of the Indian nations in our neighborhood, do not border on particular states, but incircle [sic] the Union from Maine to Georgia. The danger, though in different degrees, is therefore common. And the means of guarding against it*

ought in like manner to be the objects of common councils and of a common treasury.[76]

Note that Hamilton counts Indian nations among the foreign nations with which the United States must deal. Hamilton also shared Madison's view that the Articles of Confederation had unduly shackled the federal government's ability to deal effectively with Indian matters. As early as 1783, Hamilton observed that the "legislative right" proviso created "a constitutional possibility" of defeating treaties with Indian nations.[77]

Among those favoring the states' rights position, the North Carolina delegation would have been the logical choice to lead the opposition to the nationalization of Indian affairs. One member, William Blount, had worked to defeat congressional authority over Indian lands during the Articles of Confederation period. At the 1785 federal treaty with the Cherokee Nation, Blount attended the negotiations to lodge a formal protest on behalf of North Carolina that the treaty infringed on the legislative rights of the state under the articles.[78] Hugh Williamson, also a member of the North Carolina delegation, had served on the congressional committee that reported on the state of Indian affairs in the South in 1785.

Very little is known about the views of the other delegates, but several were involved in Indian affairs in tangential ways. During the convention, Edmund Randolph of Virginia met with a Cherokee chief, who urged him to "send a talk and a present" to the Cherokee Nation. Although the substance of the meeting is not known, Randolph paid for "a silver pipe with some symbols of Virginia and Cherokee friendship" out of his own funds.[79]

George Mason of Virginia was a strong defender of Virginia's claims to western lands and, as a result, he could be expected to oppose a congressional role in settling disputes between states and private speculators about the validity of purchases from Indians. Mason feared that states would lose their western claims if Congress were given authority to regulate the purchase of Indian lands or to resolve the competing claims of the land companies. Mason hinted at his position in 1783 when he criticized a congressional resolution providing that "unappropriated lands" ceded to the United States would be sold for the common benefit of the United States. He asked rhetorically whether this resolution would be a "sufficient bar to Congress against confirming the claims under Indian purchases. . . ."[80]

By contrast, Nathaniel Gorham of Massachusetts could reasonably be expected to favor a stronger role for Congress in Indian affairs. He had acquired the right of preemption, meaning the right to purchase land subject to congressional authority, to over six million acres of Indian land in western New York. Typically, private land speculators looked to Congress to validate their claims to Indian lands. If Congress were to lose its historic authority over Indian land purchases, Gorham's claim would have greatly diminished in value.

This variety of viewpoints notwithstanding, the desire to strengthen the federal government's powers in Indian affairs was nearly unanimous. Apparently the tumultuous years under the articles had produced a national consensus. The overriding necessity of more efficient management of Indian affairs, whether to defend against invasion or maintain peaceful relations, nearly transcended the Federalist–Anti-Federalist split that characterized so many of the other issues addressed at the convention. This unity of opinion is reflected in an Anti-Federalist document widely circulated in late fall 1787, which lumped Indian affairs with the foreign concerns that should be handled exclusively by the federal government: "Let the general government consist of an executive, a judiciary and balanced legislature, and its powers extend exclusively to all foreign concerns, causes arising on the seas, to commerce, imports, armies, navies, Indian affairs, peace and war, and to a few internal concerns of the community. . . ."[81] This view was fairly representative of the Anti-Federalist opinion that Indian affairs were an external concern requiring exclusive authority to be lodged in the central government.

The opposition that could have been expected from New York, Georgia, and North Carolina did not materialize at the convention. Georgia's inaction is puzzling. Given the bitter fight with Congress over the right to acquire Indian lands, Georgia predictably should have been a strong opponent of increased congressional authority. The surviving records of the debates, however, show that Georgia did not mount even token opposition. The probable explanation is that the war with the Creeks had reached a crisis point by 1787 and Georgia desperately needed the military assistance a revitalized national government could provide. This explanation is not entirely satisfactory, however, because Georgia protested a federal treaty with the Creeks in 1790 as an attack on its constitutional rights because it impaired Georgia's claim to the Yazoo lands.[82] Georgia had apparently decided not to oppose stronger federal authority except in specific cases that impinged on states' rights.

New York was not a strong opposition force because its Anti-Federalist delegates, Robert Yates and John Lansing, left the convention in early July before the question of Indian relations was taken up. That left only Alexander Hamilton to represent New York's views, and he was on record as a strong supporter of centralized control. Yates concentrated his efforts in working to defeat ratification by New York. His opposition was in part based on his judgment that the state's powers over Indian land purchases and the Indian trade had been competely eradicated by the new Constitution. This was a fair assessment, although Yates's assertion that the "right of regulating Indian affairs, especially with the five nations, has been in the colony of New York since the year 1664," grossly distorted over one hundred and twenty years of history.[83]

William Blount of North Carolina, perhaps the natural leader of the opposition forces, did not speak at all at the convention and apparently made few efforts behind the scenes to counter the growing sentiment for a stronger national government. Blount left temporarily on July 4 to attend Congress as that body was preparing to consider a report by Secretary of War Henry Knox on the impending military crisis in the South precipitated by state encroachments on Indian lands and violations of the federal treaties. Blount returned to the convention on August 7, several weeks before the Indian affairs power was considered, but surprisingly he did not participate in the debate. Blount might have been expected to seek a constitutional recognition of the southern states' claims to authority over Indian affairs. On 3 August 1787, a congressional committee had submitted a draft report excoriating the southern states for encroachments on Indian lands that might "produce all the evils of a general war on the frontier."[84] Despite this rebuke and the committee's strongly worded assertion of paramount federal authority, Blount did not press the issue at the convention. As a matter of conjecture, it is possible that Blount regarded Congress as a greater threat to state interests than the convention. He hesitated to sign the new Constitution because of the dispute with Congress over Indian affairs, but he eventually signed as a symbol of the unanimity of the delegates.[85] None of the delegates who refused to sign the Constitution listed objections to the Indian affairs power as a reason.

The process by which the national government acquired the sole constitutional authority over the management of Indian affairs was remarkably free of controversy. Before the delegates convened, James Madison drafted a set of resolutions to get the jump on those favoring more limited reforms. These resolutions, fifteen in number, were introduced on 29 May 1787 and became known as the Virginia Plan. Madison unexpectedly omitted any direct reference to Indian affairs in defining the powers of the national legislature he proposed. Resolution number six, however, proposed that the national legislature should enjoy all those powers that Congress had under the Articles of Confederation and, in addition, should have power to "legislate in all cases to which the separate States are incompetent, or in which the harmony of the United States may be interrupted by the exercise of individual Legislation."[86] Almost certainly Madison intended this language to include authority over Indian affairs, but the reference to congressional power under the articles left open the possibility that the same problems of enforcement would exist.

Edmund Randolph's comments in introducing the Virginia Plan confirm that it was intended to address the problems with state intrusions on Congress' Indian affairs power. Randolph listed among the defects of the confederation the inability of Congress to punish infractions of "treaties or the law of nations," to defend itself against "encroachments from the states," and to prevent state provocations of warfare.[87] Congress' experience with managing Indian affairs in the preceding thirteen years had graphically illustrated all of these defects.

Shortly after Randolph introduced the Virginia Plan, Charles Pinckney of South Carolina presented his own plan of union. Although there is some doubt about precisely what it contained, it is generally agreed that Pinckney's plan gave to Congress "exclusive power . . . of regulating Indian Affairs."[88] This plan was not considered or debated at the convention, although the Committee of Detail probably used it in drafting a constitution in late July and early August 1787.[89]

On May 31, the convention's Committee of the Whole House decided to adopt as the basis for debate the Virginia Plan, including its provision for a national legislature.[90] In another provision affecting Indian affairs, the plan empowered the national legislature to veto any state laws contravening the "articles of union." On the motion of Benjamin Franklin, this provision was amended on May 31 to extend the veto power to include state laws which violated "any Treaties subsisting under the authority of the Union."[91] The sponsorship of Franklin, who had vast experience in Indian affairs, strongly suggests that Indian treaties were intended to be covered, although there is no direct reference to them in the debates. This inference is strengthened by the support of Madison, who argued that experience had taught that the states had a tendency to "encroach on the federal authority [and] to violate national treaties."[92] This is nearly identical to the language he used in describing the problems of managing Indian affairs under the Articles of Confederation in his outline of the vices of the American political system one month earlier.

The delegates from the smaller states, such as New Jersey, Delaware, and Maryland, among others, objected to many of the nationalist provisions of the Virginia Plan, including the veto over state laws and population-based representation in the national legislature. To counter the nationalist trends, the small states drafted a separate plan of union, known as the New Jersey Plan after its sponsor William Paterson, a delegate from that state. This plan's significance for Indian affairs lies in its similarities to the Virginia Plan. It contained a provision declaring all treaties made under the authority of the United States to be "the supreme law of the respective states."[93] It also specifically authorized Congress to enact legislation "for the regulation of trade & commerce as well with foreign nations as with each other."[94] In these few ways, the

New Jersey Plan reflected a uniformity of opinion on the Indian affairs power, but in other crucial ways it mirrored too closely the structure of government under the Articles of Confederation.

For this reason, on June 18 and June 19, Hamilton and Madison respectively spoke against parts of the New Jersey Plan. Hamilton objected to the provision that Congress should depend on requisitions from the states to finance the government. Part of his argument relied on the harmful effect this would have on the military defense against Indian nations.[95] The plan contained a supremacy clause with regard to treaties, but Madison was concerned that it would not sufficiently prevent "encroachments on the federal authority." He thought it did not go far enough in establishing the principle that acts of Congress should be paramount to state laws. He noted that under the Articles of Confederation "transactions with Indians appertain to Cong[ress]," yet the articles did not prevent the states from entering into treaties and engaging in warfare with them.[96]

The convention decisively rejected the New Jersey Plan on June 19 and adopted the Virginia Plan for further consideration. During the next month, the proceedings bogged down over the question of representation in the national legislature, the smaller states favoring equal representation for each state and the larger states pushing for representation based on population. After a compromise was reached, a Committee of Detail was appointed on July 23 to draft a constitution in accordance with the resolutions the convention had approved.

The Committee of Detail, headed by John Rutledge of South Carolina, whose brother Edward had been active in Indian affairs under the articles, met for two weeks and presented a draft constitution to the convention on August 6. The committee apparently used portions of the so-called Pinckney Plan, although the document appears to have been in James Wilson's handwriting.[97] The Pinckney Plan was the only one that expressly conferred on Congress a power to regulate Indian affairs. The committee apparently discussed the power to manage relations with Indian nations, although the records are too fragmentary to learn much of the substance of the discussions. A working draft contained the simple notation "Indian Affairs" in the margin of a listing of legislative powers of the national legislature.[98] Apparently, John Rutledge made the notation.[99] The notation was placed among the list of foreign affairs powers, sandwiched between the power to punish violations against the law of nations and the power to "declare the law of piracy, felonies and captures on the high seas and captures on land."[100] The inclusion of the Indian affairs power in the committee's working draft suggests that it had been raised at some time earlier in the convention proceedings. The absence of records to show this discussion is not surprising, considering that the surviving records are believed to reflect only a small fraction of what was actually said at the convention.

The Committee of Detail draft also prohibited the states from entering into treaties or engaging in wars unless actually invaded or in imminent danger of invasion by enemies.[101] With one significant omission, this language appears to have been lifted almost verbatim from Article VI of the Articles of Confederation. Article VI's authorization for states to engage in warfare against Indian nations upon receiving "advice of a resolution being formed . . . to invade such state" was dropped by the committee. There are two possible explanations for this modification. Either the committee thought that the language in the draft constitution was broad enough to authorize state warfare against invading Indian nations, or the committee intended to remove altogether state authority to make war against Indians. Because there are no surviving records of the discussion on this point, we cannot be sure what was intended. Given the immense warfare problems caused by state-Indian relations, it is probable that the committee wanted to reduce state warfare against Indians and give Congress exclusive authority in that regard.

That Indian relations should be on the minds of the delegates is not surprising, considering the major confrontation brewing in Congress over the southern states' conduct towards Indians. In July, Secretary of War Knox had issued his sharply critical report concerning Georgia and North Carolina, and on August 3, a congressional committee had drafted a report recommending measures to strengthen Congress' hand in dealing with Indian unrest.[102] William Blount of North Carolina and William Few of Georgia had left the convention in July to be present when Congress considered this issue.

The August congressional committee report brought into sharp focus the Indian issues that threatened to tear apart the fragile government under the confederation. The committee noted that the principal source of difficulty with Indians was an "avaricious disposition in some of our people to acquire large tracts of land and often by unfair means."[103] The committee examined the legal basis for congressional intervention and found that the states' claim to authority over Indian affairs under the articles "appears to the committee, to leave the federal powers, in this case, a mere nullity."[104] The committee believed that Congress' authority over Indian affairs was "indivisible," and the states' conduct in dealing separately with Indian nations had produced "confusion, disputes and embarrassments in managing affairs with the Independent tribes within the limits of the States."[105] Although the committee avowed that Congress had ample constitutional authority under the articles to act effectively, it recommended that Congress request the states to cede their land claims to the United States in order to strengthen the political basis of congressional authority. In that way, the Indian nations would definitely be outside the limits of the states and within the ambit of congressional authority. A confrontation over the proper interpretation of the articles might perhaps be avoided.

This advice, however sound politically, exposed how weakened Congress had become; the committee admitted that it chose a cessions policy because it "appears to be the most eligible and likely to meet the approbation of the two States."[106] With a major Indian war about to break out on the frontiers, Congress was forced to rely on its persuasive powers and the willingness of the states to accede to congressional authority, an unlikely prospect. Congressional authority under the articles commanded very little respect in the South.

The August congressional committee report may have played a part in the framing of the Indian affairs power in the Constitution. Before it was issued, Indian affairs was covered only by implication in the various drafts actually discussed. During the debate on the draft constitution prepared by the Committee of Detail, Madison moved to refer twenty additional legislative powers, most of which were regarded as relatively noncontroversial, to a committee for consideration. Near the top of this list he placed a power to "regulate affairs with the Indians as well within as without the limits of the United States."[107] It may be that Charles Pinckney originally proposed this additional power, which would be consistent with his inclusion of an Indian relations power in his original plan of government.[108] Regardless of sponsorship, it is probable that an express power to manage relations with Indians was added to remedy the problems Congress was having with Georgia and North Carolina, as reflected in the August congressional report.

Between August 18 and September 4, the Indian affairs power was modified twice. The committee that studied the proposed additions to the legislative powers reported on August 22. It suggested that the Indian affairs power be added to the power of Congress to regulate commerce with foreign nations and among the states, which had been approved on August 16.[109] The committee approved the following language as an addition to the commerce clause: ". . . and with Indians, within the limits of any state, not subject to the laws thereof."[110] This language was much more restrictive of Congress' powers than the original Madison/Pinckney proposal because it used the ambiguous phrase "subject to the laws thereof." The committee probably intended to give Congress authority over all Indian nations located within the boundaries of states, but the qualifying language would have given the states a plausible basis on which to argue their authority over Indians. The delegates immediately would have recognized the inadequacies of this language from the history of contumacious state behavior during the Articles of Confederation period.

The convention postponed consideration of this and certain other aspects of the legislative powers and on August 31 referred them to a special Committee of Eleven that included Madison, John Dickinson, Hugh Williamson, and Abraham Baldwin of Georgia. This committee modified the Indian affairs power yet again, proposing that Congress be given authority simply to regulate commerce with "foreign Nations, among the several States and with Indian Tribes."[111] The doubts about the applicability of congressional power to Indians that might be subject to state law were eliminated; Congress would have authority to manage relations with Indian nations regardless of location or state claims to authority. The lessons of the Articles of Confederation period appeared to have been learned. On September 4, the convention approved this formulation of Congress' power without opposition or dissenting votes.[112]

What did the delegates mean by "commerce" with Indian tribes? It would be a mistake to rely too heavily on the debate over its meaning in the context of foreign and interstate commerce because the Indian affairs power was not introduced until two days after that debate had essentially ended. Nevertheless, there are indications that the framers thought of Indian trade as similar in many respects to other forms of commerce which needed to be regulated. Scholars have pointed out that Congress' general concern in the commerce clause was with the international aspects of commercial relations.[113] The placement of the power to regulate commerce with Indian tribes within the commerce clause is implicit recognition of the international status of Indian nations.

The scope of Congress' powers under the commerce clause may be determined with reference to the historical context in which the power was exercised. The most reliable guide to the meaning of commerce as it applied to Indian affairs during that time is found in the August 1787 congressional report on Indian affairs in the South. The committee concluded that historically the "principal objects" in managing affairs with Indians have been limited to the following: "making war and peace, purchasing certain tracts of their lands, fixing the boundaries between them and our people, and preventing the latter settling on lands left in possession of the former."[114] Add trade relations to this list and a complete picture emerges of the matters involved in Indian–United States relations during this time. This contemporaneous understanding of the scope of the federal government's powers may help illuminate the intent of the framers in granting Congress the power to conduct the United States' relations with Indian nations. Certainly it is clear that no one of that day believed that Congress had acquired the authority to violate the sovereignty of Indian nations by intruding on their internal affairs. The assumption was exactly the opposite, that Congress' authority extended only so far as necessary to manage the relations among Indian nations, the federal and state governments, and their citizens.

As the chief architect of the Indian affairs power, James Madison's views regarding the nature of the central government are relevant to this question. As one Madison scholar has observed, Madison was a nationalist to be sure, but his primary concern was to make the national government "effective and supreme within its proper sphere, which he consistently conceived as relatively small." [115] Thus, although Madison believed that Indian affairs should be the exclusive responsibility of the national government, he would have conceived of those powers as relatively limited. Certainly he would have rejected the view that Congress' powers in Indian affairs were unlimited. As Madison later observed in a slightly different context, it was a mistake to think that the term "national" as used in the early stages of the convention "was equivalent to *unlimited* or consolidated." [116] Rather, the term was used to distinguish a government that operated directly on individuals from a federal government, or one that operated through requisitions on the states and depended on the sanction of state legislatures.

There are several other sections of the Constitution that also authorized the federal government to manage relations with Indian nations. Because treaty-making was the principal means of conducting relations with Indians during the Articles of Confederation period, the framers surely intended the treaty power to apply to Indians. Indian treaties figure only marginally in the debates about the treaty power, Madison's complaint about states making treaties in violation of the articles being the only direct reference. The problem of state treaties with Indians interfering with congressional authority was sufficiently serious during the Articles of Confederation period, however, that it is safe to assume that it played a part in the framers' decision to make the treaty power exclusively a federal responsibility.

More explicit evidence of the applicability of the treaty power to Indian nations came during the debates on the ratification of the Constitution. In the South Carolina ratifying convention, Charles Pinckney argued that the treaty power under the articles was sometimes ineffectual because the assent of nine states was required. He cited an example from Indian affairs: "A single member would frequently prevent the business from being concluded. . . . This actually happened when a treaty of importance was about to be concluded with the Indians." [117]

The war powers clauses also served as a source of federal authority over Indian affairs. The framers knew that the states historically had often provoked Indian warfare and that the states were unable to defend against Indian attacks. The experience of the Continental Congress in fighting the forces of the Six Nations Iroquois Confederacy during the American Revolution convinced many delegates of the necessity of strong war powers for the national government. Presumably, the threat of an Indian alliance with Spain or Great Britain, which was widely feared and taken very seriously, was also a factor that influenced the strengthening of the federal government's war powers. On the eve of the convention, an article in the *Pennsylvania Journal* cited the need for a strong national defense to protect against Indian nations: "Let the citizens of America who inhabit the western counties of our states fly to a federal power for protection. The Indians know too well the dreadful consequences of confederacy in arms, even to admit the peaceful husbandman, who is under the cover of the arsenals of thirteen states."[118] This article was widely circulated among the convention delegates.[119]

Indian relations were expressly tied to the war powers during the debate over ratification. A key question was whether a standing army was necessary to defend against Indian attacks or invasions. The assessment of the strength of Indian forces varied according to the writer's belief about the dangers of a standing army in a democracy. The Anti-Federalists, who opposed a standing army, discounted the Indian threat, whereas the Federalists may have exaggerated it somewhat. For example, a writer in the *Virginia Independent Chronicle* defended a standing army in the most inflamatory language: "[A] standing army will be required to protect our defenceless frontiers from indiscriminating cruelties and horrid devastations of the savages. . . ."[120] On the other hand, the author of an article in the *Philadelphia Freeman's Journal* dismissed the Indian threat as a "barefaced assertion."[121]

Indians are also mentioned in the article determining the number of representatives in Congress and apportioning direct taxes among the states.[122] The framers excluded "Indians not taxed" from these computations. The origin of the phrase is rooted in an early draft of the Articles of Confederation, which provided that the colonies should fund a common treasury for defense purposes "in proportion to the number of inhabitants of every age, sex & quality, except Indians not paying taxes."[123] In the final draft of the Articles of Confederation, this phrase was deleted in favor of apportionment based on the number of "white inhabitants."[124] On 1 April 1783, however, Congress resolved that taxes should be apportioned on the basis of the number of white inhabitants, counting each slave as three-fifths and excluding "Indians not paying taxes."[125]

This resolution became the model for the apportionment clause in the new Constitution. The records of the debates do not disclose any discussion of the reasons why Indians not paying taxes were excluded from the computation. The controversial issue in this section was the treatment of slaves in the computation. Presumably, the reference to Indians was not intended to have a substantive effect on the exerise of federal power. Apparently, the framers believed that there were a number of Indians who paid taxes because they were no longer members of their Indian nations or had otherwise assimilated within the body politic of American society. Because these persons were not yet regarded as citizens, it was necessary to include them expressly in determining the basis for apportionment. Conversely, Indians not paying taxes, probably meaning those Indians who belonged to separate autonomous Indian nations, were rightly excluded from the apportionment calculation because they were not part of the community on which the tax burden would fall. There is no evidence that this clause of the apportionment section had any practical effect on the tax burdens of the states or the number of representatives in Congress. The figures used during the debates in the state ratifying conventions to explain the effect of the apportionment formula do not list the number of "Indians not taxed."

Ratification of the Constitution

The new Constitution was submitted to the states for ratification by resolution of Congress on 28 September 1787. The ratification process confirms that the framers intended to give the federal government exclusive and effective authority to conduct relations with Indian nations.

Only in Georgia did Indian relations play a direct role in ratification. The critical need for military protection against the Creeks in part stimulated a speedy ratification. Georgia ratified the Constitution by unanimous vote on 2 January 1788, the third state to approve it. The conventional wisdom of the day was that Georgia would ratify quickly because "she is at present very much embarrassed with an Indian war, and in great distress."[126] In October 1787, a Georgia county assemblyman predicted that the Constitution would be approved in order to avoid the "ruinous consequences" of fighting the Indian war alone. Even though he thought the new government's powers were too broad, "of the two evils we must choose the least."[127] Abraham Baldwin, one of Georgia's convention delegates, hoped that "these internal commotions will accelerate [Georgia's] determination on the great political question."[128]

As a matter of constitutional law, Georgia's understanding of the federal government's powers in Indian affairs was fairly broad. In June 1790, the Georgia House of Representatives responded to the governor's request for a special session to consider plans to treat with the Creeks. The legislature regarded the state's plans as "improperly directed" because, it said, the federal government now had the authority to deal with Indians. This authority included the powers of "making war and peace—raising and supporting armies—providing for the common defense and general welfare of the United States—entering into Treaties—and regulating commerce with the Indian tribes."[129] This may have been the official understanding of Congress' powers, but Georgia was not as eager to relinquish its claims to authority over Indians as the legislature's statement might suggest. As one French diplomat observed, Georgia may have been one of the first states to ratify, but "it can hardly be expected from eagerness to execute it."[130] This prediction proved to be accurate, as Georgia for many years sought to subvert federal authority over Indian affairs.

Georgia soon tested Congress' authority under the new Constitution when on 21 December 1789 it purported to sell to three private companies all the lands of the Choctaws and Chickasaws within the state's claimed boundaries. Less than a month later, Secretary of War Knox reported to President Washington that if Georgia was attempting to "extinguish the Indian claims" without the authorization of the United States, its action would violate the federal treaties with those Indian nations, the Constitution, and the newly enacted Trade and Intercourse Act.[131] Because Knox had learned that the companies were preparing to settle on the Indian lands by force if necessary, he recommended stronger military protections for that area.

New York ratified the Constitution on 26 July 1788, by a closely divided vote. There is no evidence that objections to Congress' powers in Indian relations played any part in the closeness of the vote, although Robert Yates protested bitterly that the Constitution stripped the state of its power to acquire Indian lands without authority from Congress. New York's ratifying convention recommended two amendments to the Constitution that, by implication at least, can be read as mild protests about the Constitution's grant of exclusive authority to Congress and the president in Indian affairs. The convention declared that "no treaty is to be construed so as to operate to alter the Constitution of any state."[132] The New York Constitution contained a provision asserting the right of the state to control Indian land purchases. Perhaps the delegates at the ratifying convention wished to preserve the state's authority in this regard. Equally to the point, the convention recommended an amendment stripping the federal courts of the power to hear cases involving land, "unless [they] relate to claims of territory or jurisdiction between states and individuals under the grants of different states." This amendment would have effectively disabled the federal courts from hearing cases involving disputes between the federal government and states over Indian lands.[133]

New York continued to act as if it retained exclusive authority to acquire Indian land free from federal authority. In September 1788, state officials deceived certain Oneidas into ceding over five million acres of Oneida Nation land. The Oneidas were tricked into believing that the state would return lands previously taken and protect the remaining lands against private speculators. New York was completely undeterred by the Constitution or considerations of the national welfare. In 1791, George Washington lamented to Alexander Hamilton that New York was attempting to negotiate with the Six Nations shortly after they had been assured that only the United States as a whole could constitutionally deal with them. Washington despaired: "To sum the whole up in a few words, the interferences of States and the speculations of Individuals will be the bane of all our public measures."[134]

Conclusion

The twin objectives of the framers were first to equip the national government with exclusive and effective authority to manage Indian relations, unburdened by the restrictions under the Articles of Confederation; and second, to incapacitate the states legally and politically from carrying on relations with Indian nations. All of the evidence points to the conclusion that the framers intended to strengthen, to the exclusion of the states, those powers that the national government had been exercising, however ineffectively, under the Articles of Confederation. To accomplish this end, the framers discarded the ambiguous language which had limited Congress' power vis-a-vis the states under the Articles of Confederation and gave Congress paramount authority to make treaties, conduct warfare, and regulate commerce with Indian nations.

The framers appear to have been more concerned with making federal authority supreme as against the states than with the precise scope of congressional authority. To the extent that the scope of authority was an issue, it seems that most of the delegates assumed that congressional authority would be quite limited. Indeed, most of the evidence suggests that congressional authority was understood to encompass only those matters touching on the intergovernmental relationships between Indian nations and the United States as a whole. Stated another way, the Constitution gave Congress supreme and absolute power within the narrowly defined sphere of conducting external relations with Indian governments, to the exclusion of the states separately.

By giving Congress paramount authority to make treaties, conduct war, and regulate commerce, the Constitution implicitly recognized the inherent national sovereignty of Indian nations. This acknowledgment, of course, is entirely consistent with the political realities of that day, because Indian nations began their relationship with the United States recognized and respected as sovereign nations.

The modern conception of the status of Indian nations and the scope of congressional authority is radically different from the original understanding of the framers. Recently, the United States Supreme Court declared that "the power of the federal government over Indian tribes is plenary." [135] This extraordinary statement was not regarded at the time as particularly unusual because the Supreme Court has held that view for over eighty years. "Plenary" power in this context has come to mean literally unrestricted authority over Indian nations: it is said that Congress can do whatever it pleases with the lands, governments, and cultures of Indian nations, with practically no constitutional restraint.

The manner in which a limited authority to carry on the federal government's external relations with sovereign Indian nations has been transformed into an unlimited power over Indian nations is beyond the scope of this chapter. The important point here is that the so-called doctrine of plenary power finds no support in the history or text of the Constitution or the original understanding of the framers. There is not the slightest intimation in the convention debates or the writings of the framers that the Constitution was intended to give Congress a license to encroach on the sovereignty of Indian nations. The Constitution contemplated a relationship of equality and respect for the autonomy of Indian governments. The framers simply did not conceive of a power so broad that it would extend to the domestic, or internal, affairs of Indian nations.

If the intent of the framers were the sole guide to determining the scope of congressional authority, a vast array of oppressive acts of Congress would most likely be unconstitutional. For example, Congress probably would no longer be free to abrogate Indian treaties with impunity, to terminate the powers of Indian governments, to impose federal and state laws within sovereign Indian territory, and to expropriate Indian land. In other words, the historic loss of Indian land and sovereignty under federal law has no basis whatever in the intention of the framers. Because the difference between original intent and modern day law is so striking, there are strong reasons for reevaluating current concepts of plenary power in light of the history of the writing of the Constitution, the ideas of the framers, and the status of Indian nations.

* The author gratefully acknowledges the assistance of Gail A. Lehman, Marilyn Clapp, and Robert T. Coulter in the research and preparation of this chapter.

6.
Iroquois Political Theory and the Roots of American Democracy

Donald A. Grinde, Jr.

Introduction

According to Iroquois tradition and history, the oldest continuously functioning democratic constitution is the Iroquois Confederacy, and the Confederacy served as a democratic blueprint for the creation of Western democracies, especially influencing the evolution of the American governmental systems. To many other American Indian groups, this is common knowledge as well. Speaking in 1976, the Sovereign Native Women's Conference declared:

> We, the Indian people, may be the only citizens of this nation who really understand your form of government, and respect that form of government, as this form of government was copied from the Iroquois Confederacy.[1]

Thus, in the American Indian world the fundamental principles of American government are reflections of similar concepts in native governments. However, for hundreds of years, there has only been sporadic recognition among non-Indians of this fact. This is unfortunate because it denies the "world access to the best thinking of many of the world's cultures."[2] In denying Iroquois influence upon the American government, academics, and particularly historians, do so despite documentary and oral traditions that clearly indicate a firm connection between Iroquois political theory and American instruments of government. Yet, ethnocentric attitudes laden with biased assumptions about the intellectual and moral superiority of Western civilization are still the norm in historiography. For instance, Isabel T. Kelsay's recent (1984) biography of Joseph Brant (a noted Mohawk leader) characterizes Mohawks as:

> Harmless, good-hearted creatures generally, their one great vice was drink. Male and female, old and young, they all craved rum; it was their greatest pleasure, and when really thirsty any of them would give everything he possessed for a dram of "that Darling Water." There is no reason to suppose that Joseph [Brant's] parents were any better, or any worse, than this.[3]

In the past, political scientists, legal scholars, and even politicians have pointed out the contributions of the Iroquois to American government, but historians have been largely silent. The reason for this lies in the fact that most historians of colonial America are *overseas Europeans*.

As the distinguished American Indian scholar Jack D. Forbes has pointed out, overseas Europeans are individuals "who have refused to become Americanized, who refuse to become 'nativized.' " Almost always their "loyalties remain with their Overseas European Nationality, and with its colonialist culture." More important for the purposes of this essay, as long as such scholars hold to their European colonial attitudes, they will write the "kind of history textbooks which are now in vogue. . . ." They assume that everything begins in Europe, that "the history of Overseas Europeans is the central or only theme."[4] This essay challenges this ethnocentric perception in an area that is central to both American Indian people and Euro-American people, namely the principle of democracy. Happily, this ethnocentric perception is not universal among Euro-Americans. First, elitist tendencies in Europe that stressed domination not only over non-whites but also over tribal/peasant Europeans was not totally triumphant even in the European environment. Lapps, Scotsmen, and other such groups maintained at least some of their tribal/peasant/clan identity in the face of the onslaught of divine right monarchies and other attacks. Certainly, sustained Irish protest over time against English domination is a dramatic example of ethnic resistance to colonization. Second, European philosophy has been profoundly influenced since 1492 by the values of people found in the Americas, Africa, Asia, and the Pacific. Montesquieu, in his "Spirit of the Laws," made use of African, Arab, Persian, East Indian, and Chinese concepts in his discussions of forms of government.[5] Specifically, Forbes states that

> [w]ith the writings of Rousseau, Voltaire . . . we might suggest that the traditional folk democracy of parts of Europe became viable again when merged with the actual knowledge that there were functioning democratic/communalistic societies in the world. . . .[6]

This reawakening of the idea of freedom and modern democratic ideals was born in "Native American wigwams because it was only in America" that Europeans from 1500 to 1776 knew of societies that were truly free.[7]

The genealogy of an idea is fraught with uncertainties. But American Indians are sure about the birth of freedom in North America and, as we shall see, this made them effective midwives for these ideas in another society. In fourfold fashion, we shall examine the red roots of European peace and freedom. First, there will be an examination of American Indian influences upon European political theory and the role of the Iroquois ideas. Second, we will turn to an examination of the roots of American government and then the path to union. And finally, we will look at the persistence of Iroquois contributions.

American Indian Influences on European Political Theory and the Role of Iroquois Ideas

I know histhry isn't thrue, hinessy, because it ain't like what I see ivry day in Halsted Sthreet. If any wan comes along with a histhry iv Greece or Rome that'll show me th' people fightin', gettin' drunk, makin' love, gettin' married, owin' the grocery man an' bein' without hard coal, I'll believe they was a Greece or Rome, but not before.[8]

Most studies of the modern world hold that the first significant modern democracy was established in the United States during and after the American Revolution. This assertion goes unchallenged in our history books, but there is hard evidence that the League of the Iroquois, with its representative form of democracy, not only predated the United States Constitution but also profoundly influenced the evolution and development of the document. There have been ancient forms of direct democracies which encompassed the whole corpus of citizens, such as the Greek city-state of Athens, but the success of such ventures was fleeting. Such noble experiments declined and were replaced by republics and eventually empires. The Magna Carta and the struggle over parliamentary representation were attempts to create democratic principles within an authoritarian structure, but they failed to kindle freedom and equality.[9] Consequently, for almost two thousand years after the decline of Greek city-states like Athens, there was no working democracy on European soil. So when Europeans came to the Americas, they came from divine right monarchies or oligarchies calling themselves independent republics. Once arrived, these Europeans created governmental structures with written charters sanctioned by the companies and sovereigns that ruled over the colonies on the Atlantic seaboard. From the beginning of European colonization, colonial legislative assemblies and written charters played an important part in forging a unique colonial identity while maintaining advantageous ties with the mother country.

The formation of Rhode Island demonstrates an interaction with Native American people. Roger Williams, the pariah of puritan New England, was conversant in several New England Indian languages, and his services were eagerly sought by the other colonies to moderate disputes with New England tribes. Yet, his pleas for moderation in the treatment of Native Americans went unheeded. In his arguments for religious freedom, he used American Indian practices to illustrate acceptance of diversity:

> I've known them to leave their house and mat
> to lodge a friend or stranger
> When Jews and Christians oft have sent
> Jesus Christ to the manger.[10]

With the aid of his interactions with Native Americans, Williams crafted a distinctly different government in Rhode Island. Through a constitution, Williams fixed individual rights and restricted the powers of the central government and local units. Moreover, he divided the powers of the state into central and local activities and governmental units. The central government became the "regulating, correcting and harmonizing agent for . . . all civil affairs." [11] In his arguments for freedom and autonomy, Williams critiqued puritan New England in these words:

> *Adulteries, Murthers, Robberies, Thefts,*
> *Wild Indians punish these*
> *And hold the scale of justice as*
> *That no man farthing leese.*
>
> *We weare no cloathes, have many Gods,*
> *and yet our sinners are lesse;*
> *You are Barbarians, Pagans wild,*
> *Your land's the wilderness.* [12]

Europe and the Indian Nations

In this new environment, the colonists of English North America were influenced by Native American ideas of confederation and democracy. The assumption that American democracy evolved from the English parliament or from a perusal of European political thinkers must be tempered with the realization that writers such as John Locke and Jean Jacques Rousseau derived much of their ideas about democracy in a workable form from travelers' accounts of American Indian governmental structures.

Indian democracies were working democracies that Europeans admired greatly from the first contacts. Many European theorists compared the Iroquois to the Romans, the Greeks, and the Celts in the areas of natural rights, statecraft, oratory, and public consensus. Furthermore, John Locke and others took note of the political examples of the peoples of the Americas: ". . . the kings of the Indians in America" are not much more than "generals . . . and in time of peace they . . . have . . . moderate sovereignty. . . ." Locke added that decisions of peace and war were vested "ordinarily either in the people, or in a council. . . ." [13] Despite wide European dissemination of Indian philosophy, the first democratic revolution sprang from American unrest because the colonists had partially assimilated the concepts of unity, federalism, and natural rights that existed in American Indian governments. These provided a viable alternative to the prevailing organization of European society. [14]

John Locke's interest in natural rights and the formation of British colonial governments is no casual association. From his study of aboriginal societies, Locke observed that men in their natural condition were in a state of freedom to structure their actions. In his *Second Treatise on Civil Government* Locke stated that human beings are in a natural state of equality, and so he reasoned that no person has more power and rights than another. Natural laws of tribal people teach that people are equal and independent and that no one should harm another in their life, liberty, and possessions. This concept is also a fundamental principle in the Great Law of Peace of the Iroquois.

The basis for Locke's philosophy also parallels Iroquois convictions in that he believed that everyone is bound to protect himself and protect the rest of mankind when his own preservation is not endangered. In a state of nature, people have the power to punish transgressions of the laws of nature, to protect the innocent, to restrain offenders, and to receive reparations for injuries done to them. This gave cause to the transgressor to repent, and deterred others from offensive behavior. In Locke's era, this was a protest against the autocratic monarchies.[15]

With such arguments, Locke pointed out the imperfections in his native land (particularly the "divine right" arguments of James II), and he also sought a new vision of society in his reflections on man's natural state. While Locke believed that man's natural existence involved peace, goodwill, and mutual assistance, he also stated that convenience and God made people inclined to gather into groups. According to Locke, language and understanding facilitate the formation of groups. For human beings in nature, the missing component is a settled, established common law, enforced by properly delegated authorities. Man formulates a political or civil society whenever a number of people unite in one society (an individual's executive power is relinquished under the laws of nature) to form one people, one body politic under one supreme government. Through this theoretical assumption, Locke subscribes to a form of contract theory in describing the beginnings of society.[16] It is important to understand that the experiential process detailed in the formation of the social contract for the Great Law of Peace of the Iroquois Confederacy is the same as Locke's, with at least one critical distinction. Locke's ideas were not accepted in an autocratic Europe of the late seventeenth century, while the Iroquois had lived in such a democratic state for centuries.

The social contract theory critiques absolute monarchy because it is inconsistent with the basis for a civil society. When people form a society by consent of the individuals within it, they enter into an agreement to follow the dictates of the majority. There is no real contract if one is left under no restrictions except those that bind him in nature.[17]

According to Locke, man gives up his unlimited freedom and power because the enjoyment of it is very uncertain due to corruption and aggression. To Locke, the great and main end of social contracts is the mutual preservation of lives, liberties, and estates (property). Locke reasoned that property and the organized state were the means to effect coercion.[18] This concept of private property is a major difference between Locke and the Great Law of Peace of the Iroquois, since individual property rights are not a major concern among the Six Nations.

Locke's primary natural law is the preservation of society for the public good of every person in it. Basically, the fundamental law of the commonwealth is the establishing of legislative power. It postulated that the power is not only supreme but also sacred and unalterable when placed in the hands of a popular legislative body. Because the legislature is limited to that which promotes the public good, it does not have absolute control and authority over the lives of the people.

Once a legislature is established, the laws of nature do not cease to operate in society, but stand as eternal rules for all men, legislators and others.

Government cannot rule by arbitrary decree and edict. Enduring laws are needed. Locke also enjoins the legislature against taking property without a subject's consent; and taxes can only be levied by the consent of the majority.

Finally, the legislative body cannot delegate the powers of lawmaking to other hands. The legislative body, not the prince, is the heart of the commonwealth. The legislative power embodies the will of the people, and the citizenry is the only judge as to the capability of a government to act in a society's interests.[19]

Locke's political theory was not without practical application. In 1669, he incorporated some of his equalitarian ideals into the first constitution for the Carolinas. King Charles II had granted the Carolinas to a number of English nobles, and Locke's patron, the Earl of Shaftesbury, was among the grantees.[20] Surprisingly, the document does not have the depth of democratic spirit found in some of Locke's other works.

By the end of the seventeenth century, there was a great deal of interest in Indian institutions and philosophies. In 1694, Baron Lahontan, in *New Voyages to North America*, wrote "A Conference or Dialogue between the Author and Adario, A Noted Man Among the Savages. . . ." Although written in French, it was translated into English rapidly because of its popularity. The ostensive purpose of the dialogue was to reveal Christian truths to Adario, a Huron. Indeed, the reason for the popularity of both the *Jesuit Relations* among the French people and of Lahontan in all of Europe was because they revealed the hypocrisy of European ways. On several occasions, Adario, the cosmopolitan Indian, advised Lahontan to "take my advice and turn Huron."[21] Adario pointed out that "The Great Lords . . . are slaves to their" king, and he is the only

Frenchman that is happy with respect "to that adorable Liberty which he alone enjoys."[22] In a similar manner, the Jesuits related to the French stories of "noble savages," who were nonmaterialistic and who possessed dignity and rights distinct from the powers of the state.

Fascination with American Indian freedom did not end with Locke in the seventeenth century. Although the eighteenth-century Enlightenment deified knowledge, the sciences, the arts, progress, and civilization, the French philosopher Jean Jacques Rousseau believed the sciences and the arts were the fruits of indolence and luxury and a source of moral decay. Rousseau boldly asserted that man was, by nature, good and innocent. Therefore, morality was not the product of reasoned thinking but of natural feeling. He further stated that since the origin of virtues and vices are to be found in social and political institutions, the only path for the improvement of society lies in the bettering of society.[23]

The concept of the "noble savage" was more of a hypothesis than a reality for Rousseau. His portrayals of people in the original state of nature stemmed from accounts of aboriginal tribes around the world. Essentially, the "noble savage" is a social and political fiction that enables readers to understand a universal aspect of human nature. Rousseau sought to isolate the essence and instinctive nature of man by departing from human nature as it is reflected in civilized societies, and by eliminating the influence of education and social intercourse. He held that beneath the intellectual activity—science, art, and other artificialities of civilization—there is a feeling that binds people to a common purpose.[24]

Rousseau's "return to nature" was not a naive plea to go back to nature and the simple life, but an attempt to reawaken, within the framework of a society, the necessary sentiments and feelings that nurture social justice and equality. Rousseau wanted to humanize governments and institutions in order to form a just and democratic society.[25] Moreover, he believed that "nothing is more gentle than man in his primitive state" at equal distance from the brutes and the "fatal ingenuity of civilized man." In analyzing the primitive state, Rousseau recalled Locke's axiom that there "can be no injury, where there is no property."[26] Rousseau differs from Locke in that he substitutes direct government for representative government. If all men are created free and equal, he reasons, with the same natural rights and capacities, then there is no rationale for rule or inheritance by the privileged classes. It is noteworthy that through his philosophical inquiries, Rousseau abstracted a system of government that the Iroquois had developed through strife and grief, and finally through the Great Tree of Peace. Because of this experience, the Iroquois had recognized the importance of feelings in the Condolence Ceremony and in diplomacy.

Education is the key to the creation of a more natural society. Education is a largely negative process, according to Rousseau, and it consists primarily of removing unfavorable conditions so that the child can learn to distinguish between good and evil.[27] In the final analysis, the tools for improving people are the social environment and education.

To Voltaire, North American Indians typified freedom. Borrowing from Gabriel Sagard's work, Voltaire wrote a critique of French autocracy and hypocrisy through the eyes of a Huron. Indeed, the Huron told his French companions in Voltaire's *The Huron, or Pupil of Nature* that he "was born free as the air."[28]

English observers on the eve of the American Revolution declared repeatedly that the Iroquois and other American Indians were free and scoffed at coercive authority. The famous frontier soldier Robert Rogers stated to a London audience that among American Indians "every man is free [and that no one] has any right to deprive him of his freedom."[29] David Jones, another observer, wrote in 1772 to 1773 that American Indians believed that "God made them free—that no man has the natural right to rule over another."[30] And commenting on the Iroquois during the revolutionary era, the English explorer John Long noted that "[t]he Iroquois laugh when you talk to them about obedience to kings [because] they cannot reconcile the idea of submission with the dignity of man."[31]

Essentially, the liberal ideas of the seventeenth- and eighteenth-century European philosophers were a partial reflection of Native American democratic principles. The Iroquois Constitution was a functioning political instrument in an established society rather than an abstract theory in a philosophical inquiry. However, the obsession with private property and land, especially on the part of Locke, proved to be a major point of disagreement and friction between the two societies.

Indian Governance

The People of the Longhouse (Iroquois) consisted of Five Nations (Mohawk, Oneida, Onondaga, Cayuga, and Seneca) at the time of European contact. In the early eighteenth century, a sixth brother from the south, the Tuscarora, joined the Iroquois Confederacy as they fled from Indian slave raiding in the Carolinas. The Iroquois Confederacy was a kinship state, the Iroquois being bound together by a clan and chieftain system that was buttressed by a similar linguistic base.

Through the "hearth" that consisted of a mother and her children, women played a profound role in Iroquois political life. Each "hearth" was part of a wider group called an "otiianer," and two or more otiianers constituted a clan. Such a matrilineal system was headed by a "clan mother." All the sons and daughters of a particular clan were related through uterine families that lived far apart. In this system, a husband went to live with his wife's family, and their children became members of the mother's clan by right of birth.[32] Through matrilineal descent the Iroquois formed cohesive political groups that had little to do with where people lived or from what village the hearths originated.

All authority sprang from the various clans that comprised a nation. The women who headed these clans appointed the male delegates and deputies who spoke for the clans at tribal meetings. And after consultation within the clan, issues and questions were formulated and subsequently debated in council.[33] Iroquois political philosophy was rooted in the concept that all life is unified spiritually with the natural environment and forces. Furthermore, the Iroquois believed that the spiritual power of one person is limited, but when combined with other individuals in a hearth, otiianer, or clan, spiritual power is enhanced. Whenever a person died either by natural causes or force, through murder or war, the "public power" was diminished. Consequently, to maintain the strength of the group, the dead were replaced either by newborn children or by adopting captives of war.[34] This practice of keeping clans at full strength through natural increase or adoption ensured the power and durability of the matrilineal system as well as the kinship state.

Iroquois political philosophy was transmitted through the social education of the young. The ideal Iroquois personality exhibited tribal loyalty tempered with intellectual independence and autonomy. Iroquois people were trained to enter a society that was egalitarian, with power more equally distributed between male and female, young and old than in Euro-American society. European society emphasized dominance and command structures, while Iroquois society was interested in collaborative behavior. And since Iroquois society prized competence as a hunter/provider more than material wealth, Iroquois children were trained to think for themselves and yet provide for others. The Iroquois did not respect submissive behavior.[35]

With this approach to authority, Iroquois society had none of the elaborate mechanisms to control and direct the lives of the citizenry. Instead of formal instruments of authority, the Iroquois governed behavior by instilling a sense of pride and connectedness to the group through common rituals. Ostracism and shame were the punishments for transgressions until a person had atoned for his actions and demonstrated that he had undergone a purification process. To sanctify and buttress their society, the Great Law of Peace outlined functions of tribal councils within the Iroquois Nations. The origins of the League of the Iroquois arose out of the desire to resolve the problem of blood feuds.

Before the founding of the League, revenge caused much strife. Once a clan was reduced by murder or kidnapping, relatives were bound by clan law to avenge the abduction or death of their relative, resulting in endless recriminations among clans. And as long as justice and the monopoly on violence resided in the clans, there was no hope of peace and goodwill.

Visionaries among the Iroquois such as Hiawatha, who was living among the Onondagas, tried to call councils to eliminate the blood feuds, but they were always thwarted by the evil and twisted wizard Tadodaho, an Onondaga who used magic and spies to rule by fear and intimidation. After failing to defeat Tadodaho, Hiawatha joined forces with another visionary, Deganawidah, and the two traveled to Mohawk, Oneida, and Cayuga villages with a message of peace and brotherhood. Everywhere they went, their powerful message of peace was accepted with the proviso that they persuade the formidable Tadodaho and the Onondagas to embrace the covenant of peace. Deganawidah then had a vision that gave Hiawatha's oratory increased substance,[36] and through that vision the Constitution of the Iroquois was formulated.

In his vision, Deganawidah saw a giant evergreen (white pine) reaching to the sky and gaining strength from three counterbalancing principles of life. The first principle was that a stable mind and healthy body should be in balance so that peace between individuals and groups could occur. Second, Deganawidah stated that humane conduct, thought, and speech were a requirement for equity and justice among peoples. Finally, he foresaw a society in which physical strength and civil authority would reinforce the power of the clan system.

Deganawidah's tree had four white roots that stretched to the four directions of the earth. From the base of the tree a snow-white carpet of thistle down covered the surrounding countryside, and this white carpet protected the peoples that embraced the three double principles. On top of the giant pine, an eagle was perched. Deganawidah explained that the tree was humanity, living within the principles governing relations among human beings. And the eagle was humanity's lookout against enemies who would disturb the peace. Deganawidah postulated that the white carpet could be spread to the four corners of the earth to provide a shelter of peace and brotherhood for all mankind. His vision was a message from the creator to bring harmony into human existence and unite all peoples into a single *family* guided by his three dual principles.[37]

With such a powerful vision, Deganawidah and Hiawatha were able to subdue the evil Tadodaho and transform his mind. Deganawidah removed evil feelings and thoughts from the head of Tadodaho and said, "[T]hou shalt strive . . . to make reason and the peaceful mind prevail."[38] Consequently, the evil wizard was reborn, becoming a humane person charged with implementing the message of Deganawidah.

After Tadodaho had submitted to the redemption, the Onondagas became the central fire of the Haudenosaunee and the "firekeepers" of the new Confederacy. And to this day, the Great Council Fire of the Confederacy is kept in the land of the Onondagas.[39]

After Tadodaho's conversion, the clan leaders of the Five Nations (Mohawk, Oneida, Onondaga, Cayuga, and Seneca) gathered around their council fires to fashion the laws and government of the Confederacy. The fundamental laws of the Iroquois Confederacy espoused peace and brotherhood, unity, balance of power, the natural rights of all people, impeachment and removal, and the sharing of resources. Moreover, blood feuds were outlawed and replaced by the Condolence Ceremony.

Under the new law, when a murder was committed, the grieving family could not exact clan revenge by taking the life of the murderer or a member of the murderer's clan. Instead, the bereaved family was required to accept twenty strings of wampum (freshwater shells strung together) from the slayer's family (ten for the dead person and ten for the life of the murderer himself). If a woman was killed, the price was thirty wampum strings.[40] Through this ceremony, the monopoly on legally sanctioned violence was transferred from the clan to the League/ state.

Deganawidah gave strict instructions concerning the conduct of the League and its deliberations. Tadodaho was to maintain the fire and call the Onondaga chiefs together to determine if an issue brought to him was pressing enough to call to the attention of the council of the Confederacy. If the issue proposed merited consideration, the council would assemble and Tadodaho would kindle a fire and announce the purpose of the meeting. The rising smoke penetrating the sky was a signal to the Iroquois allies that the council was in session, and the Onondaga chiefs and Tadodaho were charged with keeping the council area free from distractions. Historically, the procedure for debating policies of the Confederacy began with the Mohawks (the Mohawks, Senecas, and Onondagas are called the elder brothers). After being debated by the Keepers of the Eastern Door (Mohawks) and the Keepers of the Western Door (Senecas), the question was then addressed to the Oneida and Cayuga statesmen (considered the younger brothers) for discussion in much the same manner.

Once consensus was achieved among the Oneidas and the Cayugas, the issue was then further discussed among the Senecas and Mohawks until a consensus was reached. Next, the question was laid before the two separate bodies of the Onondagas for their decision.

At this stage, the Onondagas had a power similar to judicial review in that they could raise objections to the proposed measure if it was believed inconsistent with the Great Law of Peace. Essentially, the legislature could rewrite the proposed law on the spot so that it would be in accord with the Constitution of the Iroquois.

When the two Onondaga bodies reached a consensus, Tadodaho gave the decision to Honowireton (an Onondaga chief who presided over debates between the delegation) to confirm the decision if it was unanimously agreed upon by all of the Onondaga sachems (chiefs). Finally, Honowireton or Tadodaho gave the decision of the Onondagas to the Mohawks and the Senecas so that the policy could be announced to the Grand Council as its will.[41]

This process reflects the emphasis of the League on *checks and balances*, public debate, and consensus. The overall intent of such a parliamentary procedure is to encourage unity at each step. This legislative process is similar to the mechanisms of the Albany Plan of Union, the Articles of Confederation, and the United States Constitution. The rights of the Iroquois citizenry are protected by portions of the Great Law of Peace. Section 93 states that:

> *Whenever an especially important matter . . . is presented before the League Council . . . threatening their utter ruin, then the chiefs of the League must submit the matter to the decision of their people. . . .*[42]

The people of the League can also initiate impeachment proceedings, treason charges, and alert the council to public opinion on a specific matter. They also have the power to remove sachems of the League's council.[43]

Upon the death or removal of a Confederacy chief, the title reverts to the women of his clan. The women then have the power to determine who will assume the title, just as they have the power to decide if a chief should be removed. The process is the following: The esteemed women of a clan gather together when a title is vacant and nominate a male member to be chief. Next, the men of the clan give their approval, and the nomination is then forwarded to the council, where the new chief is installed.[44]

Public opinion is of great importance within the League of the Iroquois. Iroquois people can have a direct say in the formulation of government policy even if the sachems choose to ignore the will of the people. And the Great Law of Peace declares that the people can propose their own laws even when leaders fail to do so. It states:

> *If the conditions . . . arise . . . to . . . change . . . this law, the case shall be . . . considered, and if the new beam seems . . . beneficial, the . . . change . . . if adopted, shall be called, "Added to the Rafters."*[45]

If the council does not act on the will of the people, then it faces removal under earlier provisions detailed.

Through public opinion and debate, the Great Law of Peace gave the Iroquois people basic rights within a distinctive and representative governmental framework. The Great Law of Peace solved disputes by giving all parties an equal hearing with the Grand Council, which often functioned like a think tank. For the Iroquois, the more thinkers that were beneath the Great Tree the better, a process in marked contrast to European political and educational traditions.

The League of the Iroquois had a constitution with a fixed corpus of laws dealing with mutual defense. Since the Iroquois were not inclined to give much power to authorities, unity, peace, and brotherhood were balanced against the natural rights of all people and the necessity of sharing resources equitably. Unity for mutual defense was an abiding concept within the League. The oral tradition of the Great Law of Peace uses the imagery of a bundle of five arrows tied together to symbolize the complete union of the nations and the unbroken strength that such a unity imparts.[46]

The Iroquois also had built-in checks and balances. The notion of federalism was strictly adhered to by the Iroquois; the hereditary peace chiefs were interested only in external matters like war, peace, and treaty-making; the Grand Council could not interfere with the internal affairs of the tribe; and each tribe had its own sachems, although they were limited in that they could only deal with their tribe's relations with other tribes, and had no say in matters that were traditionally the concern of the clan.[47]

Many non-Indian people compared the Confederacy to ancient Greek and Roman states, or they viewed it as a by-product of "free" wilderness living. Americans like Benjamin Franklin and James Wilson were fascinated by its strength. The Albany Plan of Union was modeled after the Iroquois Constitution, and the Articles of Confederation reflected the importance of League principles in that, they were, in part, derived from the Albany Plan of Union. Indeed, the United States Constitution owes much of its emphasis on unity, federalism, and balance of power to Iroquois concepts.

In short, Iroquois power rested upon the consent of the governed, and was not coercive in areas of military service, taxation, and police powers. To the colonial American chafing under British authority, such a government and attitude towards freedom were powerful ideals that could be used in resisting British sovereignty and tyranny.[48]

The Roots of American Government

While during the seventeenth century there was considerable academic interest in the native democracies of North America because of thinkers such as John Locke, the eighteenth century was a time when direct experience and interaction with Indian thinkers became common on both sides of the Atlantic. The eighteenth century was a period of struggle between the empires of France and England, and the Iroquois played a crucial role in this struggle.

During King George's War (1740 to 1748), the colonists needed Iroquois support against the French. In 1742, Pennsylvania officials met with Iroquois sachems in the council at Lancaster to secure Iroquois friendship in the war. Canassateego, an Iroquois sachem, spoke on behalf of the Six Nations to the Pennsylvania officials, confirming the "league of friendship" that existed between the two parties and stating that "we are bound by the strictest leagues to watch for each other's preservation."[49]

Two years later, Canassateego would go beyond pledging friendship to the English colonist. At Lancaster, Pennsylvania, in 1744, the great Iroquois chief advised the assembled colonial governors on Iroquois concepts of unity:

> *Our wise forefathers established Union and Amity between the Five Nations. This has made us formidable; this has given us great Weight and Authority with our neighboring Nations. We are a powerful Confederacy; and by your observing the same methods, our wise forefathers have taken, you will acquire such Strength and power. Therefore whatever befalls you, never fall out with one another.*[50]

This admonition would echo throughout the colonies for over a generation, and it would be used not only as a rallying cry against French colonialism but also against British tyranny. In 1747, the royal governor, George Clinton of New York, observed that most American democratic leaders "were ignorant, illiterate people of republican principle who have no knowledge of the English Constitution or love for their country." Clearly, these unread Americans were gaining a new identity and a sense of freedom from the American environment and its native peoples long before the outbreak of the American Revolution.[51]

A major figure in this intellectual transference is Tiyanoga or Hendrick. For over fifty years, Hendrick was a man who knew both Iroquois and English cultures well. Hendrick converted to Christianity and became a Mohawk preacher about 1700.[52] As he gained prominence around Albany, New York, Hendrick became increasingly interested in English life and manners. In 1710, he became famous as one of the four "kings" that were received at the court of Queen Anne. He was painted by John Verelst and called the "emperor of the Five Nations."[53]

The quiet dignity of the four Iroquois men was in marked contrast to the demeanor of London of 1710 with its bullbaiting, dog fights, and public hangings. The sachems were said to be poised and to "have an exquisite Sense and a quick Apprehension."[54] This trip was an enlightening experience for Hendrick, who observed that one of the tragedies of English society was the poverty of some members of the society amidst the abundance of the time. Upon his return, he became a man of "spirit and striking force" in colonial affairs.[55] Although Hendrick was controversial, he saved the New York frontier and probably New England from the French in the initial stages of the Seven Years' War (French and Indian). He was mortally wounded at the Battle of Lake George in 1755, where Sir William Johnson defeated Baron Dieskau. However, through his courage and sacrifice he had set the stage for the subsequent defeat of the French by the British in North America. A year before his death, Hendrick had attended the conference at Albany that framed the Articles of Union of 1754.[56] For both military and philosophical reasons, Hendrick should be considered one of the Founding Fathers of the United States.

Hendrick, his adopted brother Abraham, and Canassateego played important roles in teaching the colonists the fundamentals of Iroquois unity. A decade after Canassateego's admonition of unity, the English colonies met in Albany, New York, to face the French threat once again. With George Washington's defeat at Fort Necessity in Pennsylvania, English prestige in North America was shattered, and the storm clouds of the Seven Years' War began to form on the horizon. French expansion into the Ohio country had to be thwarted.

Under the sponsorship of the British Crown, colonial delegates assembled at Albany in the summer of 1754 to negotiate a peace with all the Indian tribes (especially the Iroquois) and to win them over in the impending war with France.[57]

Even before the Albany Conference, Benjamin Franklin had been musing over the words of Canassateego.[58] Using Iroquois examples of unity, Franklin sought to shame the reluctant colonists into some form of union in 1751 when he addressed them in curiously paradoxical language; evidence shows that Franklin had a healthy respect for the Iroquois:

> It would be a strange thing . . . if Six Nations of Ignorant savages should be capable of forming such a union and be able to execute it in such a manner that it has subsisted for ages and appears indissoluble, and yet that a like union should be impractical for ten or a dozen English colonies, to whom it is more necessary and must be more advantageous, and who cannot be supposed to want an equal understanding of their interest.[59]

On 9 May 1753, Franklin wrote a long letter to a friend (Peter Collinson) detailing the manners and customs of American Indians and how they appealed to colonial Americans. Franklin wrote that Indian children brought up in colonial society readily returned to their people when they made but "one Indian ramble with them. . . ." However, Franklin observed that

> when white persons of either sex have been taken prisoners young by Indians, and lived a while among them, tho' ransomed by their friends . . . [they] take the first good opportunity of escaping again into the woods, from whence there is no reclaiming them.[60]

Franklin also wrote of "the Great Council" at "Onondago" in this letter and how the Six Nations educated their men in "what was the best manner."[61]

In October of 1753, Franklin attended a treaty at Carlisle, Pennsylvania. At this treaty with the Iroquois and Ohio Indians (Twightees, Delawares, Shawnees, and Wyandots), Franklin absorbed the rich imagery and ideas of the Six Nations at close range. On 1 October 1753, he watched the Oneida chief Scarrooyady and a Mohawk, Cayanguileguoa, console the Ohio Indians for their losses against the French. Franklin listened while Scarrooyady recounted the origins of the Great Law of Peace to the Ohio Indians:

> We must let you know, that there was a friendship established by our and your Grandfathers, and a mutual Council fire was kindled. In this friendship all those then under the ground, who had not yet obtained eyes or faces [that is, those unborn] were included; and it was then mutually promised to tell the same to their children and children's children.[62]

Having consoled the Ohio Indians, Scarrooyady exhorted the assembled Indians to "preserve this Union and Friendship, which has so long and happy continued among us. Let us keep the chain from rusting. . . ."[63]

The next day, the Pennsylvania commissioners, including Franklin, presented a wampum belt that portrayed the union between the Iroquois and Pennsylvania. A speech delivered by a spokesman for the commissioners echoed the words of Canassateego spoken a decade earlier at Lancaster and recalled the need for unity and a strong defense:

> [C]ast your eyes towards this belt, whereon six figures are . . . holding one another by the hands. This is a just resemblance of our present union. The first five figures representing the Five Nations [and] the sixth . . . the government of Pennsylvania, with whom you are linked in a close and firm union. In whatever part of the belt is broke, all the wampum runs off, and renders the whole of no strength or consistency. In like manner, should you break faith with one another, or with this government, the union is dissolved. We would therefore hereby place before you the necessity of preserving your

faith entire to one another, as well as to this government. Do not separate; do not part of any score. Let no differences or jealousies subsist a moment between Nation and Nation, but join together as one man. . . .[64]

This speech reflects the knowledge that Franklin and others had of the League of the Iroquois. Scarrooyady took for granted the knowledge that the Pennsylvanians had of the workings of the Great Law of Peace when he requested that

you will please to lay all our present transactions before the council at Onondago, that they may know we do nothing in the dark.[65]

Upon his return to Philadelphia, Franklin wrote to the distinguished Iroquois scholar of the age, Cadwallader Colden, that he had journeyed "to meet and hold a treaty with the Ohio Indians." Franklin promised Colden a copy of the treaty and stated he had left a copy of Colden's book, *History of the Five Indian Nations*, with a friend in Boston.[66] Franklin was now clearly steeped in Iroquois ideas.

On the eve of the Albany Conference, Franklin was already persuaded that Canassateego's words were good council, and he was not alone in these sentiments. James DeLancey, acting governor of New York, sent a special invitation to Hendrick to attend the Albany Conference so that the aging Mohawk sachem could provide insights into the structure of the League of the Iroquois for the assembled colonial delegates. On 29 June 1754, James DeLancey and Hendrick met. Hendrick advised DeLancey that the colonists should strengthen themselves and "bring as many into this Covenant Chain as you possibly can."[67]

Franklin met with both colonial and Iroquois delegates (particularly Hendrick and his brother Abraham) to construct a plan that Franklin acknowledged to be similar to the tenets of the Iroquois Confederacy. Hendrick was openly critical of the British at the Albany Conference but hinted that the Iroquois would not ally with the English colonies unless a suitable form of unity was established among them. In talking of the proposed union of the colonies and the Six Nations on 9 July 1754, Hendrick stated: "We wish this fire [tree] of Friendship may grow up to a great height, and then we shall be a powerful people."[68] In reply to Hendrick's speech, Acting Governor of New York James DeLancey said, "I hope that by this present Union, we shall grow up to a great height and be as powerful and famous as you were of old."[69] The next day, 10 July 1754, Franklin formally proposed his Plan of Union before the Congress.[70] Franklin wrote that the debates on the Albany Plan "went on daily, hand in hand with the Indian business."[71]

The Albany Plan of Union called for a "general Government . . . under which Government each colony may retain its present Constitution."[72] Basically, the plan provided that Parliament was to establish a general government in America, including all the thirteen colonies, each of which was to retain its present constitution except for certain powers (mainly mutual defense) that were to be given to the general government.

The king was to appoint a president-general for the government. Each colonial assembly would elect representatives to a grand council. And the president-general, with the advice of the grand council, would have certain powers, such as handling Indian relations, making treaties, deciding upon peace or war, maintaining troops, building forts, providing warships, and making such laws and levying such taxes as would be needed for its purposes.[73] Through this plan colonial leaders embraced a blueprint for union that Indian leaders like Canassateego and Hendrick had urged upon them for a decade or more. Thus, it can be seen that the roots of intercolonial unity are in the Indian-white relations of the early eighteenth century.

During this time, men such as Benjamin Franklin saw in the Iroquois Confederacy a model to build upon. Even before the Albany Plan of Union, Franklin's knowledge of the Iroquois Confederacy appears in his letters to Cadwallader Colden. In 1747, Franklin had requested and received copies of Colden's *History of the Five Indian Nations*, and on 27 January 1748, Franklin mentioned to Colden in a letter that he had read the *History of the Five Indian Nations*, and thought "that 'tis a well wrote, entertaining and instructive Piece," and must "be exceedingly useful to all those Colonies who have anything" to do with Indian Affairs.[74] Five years later (25 October 1753), in a letter to Colden, Franklin noted that he had seen extracts of Colden's book "in all the magazines. . . ."[75] Shortly after attending the Albany meeting of 1754, Franklin stopped to see Colden and thank him for the notes that he had sent to him while at Albany. Undoubtedly, Franklin was strongly influenced by Native American ideas, and this was reflected in his correspondence at the time.

With these facts in mind, Henry Steele Commager's remark in *Documents of American History* that preface the Articles of Confederation take on significant meaning. Commager states that the Articles of Confederation "should be studied in comparison with the Albany Plan of Union and the Constitution."[76] The interrelatedness of the three instruments of government is significant in understanding the path to union. According to Clinton Rossiter, "The Albany Plan is a landmark on the rough road that was to lead through the first Continental Congresses and the Articles of Confederation to the Constitution of 1787."[77]

The missing component in this analysis is the role of Iroquois political theory and its influence on the formation of American notions of government. Julian P. Boyd admitted a generation ago that Franklin "proposed a plan for the union of the colonies, and he found his materials in the great Confederacy of the Iroquois."[78]

In looking at Franklin's perceptions and his application of Indian thought and behavior, Boyd (editor of the papers of Thomas Jefferson) observed that Franklin left no great legacy of thought on American Indians as Rousseau had. Indeed, Rousseau examined the ways of American Indians and developed a school of romantic political thought that caused worldwide upheaval. However, according to Boyd, Franklin used analogies about Indians whenever they suited his purposes.

Franklin's bagatelle (written during the American Revolution), *Remarques su la politesse des sauvages de l'Amerique Septentrionale,* was less an examination of Indian manners than it was a commentary on civilized society that Franklin found artificial and weak. In the beginning of the bagatelle, Franklin stated:

> *Savages we call them because their manners differ from ours, which we think the perfection of civility: they think the same of theirs. The Indian men, when young, are hunters and warriors; when old, counsellors; for all their government is by counsel of the sages; there is no force, there are no prisons, no officers to compel obedience or inflict punishment.*[79]

Franklin knew that such a comparison of European and American Indian ways was exactly the kind of analysis that the romantic thinkers, recently influenced by the works of Rousseau, would want to hear.

In examining Franklin's interest in Indians, the modern reader must realize that Indians played an extremely important and central role in American history until the 1830s. American Indians had a marked impact on almost every phase of English colonial life. Tribes and confederacies such as the Iroquois often held the balance of power between the French and the British in North America. Which European nation would dominate North America was often in the hands of the Iroquois during the eighteenth century.

Indian peoples were not a subdued people. They lived in their own villages and strongholds beyond the white frontier. Their political importance as allies, counselors, and adversaries cannot be overestimated. Indeed, the process of treaty-making and protocol was often dictated by Iroquois norms.

In addition, the economic significance of native groups cannot be underestimated. New immigrants coming to the eastern seaboard of North America to settle in the fledgling cities or the frontier farms were affected by Indian power along the frontier, since Indians inhibited unbridled westward movement. Also, the fur trade was a vital part of the economy for such places as Albany and Philadelphia. In fact, the whole commercial structure of the colonial economy was dependent on Indian supply of fur to traders. And Franklin knew that Indians could subvert this commercial structure by simply refusing to trap and hunt. Hence, Indians were a factor that influenced the nature of the economy, from the wages of a Philadelphia counting-house clerk to decisions on taxation and defense policy that the British foreign ministers had to make at Whitehall in England.[80]

In fact, Native Americans influenced colonial life profoundly and far out of proportion to their relative numbers in eastern North America. The careers of colonial governors depended on their facility in handling Indians and the fur trade.

In the area of political thought, Native Americans also had a greater influence over European society than any other non-Caucasian race. Gabriel Sagard, Marc Lescarbot, and the various scribes of the *Jesuit Relations* praised the personal freedoms and democratic governments of the northeastern tribes. From these narratives, it was easy for a political analyst such as Baron Lahontan to use the American Indian as a vessel to criticize the European system of autocracy and divine right monarchies. From such accounts, Montesquieu observed that "all countries have a law of nations," including the "Iroquois . . . for they send and receive ambassadors," and they "understand the rights of war and peace."[81]

To a pragmatist like Franklin, Native American unity through confederation was a political reality, since some fifteen thousand Iroquois people held sway over a territory from Canada to Virginia and as far west as the Ohio River Valley. As a noted colonial scholar has said, "Here indeed was an example worthy of copying."[82]

The Path to Union

> *I wish I were at perfect liberty to portray . . . the course of political changes in this province. It would give you a great idea of the spirit and resolution of the people, and shew you, in a striking point of view, the deep roots of American Independence in all the colonies. But it is not prudent, to commit to writing such free speculations, in the present state of things.*
>
> *Time which takes away the veil, may lay open the secret springs of this surprising revolution. . . .*[83]
>
> John Adams to Abigail Adams, 10 July 1776

After the Albany Plan of Union, the road to revolution was long and ambiguous. Colonial Americans were growing restive under British authority. With the defeat and removal of the French from North America in 1763, the British sought to assert more authority in English North America through various revenue measures (the Sugar Act, 1764; the Stamp Act, 1765; the Townshend Taxes, 1767; and the Tea Act, 1770). From the English viewpoint, these measures were simply taxes on North Americans to pay for the cost of colonial government and defense. However, the colonists wanted no part of this taxation without some corresponding form of representation.

Colonists formed the Sons of Liberty and called a Stamp Act Congress that met in New York City in the fall of 1765 (the second attempt at colonial unity). By the spring of 1766, the Sons of Liberty had an office in New York and kept "minutes and [sent] their correspondence . . . throughout the different Provinces."[84] As the unrest grew and the British began to reinforce the troops in New York City, British intelligence accounts stated that the New York Sons of Liberty had sent "Belts of Wampum to the 6 Nations to intercept his Majesty's troops on their march" to New York City.[85] After corresponding with the Iroquois, the Sons of Liberty in New York City erected a "pine post . . . called . . . the Tree of Liberty," where they conducted their daily exercises.[86] As they had done at Albany in 1754, the colonists were once more consulting with the Iroquois about unity and military aid. According to his biographer, John Rutledge of South Carolina at the age of twenty-six was exposed to Iroquois political theory while he was attending the Stamp Act Congress in the fall of 1765. At the Constitutional Convention, Rutledge would recall his experience with the Iroquois.[87] In the eyes of the rebellious American colonists, the Iroquois symbolized autonomy and a new American identity. And these ideas and symbols of the Iroquois would become more pervasive as the revolution approached.

The burning of the British ship *Gaspee* in June of 1772 demonstrated the pervasiveness of Indian symbolism present in the American people. The *Gaspee* was a ship commanded by an unpopular captain who avidly pursued smugglers off the coast of New England, and on 9 June 1772, the ship ran aground near Providence, Rhode Island. Although the Stamp Act had been repealed, a group of local men and boys responded to the call of a drum that evening in Providence. After some discussion, they allegedly dressed up as American Indians and rowed out to the British ship and burned it as a protest to British authority. Dressing as Indians became a way to assert a new identity that was emerging as the colonists became more restive under British rule.[88]

After the burning of the *Gaspee*, committees of correspondence were created in most of the colonies by 1773. The purpose of the committees was to promote unity.[89] An article in a Rhode Island newspaper summed up the importance of unity among the colonists in 1773:

> The union of the colonies which is now taking place is big with the most important advantage to this continent. From this union will result our security from all foreign enemies; for none will dare to invade us against the combined force of these colonies, nor will a British Parliament dare to attack our liberties, when we are united to defend them. . . . In this union every colony will feel the strength of the whole; for if one is invaded all will unite their wisdom and power in her defence. In this way the weakest will become strong, and America will soon be the glory of the world, and the terror of the wicked oppressors among nations.[90]

In the spring of 1773, the British Parliament sought to shore up the insolvent East India Tea Company by authorizing the tea company to "dump" its surplus tea in the colonies. Still chafing under the tea tax, colonists saw the East India Act as a thinly disguised attempt to bribe them out of their freedoms with inexpensive tea.

In November of 1773, New Yorkers were warned by "Mohawks" that anyone aiding or abetting the landing or storage of tea in New York City would be paid an "unwelcome visit, in which they shall be treated as they deserve." Subsequently, a petition was circulated to reinstitute "The Association of the Sons of Liberty."[91]

A week before the Boston Tea Party, a "Ranger" wrote in a Boston newspaper that it would be best to let the British land with the tea so that Americans could bush fight the British and "cut off their officers . . . with very little loss" in the same way that the "Indians" had ambushed General Braddock in the French and Indian war.[92]

After reading about the "Mohawks" in New York City, on 13 December 1773, a group of Bostonians dressed as Mohawks dumped the hated tea into Boston Harbor. And several other "tea parties" were held along the eastern seaboard.

The Bostonians chose to dress as Mohawks because the Iroquois and other American Indians were increasingly being used as symbols of American liberty. From 1774 to 1775, Paul Revere did a series of engravings for the *Royal American Magazine* that portrayed Americans as Indians being oppressed by British authority. He also did an engraving showing an American Indian figure offering a pipe to the genius of knowledge (a European symbol) to demonstrate that the American people (Indian and Euro-American) had a great deal to teach the Old World. In essence, the American Indian, as a symbol of liberty and things distinctly American, was commonplace.[93]

While still in England, Franklin sponsored Thomas Paine's visit to America in 1774. Franklin's knowledge of the Iroquois led him to see the potential within Paine to articulate effectively the natural rights philosophy of the eighteenth century to an American audience that was deeply familiar with Native American images. Paine later served as a secretary to an Iroquois treaty in 1777 in Easton, Pennsylvania, and he talked of the experience for years.[94]

Paine's ideas are a good example of the transference of New World ideas to the Old World. His *Common Sense* illustrated how imbued Americans were with the "self-evident" truths of natural rights. Paine's examples of free government in a natural state exemplified the need for religious freedom in America; and in *Common Sense* he captured the essence of the American spirit by writing that civil and religious liberties stemmed from governments in a natural state. In discussing the origins of American government, Paine felt that a "convenient tree will afford . . . a State House, under which [the colonists] may assemble to deliberate on public matters." Paine believed that in the "first parliament every man by natural right will have a seat."[95]

Upon Franklin's return from England in 1775, he proposed that another League symbol, "the pine tree flag," be one of the first flags of the United States.[96] Similarly, James Wilson used Iroquois chain imagery in early 1775 when he stated that a "chain of freedom has been formed . . . to preserve the greatest of human blessings . . . liberty."[97]

On 21 July 1775, Franklin also introduced his draft of the Articles of Confederation that was obviously a revision of his earlier Albany Plan of Union. However, it was set aside until the next year.[98]

The most dramatic example of the influence of Iroquois political theories on Americans occurred in the summer of 1775, however. At German Flats, New York, on August 15 of that year, treaty commissioners from the Continental Congress met with the sachems and warriors of the Six Nations to acquaint the Iroquois with the "United Colonies dwelling upon this Island."[99] Following some preliminaries, the sachems and treaty commissioners decided to meet on 24 August 1775 at Cartwright's Tavern in Albany, New York. According to protocol, the commissioners asked the sachems to appoint a speaker, but the sachems deferred to the commissioners so the Americans picked Abraham, a Mohawk, adopted brother and successor to Hendrick.[100]

On the next day, the treaty commissioners, who had specific instructions from John Hancock and the Second Continental Congress, told the sachems that they were heeding the advice Iroquois forefathers had given to the colonial Americans at Lancaster, Pennsylvania, in 1744. At this point, the commissioners quoted Canassateego's words:

> Brethren, We the Six Nations heartily recommend Union and a good
> agreement between you our Brethren, never disagree but preserve a

strict Friendship for one another and thereby you as well as we will become stronger. Our Wise Forefathers established Union and Amity between the Five Nations . . . we are a powerful Confederacy, and if you observe the same methods . . . you will acquire fresh strength and power.[101]

After quoting Canassateego, the Americans said their forefathers rejoiced to hear his words and they sank

deep into their Hearts, the Advice was good, it was Kind. They said to one another, the Six Nations are a wise people, let us hearken to their Council and teach our children to follow it. Our old Men have done so. They have frequently taken a single Arrow and said, Children, see how easy it is broken, then they have tied twelve together with strong Cords—And our strongest Men could not break them—See said they—this is what the Six Nations mean. Divided a single Man may destroy you—United, you are a match for the whole World.[102]

The commissioners were not just engaging in diplomatic protocol with the Iroquois, but were illustrating a process of assimilating Iroquois ideas of unity.

The Americans continued and thanked the "great God that we are all united, that we have a strong Confederacy composed of twelve Provinces." The American delegates also pointed out that they had "lighted a Great Council Fire at Philadelphia and have sent Sixty five Counsellors to speak and act in the name of the whole. . . ."[103] On 26 August 1775, the commissioners stated: "We the Delegates from the twelve United provinces now sitting in Congress at Philadelphia send this talk to you." The Americans then proceeded to explain the source of their grievances with the British, and that the colonies were "necessitated to rise and forced to fight or give up our Civil Constitution. . . ." They went on to say, "We do not take up the Hatchet . . . for Honor and Conquest, but to maintain our Civil Constitution and religious privileges."[104]

After arguing for Iroquois neutrality, the commissioners asserted on 28 August 1775:

We live upon the same Ground with you—the same Island is our common Birthplace. We desire to sit down under the same Tree of Peace with you; let us water its roots, Cherish its growth, till the large leaves and flourishing Branches shall extend to the setting Sun and reach the Skies.[105]

During the deliberations on 28 August 1775, the Americans asked the Iroquois to be neutral and presented them with a white wampum belt. Next, the delegates to the Iroquois stated that when this

Island began to shake and tremble along the Eastern Shore, and the Sun darkened by a Black Cloud which arose from beyond the great water, we Kindled up a Great Council Fire at Philadelphia . . . so . . . that . . . we are now twelve Colonies united as one Man . . . and . . . as God has put it into our hearts to love the Six Nations and their allies we now make the chain of friendship so that nothing but an evil spirit can or will attempt to break it. But we hope thro' the Favor and Mercy of the good Spirit that it will remain strong and bright while the Sun shines and the Water runs.[106]

Following this statement, the Americans delivered a union belt to the Iroquois sachems.

After giving the chiefs a path belt, the pipe of peace, and six small strings, the treaty commissioners from the Second Continental Congress asked that

this our good talk remain at Onondago your Central Council House. That you may hand down to the latest posterity these Testimonials of the brotherly Sentiments of the twelve United Colonies towards their Brethren of the Six Nations and their Allies.[107]

Following several days of deliberation over what was said, the Iroquois sachems spoke to the commissioners on 31 August 1775. Abraham, the brother of Hendrick and a Mohawk sachem, was the speaker. In discussing Canassateego's speech, Abraham stated that a brother of Canassateego "is here present and remembers the Words of his Brother." Then Abraham reiterated that "your Grandfathers [have] inculcated the Doctrine into their Children," and noted the invitation to come down to the place where the Tree of Peace was planted and "sit under it and water its roots, till the Branches should flourish and reach to Heaven." He asserted that, "This the Six Nations say shall be done."[108] Abraham also agreed that the Iroquois should stay out of the "family quarrel" between the colonies and England, and stated that the Iroquois would hang up the belts at Onondaga that were presented at this meeting so that "future generations may call to mind the covenant now made between us." The Mohawk sachem also assured the Americans that "we shall send and inform all our neighbouring Council fires of the Matters now transacted."[109]

In addition, the Iroquois were concerned that the Americans maintain the council fire and the Great Tree of Peace properly. Abraham stated that there must be "some person appointed to watch it," and that the person that watches this "Council Fire is to be provided with a Wing, that he may brush off all Insects that come near it and keep it clean." Abraham instructed the Americans that this "is the Custom at our Central Council House, we have one appointed for that purpose."[110]

Obviously, this was an allusion to Tadodaho, the presiding officer of the Confederacy. (The Iroquois were quite concerned about the nature of the American presidency and demonstrated it during their visit to Congress in 1776.) By this time it was obvious that the Iroquois and the Americans were conscious of the similarities between the Iroquois Confederacy and the Continental Congress.

On 1 September 1775, the treaty commissioners answered the speech of Abraham by stating that they "return Thanks to the great Governor of the Universe that he has inclined your hearts to approve and accept of the brotherly Love offered to you. . . ." Furthermore, the Americans noted that it then "makes us happy to hear so wise and brave a people, as our Brothers of the Six Nations, publickly declare their [desire to] maintain and support peace and Friendship with the twelve united Colonies." The conference was subsequently concluded after an extended discussion of neutrality and land disputes. The Americans promised to refer the land dispute matters to "the Grand Congress at Philadelphia." Gifts were then distributed as the Iroquois prepared to go back to Onondaga.[111]

In the fall of 1775, the Continental Congress sent a delegation to speak with the Six Nations and the Western Nations (Shawnees, Wyandots, and others) at Fort Pitt in western Pennsylvania. As was the case at the conference at Albany, the Continental Congress insisted on including a member of the Continental Congress, and James Wilson became the delegate. The council at Fort Pitt mirrored the earlier conference at Albany. The Continental Congress was called "our Great United Council of Wise Men . . . at Philadelphia," and the Americans talked of transplanting "the Tree of Peace." Iroquois imagery was also quoted to explain the unity of the colonies. The Americans said that "the thirteen great colonies . . . are . . . United . . . by one lasting Chain of Friendship" and that they were not to be considered as "Distinct Nations, but as one great and strong man. . . ."[112] Offering peace and friendship to the assembled chiefs, the Americans stated that they desired to "bury in oblivion all that has past; and brighten the Chain of friendship. . . . "[113] Years later at the Constitutional Convention, James Wilson would recall these concepts in detail during the debates.[114]

The Albany and Fort Pitt conferences are notable since the imagery of the League was used repeatedly not only for the sake of diplomatic protocol when dealing with the Iroquois but also in the comparisons to the new "Grand Council" at Philadelphia. It is also noteworthy because it demonstrates that Iroquois instructions about unity as early as 1744 were remembered and heeded. The process of cultural transference of Iroquois political theory had now come full circle. Colonists were not only reading Locke and Rousseau but had also used the practical counsel of Iroquois sachems over several generations. Although it often goes undetected, Americans are indebted to Charles Thomson, secretary to the Congress (1774 to 1789) for an accurate record of the transference of Native American ideas to the Founding Fathers. As a young man, Thomson was adopted into the Delaware Nation in 1756. The Delawares called him "Wegh-wu-law-mo-end" or "the man who tells the truth." Thomson also wrote the appendix on American Indian customs and laws in Thomas Jefferson's *Notes on Virginia*, detailing the structure of the "Mingo" or Iroquois Confederacy and other American Indian customs.[115]

On 1 January 1776, Robert Treat Paine, a Massachusetts delegate to the Continental Congress, called it "the Grand Council Fire at Philadelphia" in a letter to a friend.[116] Such use of Iroquois imagery would become commonplace among many prominent Americans of the time.

On 24 January 1776, in Cambridge, Massachusetts, General George Washington, members of Washington's staff, and John Adams attended a dinner with several Caughnawaga Mohawk chiefs and their wives. During the dinner, Washington introduced Adams (one of the Massachusetts delegates to the Continental Congress) as one of the members "of the Grand Council Fire at Philadelphia," and Adams noted that the Caughnawagas were impressed with the introduction.[117]

Adams remarked that several of the Caughnawagas were part French and that one chief was English, being captured "in his infancy."[118] After the introduction, the chiefs came and shook hands with Adams. In writing to his wife, Adams stated that he was "much pleased with this day's entertainment."[119]

During this time, Adams became concerned about "constitutions for single colonies [and] a great model of Union for the whole." In April of 1776, Adams published a pamphlet entitled *Thoughts on Government*. And later Adams wrote about the "precise" separation of powers in American Indian nations on the eve of the creation of the Constitution.[120]

By February of 1776, Benjamin Franklin had designed fractional continental currency utilizing the imagery of Iroquois unity. The new one third of a dollar had an emblem of the thirteen colonies interlocked in a continuous chain of unity. The motto stated: "American Congress, We are one." This was a deliberate attempt by Franklin to invoke the Iroquois Covenant Chain imagery on the new American money. The same design would reappear on American coinage in 1787. And it is significant that the grand sachem of the Tammany Society wore a silver chain with thirteen links throughout the period immediately after the revolution.[121]

During this time two schools of political thought emerged in the Continental Congress about the nature of American government. While both schools agreed that the British should be defeated and expelled, there was no agreement as to what governmental system should be devised to replace the old order. Some members maintained that the legislative and executive powers assumed by Congress should be preserved without change. Other members believed that the unwieldy standing committee system should be modified so that an executive department outside of Congress could efficiently implement the resolutions of the legislative body.

In early 1776, Joseph Galloway, an ally of Franklin, suggested a plan of colonial union to restore harmony with England. Galloway's proposal was very similar to the Albany Plan of Union that Franklin had proposed in 1754. Those who supported Galloway's "olive branch" stalled on the issue of independence in the Second Continental Congress. The supporters of the Galloway Plan feared a lapse in governmental authority and wanted a plan for American union before imperial authority was forsaken. To allay such fears, Richard Henry Lee's independence resolution of 7 June 1776 included a clause that proposed a plan of confederation that would be transmitted to the colonies for debate.[122] During this time Indians were so plentiful in Philadelphia that Congress appointed a committee (headed by Roger Sherman) to "inquire into the cause that brings so many Indians . . . at present to Philadelphia."[123]

In the midst of this debate twenty-one Iroquois Indians met with the Continental Congress in May and June of 1776. For over a month, the Iroquois would observe the operations of the Continental Congress and its president, John Hancock.

On 27 May 1776, Richard Henry Lee reported that the American Army had a parade of two to three thousand men to impress the Iroquois with the strength of the United States. "Four tribes of the Six Nations" viewed the parade, and Lee hoped "to secure the friendship of these people." Newspaper accounts stated that generals Washington, Gates, and Mifflin, "the members of Congress . . . and . . . the Indians . . . on business with the Congress" reviewed the troops.[124]

On 11 June 1776, while independence was debated, the visiting Iroquois were formally invited into the hall of the Continental Congress, and a speech was delivered calling them "brothers" and expressing hope that the "friendship . . . between us . . . will . . . continue as long as the sun shall shine [and the] waters run." The speech also declared the Americans and the Iroquois to be "as one people, and have but one heart. . . ."[125]

After this speech, an Onondaga chief asked to give the president of the Continental Congress (John Hancock) an Indian name. The Congress consented, and the Onondaga chief gave the "president the name of Karanduawn, or the Great Tree. . . . " With the Iroquois chiefs inside the halls of Congress on the eve of American independence, the impact of Iroquois ideas on the Founding Fathers is unmistakable.[126] Shortly, plans for a confederation based on Franklin's Albany Plan of Union were formulated in committee.[127] Since it has been acknowledged by the noted historian Julian P. Boyd that Franklin's plan derived from the Great Law of Peace of the Iroquois, the question of Iroquois influence on the American governmental system now becomes one of degree.

On 26 July 1776, James Wilson of Pennsylvania argued forcefully for confederation, stating that "Indians know the striking benefits of Confederation [and they] have an example of it in the union of the Six Nations." Referring to the Albany conference of August and September of 1775, Wilson stated the "idea of the union of the colonies struck [the Iroquois] forcibly last year." Wilson was pointing out that a strong union similar to the League of the Iroquois would be crucial for the creation of a new nation.[128]

In August of 1776, a committee reported suggestions about a seal for the new nation. One depicted the colonies united by a chain; another was a frontiersman dressed in buckskin "with his tomahawk."[129]

By May of 1777, Wilson would state that liberty under the British Constitution no longer existed for Americans, but with "proper culture" in any soil, the transplanted "[b]ranch will flourish though the root be rotten."[130] However, Congress would not approve the revised Articles of Confederation until November of 1777, and it would be another four years until all thirteen states would approve it.[131]   .

The powers of the Articles of Confederation were not much more than the powers of the Congress; there was neither a judicial nor an executive branch. Congress had powers to engage in diplomacy, coin money, regulate Indian affairs, and settle disputes among the states. It only had limited power to tax or regulate trade, and the new government was expected to subsist on contributions from the states for defense. Each state had one vote, and the states retained the ordinary powers and duties assigned to governments.

As the Continental Congress was debating the proposed Articles of Confederation, a pamphlet was published by the fledgling Congress entitled: *Apocalypse de Chiokoyhekoy, Chief des Iroquois*. Written in French, the pamphlet claimed that an Iroquois prophecy of the end of the world was coming to pass. According to a prophet bird (a parrot), the prophecy stated that several beasts were fighting for the control of Iroquois territory and that the French should ally with the Americans to retain their American colonies. Furthermore, the prophecy advised all American Indians to "ally with the Americans because it will be a great victory for humanity." After a long struggle, the better beast (United States) would win out over the worst beast (Great Britain). The triumph of the Americans was supposed to allow the Iroquois to return in peace to their traditional way of life.

Just as in 1775 at the Albany conference, the Continental Congress employed a bird (*Tskleleli*, or news carrier) in the imagery of diplomacy.[132] This piece of propaganda is significant in explaining the Iroquois roots of the American government because it demonstrates the depth of knowledge that the Continental Congress had of Iroquois philosophy, spirituality, and diplomatic imagery.

Since the prophetic pamphlet was in French, it was probably meant to be used as a propaganda device in France and French-Canada to persuade the French to join the American side, while also appealing to the romantic notions about the Iroquois. In the vision, the Americans emerge as the lesser of two evils, since their way of governing is to be somewhat similar to the Iroquois ways of governing a society.

In the winter of 1777 to 1778, the ideas and imagery of the Iroquois were on the minds of the common American as well. During the bitter winter at Valley Forge, the Oneidas brought corn to George Washington's troops, thus bolstering morale and ensuring their survival as a fighting force. On 1 May 1778, with the bitter winter over, the Continental Army at Valley Forge held a Tammany Day celebration. After poles were erected on the evening of 30 April, there was a ceremony on 1 May that incorporated the arrow imagery of the Iroquois. Reports of the time stated that

> [t]he day was spent in mirth and jollity, the soldiers parading, marching with fife and drum and Huzzaing as they passed the poles, their hats adorned with white blossoms. The following was the procession of the 3d J Regt on the aforesaid day first one Serjeant drest in an Indian habit representing King Tammany. Second Thirteen Serjeants drest in white each with a bow in his left hand and thirteen arrows in his right.[133]

The Indian imagery of the bundle of arrows, symbolizing federated strength and unity, became a common theme in propaganda and in the customs of the American soldier.

In 1778, the Continental Congress negotiated a treaty of alliance with the Delawares. The treaty is informative because it focused on three concerns: trade, land, and political relationships. After discussing the regulation of unscrupulous traders, Article VI of the treaty sought to guarantee to the "nation of Delawares, and their heirs, all their territorial rights." However, the treaty commissioners took a dramatic step when they stated:

> And it is further agreed . . . should it . . . be found conducive for . . . both parties to invite any other tribes who have been friends to the interest of the United States, to join the present confederation, and

*to form a state whereof the Delaware nation shall be the head, and
have a representation in Congress. . . .*[134]

Aside from the diplomatic opportunism of the statement, the treaty
demonstrated that the Continental Congress respected the stature and
power of Indian nations as the new nation struggled to emerge and
create a new identity for itself. With all of this interaction with the
Iroquois and other Indians, George Washington could state at the end
of the revolution:

*I have been more in the way of learning the sentiments of the Six
Nations than of any of the other tribes of Indians. . . .*[135]

During the American Revolution, the weaknesses of the Articles of
Confederation were not readily apparent. Except for taxation, there were
no attempts to augment the powers of Congress. However, after the revolution the absence of an executive, or as the Iroquois would say, someone
to "kindle the fire" became critical. Absenteeism was also a problem.
The articles stipulated that no delegate could serve any more than three
years in six, but this misguided effort to promote rotation in office
backfired. In fact, delegates moved in and out of office more frequently
than the restrictions prescribed. It was a government of amateurs. Public
service was burdensome since it meant that planters, merchants, and
others had to leave their business affairs for extended periods of time.[136]

Under these conditions, James Madison, a major architect of the
United States Constitution, tired of Virginia politics and traveled to
Iroquois country in 1784.[137] He was accompanied by the Marquis de
Lafayette, the Chevalier de Caraman (Lafayette's aide), and François de
Marbois, French charge d'affaires.

During his visit, Madison and his French companions were greatly
enlightened by the Oneidas on the virtues of American Indian life. One
of the Oneida bearers accompanying Madison on the journey identified
himself, in excellent French, as Nicolas Jordan from a French village
near Amiens. Jordan related how he had been captured during the
French and Indian War and had married a chief's daughter. He confessed
that he missed France occasionally, but he had lived among the Oneidas
so long that "my age, my . . . children, fix me here, forever." As soon as
the Oneidas adopted him, he "experienced great humanity from them."
Jordan confessed, ". . . I no longer think of leaving them."[138] Such a
revelation surprised Madison and his companions.

Even more surprising was the discovery of a white woman living
among the Oneidas with strong opinions about the virtues of Oneida
life. Noticing a woman that was fairer than other Oneidas, Madison and
his companions badgered the Indian woman in English until she admitted

that she was white. She told them that she had been a servant girl in a New York planter's house and had fled. The Oneidas had welcomed her, and she had lived happily among them. She told the puzzled Frenchmen and Madison that

> [t]he whites treated me harshly. I saw them take rest while they made me work without a break. I ran the risk of being beaten, or dying of hunger, if through fatigue or laziness I refused to do what I was told. Here I have no master, I am the equal of all the women in the tribe, I do what I please without anyone's saying anything about it, I work only for myself—I shall marry if I wish and be unmarried again when I wish. Is there a single woman as independent as I in your cities? [139]

These remarkable accounts no doubt had an influence upon Madison as he sought to create a new government for America. In addition to these experiences, Madison renewed his acquaintance with the Oneida chief, Grasshopper, who had visited Philadelphia in 1781. More importantly, Madison was exposed to the governmental structure of the Iroquois people and their ideals of freedom. [140]

After the revolution, American Indian societies became even more popular. The most prominent among them was the Society of the Sons of Saint Tammany of Philadelphia (although there were many Tammany societies in a variety of American towns and cities). According to local custom in Philadelphia, Saint Tammany's Day was 1 May. Originally called the Sons of Liberty of Philadelphia in the 1760s, by 1772 the Society of the Sons of Saint Tammany became the successor to that patriotic organization. [141]

This society functioned as a patriotic organization throughout the revolution. Its members often used the rhetoric of Indian nations in public speeches, and delighted in welcoming American Indian delegations to the city of Philadelphia. [142] By the end of the revolution, the society was called the Constitutional Sons of Saint Tammany. On 1 May 1783, to celebrate the coming of peace in Philadelphia, the society organized a parade (reminiscent of the 1778 Valley Forge Tammany parade) that had "thirteen sachems" dressed as Indians and utilized many American Indian symbols. [143]

In 1784, the Tammany Society toasted the Pennsylvania Constitution and cheered a visiting George Washington. [144] And in May of 1785, George Washington arranged his business so that he could attend a meeting of the Tammany Society in Richmond, Virginia. [145]

By 1786, the Tammany Society was a significant factor in American politics. In April of that year, the society welcomed Cornplanter and five other Senecas to Philadelphia. In a remarkable ceremony, the Tammany sachems escorted the Senecas from their lodgings at the Indian Queen Tavern to Tammany's wigwam on the banks of the Schuykill River for a conference. Cornplanter's address to the assemblage was eloquent:

> This great gathering of our brothers is to commemorate the memory of our great-grand-father. It is a day of pleasure (pointing to Saint Tammany colors). . . .
>
> The business I am come on is to have us all united as one man, and it may be my happiness to have it so. Let us keep fast the chain of friendship, and put the same around us. Then we shall have nothing to fear from the great kings on the other side of the waters. Brothers, if we can effect this to become brothers united as one man, there is no people that shall think evil of us that a frown from us will not intimidate. I heard it said that our great-grand-fathers are dead. They are not dead. They now look down upon us and know what we are doing.[146]

After this speech, Cornplanter said that it was fitting that Saint Tammany should have a glass of wine and if we pour it "on the ground, the ground will suck it in and he will get it."[147] After pouring wine on the ground, Cornplanter and his companions then gave a war dance, and afterwards were joined by the Tammany sachems and the officers of the militia in a peace dance and a dance of "mirth." After the dancing, a Tammany sachem addressed the Senecas:

> We meet as brothers, and it is to us a day of pleasure. We meet here every year to remember our great-grand- father Tammany, and three years ago we buried the hatchet in a great deep hole near that stump; we covered it with heavy stones because we wished it never to rise again. You will see great trees growing over it under which we wish our children to sit. We kindled a fire here, it is a bright fire, for our young men to sit by, and there are twelve other fires. But there is a greater fire than all of them. We are glad you are going to that great fire. You will find the road plain and bright. They will bind the chain of friendship round their bodies, and it cannot be broken, but by cutting them in two. We have nothing to fear. Our great men will dry the tears from your eyes. We are pleased that you came; to effect this God sent you. He loves peace and friendship. We love you because you are from the great-grand-father, and we shall never forget that you visited our wigwam.[148]

Following the festivities, Cornplanter and the Senecas were escorted back to their lodgings at the Indian Queen.

Within a few days, Cornplanter and the Senecas proceeded to New York City to address Congress. In his address to Congress on 2 May 1786,

Ki-On-Twog-Ky, or Cornplanter, as painted by F. Bartoli in 1796. The Seneca
leader made important addresses to the Saint Tammany Society and to the
United States Congress. (Courtesy of the New York Historical Society.)

Cornplanter expressed concern about the unity of the United States and stated:

> *Brothers of the Thirteen Fires, I am glad to see you. It gives me pleasure to see you meet in Council to consult about public affairs. May the Great Spirit above direct you in such measures as are good. I wish to put the chunks together to make the Thirteen Fires burn brighter.*[149]

Even a casual examination of public sentiments in America demonstrates that Cornplanter's counsel was respected and widely reported in American newspapers of the time.

In Philadelphia on 1 May 1786, Saint Tammany's Day was commemorated. After the usual celebrations and feasts, a portrait of Cornplanter was given to the Tammany Society and such toasts as the following were given: "The Great Council Fire of the United States—May the 13 fires glow in one blended blaze and illumine the Eagle in his flight to the stars," and "Our great grand sachem George Washington, Esq." Then the Tammany sachems and a great number of spectators proceeded to the residence of "brother Benjamin Franklin who appearing was saluted . . . ," and Franklin thanked them for the "honour paid him, then the brothers all retired to their own wigwams. . . ."[150] In May of 1786, such celebrations were noted as far away as Savannah, Georgia, and Richmond, Virginia. On 1 May 1787, Saint Tammany's Day was celebrated in Philadelphia and for the first time in New York City with the toast: "May the American chain never be tarnished by the rust of discord."[151] In connection with all this activity, it is interesting to note that as the Constitutional Convention began in May of 1787, a Philadelphia publication referred to George Washington as the "great chief."[152]

As America struggled to form a new government, John Adams once again turned his attention to a study of governments of the world. In January of 1787, Adams published his *Defence of the Constitutions of Government of the United States,* a work so popular and important that it was printed in Boston and Philadelphia. Indeed, it was widely distributed and used extensively at the Constitutional Convention.

Adams's discourse discussed ancient and modern forms of government, and it included an analysis of Germanic tribal traditions and American Indian traditions.[153] At the same time that Adams wrote about the advantages and disadvantages of monarchies, republics, and democracies around the world, he also acknowledged that some of the "great philosophers and politicians of the age [want to] set up governments of . . . modern Indians."[154]

French thinkers like Turgot examined the new American constitutions brought by Franklin to France in 1777 and found that they were "an unreasonable imitation of the usages of England." Turgot objected to the perpetuation of bicameral legislatures by the American states and reserved praise only for the unicameral legislature found in the new Pennsylvania State Constitution. Adams stated that Turgot's preference was probably the result of conversations with Franklin. No doubt Franklin favored a unicameral legislature that he believed to exist among the Iroquois.[155]

Adams felt that instead of attempting to implement Indian governments as Franklin saw them it would be more helpful to have "a more accurate investigation of the form of governments of the . . . Indians."[156] In addition, Adams believed that it would be "well worth the pains . . . to collect . . . the legislation of the Indians" while developing a new constitution for the United States.[157] Adams urged leaders of the time to investigate the "government of . . . modern Indians," since the separation of powers in their government "is marked with a precision that excludes all controversy." Indeed, Adams remarked that the legislative branch in modern Indian governments is so democratic that the "real sovereignty resided in the body of the people."[158]

Personal liberty was so important to American Indians, according to Adams, that Mohawks have "complete individual independence."[159] Moreover, Adams also pointed out that every American Indian nation in North America had three distinct branches of government. In an obvious reference to the Iroquois, Adams wrote that a sachem is elected for life and lesser "sachems are his ordinary council." In this ordinary council, all the "national affairs are deliberated and resolved," except when declaring war the "sachems call a national assembly round a great council fire. . . ."[160] Adams's discussions on American Indian governments also included references to Peru and Incan polity.[161]

While Adams admired some of the qualities of American Indian governments, he was critical of European thinkers like Turgot, John Locke, and David Hume. Adams felt that they were too abstract and did not know much about tribal society and republican governments.[162] Further, Adams held the view that American Indian governments were a window to the pre-monarchical past of Europeans, and that the study of American Indian ways by the Founding Fathers was more fruitful than discussing the theoretical democratic misperceptions that European thinkers, such as Locke and Turgot, saw in American Indian polities.

Since Adams discussed the advantages of American Indian governments in his *Defence of Constitutions* on the eve of the Constitutional Convention, it is clear that Iroquois political theory played a role in the debate and framing of the Constitution, since his *Defence of Constitutions* was used and quoted extensively at the Constitutional Convention.

Probably the greatest achievement of the Articles of Confederation was the passage of the Northwest Ordinance of 1787, which provided for gradual statehood of western lands and outlined the procedures for Indian-white relations. It was literally passed while the Constitution was being framed. It is generally recognized that Charles Thomson (adopted Delaware and secretary to Congress) was responsible for this legislation. While this critical piece of legislation was in progress, Thomson went to Philadelphia to consult with his friends at the Constitutional Convention. Thomson was a Pennsylvanian and, of course, was close to James Wilson and Benjamin Franklin, but he also knew most of the other convention delegates that had served in the Continental Congress and confederate government.[163]

The Northwest Ordinance also contained an extensive Bill of Rights. It is important to stress that a bill of rights is an American idea, and whereas the Iroquois Constitution is very sensitive to the rights of individuals and the potential abuses of the state, most European governments were still either divine right monarchies or commercial oligarchies controlled by the middle and upper classes. As the Northwest Ordinance was clearing Congress in July of 1787 in New York, a convention was meeting in Philadelphia to draft a blueprint for the government that would replace the Articles of Confederation.[164] No one has ever examined the agenda that the Northwest Ordinance and its Bill of Rights established in the ratification process. Did Thomson and others generate the issue to ensure citizen debate and input into the new Constitution?

For various reasons, the Founding Fathers rejected ancient and modern European models. Charles Pinckney of South Carolina recalled the dilemma that the delegates faced when they found no precedents in Europe:

> From the European world no precedents are to be drawn for a people who think they are capable of governing themselves. . . . Much difficulty was expected from the extent of country to be governed. All the republics we read of, either in the ancient or modern world, have been extremely limited in territory—we know of none a tenth so large as the United States. Indeed, we are hardly able to determine . . . whether the governments we have heard of under the name of republic really deserve them, or whether the ancients had any just or proper ideas on the subject.[165]

Since South Carolina was one of the most informed states on American Indian affairs, it would be easy for their delegates to entertain Native American ideas at the Constitutional Convention. Moreover, it seems likely that Pinckney was also echoing John Adams's conclusions in his *Defence of Constitutions*.[166]

On 20 May 1787, George Mason (Virginia delegate to the Constitutional Convention) observed that the "most prevalent idea" at the convention was to create "a great National Council." Mason also stated that among the delegates there were "some very eccentric opinions upon this subject."[167] A few weeks later, Mason observed that Adams's idea of a "legislative, a judiciary & an executive [in a] Great National Council" was "still the prevalent one."[168] Certainly, Adams's *Defence of Constitutions* and his discussions about their separation of powers was having its effects on the delegates.

By June of 1787, the delegates to the Constitutional Convention were engaged in a debate about the fundamental nature of the American union. A Philadelphia magazine openly addressed a poem to the "members of the Continental Convention" using Native American imagery:

> To bid contending states their discord cease;
> To send through all the calumet of peace.[169]

Many delegates appeared to agree with James Wilson when he stated, on 1 June 1787, that he would not be "governed by the British model which was inapplicable to ... this country." Wilson believed that America's size was so great, and its ideals so "republican, that nothing but a great confederated republic would do for it."[170]

Iroquois rhetoric and imagery were already an important part of the political awareness of the times because of the activities of the Saint Tammany Society. On 8 June 1787, James Wilson (according to James Madison's notes) used an interesting argument about unity that surely must have harkened back to his experiences with the Iroquois at Fort Pitt in 1775:

> Among the first sentiments expressed in the first Congress, one was that Virginia was no more, that Massachusetts was no more, that Pennsylvania is no more &c. We are now one nation of brethren. We must bury all local distinctions. This language continued for some time [n.b. Madison's sentence about "language" shows that he probably cut off notetaking of Iroquois rhetoric here since it was so well known]. The tables at length began to turn. No sooner were the state governments formed than their jealousy and ambition began to display themselves ... till at length the confederation became frittered down to the impotent condition in which it now stands. Review the progress of the Articles of Confederation thro' Congress and compare the first and last draught of it. To correct its vices is the business of this convention. One of its vices is the want of an effective control in the whole over the parts.[171]

As we shall see later, this instance was just one of several that demonstrated the presence of Iroquois ideas in Philadelphia during the summer of 1787, in part because of the experiences of the framers such as William

Livingston of New Jersey, who had lived for a year among the Mohawks when he was fourteen.[172]

Benjamin Franklin, near the end of the debates, made an impassioned plea for unity and pragmatic compromise:

> I confess that there are several parts of this Constitution which I do not at present approve ... but ... the older I grow, the more apt I am to doubt my own judgment, and to more respect the judgment of others. ... I doubt whether any Convention we can obtain may be able to make a better Constitution ... so near to perfection as it does; and I think it will astonish our enemies who are waiting with confidence to hear that our councils are confounded like those of the Builders of Babel; and that our States are on the point of separation, only to meet for the purpose of one another's throats.[173]

Franklin never forgot the Iroquois roots of the United States Constitution and the need for unity. On 30 June 1787, while the Constitutional Convention was resolving the bitter dispute on proportional representation, he wrote to Indian leaders using direct references to the "Great Spirit" and the council fire of the American government.[174] And by this time, he was commonly held to be the "philosopher as savage."[175] He stated:

> I am sorry that the Great Council fire of our Nation is not now burning, so that you cannot do your business there. In a few months, the coals will be rak'd out of the ashes and will again be rekindled. Our wise men will then take the complaints of your nation into consideration. ...[176]

In July of 1787, another noted Pennsylvanian, Benjamin Rush, M.D., published a letter stating that Independence Hall was filled with "legislators astonishing the world with their wisdom and virtue" on the same site "where had been seen an Indian council fire."[177] In that same month *The American Museum*, a Philadelphia magazine read by most of the members of the Constitutional Convention, republished an article by Franklin entitled "The Origin of Tobacco," which ridiculed European cultural and religious arrogance. In the story, a Susquehannah Indian and a Swedish minister exchange accounts of the origins of their respective religions. After the Indian had recounted his story, the Swedish minister scoffed at the Indian story and called it "fable, fiction, a falsehood," while characterizing the Christian version as "sacred." In replying to the rude minister, the offended Indian asserted that his people believed the minister's stories, and so ". . . [w]hy then do you refuse to believe ours?"[178] It is clear that American Indian images swirled around the delegates at the height of their constitutional deliberations.

On 26 July 1787, the Constitutional Convention adjourned for ten days while a Committee of Detail (John Rutledge of South Carolina, chairman; Edmund Randolph of Virginia; Nathaniel Gorham of Massachusetts; Oliver Ellsworth of Connecticut; and James Wilson of Pennsylvania) met to "arrange and systematize the materials" that the convention had collected.[179] For ten days, the committee met, sometimes at Independence Hall, occasionally at James Wilson's house, and once at the Indian Queen Tavern. At the beginning of the committee's deliberation, John Rutledge read aloud some excerpts from Iroquois Indian treaties that reflected on the will of "the people," and according to his biographer, Rutledge was impressed with the government of the Iroquois from the time of the Stamp Act Congress.[180]

An examination of James Wilson's "Notes on Drafting a Constitution" reveals that there was a great deal of committee discussion "on the original authority of the people. . . ." Wilson's notes say there was uncertainty about "what the sense of the people is" and how "long it existed . . . in an improper manner . . . and from improper sources." However, Wilson noted that the committee meant to discuss

> the different points in question 1. on principle 2. by the Ind[ian] sense of the States in Common. 3. By some striking instance which may happen if the plan be adopted.[181]

In August of 1787, an "American Indian" fable was published in *The American Museum* that recalled Iroquois admonitions of unity to the American people. Using the imagery of the bundle of arrows and portraying the Iroquois as "sires," the fable is a striking example of the use of Iroquois imagery during the Constitutional Convention; this imagery is a direct reference to a section of the Constitution of the Iroquois.[182] This fable is unique since it is one of the few direct admonitions in the press to the delegates of the Constitutional Convention while they were in secret session. And it is significant that the fable did not refer to ancient or modern European models of state; it read:

Unanimity recommended to Americans
—A Fable—
Addressed to the Federal Constitution

A careful sire, of old, who found
Death coming, call'd his sons around.
They heard with reverence what he spake,
Here, try this bunch of sticks to break.

They took the bundle: ev'ry swain
Endeavour'd but the task was vain.

"Observe," the dying father cry'd;
And took the sticks himself and try'd;

When separated, lo! how quick
He breaks asunder ev'ry stick
"Learn my dear boys, by this example,
So strong, so pertinent, so ample,
That UNION saves you all from ruin,
But to divide is your undoing:

For if you take them one by one,
See, with what ease the task is done!
Singly, how quickly broke in twain,
How firm the aggregate Thirteen!"

Is not the tale, Columbians, clear?
What application needs there here?
This motto to your hearts apply,
Ye Senators, UNITE, OR DIE.[183]

Another article in the same issue of *The American Museum* criticized the state of the union and stated: ". . . we are no longer united states [since every] link of the chain of union is separated from its companion."[184] Similarly, in November of 1787, James Wilson used the "Unite or Die" phrase at the debates of the Pennsylvania Ratification Convention.[185]

Iroquois imagery was also used by James Wilson to explain the process of territorial expansion and the establishment of new states. Wilson made it clear that the eastern states should not expand their western boundaries and instead new semi-independent states ought to be created. He believed that in order to have the respect of western settlers, new government officers should be

> chosen by the people to fill the places of greatest trust and importance in the country; and by this means, a chain of communication and confidence will be formed between the United States and the new settlements. To preserve and strengthen this chain it will, I apprehend, be expedient for Congress to appoint a minister for the new settlements and Indian Affairs.[186]

In 1788, an editorial on the Constitution appearing in South Carolina also recalled the "Unite or Die" motto and urged the people to be "of one heart and mind."[187] In November of 1788, *The Columbian Magazine* (one of the foremost magazines of the day) published an article on Canassateego's version of the origin of the Five Nations.[188] Clearly, Iroquois concepts and rhetoric were present in the American press at the time of ratification.

David Ramsay of South Carolina argued during ratification that the American union was a kinship state; he had been president of Congress on 2 May 1786 when Cornplanter spoke on Iroquois unity. Ramsay stated:

> When thirteen persons constitute a family, each should forego every-thing that is injurious to the other twelve. When several families constitute a parish or county, each may adopt what regulations it pleases with regard to its domestic affairs, but must be abridged of that liberty in other cases, where the good of the whole is concerned.
>
> When several parishes, counties, or districts form a state, the separate interests of each must yield to the collective interest of the whole. When several states combine in one government, the same principles must be observed. These relinquishments of natural rights are not real sacrifices; each person, county, or state gains more than it loses, for it only gives up the right of injuring others, and obtains in return aid and strength in securing itself in the peaceful enjoy-ment of all remaining rights.[189]

Ramsay and other intellectual leaders of the time led a movement to de-velop a distinct American character that was different from Europe. Like Charles Pinckney of South Carolina, Ramsay felt that few European ideas were really applicable to the American environment. And it is only logical that these thinkers turned to their "native" roots for inspiration.

In early 1789, *The American Museum* called attention to the similar-ities of Franklin's Albany Plan of Union and the new Constitution. The article said that the Albany Plan of 1754 had a "strong . . . resemblance to the present system." The essay further observed that an examination of the similarities of the two documents will "convince the wavering, the new constitution is not the fabrication of the moment." In addition, it stated that Franklin never lost sight of his favorite system until the end of his life, when he "lived to see it accomplished. . . ."[190]

After this article, the same publication launched a three-part series entitled "Albany Papers with Notes by Franklin" that explored the evolu-tion of American government from the Albany Plan of Union to the framing of the Constitution. It is interesting to note that *The American Museum* also carried several essays on American Indian manners and customs during this time.

When the ratification process was in its last stages, *The American Museum* reprinted the major speech by the Americans to the Iroquois at the Albany conference in the summer of 1775. The reprinted speech contained the "tree of peace" imagery and many other familiar references. Another obvious reference was a poem entitled "Character of St. Tammany" that idolized the old Delaware chief who wanted "to live in freedom or with honor die."[191]

The monthly magazine's list of subscribers included almost every major political figure of the era (Washington, Madison, Jefferson, Franklin, and others); consequently, it had an enormous impact. The clustering of the Albany Plan of Union, the Albany conference of 1775, and a poem about Saint Tammany during the ratification process seems to have been deliberate. It sent a clear message to the American people about the nature of American government and its origins.

Thus, in the formative years of the American nation, the use of Iroquois ideas and phrases was common, and relations with Indians, in general, were often on a basis of equality and mutual respect. In 1785, at the Treaty of Hopewell, the Congress actually invited the Cherokees "... to send a deputy of their choice ... to Congress." [192] Political discussion was often cloaked in Native American terms, pseudonyms, or fables. And the synthesis of Native American and European ideas is demonstrated clearly in the activities of the Tammany Society and its interaction with political leaders of the time. Moreover, the editorial policy of The American Museum clearly recognized and reflected the intercultural exchange that was a crucial part of the building process of our nation.

The Persistence of Iroquois Contributions

I am an Indian. . . .
> Robert Beverley,
> Virginia's first native-born historian, 1705.[193]

The American Indian as a symbol of liberty and unity fostered an imagery manifested in the American consciousness before, during, and after the revolution. This symbol was used effectively during the Boston Tea Party and in Thomas Paine's natural rights arguments in Common Sense. The free use of "Great Tree," "Unite or Die," "chain of friendship," and "league of friendship" indicates that such imagery and symbolism were present in the collective mind and in the vocabulary of the leaders of the era.

A dramatic example of this symbolism was recorded in 1790. President George Washington, seeking to negotiate a favorable treaty with the Creek Nation, asked the New York Saint Tammany Society to escort and entertain the Creek leaders in New York City in July and August of 1790, just as they had Cornplanter and the Senecas. On 21 July 1790, the Creek leaders (headed by Alexander M'Gillvray of Scottish and Creek extraction) arrived in New York City and were escorted throughout the city by three officers of "The Society of Saint Tammany, in their proper dresses. . . ." Toasts were made to a "strong and perpetual chain of friendship between the United States and the Creek Nation" and to the "[o]blivion of all prejudices and resentments."[194]

On 2 August 1790, the Saint Tammany Society sought to explain their purpose to the Creeks. Their great objective, it was said, was to "cherish—to spread abroad, and to maintain the love of freedom." According to tradition, their two great leaders (Tammany and Columbus) were supposed to direct the society in all of its proceedings, and they lived "together in the world of the spirits in great harmony." With pride, the society told the Creeks that they had welcomed a delegation of Oneida chiefs "not long ago" in a similar ceremony. While pointing out that M'Gillvray was both white and Indian, the sagamore of the society stated that we "are altogether children of one father."[195]

Subsequently, the scribe of the Tammany Society asserted:

> Our institution, erected on the basis of natural freedom, records, in its formation, the noblest sentiments . . . public virtue and political friendship; men actuated by a sameness of principle, become our brethren, and we embrace them as friends. . . .
>
> [I] . . . present to you our public constitution. In it you will behold the strong features of political freedom, and that a sacred regard for the rights of human nature originated in our institution. . . . Let these [principles] prove a covenant chain between us, the brightness of whose links will never know rust, and . . . let us take hold of it, and, as we are all children of the same soil, let one tree of peace shelter us with its branches of union. . . .
>
> The . . . constitution . . . was then presented by him to the acceptance of Col. M'Gillvray.[196]

Following this speech, everyone shook hands and sang patriotic songs, and the Creeks danced. Several toasts were offered to "Washington—the beloved sachem of the 13 fires," and to universal peace and happiness, or the "Tammanical Chain extended thro' the Creek Nations and round the whole earth."[197]

The Creeks were pleased with the ceremony and enjoyed the rhetoric of their grandfathers, the Iroquois. Notables in attendance at this remarkable event included: Thomas Jefferson (secretary of state), John Jay (chief justice of the Supreme Court), and Henry Knox (secretary of war).[198]

After ratification, the political ideas of the Iroquois and their influence on the American mind persisted for most of the nineteenth century. Often, the Iroquois League's ideas were welded to the classical imagery that was so evident in the first decades of the federal period.

Speaking before the New York Historical Society in 1812, De Witt Clinton (a member of the New York Tammany Society) stated that all of the proceedings of the Iroquois "were conducted with great deliberation and were distinguished for order, decorum, and solemnity." Clinton also asserted that in "eloquence, in dignity, and in all characteristics of profound policy, they surpassed an assembly of feudal barons, and were perhaps not far inferior to the great . . . Council of Greece."[199] References like this helped America to develop a separate identity that was not tied to the British parliamentary tradition and served to nurture a distinct democratic tradition that was not British in origin.

As a result of his travels in Iroquois country, Clinton asserted that the Iroquois were "the Romans of the Western World."[200] Comparing Iroquois political theory to the Roman republic was a common theme. In April of 1792, *Freneau's National Gazette* in New York corrected a report that President George Washington was negotiating with Iroquois leaders that were "princes" but in reality the Iroquois "were republicans, rather than aristocrats or monarchy men."[201] And in commenting on their government, Clinton observed that the Iroquois

> look upon themselves as sovereigns, accountable to none but God alone, whom they call the Great Spirit. They admitted of no hereditary distinctions. The office of Sachem was the reward of personal merit— of great wisdom or commanding eloquence—of distinguished services in the cabinet or in the field. . . . [202]

By 1812, aging patriots like Thomas Jefferson and John Adams looked upon their American Indian experiences with nostalgia. Jefferson wrote to Adams that

> in the early part of my life, I was very familiar, and acquired impressions of attachment and commiseration for [Indians] which have never been obliterated. Before the Revolution, they were in the habit of coming often and in great numbers to the seat of government [at Williamsburg], where I was very much with them.[203]

Adams replied to Jefferson:

> I have also felt an interest in the Indians . . . [they] were frequent visitors . . . at my father's house, and I, in my boyish rambles, used to call at their wigwam. . . .[204]

The interest in American Indians continued throughout the nineteenth century. Tammany Hall, in New York City, remained a political force, even though it would forsake its idealistic origins; when it was founded it had different lodges called tribes, its leaders were called "sachems," and the meeting place was a "wigwam."

The Tammany Society's original purpose was admirable. After the revolution, it dedicated its activities to liberty, independence, and federal union. And it worked against powerful forces that wanted to institute an oligarchy or monarchy in the new nation. In addition, the society also advocated other libertarian ideals. For example, in 1826 Tammany Hall was instrumental in developing a law to abolish imprisonment for debt in New York City.[205] The eventual corruption of the society stands in contrast to its early record of notable dedication to Indian ideals and traditions.

Prominent political theorists and politicians in America found the Iroquois paradigm useful in their work. John C. Calhoun, in his "A Disquisition on Government and a Discourse on the Constitution and Government of the United States," stated that "governments of concurrent majority" were practical since the Iroquois utilized them. Calhoun believed that the "federal, or general government" of the Six Nations constituted a "council of union," where each member possessed a veto on its decision so that nothing could be done without the united consent of all. But this, instead of making the Confederacy weak, or impracticable, had the opposite effect. It secured harmony in council and action, and with them a great increase of power. The Six Nations became the most powerful of all the Indian tribes within the limits of our country. They carried their conquest and authority far beyond the country they originally occupied.[206] To Calhoun and his contemporaries, it was appropriate to discuss the Iroquois when advancing ideas about the revision of the Constitution, since the Founding Fathers had done so in the eighteenth century.

By the mid-nineteenth century, the folklore of Indian democracy and American government was still strong. Governor Horatio Seymour of New York (1853 to 1855) stated while in office that

> [g]overnment of the whole, by the whole and for the benefit of the whole are native here, and are no more to be traced back to the old world than are the granite rocks on which we stand.[207]

It has been established that Governor Seymour was a frequent visitor to the Onondaga Indian Reservation.[208]

A generation later, Lewis Henry Morgan, the pioneer anthropologist, would emphasize the importance of Iroquois contributions to the American government in his *Houses and House-Life of the American Aborigines*:

> Each [tribe] was in vigorous life . . . presenting some analogy to our own States within an embracing Republic. . . . The Iroquois commended to our forefathers a union of the colonies similar to their own as early as 1755. They saw in the common interests and common speech of the several colonies the elements for a confederation.[209]

By the late nineteenth century, noted feminists such as Elizabeth Cady Stanton and Matilda Jocelyn Gage were using detailed descriptions of Iroquois society to demonstrate that a nonsexist society was possible and that one did indeed exist among the Iroquois in western New York. These feminists knew Iroquois people and were familiar with the work of Henry R. Schoolcraft and Lewis Henry Morgan. Both Stanton and Gage believed that the American form of government was "borrowed from . . . the Six Nations."[210]

Moreover, in 1894 the Hon. Elliot Danforth, former New York State treasurer, asserted before the Oneida Historical Society that

> [t]he five nations were confederated in a barbarian republic upon the unique plan afterward adopted by our states and our national republic.[211]

At the beginning of the twentieth century, the "Six Nations" article in the *Encyclopedia Americana* would state that the Founding Fathers

> in framing a Constitution for the United States honored these people by the adoption of their general constitutional system.[212]

The list of scholars and students of the Iroquois roots of the United States Constitution does not end there. In 1937, Matthew W. Stirling, chief and later director of the Bureau of American Ethnology (1928 to 1958), stated in an article in the *National Geographic* that the Albany Plan of Union was greatly influenced by the League of the Iroquois, and that the Iroquois had a profound impact on the formation of the American state.[213] Stirling reiterated his respect for American Indian ways when he stated in congressional testimony in the 1950s that "perhaps we can learn the elusive secret to worldwide peace from [the Iroquois]."[214]

In the 1950s, the distinguished American legal scholar Felix Cohen argued that

> it is out of a rich Indian democratic tradition that the distinctive political ideals of American life emerged. Universal suffrage for women as for men, the pattern of states that we call federalism, the habit of treating chiefs as servants of the people instead of their masters, the insistence that the community must respect the diversity of men and the diversity of their dreams—all these things were part of the American way of life before Columbus landed.[215]

Cohen was a law professor at CUNY and Yale, and he wrote the *Handbook of American Indian Law* (1942) when he worked for the Department of the Interior as associate solicitor.

Contemporary anthropologists and other academics are generally less enthusiastic about the Iroquois roots of the United States Constitution. William N. Fenton makes the following statement about Iroquois influences on American government:

> *Although the United States Constitution was not modeled on the League, its authors, particularly Franklin, were aware of the existence of the Iroquois Confederacy and used it to whip their fellow countrymen into line. On the eve of the American Revolution both the representatives of the Continental Congress and the Iroquois recalled the connection.*[216]

Thus, Fenton admits some connection, but he is unable or unwilling to examine the evolution of that cultural nexus between the Iroquois and the American colonists.

Contemporary historians largely ignore or downplay the Iroquois roots of American government. Francis Jennings in his *The Invasion of America* believes that

> *modern American society owes more of its apparent features to European antecedents than to Indian . . . traits. . . .*[217]

Jennings further asserts that Indian agriculture offered new crops, but Europeans did not give up the plow; that Indian medicines were adopted without modification of the role of the European physician; and that Europeans learned Indian guerrilla tactics without changing the discipline and command structure of modern military forces. In the realm of political theory, Jennings admits that

> *Indian voluntarism and equalitarianism struck the European political imagination, but the nation-state grew ever more centralized and bureaucratic and acquired new techniques for compelling its subjects to obedience and conformity.*[218]

Hence, Jennings follows the reasoning of Fenton in recognizing the fascination of Europeans and Euro-Americans for American Indian political systems, but he implies that whatever concepts were incorporated into the American political system were subordinate to the hierarchical structures that were maintained in transplanted governmental systems. However, this analysis does not, for example, take into account the change in the military structure that contact with American Indians helped to precipitate.

Even before independence, the issue of the election of military leaders forced major changes in the American Army. When a British general recruited, it was with little regard for the rights of individuals. And British officers bought their rank, a practice that made morale very low. In contrast, Americans expected to elect their leaders, advocating an organizational philosophy that they could have only learned from American Indians.[219] Indeed, Ethan Allen of Vermont tried to recruit American Indians by stating that American military discipline and strategies were very similar to that of American Indians. He asserted that he knew how to "shute and ambush just like [an] Indian." He also asked Indians to help him fight British regulars, since they stand in close together "[r]ank and file and my men fight so as Indians do and Ambush the Regulars. . . ."[220] Thus, the early American military leaders emulated American Indian traditions.

While asserting the dominance of European roles and command structures in American society, Jennings admits that Europeans did

> enter into symbiotic relations of interdependence with Indians (and Africans), involving both conflict and cooperation, that formed the matrix of modern American society.[221]

Jennings is largely concerned with pioneering in his analysis, and he thinks that in this area "the European vanguard were pupils in the Indian school." Further, Jennings feels that Indian pioneering techniques taught to Europeans were one of the American Indian's most significant contributions to American society. In fact, Jennings states that what Euro-American society owes "to Indian society, as much as to any other source, is the mere fact of its existence."[222]

In the writings of both Fenton and Jennings, we see the importance of dominance as a theme in Western civilization. Both scholars admit Native American interaction, but they feel that the maintenance of a European hierarchical structure negates or supersedes the importance of Native American political theories concerning natural rights and equality.

However, at least Fenton and Jennings are concerned about historical and contemporary interactions with native peoples and engage in debate and analysis with American Indian people on a variety of topics. By contrast, younger ethnohistorians such as James Axtell believe that

> historians need not feel unduly sensitive about their lack of personal research among contemporary tribal cultures. Often the descendants of their historical subjects no longer survive, or, if they do, have lost much of their historical cultural character.[223]

It is striking testimony to the state of American Indian history that a contemporary ethnohistorian such as Axtell, in this neo-conservative age, would feel confident to make such a statement about Native American people. Such rhetoric often betrays deep-seated animosities towards American Indians.

In discussing the entry of American Indian scholars into the fields of anthropology and ethnohistory, Axtell talks of the "Indian threat," and fears that people will accept the "genetic fallacy" that American Indians are the only people capable of understanding their history (one wonders if Axtell has pondered the Anglo-American threat to the study of the Anglo-American Founding Fathers).[224] It is certainly a unique methodological approach to assert that a scholar of American Indian history need not know the language, culture, and tradition of the people studied, and can claim the absence of such knowledge is desirable in the pursuit of objectivity.

Anthropologists have also joined the debate over the influence of Iroquois ideas on American government. Elisabeth Tooker, in her article "The United States Constitution and the Iroquois League," states that the League of the Iroquois was not a "model for the United States Constitution," and that "a review of the evidence in the historical and ethnographic documents . . . offers virtually no support for this contention."[225] However, Tooker ignores Franklin's presence at a Condolence Ceremony less than a year before the Albany Conference of 1754, and also ignores the fact that Franklin had corresponded with Peter Collinson at length on Indian customs and the "Grand Council" at Onondago in 1753.[226] In general, Tooker fails to address the historical evidence at hand. Although she quotes a few passages from Franklin's papers and from the Albany meeting of 1775 in which the Americans note Iroquois admonitions of colonial unity for over a generation, she does not pursue the historical evidence further.[227] Instead, she shifts the argument to the "ethnographic evidence" with which she is much more comfortable. After a detailed description of the League, she then proceeds to a discussion of the "development of the myth" of the connection between the Iroquois and the United States Constitution, maintaining that the Iroquois League was either unfathomable to the Founding Fathers, or that the League as we know it today did not exist several hundred years ago.

Moreover, Tooker believes that the Iroquois League and the Constitution are so structurally dissimilar that there is no relationship between the two governments. She quotes various scholars on the topic and asserts that such a "positive stereotype" is as damaging to American Indians as a negative one. Tooker concludes her essay with the patronizing statement: "We owe our fellow residents on this continent better."[228]

Tooker's article fails to address significant historical evidence from the years 1776 to 1789, an omission that is understandable since she is an anthropologist, not a historian. However, if she had consulted the *Journals of the Continental Congress*, she would have known that Iroquois chiefs were present in May and June of 1776 and that an Onondaga sachem gave John Hancock the title "Great Tree" at that time. On 12 June 1776, the day after the naming ceremony, a revised version of Franklin's Albany Plan of Union (acknowledged by the editor of Franklin's treaties to be based on the League of the Iroquois) was laid before the Confederation Committee of the Continental Congress. The editors of the *Letters of the*

Delegates to Congress point out that "the 4th, 7th, 8th, and 12th of Franklin's Articles are conspicuously incorporated into the committee's work."[229]

In addition, Tooker seems unaware that in 1777 the Continental Congress used an Iroquois prophecy in developing propaganda.[230] She ignores John Adams's admonitions to the Constitutional Convention that they study the "governments of . . . modern Indians," and she refuses to deal with Adams's assertion that the French philosophers were advocating a government like those of contemporary Indians and that American Indian governments were an excellent example of the precise separation of powers in government.[231] Tooker also fails to take into account the suggestions by the media at the time of the Constitutional Convention to use parts of the Iroquois Great Law of Peace in the formation of our United States Constitution.[232] And she does not seem to be aware of the fact that the New Jersey Plan introduced at the Constitutional Convention was derived from the Articles of Confederation;[233] nor does she address the idea that the Society of the Sons of Saint Tammany believed America to be a synthesis of American Indian and European concepts.[234]

Further, Tooker argues that the structure of the Iroquois League is not similar to the structure of the United States Constitution. However, using this criterion, one could also argue that the British Constitution does not qualify as a precursor to the United States Constitution because its structures and concepts are different. Since the British Constitution is unwritten, provides for a monarch, has no declaration on the rights of citizens (subjects) and regional governments, no judicial independence, few checks on the executive, and no time schedule for elections, one can conclude by Tooker's methods that it is a "myth" that the United States Constitution is derived, in part, from the British Constitution. Moreover, the British Constitution is based on the assumption that government is benign, while the United States Constitution is based on the assumption that all government is potentially oppressive and thus must have its powers clearly defined and limited.

Ultimately, Tooker's methodology would lead us to the conclusion that the United States Constitution has no historical roots. Tooker's inability to address the documentary evidence that reflects the influence of Iroquois and other Native American ideas on the evolution of American government gives us an impoverished view of American history that ignores the richness and diversity of our heritage. In the end, scant evidence, arguments about "myth," and appeals to authority make her research and conclusions unreplicable.

Unfortunately, Tooker's orientation is not uncommon in contemporary historiography. Although contemporary American political scientists like Vine Deloria, Jr., and Clifford M. Lytle recognize that "the Iroquois Constitution provided a written preview of some of the governmental values to be adopted by the whites in America,"[235] most American history is still written as if American culture derived from European culture. Writing about this approach, the distinguished historian Bernard DeVoto stated in 1952 that despite the fact that

> *well into the nineteenth century the Indians were one of the principal determinants of historical events. . . . American historians have made shockingly little effort to understand the life, the societies, the cultures, the thinking, and the feeling of the Indians and disastrously little effort to understand how all these affected white men and their societies.*[236]

It is important to ask why Native American contributions to society are still being largely ignored. The noted American Indian historian Virgil Vogel believes that historians have used four methods to create or perpetuate incorrect interpretations about Native Americans. First, historians simply do not deal with the historical treatment of American Indians; thus, Native Americans are obliterated as valid themes in American history. Second, native people were often depersonalized, made into dehumanized abstractions. Consequently, the "civilizing Europeans" had a moral right to usurp American Indian resources. Third, some historians claimed that Indians were inferior, nomadic (in fact, American Indians were, and are, far less mobile than non-Indian Americans), and had no virtues. This defamation of Indians is not as popular as it was several generations ago, but it surfaces in land claims suits and lingers on in the public mind. Finally, the contributions of Native Americans to the development of North American culture are denied through disparagement.[237] Assimilation is thought to be a one-way street—that American Indians received the benefits of European civilization but that Europeans had little to learn from the native people of North America. This biased assumption is based on an idea of cultural and/or racial superiority. In general, historians have assumed that military conquest rationalized superiority in all areas relating to culture, intellect, and technology. In many cases, American Indian ideas are hidden from the American people through indifference, stereotyping, and assertions of superiority. Vine Deloria, Jr., believes that a reexamination of the history of mankind "in terms of a universe that is alive and not dead is asking too much of the American people."[238] If such a view is valid, it may be left to American Indians to catalyze and disseminate such a reexamination.

Conclusion

> *All the history books have been written by the white man, and it is slanted to justify his behavior in our lands. The sin of omission is rampant throughout the history books. . . .*
> Onondaga Council of Chiefs of the Iroquois Confederacy[239]

In essence, American democracy is a synthesis of Native American and European political theories; there is an abundance of inferential and direct evidence to support the thesis that American government was influenced by Native American political concepts. To pretend that America's intellectual tapestry is woven only from European threads is a colossal myth. Those scholars that refuse to acknowledge the influence of Native American government on the evolution of American government demean American Indians, the Founding Fathers, and the common sense of the American people. The Founding Fathers did not "copy" the British Constitution, the Magna Carta, the governments of the ancients, or the Iroquois Confederacy, but they did examine and use European and American Indian ideas in the creation of our American government. The fundamental ideas that form the basis of our political identity arose out of a blending of European and American antecedents, acting in concert. Our political traditions are not the product of any single heritage, but of a unique amalgam that remains incomplete without an awareness of our American Indian roots. In the final analysis, the grand intellectual document that is the United States Constitution is rich with both Old World and New World concepts.

7.
The Application of the Constitution to American Indians

Vine Deloria, Jr.

Introduction

Although American Indians are mentioned by name twice in the Constitution of the United States, they were clearly not within the citizenry contemplated by this document at the time of its adoption. In the two centuries during which the United States has developed into a major world power and settled a substantial portion of North America, constitutional amendments have brought black citizens and women into the American social contract and made them an integral part of the body politic.

American Indians, however, still stand outside the protections of the Constitution as tribes and only have partial protection as individual citizens. While Indian lands have become part of the United States, Indian communities have neither been allowed to remain isolated as independent political entities nor have they been granted full status within the American political system. Consequently, American Indians have been forced to live within a political/legal no man's land from which there seems to be no possibility of extrication. This chapter will explore the systematic exclusion and occasional application of the Constitution of the United States to American Indians.

The Historical Context of the Constitution

The Constitution of the United States was adopted in 1787 after the nation had been successful in a revolution against the king of England and had governed itself for nearly a decade under the Articles of Confederation. At the time the Constitution was adopted, it was accepted law that European nations discovering new and uninhabited lands in the Western Hemisphere could lay claim to the legal title to these lands in defiance of whatever title was asserted by the original inhabitants of the New World. The United States laid claim to the English title to the lands which the thirteen colonies occupied and believed to be theirs under colonial charters issued earlier by the king of England.

The Indian nations were believed to possess an equitable title of occupancy over lands upon which they lived, and this occupancy was not to be disturbed except by voluntary and lawful sales of lands to the European country claiming the legal title to the area in question. The British and French had adopted the practice of dealing with the Indian nations through formal treaties, and the colonies and later the United States continued this practice.

The Indian nations were regarded as possessing sufficient political status to wage war and make peace, and had been regarded as valuable allies in the colonial wars between the competing European powers. The American Revolution left three major political competitors in North America: the United States, Great Britain, and Spain. Since the English and Spanish continued to treat Indian nations as nations, the United States had no choice but to accept and recognize the Indian nations as nations capable of entering into treaty relationships. Only at the conclusion of the War of 1812 did the United States feel powerful enough to insist that the Indian nations of the interior recognize it as the solitary sovereign to whom they should be accountable. This exclusive relationship gave the United States a claim to the title of all lands then occupied by the Indians that were not subject to the superior claim of any other sovereign. Subsequent historical developments eventually allowed the United States to claim all the lands presently encompassing the continental land area of the contiguous forty-eight states.

The debates between advocates and opponents of the Constitution reveal that Indian nations were viewed as entirely outside the scope of constitutional powers and protections. Alexander Hamilton best summarized the status of Indian nations in No. 24 of *The Federalist* as foreign and perhaps even hostile nations to the United States:

> On one side of us, stretching far into our rear, are growing settlements subject to the dominion of Britain. On the other side and extending to meet the British settlements, are colonies and establishments subject to the dominion of Spain. This situation and the vicinity of the West Indian Islands, belonging to these two powers, create between them, in respect to their American possessions and in relation to us, a common interest. The savage tribes on our Western frontier ought to be regarded as our natural enemies, their natural allies, because they have most to fear from us, and most to hope from them.[1]

Americans brought into the constitutional setting from their colonial and revolutionary experience two principles which have dominated and defined the subsequent relationship of Indian nations with the United States. First, there was no question that the United States claimed title to the lands possessed and occupied by the Indian nations and would assert this title against the Indians when the opportunity presented itself or the occasion demanded it. Second, the best and most efficient way of dealing with the Indian nations was through treaty-making and negotiations. The first principle has continued until the present time and has been both helpful and harmful to Indian aspirations. The second principle was abandoned by congressional fiat in 1871 with the subsequent drastic decline in Indian fortunes and conditions.

Constitutional Relationships

In discussing the applicability of the Constitution to the Indian nations we face a multi-stage sequence of examination. The constitutional clauses that have some relationship to American Indians can be classified as (1) explicit clauses in which Indians are directly mentioned, (2) implicit clauses where the government assumed that its powers enabled it to deal with Indians because past practices dictated that these were the proper courses of action, (3) implicit clauses in which the logical analysis of the authority led to the conclusion that the power to deal with Indians was present, and finally, (4) clauses which had peripheral importance and were seldom if ever used to deal with Indian matters.

The Constitution divides the sovereign political power of the United States between the national government and the constituent states, and then takes the body of federal authority and distributes it among three independent yet interrelated branches of government. Each state in turn subdivides its sovereignty into the same three branches modeled closely after the structure of the federal government. Political power in the United States is thus carefully distributed among six different entities of government: the executive, legislative, and judicial branches of state and federal governments. In maintaining a relationship with the United States, it has been necessary for Indian nations to deal with any one of these branches or with different combinations of these subdivisions. Often Indian nations must deal with the separate branches in a predetermined sequence in order to get decisions made and problems resolved.

The very structure of the constitutional framework of government has created immense difficulties for Indian nations. No single branch of either state or federal government can be said to represent the whole functioning of that political entity unless the two remaining branches refuse to become involved in the issue under consideration. Therefore, the Constitution itself is the greatest barrier Indians have faced in attempting to deal with the United States.

The structure of the federal and state governments is critical to the political posture of the United States toward Indians. Therefore, we will first discuss how this structure has functioned before we examine how the powers authorized in the Constitution have been applied to Indians; in doing this, it will then be possible to distinguish between the latitude available to the respective branches of government and the power contained in the document itself.

Indians and the Executive Branch

The president of the United States, as its chief executive officer, has no direct constitutional responsibility for American Indians. He does, however, have the primary role in the conduct of foreign affairs, and since Indians were considered a part of the external affairs of the United States at the beginning of the republic, the president came to have an important function in Indian treaty-making. Either on his own initiative or following instructions from the Congress, the president nominates treaty commissioners, supervises the preparation of treaty provisions, and submits the treaty for senatorial advice and consent prior to ratifying the treaty.

The substance of treaty provisions, therefore, originates in the executive branch. Specific goals may be identified prior to treaty negotiations, and specific promises may be suggested as a means of securing the agreement of the Indians, but the treaty process itself is almost exclusively an executive function. Following the ratification and proclamation of an Indian treaty, the president is responsible for seeing that the provisions are carried out, and since the trend of treaties moved in the direction of providing services to the tribes, the president quickly became the chief administrative officer of the government as well. Fulfillment of the treaties was initially almost wholly an executive responsibility, with the president having the power of appointment of subordinate officers, preparing and submitting a budget for Indian affairs, and resolving conflicts between federal officials and state officers over the conduct of Indian affairs in the states and territories.

The trend of American history was to expand the administrative function of the executive branch while reducing the active role of the president in Indian matters. The Act of June 30, 1834 (4 Stat. 735), provided for the organization of the Department of Indian Affairs, and this statute marks a fundamental change in the role of the president. While he continued to play an important part in the treaty-making process, the establishment of a separate agency for Indians made it inevitable that he become a symbolic representation of the United States and less personally involved in Indian matters. From that time forward the expansion of the federal government's programmatic agencies moved the president to the periphery of Indian affairs.

With the election of Andrew Jackson, the role of the president shifted in another direction. Jackson favored removing the Indians west of the Mississippi and clearing the area east of that river of all Indian title. Part of his campaign for the presidency was based upon that pledge, and the passage of the Removal Act in 1830 (Act of May 28, 1830, 4 Stat. 411) meant that the executive branch could use Indians in any way it wished to fulfill political promises to particular constituencies. This use, or rather misuse, of the office of the presidency was not contemplated by the Constitution, but it was not challenged by the other branches of government and so became an accepted practice of the executive branch.

With an occasional ebb and flow, depending on the historical circumstances, Indian affairs became part of the internal and domestic political agenda of the United States even though Indians themselves were not part of the body politic. Administrations were expected to have a "policy" on Indian matters, and this policy was supposed to be reflected in the kinds of administrative appointments made by the president in the Department of the Interior and Bureau of Indian Affairs, and in the kinds of legislative initiatives drawn up and submitted to the Congress. Since it is impossible to predict how the respective incumbents in the White House will actually view Indians, federal Indian policy fluctuates according to the perspective of each president and his supporters and advisors. Indian affairs within the executive branch are a matter of man and not of law.

Some presidents have exercised certain kinds of constitutional power on behalf of American Indians in a manner quite unexpected. Beginning in May 1855 and continuing until Congress prohibited the practice in 1927, a succession of presidents used their power of issuing executive orders to set aside Indian reservations for Indian tribes in the western United States.[2] This practice was particularized by instructions to the president in the General Allotment Act (24 Stat. 388), but the power to set aside public lands for the specific use of tribes of Indians was constitutionally suspect although never questioned by the other branches of government. Congress was content, long after the fact, to pass legislation that sought to limit the use of this power to instances in which the Congress had a voice in the decision to exercise it.

Abraham Lincoln used the power granted to him under the Constitution to grant reprieves and pardons to rescue some Sioux Indians from a death sentence passed by a military court. In 1862, in the Minnesota war between the Sioux and the settlers, the Sioux were quickly routed, and a sizeable group was imprisoned at Fort Snelling, where 303 Sioux men were found guilty of murder and ordered to be executed. Lincoln insisted on reading the trial record, and he assigned two men to go over the proceedings to determine which of the Indians might actually be guilty of this offense and which Indians were simply victims of army vengeance. Lincoln pardoned all but 40 of the Indians. In this incident we have the exercise of constitutional authority on behalf of the Indians, but it is not the Indian aspect of the affair that called forth the use of the constitutional protections. Rather, the latitude of the other two branches, and the absence of an overwhelming political rejection of the course of action, made the exercise of this power possible.

The executive branch, in summary, generally provides the content of Indian programs and treaty rights, and the presidency itself provides the symbolic and moral focus of policy in the field of Indian affairs. The constitutionality of presidential acts with respect to Indians is rarely challenged because Indians are not a major political constituency within the United States. The executive branch has unusually wide discretion in its administration of Indian affairs, and since one theory of the status of Indians is that they are wards of the government, almost any action taken by the executive branch can be justified under this rubric. There is *nothing* in the constitutional establishment of the executive branch that places any limitation on the actions of this arm of government toward Indians. Any limitations imposed are wholly as a result of the moral perception of the condition of Indians at the time decisions are made.

Indians and the Legislative Branch

The commerce clause, Section 8, clause 3 or Article I of the Constitution, gives Congress the power to regulate commerce with foreign nations, and among the several states, and with the Indian tribes. In theory, Congress should have *no greater power* over Indian nations than it does over states, but in historical practice such has not been the case. The initial tendency of Congress was to establish the rules and regulations under which citizens of the United States could have trade and intercourse with Indian nations. Early statutes reflect this narrow view of the power and responsibilities of the legislative branch. Within two decades of the adoption of the Constitution, however, Congress began to appropriate funds for the "civilization" of Indians, and the creation of these kinds of funds represented a fundamental shift in Congress' view of its powers under the commerce clause. The goal was wholly humanitarian. Faced with the fictional dilemma of either exterminating or assimilating the Indian tribes, Congress chose the latter course, and it began to develop a policy that would accomplish this goal.

In 1830, at the urging of southern and western congressmen and senators, the Indian Removal Act was passed, and this act marks the emergence of the legislative branch as the dominant actor in the formulation of Indian policy. Four years later Congress enacted a comprehensive statute to regulate trade and intercourse with the Indian tribes (Act of June 30, 1834, 4 Stat. 729), which summarized, updated, and expanded all existing federal Indian law, generalized the concept of "Indian country," and established the beginnings of a code of civil and criminal law applicable to the areas of conflict between whites and Indians. Thereafter, with the possible exception of a few presidential policy initiatives, which had to be approved by the Congress, the legislative branch determined the shape and direction of federal Indian programs and every aspect of the relationship between the United States and the Indian tribes. In 1871, Congress foreclosed the power of the executive branch to make further treaties with Indian nations, and later in the General Allotment Act reopened the treaty process in order to secure massive land cessions and the allotment of Indian lands.

Neither the executive branch nor the judicial branch did anything to exert their constitutional powers against this usurpation of power by the Congress. No president wished to place his own program or political career in jeopardy by opposing Congress on behalf of Indians; the federal courts, led by the Supreme Court, merely shrugged and espoused the doctrine that Congress possessed plenary power in the field of Indian affairs. The carefully designed system of checks and balances that would have prevented the abuse of citizens simply did not function for American Indians.

Indians and the Judicial Branch

It was contemplated in *The Federalist* arguments that the Supreme Court was necessary to provide a solitary and conclusive interpretation of American treaties, foreclosing the possibility that each state supreme court would render its own version of the responsibilities of the United States toward foreign nations. In 1831, the Cherokees approached the United States Supreme Court as a court of original jurisdiction, claiming that they could pursue their complaint against Georgia because they were a foreign nation (*Cherokee Nation v. Georgia*, 5 Pet. 1). The Court turned aside the argument, ruling instead that they were a "dependent domestic" nation. In *Worcester v. Georgia*, 6 Pet. 515, a year later, the supremacy of Indian treaties and federal laws fulfilling those treaties was upheld, but the description of the status of Indian nations was not changed.

The only reason Indian tribes would approach the federal court system in the nineteenth century was to ensure that treaty rights were enforced. In 1863, however, Congress prohibited the Court of Claims from hearing any suits involving Indian treaty claims without a special jurisdictional act admitting the Indian nation to the court (Act of March 3, 1863, 12 Stat. 765, 767). This prohibition meant that Indian nations had to have their claims against the United States examined by Congress prior to seeking relief, and as it developed, jurisdictional acts severely restricted the causes of action that Indian nations could bring and the latitude which the courts were given in resolving disputes.

The Constitution authorizes the creation of lesser courts, and in 1891 Congress established a forum for claims against the Indian nations in passing the Indian Depredations Act (Act of March 3, 1891, 26 Stat. 851). White settlers could recover damages against the Indian nations for acts committed in the Indian conflicts on the frontier, but Indian nations were barred from similar suits for damages they suffered. In 1946, after several decades of controversy, Congress established the Indian Claims Commission (Act of August 11, 1946, 60 Stat. 1049), which was supposed to function as a commission to review past dealings between the United States and Indian tribes, and remedy any injustices that might have occurred. Unfortunately, in order to file a claim in this commission, Indian nations had to allege that the United States had "taken" its lands illegally and seek monetary redress. Since many large areas of land had not been formerly or formally ceded by the Indian nations, the effect of the work of the Indian Claims Commission was to retroactively transfer title to large tracts of land owned by the Indians to the United States by using the fictional device which asserted that the lands had been permanently lost. Deprived of the right to sue for title to their lands, the Indian nations were simply stripped of their legal rights for a pittance.

In recent years Indian nations have made increasing use of the federal courts system, but in doing so they have had to make substantial reductions in the remedies they seek. Indian nations have not been allowed to challenge the constitutionality of any congressional act, and the courts have given themselves the broadest latitude in constructing an alleged "intent" of Congress when examining federal statutes dealing with Indians. As a result, many incidents of the American past have been literally revised in order to make the cases reach a predetermined conclusion. The role of the judiciary in the checks and balances system is to seek to reconcile the acts of the legislative and executive branches with constitutional principles. In virtually rewriting American history, the federal judiciary has become unreliable, antagonistic, and a barrier to the Indian quest for justice.

Constitutional relationships are determined by the nature of the Constitution itself. The system is designed to protect the political minority from an aggressive majority, and to place limits on the exercise of constitutional powers by the other two branches. There are no checks and balances, however, when Indians have dealt with the federal government. By expanding the powers of Congress at the expense of the executive branch, whatever balance might have existed has been destroyed. When we examine the constitutional clauses that authorize the federal government to deal with Indians, we must keep in mind the fact that the only limitations placed on dealings with Indians are the perceptions of power held by the branches of the federal government and the self-control exercised by the federal government itself. Unfortunately, American history demonstrates that there has been precious little self-restraint.

The Constitutional Powers

In *Worcester v. Georgia*, Chief Justice John Marshall declared that the Constitution

> *confers on Congress the powers of war and peace; of making treaties; and of regulating commerce with foreign nations, and among the several states, and with the Indian tribes. These powers comprehend all that is required for the regulation of our intercourse with the Indians. They are not limited by any restrictions on their free actions; the shackles imposed on this power, in the confederation, are discarded.*[3] *(Emphasis added.)*

Marshall's analysis reflects the original understanding of the number and scope of federal powers for dealing with Indians. Quite late in the nineteenth century, however, the Supreme Court discovered another power, that of the property clause, which it cited to justify massive changes in the status and condition of Indians. Of the constitutional clauses most often cited as justification for federal involvement with Indian nations, only the commerce clause specifically mentions Indian tribes. The other clauses are believed to affect Indians because these powers were traditionally exercised prior to the Constitution or, with the property clause, they were based upon doctrines which preceded the Constitution. So the major constitutional clauses authorizing the federal government to deal with Indians have consisted of powers *assumed* or *implied* and not specifically articulated in the document itself.

The Powers of War and Peace

Although the power to make war has been frequently cited in connection with Indians, the power to make war has never officially been used against an Indian tribe as a formal procedure by the Congress. There were Indian wars aplenty during the nineteenth century but never a formal declaration of war. The nature of the frontier precluded the formalities of declaring war. Skirmishes would break out, and the army would be ordered to pursue and attack the warring Indians in the vicinity. After several battles there would be a call for peace, and a treaty would be made, usually with the Indians ceding lands or promising to restrict their movements to certain areas and allowing the settlers to move into the abandoned lands or pass through their lands on the journey westward.

After the War of 1812 the United States was required to make peace with all the Indian tribes which had opposed it in the late war, and from 1815 to 1820 small delegations visited the Indian nations in the Great Plains, making peace treaties and establishing new trade relationships.

In 1862, when the Sioux fought the settlers in Minnesota, Congress authorized the abrogation of treaties with the nations engaged in hostilities against the United States (Act of July 5, 1862, 12 Stat. 512, 528; and Act of March 2, 1867, 14 Stat. 492, 515) and authorized withholding annuities from hostile nations. But apart from these specific acts directed at specific nations, there is no evidence that the war power was ever exercised against or on behalf of Indians. Most probably, since the early frontier was in a constant state of turmoil, John Marshall saw the war power as an important part of Indian relations. If anything, exercise of the war power was a wholly executive function determined by other more practical considerations and was not regarded as giving the United States unlimited power to force the Indians to conform to its wishes.

The Treaty-Making Power

The treaty-making power is assumed, rather than explicit or implied, in the sense that the president naturally followed this course of action already established by the French, English, and individual colonies in dealing with Indian tribes. Initially, the president played a dominating role in Indian treaty-making. George Washington, in a message to Congress on 17 September 1789, asked for clarification on instructions given him by Congress regarding then pending Indian treaties. Informed that he would execute and enjoin the observance of a treaty, Washington inquired:

> If, by my executing that treaty, you mean that I should make it (in a more particular and immediate manner than it now is) the act of Government, then it follows, that I am to ratify it. If you mean by my executing it, that I am to see that it be carried into effect and operation, then I am led to conclude, either that you consider it as being perfect and obligatory in its present state, and, therefore, to be executed and observed; or, that you consider it as to derive its completion and obligation from the silent approbation and ratification which my proclamation may be construed to imply.[4]

The Senate responded the following day that it was not necessary for the treaty to be formally ratified, and that a Senate resolution approving the actions of the president was sufficient to make the treaty operable.

The early stage of treaty-making relied heavily upon the activities of the executive branch. The president, on his own initiative or sometimes on instructions from the Senate, would seek appointment of treaty commissioners and, having them approved by the Senate, commission them to negotiate with the nation whose agreement was sought. Negotiations completed, the president would send the completed treaty with his comments to the Senate for advice and consent of that body. The

Senate then would examine the message and the treaty itself and, after offering its advice on changing terms, would pass a resolution to affirm the treaty. A typical early resolution, dealing with the treaty of Hopewell with the Cherokees, illustrates the form of consent used by the Senate to give its approval:

> Resolved, That the Senate do advise and consent, that the President of the United States do, at his discretion, cause the treaty concluded at Hopewell, with the Cherokee Indians, to be carried into execution according to the terms thereof, or to enter into arrangements for such further cession of territory, from the said Cherokee Indians, as the tranquillity and interest of the United States may require.[5]

Congress has a minor role in this process, and the treaty-making function of the president largely determines the substance of the posture and promises of the United States. The president and/or his advisors draw up the text of the treaty, conduct all negotiations, submit the signed treaty to the Senate, with its approval ratify it, proclaim it to be a binding obligation on the United States, and give direction under which it is put into operation. Thereafter, Congress appropriates the necessary funds and authorizes the necessary government personnel to put the treaty into effect.

With the increase in treaty-making and the expansion of the United States into the western lands, the Senate played an increasingly active role in treaty-making, examining the text of the treaty with more scrutiny and suggesting additional changes in the promises made. By 1851, when the Senate substantially changed the terms of the treaty of Fort Laramie, treaties were handled like a peculiar form of legislation with material changes in the provisions, primarily in response to pressures from private pressure groups and territorial governments. In 1867, Congress finally took the initiative and authorized a peace commission to make treaties with the warring Indian nations of the Great Plains (15 Stat. 17). Congress specifically named several of the commission members and allowed the president to appoint several members, thus preempting some of the prior executive power and sharing some of the prior legislative prerogative, making the treaty commission a major government effort to achieve peace with the Indian nations.

Although the 1867 to 1868 Indian Peace Commission had the full support of the Senate and the president, it proved to be very controversial and led to the prohibition of treaty-making. Members of the House of Representatives loudly objected to the provisions of these treaties, and so a rider was attached to the appropriation bill of 1871 which read: "That nothing in this act contained shall be construed to ratify any of the so-called treaties entered into with any tribe, band, or party of Indians since the 30th of July, 1867."[6] After much debate and negotiation in the conference committee, which sought to reconcile the Senate and House versions of the appropriation bill, language prohibiting any further treaty-making with Indians was adopted:

> That, hereafter no Indian nation or tribe within the territory of the United States shall be acknowledged or recognized as an independent nation, tribe, or power with whom the United States may contract by treaty: Provided further, That nothing herein contained shall be construed to invalidate or impair the obligation of any treaty heretofore lawfully made and ratified with any such Indian nation or tribe.[7]

The conference report set off a great controversy when it reached the Senate. The House of Representatives had been using the device of forcing a conference report on policy matters and getting the Senate to modify its posture on many pieces of legislation, and some of the senators objected to using this method to change the manner of dealing with Indians. Senator Casserly of California reviewed the history of the treatment of Indian nations and cited approvingly the words of the Supreme Court in the *Kansas Indians* case (5 Wall 755, 1866), which described the Indians as a "people distinct from others, capable of making treaties."[8] Referring to the House amendment, Casserly complained that

> the objection, or sting, is not in the word "independent," so much as in the assertion that the Indians are not a people with whom the United States may contract by treaty. I deny the right of either or both Houses of Congress to pass such a law. The Indians are not a part of the people of the United States; still less are they a portion of the citizens of the United States. I speak now of course of the Indians as tribes. It is not easy to define expressly their political relation to the United States, but I shall speak with sufficient accuracy when I say that their relations are those of a State having an existence of its own, having a certain independence of its own, but still under the protection and control of the United States according to treaty stipulations.[9]

Casserly then cited approvingly John Marshall's characterization of the Cherokees as more independent than states, but less independent than foreign nations:

> It is more than doubtful whether Congress, dealing with a people like the Indians, whose relations with us are so well established by treaty after treaty, and the whole practice of the Government, can annul, as to them, the treaty-making power vested in the President and the Senate. But the main objection is that the tribes are under

the protection of the Constitution and the treaties and the laws made in accordance therewith. Of that protection they cannot be deprived but with their own consent.[10] (*Emphasis added.*)

In other words, the commerce clause vested a constitutional protection for the Indians, and any change in their status required their consent.

Casserly suggested an alternative course of action for Congress to take:

> It is this: that instead of attempting to abrogate the provisions express and implied, of the Constitution, and to override the unvarying current of authorities in our own courts and of practice in our Government, we should let time solve it. Time will solve it if we have patience, either by the disappearance of these dwindling races or by their own voluntary acceptance of the relations of citizenship. In my judgment, it is only in this way that you can ever undertake to deal with these tribes. The United States has no peaceful control over them for any purpose whatever except through treaties made with them. It is by treaties that you exercise your authority. It is by treaties or by war that you regulate your relations with them; and yet here is a provision that we shall not again make treaties with them.[11]

Other senators were more concerned about the effect on the treaty-making powers of the Senate and the president than about the effect of the provision on Indian relations. Senator Pomeroy argued that

> it would be difficult by a law of Congress to limit the power of the President and Senate over treaties as provided in the Constitution. The Constitution of the United States defines and fixes the powers of the Executive and the Senate in regard to treaties; they are the treaty-making power. Now, you come in here on an appropriation bill, and by an act of Congress prohibit that power, contract it, limit it, when no law can have anything to do with it.[12]

Senator Davis was even more specific:

> Now the principle is this: the whole treaty-making power is vested by the Constitution in the President and the Senate. The House of Representatives have nothing to do with it except to pass appropriation bills that may be necessary to execute treaties. Beyond this power of appropriation the House has nothing to do with the subject of treaties either with foreign nations or with the Indian tribes.[13]

And Davis's argument was sound constitutional law. No one supposed that the House could direct the recognition of countries or the signing of treaties by a simple refusal to appropriate funds if they disliked the actions of the president. Yet, there was a considerable issue at stake here. If the House had an equal voice in determining the federal Indian policy, a great many benefits could accrue to the constituents of congressmen, benefits which they saw as being the privilege of the Senate alone and which they believed they should share.

Davis had some prophetic words to say regarding the future course of Indian affairs:

> *Is not the President of the United States competent to execute the power, according to his discretion, of negotiating a treaty with an Indian nation? Do we not all know that there are about eighty thousand Indians in the Southwest part of the United States, who are civilized, who are advancing in civilization and in all the developments of civilization, where they have their own government, their own constitution, their own language, their own alphabet, their own literature, and where they are making rapid progress in human improvement? Well, what is the effect of this article in the report of the committee of conference in relation to them? That the President in the future shall not have the power to negotiate a treaty with those Indians, either as tribes or as a confederate nation?*

And Davis concluded his speech dramatically:

> *I deny the power of the committee of conference to concede that great principle. I deny the power of the Senate to sacrifice it. I deny the power of the Congress of the United States to expunge it from the Constitution. It is as deeply moored, as fixed and immutable in the foundations of the Constitution as any other power whatever or any other principle established by it.*[14] *(Emphasis added.)*

The language recommended by the conference committee prevailed, and the Congress prohibited further Indian treaty-making, but it promptly continued making treaties and agreements with the tribes and authorized the president, in section 5 of the General Allotment Act (Act of February 8, 1887, 24 Stat. 388, 389–390) to negotiate with the Indian nations, in conformity with existing treaties and statutes for a sale of a portion of their lands after they had received allotments. Consequently, the various commissions to deal with the Indians—the Dawes, Jerome, and Crook commissions—were appointed using the same form of practice which had always been used. Indians were told that their agreements concerning the cession of lands were treaties, and the federal courts in interpreting the agreements gave them the same status as treaties. In this century securing Indian agreement has become an informal yet important part of the legislative process. Even in passing the termination acts of the 1950s, when Congress most aggressively asserted its plenary powers over Indians, there was a concerted effort to secure Indian consent to the legislation.

There is no question that constitutional issues of great importance still exist with respect to the termination of treaty-making with the Indian tribes. Two constitutional principles are involved: (1) does the treaty-making power, bolstered by the long practice of the federal government in using the treaty format to deal with Indian nations, constitute a vested power or determine a specific manner in which the actions of the federal government and/or any of its branches must relate to Indian nations? And (2) can the Congress, by statute, deprive the president and the Senate of a portion of the treaty-making power by specifically narrowing the number of entities with whom the United States can make treaties?

It is doubtless too late in American history to attempt to prove that there is a vested power which must be used to deal with Indian tribes. The second constitutional question, however, still has considerable relevance. Limiting the discretionary power of the president in treaty-making is much different than limiting the subject matter over which federal courts have jurisdiction; it involves the very essence of the president's constitutional responsibilities in recognizing political entities with whom the United States may contract by treaty. A good test of this question would be the submission of a newly negotiated Indian treaty to the Senate for ratification. If rejected on the basis of the 1871 act, the issue could then be taken to the Supreme Court for a definitive ruling.

The Power to Regulate Commerce

The commerce clause is the heart and soul of modern constitutional law and the cornerstone of federal plenary powers in Indian affairs. Initially Congress saw its responsibilities as twofold: (1) to pass legislation fulfilling treaty obligations and (2) to provide a means of civilizing the Indians with the eventual goal of assimilating them into American society. The first responsibility naturally follows from the nature of treaty-making, but the second responsibility is a policy decision woven wholly out of an extra-constitutional cloth. It is an effort to reduce tensions on the frontier between Indians and whites while maintaining some kind of accommodation to the changing nature of Indian life.

Most legislation in the period 1785 to 1834 reflected the belief that the federal government needed to control and police its own citizens in their intercourse with the Indian tribes, and it dealt primarily with establishing trading houses or factories, with issuing licenses for the Indian trade, and with fulfilling specific treaty provisions that spoke to the question of commerce. These acts show a careful delineation of the boundaries between the powers of the Indian tribes and the powers and responsibilities of the federal government.

One statute, however, the "Civilization Act" of 3 March 1819 (3 Stat. 516), provided for the gradual assumption of Indians into American society by enabling the president to use a special fund to provide education and agricultural assistance to the Indians at his discretion. Basically, the ideology of this program was simply a reversal of the commerce clause in that it saw culture as a function of commerce and not commerce as a part of culture. Expenditures under this provision were wholly gratuitous, and yet much later when the Indian tribes were able to file claims against the United States for loss of lands, these expenditures were credited to the United States as off-setting expenses. In effect, the tribes paid for the policy of assimilation, which was not a direct logical consequence of the power to regulate commerce.

It was assumed by most observers that Congress was functioning under the broad provisions of the commerce clause in directing the internal affairs of the reservations. No statute or court decision directly raised the question of the extent of the exercise of the commerce clause until *United States v. Kagama* (118 U.S. 375) in 1885, when the Seven Major Crimes Act was challenged. The Court rejected the argument that Congress derived broad plenary powers from the commerce clause. "The mention of Indians in the Constitution which has received most attention is that found in the clause which gives Congress 'power to regulate commerce with foreign nations, and among the several States, and with the Indian tribes,' " the opinion stated, commenting further that

> [t]his clause is relied on in the argument in the present case, the proposition being that the statute under consideration is a regulation of commerce with the Indian tribes. But we think it would be a very strained construction of this clause, that a system of criminal laws for Indians living peaceably in their reservations, which left out the entire code for trade and intercourse laws justly enacted under that provision, and established punishments for the common-law crimes of murder, manslaughter, arson, burglary, larceny, and the like, without any reference to their relation to any kind of commerce, was authorized by the grant of power to regulate commerce with the Indian tribes.[15] *(Emphasis added.)*

In view of the extensive body of federal law dealing with the Indian nations and the unbroken tradition of congressional legislation dealing with Indians, the rejection of the commerce clause by the Supreme Court is nothing short of astounding. It seems to be suggesting that only a narrowly drawn and rigidly interpreted code of commercial laws dealing with Indian matters can properly be the result of the exercise of the commerce clause, an interpretation that many Indians would willingly support. It further suggests that efforts by the federal government to dominate the internal workings of an Indian tribe are efforts which go beyond the scope of the powers allocated to the federal government by the Constitution.

In place of the commerce clause, the Supreme Court offered a new basis for justifying federal relationships with the Indian tribes:

> [T]hese Indians are within the geographical limits of the United States. The soil and the people within these limits are under the political control of the Government of the United States, or of the States of the Union. . . . What authority the State governments may have to enact criminal laws for the Indians will be presently considered. But the power of Congress to organize territorial governments, and make laws for their inhabitants, arises not so much from the clause in the Constitution in regard to disposing of and making rules and regulations concerning the Territory and other property of the United States, as from the ownership of the country in which the Territories are, and the right of exclusive sovereignty which must exist in the National Government, and can be found nowhere else.[16] (Emphasis added.)

The final meaning of the *Kagama* case, and a conclusion that most legal scholars and judges are reluctant to draw, is that the Supreme Court has held a federal statute applying to Indians to be constitutional, while rejecting every possible constitutional clause and phrase that would connect it to the document. Property ownership but not the constitutional property clause is believed to be sufficient to justify this statute as a valid legislative act. So the commerce clause must be restricted to apply only to those provisions which are required of Congress in the regulation of Indian trade and intercourse.

The primary responsibility of Congress under the commerce clause, that of passing legislation to fulfill the treaty provisions, has never been clearly distinguished from the charitable and gratuitous acts of humanity, also the product of congressional action. Therefore, American legal thought regarding the commerce clause is hardly definitive. At best the commerce clause merges with the treaty-making and property clauses to provide a general authority to deal with Indians. But this general authority has no clearly defined boundaries or limits, and consequently almost anything that touches upon the Indian situation is believed to fall within the purview of this power.

The Property Clause

Although it never seems to play a prominent role in the deliberations of either Congress or the federal courts when they deal with Indian matters, an analysis of the critical decisions of the Supreme Court suggests that the property clause and/or the fact of American claims to legal title to lands in North America underlie the posture and actions of the United States towards Indians. The clause itself is a model of restraint:

> The Congress shall have Power to dispose of and make all needful Rules and Regulations respecting the Territory or other Property belonging to the United States; and nothing in this Constitution shall be so construed as to Prejudice any Claims of the United States, or of any particular State.[17]

Through negotiation after the American Revolution, the United States acquired the colonial charter claims of its constituent states, and these claims formed the basis of the national public domain. Apart from these claims, however, there was no basis for making any extensive claims to territory based on national existence until Chief Justice John Marshall provided it in the 1823 case of *Johnson v. McIntosh* (8 Wheat 543). At issue was the question of whether a land title, given by the Indians under British supervision at an open public sale, was superior to a title derived from the United States through a sale by designated federal land officers.

John Marshall argued:

> On the discovery of this immense continent, the great nations of Europe are eager to appropriate to themselves so much of it as they could respectively acquire. Its vast extent offered an ample field to the ambition and enterprise of all; and the character and religion of its inhabitants afforded an apology for considering them as a people over whom the superior genius of Europe might claim an ascendency. The potentates of the old world found no difficulty in convincing themselves that they made ample compensation to the inhabitants of the new, by bestowing on them civilization and Christianity. . . . So the Europeans agreed on a principle of law that discovery gave title to the government by whose subjects, or by whose authority, it was made, against all other European governments.[18] (Emphasis added.)

This line of reasoning came to be known as the Doctrine of Discovery, and it is the primary basis for the American claim to own its lands in North America. It is wholly a fiction deriving from earlier claims by Spain and Portugal that the pope, as Christ's representative on earth, had given them claim to the lands of the Western Hemisphere.

The aboriginal inhabitants in this scheme

> were admitted to be the rightful occupants of the soil, with a legal as well as just claim to retain possession of it, and to use it according

to their own discretion; but their rights to complete sovereignty, as independent nations, were necessarily diminished, and their power to dispose of the soil at their own will, to whomsoever they pleased, was denied by the original fundamental principle that discovery gave exclusive title to those who made it.[19] *(Emphasis added.)*

Since the culture and religion of the aboriginal peoples become the impediment standing between them and the Europeans, and since Christianity and civilization, even if forced upon the natives, are believed to be fair consideration for recognizing the Europeans' title, it is not difficult to see why and how the commerce clause gets confused with the property clause and the desire of Congress to civilize the Indians. Discovery suggests that culture is a tangible commodity which can be exchanged within a system of property laws to confirm an interest in lands.

Marshall argued that the United States, in its successful revolution against Great Britain, had succeeded to whatever claims and titles England had possessed in the area east of the Mississippi. All titles to land, therefore, must follow a path from the Indians to the United States and thereafter to the individual states and citizens. The Indians could not sell their lands without the permission or approval of the United States. And Marshall justified this theory by declaring that

> *[h]owever this restriction may be opposed to natural right, and to the usages of civilized nations, yet, if it be indispensable to that system under which the country has been settled, and be adapted to the actual condition of the two people, it may, perhaps, be supported by reason, and certainly cannot be rejected by courts of justice.*[20] *(Emphasis added.)*

In other words, this claim to property titles was valid because to do otherwise would disrupt everything that had previously occurred.

In theory, then, the United States could not have had any property unless it was derived from the Indians. It might have a great expectation of land ownership based upon the obvious degeneration of the Indian nations, but it could not have complete title to its lands until the Indian title was extinguished. To argue, then, as the Court did in *Kagama*, that the United States possessed power to deal with the Indian nations because of its ownership of lands, is entirely beside the point, since it could not own lands unless and until the Indians were removed, and if the Indians were removed, there was no responsibility for them on lands which they had ceded.

In order to deal with the Indians on the basis of the property clause, it would be the responsibility of the United States to ensure the proper functioning of Indian governments and to secure to the Indian nations a climate in which they could act relatively independent so that their cession of land, when it occurred, would have a ring of legality to it. There is no question that the property clause acts to exclude Indians from the constitutional umbrella, and that if the Doctrine of Discovery vested the United States with some interest in the land, it operated before and outside of the Constitution. The only just resolution of this problem, therefore, would be an international forum or tribunal to which the United States and the Indian nations would submit their dispute. Within the constitutional framework alone, the United States can only own property when it has extinguished Indian title, and once extinguishing this title Indians are by definition excluded from the operation of the powers provided by the property clause.

Miscellaneous Constitutional Clauses

Although the Constitution clearly excludes American Indians, and a few constitutional phrases have been used to justify actions toward Indians by the three branches of the federal government, it can be argued that the document as a whole articulates a pattern of behavior which has often been applied to American Indians. There have been instances in which a branch of the government has exercised its powers on behalf of or in a manner which affected Indians. These occasions are peripheral to the central theme of receiving authority to deal directly with Indian matters, and can be understood as including Indians within the normal exercise of powers designed to solve other problems.

The presidential power to grant reprieves and pardons has been used once to benefit Indians. In 1862, the Sioux of Minnesota, after suffering much abuse from their agent, attacked the settlements in that state. Overwhelmed by whites after a few weeks of conflict, the Sioux found themselves imprisoned at Fort Snelling and other military outposts, where they were given the semblance of a trial and sentenced to death. As previously noted, President Lincoln insisted on reviewing the trial record, unable to believe that 303 Sioux had committed capital crimes. He assigned two men to go over the proceedings to determine which of the Indians might actually be guilty of a crime and pardoned all but 40 of the Indians.[21]

In exercising the power to admit new states, Congress included Indian provisions in the enabling acts so that the new states, lacking a large population and with major Indian reservations inside their borders, would not look to Indian property for their income. In the enabling acts for North Dakota, South Dakota, Montana, and Wyoming (Act of February 22, 1889, 25 Stat. 399); for Washington (Act of February 22, 1889, 25 Stat. 677); for Oklahoma (Act of June 16, 1906, 34 Stat. 267); and for Arizona and New Mexico (Act of June 20, 1910, 36 Stat. 557), Congress exempted Indian property and rights from state control. States have argued, with no success, that these limitations have placed them on a less than equal status with respect to the existing states in the union when they were admitted. In 1953, Congress passed PL-280 (Act of August 15, 1953, 67 Stat. 588), which gave states permission to amend their constitutions to omit the exclusionary clauses. But in 1968, in the Indian Civil Rights Act (82 Stat. 73), these provisions were again amended to provide for Indian consent to this change of status in state law.

The two clauses granting the power of judicial review and the power to constitute the necessary inferior tribunals must be discussed together. Judicial review is the only avenue open to the tribes to secure a determination of their rights once treaty and agreement making are prohibited. Approaching the federal courts in this respect, however, means that Indian rights are viewed as equal to the rights of citizens even while Indians do not have the protections granted other citizens. Courts therefore balance treaty rights which occur prior to the Constitution with civil rights of citizens often granted only months before the Indians approach the court. In general, the federal judicial forum sees its task as that of reconciling Indian rights to the existing situation, not in the protection and enforcement of them.

In 1855, Congress established the Court of Claims (Act of February 24, 1855, 10 Stat. 612) as a means of eliminating the hundreds of requests from private citizens for redress from real and imagined wrongs visited upon them by the federal government. But a decade later, to forestall suits by Indian tribes in this forum, Congress changed the jurisdiction of the court by prohibiting it from hearing claims based upon treaties (Act of March 3, 1863, 12 Stat. 765, 767). Thereafter, Indians could only sue the government with the legislative permission of Congress in a special jurisdictional act. The United States thus prejudged the causes of action which a tribe could bring against it and screened out any claim that might have been embarrassing or which might have become the basis for a real solution to the question of treaty violation. In the jurisdictional acts the Indian nations had to allege that their lands had been "taken" by the United States, either legally or illegally, and that they would accept monetary compensation.

In 1891, after processing numerous claims made against the Indian nations as a result of actions in the final wars on the Plains, Congress decided to allow the Court of Claims to hear all cases brought against the Indian nations for the violation of treaties (Act of March 3, 1891, 26 Stat. 851). The result was decidedly unjust: white citizens could sue the Indians for depredations, but the Indian nations could not sue whites for depredations they had suffered. Meanwhile, petitions for permission to sue the United States increased with each session of Congress so that in 1946 Congress finally authorized the Indian Claims Commission (Act of August 8, 1946, 60 Stat. 939) to handle all Indian claims. Although it was designed to be a commission, the ICC quickly adopted all the judicial procedures of a court and processed over 600 claims against the United States using a rigorous definition of what "taking" lands of the Indians actually meant, frequently obliterating treaty rights. In 1978, after much controversy, Congress let the authorization for the Indian Claims Commission lapse and sent all remaining claims to the Court of Claims, later reconstituted as the Claims Court (Act of October 8, 1976, 90 Stat. 1990).

As a rule, the inferior tribunals of the judiciary have not protected Indian rights but have seen their role as rewriting American history to protect the federal government. They have often been refused the power to deal with intangible treaty rights and have been forced to reduce treaty provisions to simple contract law, finding no inherent liability by the United States for promises to provide education, health services, and other benefits.

The Constitutional Amendments

The constitutional amendments represent a special situation in their applicability to American Indians. The Bill of Rights was added to the Constitution at a time when many Indian nations did not recognize the United States as a superior sovereign to whom they owed allegiance. The Thirteenth, Fourteenth, and Fifteenth Amendments were added during the treaty-making period when it was anticipated that Indians would always remain separate from American society. The Sixteenth, Eighteenth, and Twenty-First amendments were adopted long after the end of treaty-making when everyone assumed that the federal government had a plenary power over Indians which precluded the operation of these amendments with respect to Indians.

The Bill of Rights

The Bill of Rights did not come into effect until Indians were made citizens in 1924 (43 Stat. 253), and even then they have been regarded as applicable primarily when Indians are off their reservations. Of importance in this respect are: the First Amendment, which prohibits Congress from making any law "respecting the establishment of religion, or prohibiting the free exercise thereof," and guaranteeing the freedom of speech, assembly, press, and the right to petition the government for redress; the Fourth Amendment, prohibiting unreasonable searches and seizures; and the Fifth Amendment, prohibiting double jeopardy and providing just compensation when property is taken for a public purpose. The provisions dealing with religion have the most relevance for American Indians.

The First Amendment: The Establishment of Religion

Although some early treaties have provisions establishing a mission school, and the federal government made free use of missionaries in providing services to the Indians, it was not until 1869 with the Peace Policy of President Grant that church and state were forcibly mixed on Indian reservations. The Act of April 10, 1869 (16 Stat. 40), established a Board of Indian Commissioners to oversee the administration of Indian affairs. President Grant solicited nominations from the churches and appointed lay churchmen who had the belief that the agencies should be parceled out to the various Christian denominations. "What the government wanted from the churches," Francis Paul Prucha observed, "was a total transformation of the agencies from political sinecures to missionary outposts."[22] And, he noted, "maintaining a position against a conflicting group was . . . often a more powerful motivation than concern for the welfare of the Indians."[23]

Not only was the establishment clause violated, the missionaries did everything they could to eliminate the native religions. "What was more serious," according to Prucha,

> *was the complete disregard for the religious views and the religious rights of the Indians themselves. Quakers, Methodists, Episcopalians, and all the other Protestants, fighting for the religious liberty of their own groups on the reservations, made no move to grant so much as a hearing to the Indian religions. The record of the Catholics was no better. They criticized Protestant bigotry and called for freedom of conscience, but that freedom did not extend to native religions, which were universally condemned. The missionaries were not interested in the Indians' right to maintain and defend their own religion. By religious freedom they meant liberty of action on the reservations for their own missionary activities.*[24] *(Emphasis added.)*

The two protections of the First Amendment were simply not a matter of concern when federal reservation policy was formulated.

Competition among the churches became so fierce that after the practice of giving denominations virtual franchises with agency appointments, the conflict spread to the question of federal funding of sectarian schools. In 1895, the Protestants began agitating for the prohibition of funding for church schools, and in 1897 the Congress inserted a phrase accomplishing this goal in an appropriation act (30 Stat. 62, 79). After several years of severe reductions in federal funds, the Catholics devised a plan whereby they could be given tribal funds for their mission schools. In 1908, this practice was challenged in *Quick Bear v. Leupp*, 210 U.S. 50, when Reuben Quick Bear, a Protestant Sioux Indian on the Rosebud Reservation in South Dakota, objected to the practice of transferring a per capita share of tribal funds on deposit in the federal treasury to the Catholic school programs. The Court, in an ironic decision, declared that

> *it would be unjust to withhold from an Indian or community of Indians the right, within reasonable limits, in good faith, and under the safeguards provided by the President's instructions, to choose their own school and to choose it frankly because the education therein is under the influence of the religious faith in which they believe and to which they are attached, and to have the use of their proportion of tribal funds applied under the control of the Secretary's discretion to maintain such schools.* Any other view of the case perverts the supposed general spirit of the constitutional provision into a means of prohibiting the free exercise of religion.[25] *(Emphasis added.)*

The establishment clause has another dimension to it. In the 1890s, Congress granted a right-of-way through Osage lands to the Missouri, Kansas and Texas Railway Company. The Indians loudly protested, and the case went to the Supreme Court.[26] In upholding the powers of Congress to deal with Indian property in this manner, the Court declared that

> *though the law as stated with reference to the power of the government to determine the right of occupancy of the Indians to their lands has always been recognized, it is to be presumed, as stated by the Court in the Buttz case, that in its exercise the United States will be governed by such considerations of justice as will control a Christian people in their treatment of an ignorant and dependent race. . . .*[27] *(Emphasis added.)*

If the tenets of Christian doctrine, morality, or concepts of justice are the criteria for judging the propriety of federal acts towards the Indians, has the United States *established* the Christian religion and abandoned neutrality in this respect? Only if the United States Constitution protects denominational differences, not substantive religious differences, could this criterion be in accord with the intent of the Constitution.

The First Amendment: The Free Exercise Clause

The free exercise of traditional Indian religions has been inhibited by administrative action and has not, until very recently, been the subject of court litigation. Discretionary actions on the part of the Indian agents suppressing tribal ceremonies have been a constant feature of reservation life, and these actions have always been directed from the commissioner's office. An example of the kinds of suppression experienced by Indians can be seen in the language of an Office of Indian Affairs circular (No. 1665) dated 26 April 1921:

> The sun-dance, and all other similar dances and so-called religious ceremonies are considered "Indian offences" under existing regulations, and corrective penalties are provided. I regard such restrictions as applicable to any dance which . . . involves the reckless giving away of property . . . frequent or prolonged periods of celebration . . . in fact any disorderly or plainly excessive performance that promotes superstitious cruelty, licentiousness, idleness, danger to health, and shiftless indifference to family welfare.[28]

Indians received some relief from administrative suppression in the 1930s under the general New Deal reforms, but it was not until 1978 when the American Indian Religious Freedom Resolution was passed (92 Stat. 469) that Congress felt it necessary to make a formal statement on the protection of Indian religious practices.

This resolution, however, was intended primarily as an administrative directive to federal agencies to bring their rules and regulations within the existing scope of constitutionally exercised powers. Subsequent litigation involving the resolution demonstrated that Indian religious practices would simply be balanced against the interests of federal agencies when a conflict arose; there was no effort to examine the tribal religious claims or to ensure that federal agencies did not unduly interfere with traditional practices. Opponents of tribal religions have gone so far as to suggest that the resolution *establishes* tribal religions, thus violating the constitutional prohibition in that respect. Insofar as Indians have constitutionally protected rights to practice their religion, they remain outside the Constitution.

The First Amendment: Freedoms of Speech and Assembly

The freedoms of speech and assembly have a strange history on Indian reservations. The Trade and Intercourse Act of 1834 (4 Stat. 729) greatly expanded the powers of the United States to take actions in Indian country against disruptive persons and activities there. Section 6 required foreigners to obtain passports in order to enter Indian country; Section 10 empowered the superintendent of Indian affairs to remove persons illegally in Indian country; and Sections 21 and 23 gave the president great leeway in employing military force and in arresting Indians. In 1858, Congress expanded these powers by authorizing the commissioner of Indian affairs to remove any person from the reservation whose presence, in his judgment, might be detrimental to the peace and welfare of the Indians (11 Stat. 329).

Although intended to protect Indians against foreigners, the authority to police the reservations was quickly turned against the Indians. Free speech and free assembly were prohibited at the whim of the agent.

The condition of Indians during the nineteenth century is best described by a Claims Court case:

> *These Indians, indeed, in 1878 occupied an anomalous position, unknown to the common or civil law or to any system of municipal law. They were neither citizens nor aliens; they were neither free persons nor slaves; they were wards of the nations, and yet, on a reservation under military guard, were little else than prisoners of war while war did not exist. Dull Knife and his daughters could be invited guests at the table of officers and gentlemen, behaving with dignity and propriety, and yet could be confined for life on a reservation which was to them little better than a dungeon, on the mere order of an executive officer.*[29]

As late as 1952, the Bureau of Indian Affairs was still attempting to deny Indians the right of free speech and assembly. In that year a bill was introduced (H.R. 6035, 82d Cong., 2d Sess.) which would have authorized employees of the Bureau of Indian Affairs to carry arms and to make arrests, searches, and seizures, without warrant, for violation of bureau regulations, on or off Indian reservations. That any administration could seriously sponsor such legislation is prima facie evidence that insofar as First Amendment speech and assembly rights are concerned, Indians have at best a tenuous claim to constitutional protections.

The Fourth Amendment: Search and Seizure

It goes without saying, in light of the discussion above, that Fourth Amendment protections were believed to have no application to Indians from the very beginning. Seizure is probably more important in this respect, since it was a common practice, when the tribes went on the reservations, for the army to confiscate their horses, weapons, household goods, and religious medicine bundles. Of a more ghoulish nature, however, was the army practice of shipping Indian bodies to the Smithsonian Institution for its museum exhibits and anthropological research. A more profound and distasteful violation of both the spirit and letter of the Fourth Amendment prohibition against unlawful seizure cannot be found.

The Fifth Amendment: Double Jeopardy

The confusing relationship between the federal government and Indian governments has created a situation which seems to be desperately close to a violation of the Fifth Amendment prohibition against double jeopardy. Since the federal government, the states, and tribal governments can all promulgate criminal codes, it is possible to have one criminal act fall into three distinct criminal codes and subject the defendant to three possible prosecutions. In *United States v. Wheeler*, 435

U.S. 313 (1978), a Navajo defendant appealed convictions under both Navajo and federal law on the double jeopardy clause but was denied. The Supreme Court held that the Navajo tribe had power to punish offenses under its "retained sovereignty" and denied that the tribal court was an arm of the federal government.

An earlier case, however, *Colliflower v. Garland*, 342 P.2d 369 (1965), had seen an appeals court declare that

> it is pure fiction to say that the Indian courts functioning in the Fort Belknap Indian community are not in part, at least, arms of the federal government. Originally they were created by the federal executive and imposed upon the Indian community, and to this day the federal government still maintains a partial control over them.[30]

The unpredictability in determining the status of the tribal court system, coupled with the broad discretionary powers of prosecuting attorneys, makes the possibility of multijurisdictional prosecution a de facto condition of double jeopardy.

The Fifth Amendment: Due Process and Just Compensation

Federal courts have never reached the question of due process for American Indian nations because it has been the rule that the Congress has plenary powers over Indian affairs. Consequently, when treaties or specific Indian statutes conflict with general statutes of the United States, the tendency of the federal courts is to construct a fictional intent of Congress that has already taken the Indian interests into consideration and subjected them to general domestic legislation. Due process in this setting is purely at the whim of judges. A court may rule that general legislation affects Indians because they are not specifically excluded, or it may decide that it does not affect them because they are not specifically included. No acceptance doctrines dealing specifically with Indian rights are universally respected in the federal courts. Consequently, nothing approaching the idea of due process exists in Indian law.

Just compensation under the Fifth Amendment has a history of inconsistency when applied to Indian tribes. Occasionally, as in the case of the *Tee-Hit-Ton Indians v. United States*, 348 U.S. 272 (1955), the courts simply hold that Indians do not have sufficient title in their lands to qualify as "property" under the amendment.

Between *Lone Wolf* and its plenary power doctrine and *Tee-Hit-Ton* with its disclaimer of compensable title, Indians had neither due process nor just compensation. In 1968, the Court of Claims attempted to reconcile these doctrines and introduce a means of avoiding a complete denial of Indian claims. In *Fort Berthold Reservation v. United States*, 390 F.2d 686 (1968), the court observed that it is obvious that Congress cannot simultaneously (1) act as a trustee for the benefit of the Indians, exercising its plenary powers over the Indians and their property, as it thinks is in their best interests, and (2) exercise its sovereign power of eminent domain, taking the Indians' property within the meaning of the Fifth Amendment to the Constitution. In any given situation in which Congress has acted with regard to Indian people, it must have acted either in one capacity or the other. Congress can own two hats, but it cannot wear them both at the same time.[31]

The ultimate test, according to the Claims Court, is that Congress must act "in good faith" when taking Indian property. It must make a reasonable effort to transmute Indian property from land to money, otherwise the Fifth Amendment applies. Later, in *United States v. Sioux Nations*, 448 U.S. 371 (1980), involving a history of duplicitous dealings with an Indian nation, the Supreme Court expanded the *Fort Berthold* concept to require an Indian nation to overcome the presumption of good faith in order to receive Fifth Amendment compensation. In view of the commonly known incidents of American history, it would seem that the presumption of good faith is simply a fictional hurdle placed before Indian litigants to narrow the application of the Fifth Amendment to so few occasions as to be meaningless as a protection for the Indian nations.

Summary

The protections of the Bill of Rights, available to all other Americans, have not been available for American Indians. Not only have the federal courts studiously avoided considering the application of these protections, but Congress and the executive branch have frequently acted as if there were no limitation whatsoever in their power to deal with Indians, and the courts have deferred to this assertion of naked authority. In 1968, the American Indian Civil Rights Act (82 Stat. 73) was passed, but this act only served to extend some Bill of Rights protections to tribal members in their relationship with Indian governments. Nothing was authorized that would protect American Indian nations or individuals against the arbitrary actions of the federal government, protections that both states and individuals enjoy.

The Later Amendments

Five later amendments have peripheral relationships with Indians: the Thirteenth, which abolishes slavery and involuntary servitude; the Fourteenth, which defines national citizenship; the Sixteenth, which establishes a federal income tax; and the Eighteenth and Twenty-First, which deal with the prohibition of alcoholic beverages in the United States. These amendments have no bearing on Indians, or Indians are specifically excluded from their provisions.

The Thirteenth Amendment

This amendment, adopted in 1865, prohibited slavery and involuntary servitude within the United States or any place subject to its jurisdiction. Slavery within the Five Civilized Tribes, however, was abolished only by treaty provision, since the amendments did not apply to Indian nations. The treaty of 21 March 1866 with the Seminoles (14 Stat. 755) is an example of how slavery was handled in the Indian context. Article 2 stated:

> The Seminole Nation covenant that henceforth in said nation slavery shall not exist, nor involuntary servitude, except for and in punishment of crime, whereof the offending party shall first have been duly convicted in accordance with law, applicable to all the members of said nation.[32]

Similar provisions occur in the treaties of the other Five Civilized Tribes.

Three years after the ratification of the amendment Congress found it necessary to pass Joint Resolution No. 83 (15 Stat. 264, 27 July 1868), which prohibited peonage of women and children of the Navajo Tribe and was designed to stop the profitable slave trade of the Southwest in which Americans and Mexicans were engaging. Involuntary servitude in Alaska did not cease until *In re Sah Quah*, 31 Fed. 327, finally prohibited customary slavery in 1886. The federal government, however, required a form of involuntary servitude of all reservation Indians when it required them to work in order to qualify for treaty negotiated rations. Felix Cohen cited the Act of June 22, 1874, Section 3, requiring Indians to work, and noted: "The popular outcry that would have followed the application of a similar rule to white holders of Government bonds or pensions may well be imagined."[33] This practice was followed at most agencies for many years.

The Fourteenth Amendment

This amendment was adopted in 1868, and in April of 1870 the Senate Judiciary Committee issued a report on its applicability to Indian nations. The committee found that Indians were born subject to the jurisdiction of their own tribes and not the United States. And with respect to the operation of the amendment, the report said:

> To maintain that the United States intended, by a change of its fundamental law, which was not ratified by these tribes, and to which they were neither requested nor permitted to assent, to annul treaties then existing between the United States as one party, and the Indian

A meeting on Native American sovereignty issues between Lakota and Hopi representatives and Haudenosaunee chiefs at the Onondaga Nation Longhouse in 1974. Second from left, Thomas Banyaca (Hopi); sixth from left, Leon Shenandoah (Onondaga), chief of the Iroquois Confederacy; second from right, Chief Oren Lyons (Onondaga). (Photograph by Marcia Keegan.)

tribes as the other party respectively, would be to charge the United States with repudiation of national obligations, repudiation doubly infamous from the fact that the parties whose claims were thus annulled are too weak to enforce their just rights, and were enjoying the voluntarily assumed guardianship and protection of this Government.[34] *(Emphasis added.)*

In 1884, in *Elk v. Wilkins*, 112 U.S. 94, the Supreme Court relied heavily upon this report in denying that the Fourteenth Amendment had made citizens of Indians who had voluntarily abandoned their tribal relations. It was not until 1924 (43 Stat. 253) that Indians were finally declared to be citizens. But this citizenship does not change the relationship between Indians and the federal government. According to *United States v. Nice*, 241 U.S. 591 (1916),

[c]itizenship is not incompatible with tribal existence or continued guardianship, and so may be conferred without completely emancipating the Indians or placing them beyond the reach of congressional regulations adopted for their protection.[35]

So in this instance also, the Constitution does not come between the federal government and the Indians to provide them with protection and rights.

The Sixteenth Amendment

In the popular mind, the constitutional phrase "Indians not taxed" created a kind of immunity from federal and state taxation. Although the amendment speaks of "income from whatever source derived," it has generally been acknowledged that unless and until the United States releases Indian lands from their trust status, the United States cannot and should not levy a tax against them (*Squire v. Capoeman*, 351 U.S. 1, 1956). More important for our purposes here is the question of whether the United States ever took sovereign immunity away from Indian nations in the field of taxation. In *McCulloch v. Maryland*, 4 Wheat. 316 (1819), John Marshall identified the taxing power as a power to destroy. Arguably, since the tribes are under a federal protectorate, again in Marshall's view, this status inhibits the federal government from attempting to exert that taxing power against the Indian nations. The cumulative effect of the Indian status, whether considered as a ward or dependent sovereign, is to remove Indian tribes from the all-inclusive phrases of the Sixteenth Amendment.

The Prohibition Amendments

The Eighteenth and Twenty-First amendments deal with the prohibition and sale of intoxicating liquors and the subsequent repeal fourteen years later. The liquor prohibition affecting the Indian tribes was a

Onondaga Chief Oren Lyons speaking in Washington, D.C., during *The Longest Walk*, 1978, in defense of Native American sovereignty. Standing to his right is Chief Jake Swamp (Mohawk); to his left is Chief Vince Johnson (Onondaga). (Photograph by Marcia Keegan.)

combination of early laws regulating trade and treaty provisions desired by the tribes. During prohibition, when it would have been possible to merge the national prohibition and earlier specific federal prohibitions regarding Indians, the prosecution of Indians continued under old statutes, and repeal of the Eighteenth Amendment had no effect on the prohibition for Indians. In 1953, some twenty years after the adoption of the Twenty-First Amendment, Congress finally repealed the Indian liquor prohibition, allowing what amounted to local option on the basis of tribal consent (Act of August 15, 1953, 67 Stat. 586).

The Relationship of Indian Tribes and the Constitution

In *Talton v. Mayes*, 163 U.S. 376 (1896), the Supreme Court turned aside the appeal of a Cherokee citizen claiming Fifth Amendment protections, declaring that

> as the powers of local self-government enjoyed by the Cherokee Nation existed prior to the Constitution, they are not operated upon by the Fifth Amendment, which, as we have said, had for its sole object to control the powers conferred by the Constitution on the National Government.[36]

Again, in *Native American Church v. Navajo Tribal Council*, 272 F.2d 131 (1959), the Tenth Circuit ruled that the Navajo tribal council could prohibit the use of peyote on the reservation because First Amendment limitations applied only to the federal government, and Fourteenth Amendment protections dealt primarily with states. The Indian tribes were neither. The court declared:

> Indian tribes are not states. They have a status higher than states. They are subordinate and dependent nations possessed of all powers as such only to the extent that they have been expressly required to surrender them by the superior sovereign, the United States.[37]

The underlying theme of these cases is that Indian nations are not subject to the Constitution because they existed prior to its adoption and have inherent powers, whereas the Constitution is a document of delegated and ceded powers. And, although tribes are comparable to states, they have a higher status than states because they are dependent domestic nations, not the originators of the constitutional social contract or creatures of the national government. The principle announced by the Senate Judiciary Committee in 1870, in finding that Indian nations were excluded from the operation of the Fourteenth Amendment, was that it would be unfair and unjust to subject them to a rule of law to which they had not consented.

Consent, the basis of modern Western social contract theory, can only be found in the Indian treaty relationship with the United States. A strong analogy exists, therefore, between the status of Indian nations and the states of the union with respect to the Constitution. Under the Tenth Amendment, all powers not delegated to the federal government by the states are reserved to the states and the people respectively. It is standard treaty law that everything not specifically ceded to the United States by an Indian nation in a treaty remains vested in the Indian nation (*United States v. Winans*, 198 U.S. 371, 1905). The proper relationship of Indian nations and the Constitution is, therefore, also one of delegated rights and powers with the Indian nations, like the states, reserving and preserving everything not specifically ceded by treaty. Only by using this analogy can existing case law and the history of constitutional exclusion of Indian tribes make sense.

8.
Congress, Plenary Power, and the American Indian, 1870 to 1992

Laurence M. Hauptman

Introduction

During the two-hundredth anniversary of the United States Constitution five years ago, Americans commemorated the drafting of this historic document of 1787 as well as its legacies. American Indians could find things to celebrate in the original document; however, they could find much less to applaud concerning constitutional development, especially over the past one hundred and twenty years. Until 1871, the United States government made treaties with American Indian nations. Even before the suspension of federal Indian treaty-making, a new era had begun, one marked by wholesale congressional intervention, resulting in the near extinction of meaningful Indian autonomy and Indian national self-government.

For well over one hundred years, the United States federal court system has recognized the doctrine of plenary power, namely the right of Congress to unilaterally intervene and legislate over a wide range of Indian affairs, including the territory of the Indian nations. A century of abuse of this doctrine by Congress has motivated some American Indians to suggest that federal Indian treaty-making be reinstituted, thus reinstating the original intent of the framers of the United States Constitution.[1] The noted attorney Alvin J. Ziontz has observed that the doctrine of plenary power "in practice means that Congress has the power to do virtually as it pleases with the Indian tribes. It is an extraordinary doctrine for a democracy to espouse. It would justify abolishing the political existence of the tribes." Ziontz added: "Short of that, it justifies the imposition of controls over the lives and property of the tribes and their members. Plenary power thus subjects Indians to national powers outside ordinary constitutional limits."[2]

Plenary power has an interesting history. In 1868, the Internal Revenue Act provided for the imposition of federal taxes on distilled spirits, tobacco, and so forth produced anywhere, within a collection district or not. Despite apparent provisions of exclusion in the Federal-Cherokee Treaty of 1866, the United States applied the act to the Cherokee Nation in Indian Territory. In 1870, the United States Supreme Court in the *Cherokee Tobacco* case held that an act of Congress can supersede a prior treaty, setting the precedent for the doctrine of plenary power. According to the Court:

A treaty may supersede a prior act of Congress and an act of Congress may supersede a treaty. In the cases referred to these principles were applied to treaties with foreign nations. Treaties with Indian nations within the jurisdiction of the United States, whatever considerations of humanity and good faith may be involved and require their faithful observance, cannot be more obligatory. They have no higher sanctity; and no greater inviolability or immunity from legislative invasion can be claimed for them. The consequences in all such cases give rise to questions which must be met by the political department of the government. They are beyond the sphere of judicial cognizance.[3]

In 1883, the United States Supreme Court decided a case, *Ex Parte Crow Dog*, that set in motion the development of the doctrine of plenary power. Crow Dog, a Brule Sioux Indian, had been sentenced to death by a Dakota territorial court for murdering Chief Spotted Tail; nevertheless, the United States Supreme Court ordered Crow Dog's release because the Court claimed the United States had no jurisdiction over Indian crimes on a reservation.[4] In response to what the non-Indian world considered to be a "state of lawlessness" on Indian reservations, the Congress in 1885 passed the Seven Major Crimes Act extending federal jurisdiction to specific crimes—murder, manslaughter, rape, assault with intent to kill, arson, burglary, and larceny "within any territory of the United States, and either within or without an Indian reservation. . . ."[5] The act for the first time extended federal jurisdiction "over strictly internal crimes of Indians against Indians, a major blow at the integrity of the Indian tribes and a fundamental readjustment in relations between the Indians and the United States government."[6]

The following year, the United States Supreme Court in *United States v. Kagama*, a case involving the murder of one Indian by another within the limits of the Hoopa Valley Reservation in California, upheld the right of Congress to pass such legislation.[7] The decision, according to legal scholars Russell Barsh and James Henderson, "provided a sweeping legal theory for a new epoch of federal Indian legislation."[8] The Court held that "Indian tribes *are* wards of the nation. They are communities *dependent* on the United States. Dependent largely for their daily food. Dependent for their political rights. They owe no allegiance to the States, and received from them no protection."[9] Although the Hoopas had been under Mexican domination until 1848 and did not have a treaty relationship with the United States, the Treaty of Guadalupe Hidalgo between Mexico and the United States ceded California, which, according to the Court, brought them under American jurisdiction. Barsh and Henderson have observed the following about this important decision:

Strictly construed, therefore, Kagama applies only in the absence of treaties or analogous forms of limited tribal consent to federal jurisdiction. Loosely interpreted, as it later was, Kagama reclassified all tribal areas as parts of the territory of the United States, and thereby authorizes Congress to abolish tribal governments and create new ones.[10]

Although the outline of the doctrine of plenary power had been sketched in the last three decades of the nineteenth century, starting with the Cherokee Tobacco decision, its place in American law had not been stated as clearly as it was in 1903. In that year, the United States Supreme Court in Lone Wolf v. Hitchcock gave the doctrine its most extensive definition, one which has affected the status of American Indian nations and their treaty rights down to the present day.[11] Under the Treaty of Medicine Lodge Creek of 1867, no part of the Kiowa and Comanche Reservation could be ceded without approval of three-fourths of the adult males; nevertheless, a three-man federal commission headed by David Jerome arranged an agreement for the allotment of tribal lands and the opening up of "surplus" reservation lands to non-Indians. The Jerome Commission failed to obtain three-fourths approval. On 6 June 1900, Congress confirmed the agreement. Lone Wolf, a prominent Kiowa, then sued the secretary of the interior, the commissioner of Indian affairs, and the commissioner of the General Land Office, attempting to enjoin the implementation of allotment under the act of 1900. Despite support from the Indian Rights Association, Lone Wolf lost the case. On 5 January 1903, the United States Supreme Court held that the plaintiff's contention "in effect ignores the status of the contracting Indians and the relation of dependency they bore and continue to bear toward the government of the United States." The Court added:

To uphold the claim [of Lone Wolf] would be to adjudge that the indirect operation of the treaty was to materially limit and qualify the controlling authority of Congress in respect to the care and protection of the Indians, and to deprive Congress, in possible emergency, when the necessity might be urgent for a partition and disposal of the tribal lands, of all power to act, if the assent of the Indians could not be obtained.[12]

One wonders about the nature of the "possible emergency" herein mentioned. The Court, misreading history, stated its view on Congress' authority over Indian affairs: "Plenary authority over the tribal relations of the Indians has been exercised by Congress from the beginning, and the power has always been deemed a political one, not subject to be controlled by the judicial department of the government."[13] (Emphasis added.) Although the Court indicated that the breaking of a federal treaty should occur only when it is in the interest of the country and the Indians themselves, the decision made it clear how the jurists on the nation's highest court read the past history of Indian-white relations: "When, therefore, treaties were entered into between the United States and a tribe of Indians, it was never doubted that the *power* to abrogate existed in Congress, and that in a contingency, such power might be availed of from considerations of governmental policy, particularly consistent with the perfect good faith towards the Indians." [14]

In effect, the *Lone Wolf* decision produced judicial laissez-faire in cases involving Congress' relationship with the Indians well into the future. From 1903 onward, the nation's highest court has always been reluctant to oppose Congress and has been deferential to Capitol Hill's control over Indian affairs. On the other hand, the Court has frequently recognized Indian interests when they were not inconsistent or in direct conflict with federal interest. [15]

Congress' Renewed Attack on Indian Sovereignty

The doctrine of plenary power over Indians gave Congress almost a completely free hand to operate as it wished in the internal affairs of Indian nations; nevertheless, even before the *Lone Wolf* decision, Congress was extending its statutory authority over Indian nations. From the (Dawes) General Allotment Act of 1887 onward, the Congress consciously tried to break up the Indian land base and attempted to absorb native peoples into the body politic. Within a year of the *Kagama* decision, Congress passed the (Dawes) General Allotment Act, which codified as national policy what had been taking place for many years. The president of the United States was given the discretion to allot reservation land to Indians, the title to be held in trust for twenty-five years. American Indians accepting allotment were to receive United States citizenship. Heads of families were to receive 160 acres with smaller plots going to other Indians. All "surplus" reservation lands after the allotment process was completed would be up for sale. This idea of surplus land was obviously a way of rationalizing the theft of Indian land. The act excluded many native people occupying the Indian Territory, as well as the reservations of Senecas in New York and Native Americans occupying "that strip of territory in the state of Nebraska adjoining the Sioux Nation on the south added by executive order." [16]

This act was the culmination of lobbying by eastern reform groups such as the Indian Rights Association, the Women's National Indian Association, and the Lake Mohonk Conference of the Friends of the Indian. According to the reformist mentality of the late nineteenth century, American Indians had to be transformed for their own good. American Indians could not long endure anymore as separate enclaves in the dominant white world and must learn to cope with the larger society. Reformers believed in bringing "civilization" to the Indians in order to absorb them into American society through a four-pronged formula of forced assimilation. This "Americanization" process included the proselytizing activities of Christian missionaries on reservations in order to stamp out "paganism"; the exposure of the Indian to the white Americans' way through compulsory education and boarding schools; the breakup of tribal lands and allotment to individual Indians to instill personal initiative, allegedly required by the free enterprise system; and finally, in return for accepting land-in-severalty, the rewarding of United States citizenship. To Henry S. Pancoast, one of the founders of the Indian Rights Association, American Indians had to be educated and prepared for United States citizenship. Writing in 1884, Pancoast added:

> Nothing [besides United States citizenship] will so effectively do away with contempt for the Indian and prejudice against him, as the placing him on a political equality. Nothing will so tend to assimilate the Indian and break up his narrow tribal allegiance, as making him feel that he has a distinct right and voice in the white man's nation.[17] (Emphasis added.)

To the bill's author, Henry L. Dawes of Massachusetts, United States citizenship was an enticement for the Indian to turn his back upon the "savage" life.[18] Thus, the Dawes Act was the first congressional statute to provide United States citizenship to American Indians; however, it extended citizenship at the expense of sacrificing the Indians' wishes to retain a separate national identity. Since few Indians and Indian governments were consulted about whether they wanted the act or not, the Dawes Act added to the growing trend toward federal control over Indian affairs and was another attempt at acculturation under duress. Between 1887 and 1934, American Indian landholdings shrank from an estimated 138 million to 52 million acres under the land theft machinations of the allotment policies, which facilitated outright murder, guardianship frauds, and tax foreclosures, all of which separated the allottee from his or her lands.[19]

The Dawes Act was soon followed by the congressional passage of the Indian Territory Naturalization Act of 1890. According to this most important piece of federal legislation, any member of an Indian nation in Indian Territory could become a United States citizen by formally applying for such status in federal courts. Quite significantly, the act maintained that the Indian did not lose his Indian citizenship or the right to share in his nation's assets if and when he accepted United States citizenship. Thus, this statute is the basis for much of the Oklahoma Indians' concept of citizenship, namely that they hold *dual citizenship*, or could do so by an appearance in a federal court.[20]

In 1906, Congressman Charles H. Burke of South Dakota introduced an amendment to the Dawes Act, delaying the granting of United States citizenship to Indian allottees until the end of the twenty-five year trust period in order to safeguard the Indians' personal welfare; however, the act, which passed in May of that year, did not affect those Indians who had received their allotments prior to that date and who were already considered citizens. Thus, although the Burke Act was intended to clarify the Dawes Act, it instead compounded an already complicated situation; in effect, it put the Indians into two categories: (1) those who had received land allotments prior to 1906 and who were citizens, subject to no more federal authority than white citizens except in the matter of their land; and (2) those who had received allotments after that date and who were subject to federal authority as wards, not citizens, until they acquired land patents in fee at the expiration of the trust period.[21]

On 6 November 1919, Congress passed an act allowing Indians who had served in the army or navy during World War I and had received honorable discharges to become United States citizens. In order to receive citizenship, Indians had to apply to "courts of competent jurisdiction." Although approximately 9,000 Indians had participated in the American Expeditionary Forces during World War I, few sought this route to United States citizenship.[22] Despite the legal protections associated with acquiring citizenship, few Indians refused to turn their back on their heritage or go through the demeaning process of being declared "competent." One hundred years after the Cherokee Treaty of 1817, many Indians, although not all, associated acquisition of United States citizenship with their denationalization or loss of sovereignty. Having survived the minefields for a century, the Indians, already suspicious, saw an assertive Congress as continually tying United States citizenship to the removal of trust restrictions on Indian lands and subsequent loss of sovereignty. As Vine Deloria, Jr., and Clifford Lytle have perceptively observed: "This requirement actually meant that citizenship, which is supposed to be a personal right of the individual, was really a function of the status of whatever real estate the Indian might possess."[23] Thus, to certain American Indians such as the Iroquois in New York, United States citizenship was always, then and now, viewed as the first step toward taxation and the loss of their political and territorial sovereignty.[24]

The culmination of congressional efforts to extend United States citizenship to American Indians occurred on 2 June 1924, when President Calvin Coolidge signed the Indian Citizenship Act:

*That all non-citizen Indians born within the territorial limits of the
United States be, and they are hereby, declared to be citizens of the
United States.*[25]

The act added an important disclaimer: "That the granting of such
citizenship shall not in any manner impair or otherwise affect the right
of any Indian to tribal or other property."[26] Despite decades of lobbying,
this act was the creation of the lingering Progressive reform spirit of the
1920s. Senate Progressives, seeking to protect Indians from the rapacious
and unscrupulous politicians of the Harding era, pushed for regulations
over the scandal-ridden Department of the Interior, an agency beset by
lingering memories of the Teapot Dome and the Bursum Pueblo Land
Bill. Gary Stein, in a most insightful article on the origins of the Indian
Citizenship Act, has observed:

*[The Progressives hoped that granting] automatic citizenship to all
Indians would prevent anyone in the Interior Department or the
Bureau of Indian Affairs from profiting as a result of unjust citizenship regulations, would hopefully reduce bureaucratic inefficiency,
and might even cause some embarrassment to the administration
should the House refuse to accept the Senate amendments.*[27]

Major western Progressives Robert M. LaFollette, Burton K. Wheeler,
Lynn Frazier, Charles McNary, Henry Ashurst, C.C. Dill, and Robert
Owen, a Cherokee Indian, all of whom had attended the Progressive
Conference of 1922, were all on the Senate Committee on Indian Affairs
in 1924. They "forged an act to strike a blow at big bureaucracy in the
way earlier Progressive legislation had struck at big business."[28] The act
of 1924 was in the spirit of the gospel of efficiency and reform advocated
by the Progressives since the period prior to World War I. Thus, congressional monitoring of the Interior Department rather than human rights
concerns or the lobbying of American Indians in the Society of American
Indians was the major reason for this legislation, since there appears to
have been little lobbying for or against the act.[29]

For certain Indian nations, the Indian Citizenship Act proved to be
a major thorn in their side and was openly challenged in the federal
courts. The Grand Council of the Six Nations Iroquois Confederacy
promptly sent letters to the president and Congress of the United States
respectfully declining United States citizenship, rejecting dual citizenship, and stating that the act was written and passed without their
knowledge or consent.

A crisis of monumental proportions was to occur after the passage
of the United States' Selective Service Act of 1940, an act that was
challenged by the Iroquois in New York, the Seminoles in Florida, and

others. Despite Indian willingness to participate actively in the war effort, the Iroquois in New York were uniformly against the application of the act to them. For the first time in the United States, the federal government conscripted Indians against their will into the armed services. These Iroquois, following their own views of sovereignty, insisted that the Selective Service Act and the earlier Indian Citizenship Act did not apply to them, since they had never accepted the 1924 law and considered themselves foreign nationals, not United States citizens. Both laws, they maintained, had been *promulgated unilaterally* by Congress and *without their consent*; thus, the Iroquois rejected the doctrine of plenary power or federal supremacy over Indians and Indian affairs, insisting they were Six Nations citizens, not United States citizens. They claimed to be sovereign nations and brothers of the United States, and that neither could tell the other what to do, as they were, and are, equals. Even though many willingly enlisted to help the war effort, a significant number of Indians, clinging to traditional beliefs about sovereignty, were arrested and some were prosecuted as draft evaders.[30] The Six Nations Grand Council rejected the right of the United States to draft its members: (1) Because they were separate nations, (2) because their treaties with the United States forbade either nation from drafting the members of the other, and (3) because the chiefs could not, under their own laws, draft their own people.

Subsequently, to test their status, the Iroquois brought a case, *Ex Parte Green* (1941), to federal court. The United States Court of Appeals for the Second Circuit rejected Iroquois contentions and upheld the application of the Selective Service Act to these Indians.[31] In two later draft cases, *United States v. Claus* (1944) and *Albany v. United States* (1945), involving Mohawk Indians from the Six Nations and Caughnawaga reserves, the federal courts went even further, holding that the Selective Service Act was applicable to Indian non-citizen aliens from Canada residing in the United States. The courts rejected arguments by the Mohawks that, since Canada did not conscript Indians during World War II, the United States had no right to draft Canadian Indians. Moreover, the courts dismissed the Mohawks' contention that the Jay Treaty, granting the right of free passage back and forth across the international boundary, exempted them from being drafted into military service in the United States.[32]

In spite of the Iroquois failure to gain recognition for their views of conscription and United States citizenship, these legal appeals reinforced the Indian belief about their sovereignty and nationhood at a time when the dominant white society was beginning to talk about absorbing the Indian peoples into the mainstream. In order to counter the unfavorable effects of media coverage of Iroquois draft resistance, which were largely misunderstood by the American public at large, a group of six well-known Iroquois, without formal approval of most of the Six Nations, "declared war" against the Axis on the Capitol steps in Washington, D.C., on 11 June 1942.[33]

The Iroquois critique of the application of the congressional acts of 1924 and 1941 was later best summarized by Tuscarora Chief Clinton Rickard:

> The Citizenship Act did pass in 1924 despite our strong opposition. By its provisions all Indians were automatically made United States citizens whether they wanted to be so or not. This was a violation of our sovereignty. Our citizenship was in our own nations. We had a great attachment to our style of government. We wished to remain treaty Indians and reserve our ancient rights. There was no great rush among my people to go out and vote in white man's elections. Anyone who did so was denied the privilege of becoming a chief or a clan mother in our nation.[34]

The Indian Reorganization Act and Its Legacies

Congressional intrusion into the lives of American Indians continued throughout the 1930s. Legislation passed in that era has affected American Indian communities down to the present day. The Indian Reorganization Act (IRA) of 1934, the most important piece of legislation affecting American Indians in this century, has been the subject of heated debate since its passage.[35]

To some Native Americans—such as the Oneidas of Wisconsin, who had lost a 65,000-acre reservation because of allotment provisions under the Dawes Act, and had less than 90 acres of land in tribal ownership at the beginning of the New Deal—the IRA seemed to provide the mechanism for beginning tribal economic and political restoration.[36] Yet, not all Indians benefited from the IRA. The New Deal years marked an era of increased discord and factionalism between traditional Indian leadership and leaders under the new systems of tribal/elective government created under the IRA.

Whether traditional or newly elected, Indian leadership often felt subjected to undue non-Indian tampering with the existing native political systems.[37] In the mid-1970s, the American Indian Policy Review Commission (the Abourezk Commission) observed that, under the IRA in a forty-year period, only 595,157 acres were purchased for tribal use, while government agencies condemned 1,811,010 acres of Indian land for other purposes during this period.[38]

The blame, of course, largely rests with the Congress, which not only subverted the major reformist provisions of the original bill, but never funded the IRA programs for significant land purchase.

The IRA as passed in 1934 provided for the establishment of tribal elections to accept or reject the provisions of the legislation and of tribal constitutions and corporations. It established a revolving loan fund to assist "organized" tribes in community development, and by waiving civil service requirements, it offered preference to Indians who sought employment in the Bureau of Indian Affairs. The act also created an educational loan program for Indian students seeking a vocational, high school, or college education.

Perhaps most importantly, the act ended the land allotment policies of the Dawes Act for those nations accepting the new provisions, and provided for the purchase of new lands. Unallotted surplus lands were authorized to be returned to elective governments. Conservation efforts were encouraged by the establishment of Indian forestry units and by herd reduction on arid land to protect range deterioration. This later program cost the federal government the support of the Navajos because the United States government radically reduced their sheep herds with disastrous results.[39]

Congress, in passing the IRA, also dramatically increased federal supervision over Indian nations. Sections 16 and 17 were the heart of the IRA. According to Section 16:

> Any Indian tribe, or tribes, residing on the same reservation, shall have the right to organize for its common welfare, and may adopt an appropriate constitution and by-laws . . . at a special election authorized by the Secretary of the Interior. . . . Amendments to the constitution and by-laws may be ratified and approved by the Secretary in the same manner as the original constitution and by-laws. . . . In addition to all powers vested in any Indian tribe or tribal council by existing law, the constitution adopted by said tribe shall also vest in such tribe or its tribal council, the following rights and powers: To employ legal counsel, the choice of counsel and fixing of fees to be subject to the approval of the Secretary of the Interior; to prevent the sale, disposition, lease, or encumbrance of tribal lands, interest in lands, or other tribal assets without the consent of the tribe; and to negotiate with the Federal, State, and local Governments. The Secretary of the Interior shall advise such tribe or its tribal council of all appropriation estimates or Federal projects for the benefit of the tribe prior to the submission of such estimates to the Bureau of the Budget and the Congress.[40] (Emphasis added.)

Section 17, which was concerned more with business organization, allowed the secretary of the interior to issue a charter of incorporation upon request and to establish the electoral machinery to vote on it. If approved, the incorporated tribe could "purchase, take by gift, or bequest, or otherwise, own, hold, manage, operate, and dispose of property of every description, real and personal, including the power to purchase restricted Indian lands and to issue in exchange therefor [sic] interests in corporate property, and such further powers as may be incidental to the conduct of corporate business" as long as it was not inconsistent with the law. It added that "no authority shall be granted to sell, mortgage, or lease for a period exceeding ten years any of the land included within the limits of the reservation," with a caveat that this provision could be revoked only by congressional legislation.[41]

The IRA achieved some noteworthy initial successes. It helped some tribes increase their tribal landbase, and (especially when contrasted with the allotment period) helped some gain better control of tribal property. Yet, according to Commissioner John Collier, the act was designed to overcome a situation where "the Department has absolute discretionary powers over all organized expressions of the Indians. . . . Tribal Councils existed by the Department's sufferance and had no authority except as . . . granted by the Department."[42] Sections 16 and 17 indicate that the attempt to provide the tribes with self-rule served mainly to *increase* the personnel and supervisory responsibilities of the Interior Department and its agency, the BIA. In effect, the IRA "added a new layer of permanent administration to the agency [BIA], while all the staff and activities established by the General Allotment Act were continued for the benefit of the remaining allottees."[43]

Collier had claimed that the bureaucratic nature of Indian affairs and the lack of home-rule was the real issue in designing the Indian Reorganization Act. During congressional hearings on the bill, the commissioner maintained its aim was to "extend to all Indians that minimum of home-rule in domestic and cultural matters which is basic to American life."[44] On a separate occasion, he added: "Any American community that was at the mercy of such a bureaucracy would move out or rise in rebellion."[45] Yet ironically, Collier gave the BIA, an agency already viewed by many Native Americans as the germ responsible for the sickly state of Indian affairs, increased authority in its supervision.

Thus, even when the majority of an Indian nation valued the opportunity to rebuild a landbase or participate in the revolving loan program, many viewed the increased federal supervision as a necessary but unpleasant trade-off.

It is little wonder that some of the tribal business committees created under the IRA were labeled by some Indians as the tools of the federal government, and that the IRA represented "a blueprint for elected tyranny."[46] As early as October 1946, the secretary of the Sioux Indian Rights Association wrote to Ben Dwight, then acting secretary of the National Congress of American Indians, that thirty percent of the Oglala Sioux, who had opposed the IRA, were boycotting all tribal elections conducted under the provisions of the act.[47] It is little wonder that by the 1970s these "IRA councils" became the focus of "Red Power" militancy that sought to restore traditional government to some reservations.

Thus, the road to the takeover of Wounded Knee in 1973 was blazed by the paradoxes and inconsistencies of the Indian Reorganization Act and Bureau of Indian Affairs (BIA) land policy. Although today's critics of the act should remember that *self-government* was a radical policy for the 1930s, there is no question that the IRA was and is a seriously flawed piece of legislation.

The IRA was not designed to recognize native sovereignty, nor did its operations encourage it. The secretary of the interior, after all, had the final voice in every major policy decision made by Indians. It is no wonder that many Indians believed the BIA, under the IRA, "set up puppet governments on the reservations and somehow mysteriously govern[ed] all aspects of tribal life by remote control."[48]

The Age of Termination

Nowhere was the Congress' omnipotent power in Indian affairs more apparent than in the development and implementation of Indian policy after World War II. Although policymakers used varied expressions to describe postwar American Indian policy, including "emancipation," "federal withdrawal," or "readjustment," the most frequently employed, and perhaps the most descriptive word to characterize the shift was "termination."

In actuality, termination was both a philosophy and a specific legislation applied to Indians. As a philosophy, the movement encouraged assimilation of Indians as individuals into the mainstream of American society and advocated the end of the federal government's responsibility for Indian affairs.

To accomplish these objectives, termination legislation fell into four general categories: (1) the end of federal treaty relationships and trust responsibilities with certain specified Indian nations; (2) the repeal of federal laws that set Indians apart from other American citizens; (3) the removal of restrictions of federal guardianship and supervision over certain individual Indians; and (4) the transfer of services provided by the Bureau of Indian Affairs to other federal, state, or local governmental agencies, or to Indian nations themselves. These "termination laws" of the Truman and Eisenhower administrations ended federally recognized status for 109 Indian groups, totaling 13,263 individuals owning 1,365,801 acres of land; removed restrictions on Indian trust lands to allow for easier leasing and sale; shifted Indian health responsibilities from the BIA to the Department of Health, Education and Welfare; and established relocation programs to encourage Indian outmigrations from reservations to urban areas. Even the creation of the Indian Claims Commission in 1946 became tied with the congressional efforts at "getting the United States out of the Indian business."[49]

Historians examining the postwar policy of termination have exclusively focused on those groups such as the Menominees of Wisconsin and the Klamaths of Oregon, who were disastrously affected by these official initiatives. Yet, every federally recognized tribe had to contend with this readjustment of Indian affairs during the Truman-Eisenhower years. Indeed, the Bureau of Indian Affairs, under congressional budgetary pressure, prepared a federal withdrawal plan for each tribe under its administrative aegis. What is remarkable is not that some Indian groups were terminated but that so many successfully thwarted these moves.

By 1950, American Indians also had to contend with a new commissioner of Indian affairs, Dillon S. Myer, appointed to office by President Truman. Myer, a career administrator who had served in numerous posts in the Department of Agriculture, headed the War Relocation Authority from 1942 to 1944, and had been a commissioner of the Federal Housing Authority since 1946. His wartime experience as head of the War Relocation Authority, supervising the removal and detention of tens of thousands of Japanese-Americans, led to his appointment as commissioner of Indian affairs. According to the recommendation of the secretary of the interior, Myer "did an outstanding job in the maintenance and relocation of the Japanese evacuated from the Pacific Coast region. . . ." He added that he felt that "this total experience well fits him for the position of Commissioner of Indian Affairs."[50]

Armed with congressional support and the recommendation of the Special Presidential Commission on the Organization of the Executive Branch of Government, better known as the Hoover Commission, which filed a task force report on Indian affairs in 1949, Myer and his successor Glenn Emmons pushed termination policies: the transfer of federal programs to the states; the federal relocation of Indians off the reservations; and the "ending of tax exemption and of privileged status for Indian-owned land and the payment of the taxes at the same rates as for other property in the areas."[51] Almost immediately upon assuming office, Myer focused his agency's attention on these areas, as well as on the step-by-step transfer of BIA functions.

The cooperation between congressional leaders and Interior Department personnel continued even after Myer left office in 1953. Since Indian affairs and policies were a backwater area to most congressmen in the postwar period, a few single-minded conservative individuals, operating through the subcommittees of the Senate and House Interior and Insular Affairs committees, and the Senate Public Lands Committee, emerged to mold Indian policy in the late 1940s.

Congressional liberals, although often in conflict on other matters, were increasingly swayed by their conservative colleagues about the malfeasance of the Indian office and the need to provide civil liberties to another oppressed minority group. Moreover, in the postwar years, both Democrat and Republican congressmen sought to promote parks, dams, and other development projects that often impinged upon Indian tribal rights and landholdings. The policies, with the reluctant, tacit, or open support of the Department of the Interior, lent fuel to so-called termination legislation.

Glenn Emmons, who became commissioner of Indian affairs in 1953 and an ally of pro-terminationist Senator Clinton Anderson of New Mexico, agreed with much of Myer's thinking, believing that Congress should speed up removing the excessive restrictions on Indian trust lands, dismantle the bureaucracy of Indian affairs, discourage Indian dependence, and promote Indian "progress" by assimilating Indians into the mainstream white society. Thus, by August 1953 the Congress was to respond by the passage of House Concurrent Resolution 108 and Public Law 280, the two cornerstones to the policy of termination.

House Concurrent Resolution 108, which became the basis of the federal termination legislation for the Menominees and other Indian nations, stated:

> [I]t is the policy of Congress, as rapidly as possible, to make the Indians within the territorial limits of the United States subject to the same laws and entitled to the same privileges and responsibilities as are applicable to other citizens of the United States, to end their status as wards of the United States and to grant them all the rights and prerogatives pertaining to American citizenship.

It added that certain tribesmen "be freed from federal supervision and control and from all disabilities and limitations specifically applicable to Indians."[52]

Public Law 280 was largely based on the earlier congressional acts of 1948 and 1950, which specifically gave New York State jurisdiction over Iroquois affairs. The 1953 act transferred criminal and civil jurisdiction over Indian affairs to the states of California, Minnesota, Nebraska, Oregon, and Wisconsin.[53]

The age of termination, which waned in the late 1950s and finally came to an end in 1970, had another more disastrous effect on Indian communities. The doctrine of plenary power was used to condemn substantial Indian lands. In the postwar era, the Congress, with judicial acquiescence, allowed the Army Corps of Engineers and/or the Interior Department's Bureau of Reclamation to condemn sizeable parts of Fort Mohave, Chemehuevi Valley, the Colorado River, and the Yuma and Gila Bend reservations in Arizona in order to harness the power and manage the water of the Colorado River basin.

Their joint Pick-Sloan Plan, originally conceived in 1944 for the Missouri River basin, also took Chippewa, Mandan, Hidatsa, and Arapaho land in Wyoming; Crow, Cree, Blackfoot, and Assiniboine land in Montana; and over 200,000 acres of Sioux land in North and South Dakota, land that was also flooded for the building of the Fort Randall, Oahe, and Big Bend dams. In each case, the federal government uprooted Indian peoples and relocated them from their homelands, disturbing sacred sites, seriously affecting the ecology of each region, and showing too little concern for treaty and human rights.[54]

No event of the postwar era symbolizes the extension of the doctrine of plenary power over Indians more than the tragedy that befell the Seneca Nation from 1957 to 1966. The building of the $125 million Kinzua Dam in that period broke the Pickering Treaty of 1794; flooded more than 9,000 acres of top quality farmland, thus destroying the livelihood of the Seneca farmers and a major source of food for those who planted; ruined the old Cold Spring Longhouse, the ceremonial center of Seneca traditional life; caused the removal of 130 Indian families from the "take area"; and resulted in the relocation of these same families from widely spaced rural surroundings to two suburban-style housing clusters, one at Steamburg and the other at Jimersontown, adjacent to the city of Salamanca.

In compensation, Congress awarded the Seneca Nation $15,000,573 by a law passed, belatedly, in 1964. This act provided $1,289,060 for direct damages by land loss; $945,573 for indirect damages, compensating the Indians for relocation expenses, loss of timber, and destruction of wildlife; $387,023 for "cemetery relocation"; $250,000 for Indian legal and appraisal fees; and $12,128,917 for "rehabilitation," which was directed at meeting the Senecas' urgent need for community buildings, economic development, education, and housing.[55]

It is also important to note that Section 18 of the compensation bill of 1964, although not implemented, put in by Senator Clinton Anderson of New Mexico, required the secretary of the interior to submit to Congress within three years after consultation with the Seneca Nation a plan for complete withdrawal of federal supervision over the property and affairs of the nation and its members.[56]

On 3 January 1957, the Department of Justice filed a condemnation proceeding at the insistence of the secretary of the army in order to acquire the use of certain Seneca lands for the purpose of making surveys and appraisals essential in the development of the project, citing eminent domain provisions of various flood-control statutes from 1888 to 1941.[57]

Eight days later, the Federal District Court for the western district of New York, in the first of a series of legal decisions, held that, despite the Pickering Treaty of 1794, the United States had the right to condemn any land essential for the purposes of the project. The court rejected the Seneca Nation's plea about the primacy of their treaty by maintaining that Indian lands were subject to the power of eminent domain, just as are all lands privately held in the United States. The court added that a federal-Indian treaty could not rise above the power of Congress to legislate.[58]

This and later decisions repeated the arguments made by Department of Justice attorneys in their memoranda of law and briefs. Citing *Lone Wolf v. Hitchcock* (1903) and other key decisions, these attorneys questioned the power of treaties to control the power of Congress to legislate, and insisted that "treaty rights do not forbid the taking, by the United States, of lands within the Allegany Reservation."[59] Department of Justice officials throughout Eisenhower's second term repeated this argument and, like Department of Interior officials, never questioned the morality or the legality of the federal government's actions.

The legal battles between the Seneca Nation and the army and its ally the Department of Justice raged until the United States Supreme Court denied the Indians a writ of *certiorari* in June 1959. In each of the lower federal courts, attorney for the Senecas Edward O'Neill argued that general legislation earmarking congressional funds for construction of an Allegheny Reservoir project was not sufficient to overthrow the sanctity of the treaty of 1794. Although recognizing the power of Congress under federal law to break treaties, he insisted that specific legislation, not pork-barrel appropriations, was needed for Congress to unilaterally change the federal-Indian treaty relationship.[60]

At the district court level, Judge Joseph McGarraghy described the Senecas' contention: "The Seneca Nation *does* claim that the rights covenanted under such a treaty—especially one with an Indian tribe— cannot be destroyed by implication, innuendo, or unauthorized act of the Executive. To destroy such rights Congress must specifically say so." McGarraghy then went on to maintain that the congressional intent in passing the Public Works Appropriation Act of 1958 was sufficiently clear to set aside a treaty consummated 163 years earlier.[61]

On 25 November 1958, in what proved to be the last major rendering by a federal court in the Kinzua Dam matter, the three judges of the United States Court of Appeals for the District of Columbia unanimously affirmed McGarraghy's decision and denied the Senecas an injunction against the army. Citing congressional testimony throughout 1958, the courts clearly found that the Congress was aware of what it was doing to Indians and their lands when it passed the Public Works Appropriation Act of 1958.[62] Thus, the doctrine of plenary power reached its apogee in the federal courts' acquiescence to the taking of Seneca lands.

Plenary Power in an Age of American Indian Activism, 1968 to the Present

In response to decisions such as the one regarding Kinzua Dam, a new style of politics arose in Indian country. American Indian political activism increased from the late 1960s onward with takeovers of Alcatraz Island in 1969, the Bureau of Indian Affairs building in Washington, D.C., in 1972, and Wounded Knee in 1973. Moreover, American Indians have also used a variety of legal strategies to assert their rights or win back their lands. In 1974, and again in 1985, the Oneidas won two United States Supreme Court cases, winning access to the federal courts to sue for lands taken after 1790.[63] These victories have furthered out-of-court Indian land settlements for the Penobscot, Passamaquoddy, and Houlton Band Indians of Maine; the Narragansets of Rhode Island; the Mashantucket Pequots of Connecticut; and the Gay Head Wampanoags of Massachusetts. All of these settlements have been confirmed by Congress over the past decade.[64] Moreover, certain Indian groups such as the Narragansets, the Mashantucket Pequots, the Porch Band of Creeks, and the Tunica-Biloxi Indians have secured federal recognition, struggles they had been waging for many years.[65]

In response to Indian protests, Congress has also overturned some of its policies made in the age of termination. In 1973, the Congress restored the Menominee Indians to federal recognition. Throughout the late 1970s, other "terminated" Indian groups were also returned to federal recognition, including the Ottawa, Peoria, and Wyandot Indians in Oklahoma; certain bands of Paiutes in Utah; and the Confederated Tribes of Siletz Indians of Oregon.[66]

With the new spirit of legal activism came efforts by tribal attorneys to expand governmental activities and employ litigation to rebuild sovereign power. In 1973, because of this, the United States brought suit against the state of Washington on behalf of Northwest Indian tribes' fishing rights. In an historic decision, Federal Judge George Boldt affirmed the Indians' right to share equally in the salmon harvest.[67] Although the Boldt decision was a measured victory for Indian sovereignty, Indians of the Northwest such as the Lummi are still faced today with federal attempts at limiting their sovereignty, this time squaring off with the Internal Revenue Service.[68]

Despite significant changes since 1968, a new day is not fully at hand. In the late 1970s, congressmen from the Pacific Northwest introduced new versions of termination legislation. In the early 1980s, Congressman Gary Lee of New York and senators Strom Thurmond of South Carolina and Alfonse D'Amato of New York introduced legislation to extinguish Indian land claims. Moreover, other congressional actions indicate the continuity, not the break, with past policies. Three pieces of legislation, all presented as needed reforms, illustrate this point.[69]

In 1971, the Alaskan Native Claims Settlement Act (ANCSA) was passed by Congress. By the act of 1971, Congress legislated a settlement guaranteeing Alaska natives title to 44 million acres of their own land and payment of $962.5 million for the balance of their land.[70] Nevertheless, in ANCSA Congress did not convey the land to tribal entities, considering tribal governments "to be an impediment to assimilation."[71] Thus, ANCSA mandated the natives to establish village and regional *corporations* as title holders to the land. The land so conveyed belongs to these corporations, not to the Alaska natives. Alaska natives, fully aware that these corporations would "go public" in 1991 and be opened up to non-native investors, feared that "through corporate failure, corporate takeovers, and taxation, they could lose their land."[72] Recently, Congress has acted to correct the situation by placing a moratorium on the 1991 deadline in response to overwhelming criticism of the 1971 act.

Congressional interventionist legislation to provide "solutions" has also exacerbated Indian-Indian relations, the most publicized being the passage of PL 93-531, the Navajo-Hopi Land Settlement Act of 1974. Although the act provided for the process by which the so-called Joint Use Area would be partitioned and for the federal government to pay for the relocation of upwards of 10,000 Navajos, the Congress has had little concern for the cultural and religious sensitivity of the Indians being removed.[73] At the time of this writing, the process of relocation, which has already cost nearly $1 billion, has continued to generate headlines and engender tense relations between the two Indian groups.[74]

In 1975, Congress passed the Indian Self-Determination and Education Assistance Act.[75] Although heralded by its congressional sponsors as a major development in Indian policy, the act was actually only a footnote to the original ideas of "self-government" promulgated by Commissioner John Collier four decades before. Although the 1975 act allowed and encouraged Indian contracting, in actuality it only formalized the tenuous relationships which had grown up in the 1960s when Indian tribes became sponsoring agencies of federal poverty programs.

Conclusion

Many of the problems faced by American Indian nations today stem from a pattern of congressional intrusions and manipulations over the past two centuries. Nearly every congressional change in Indian policy has been presented as a reform or a "benefit" to Indians regardless of their wishes. From the (Dawes) General Allotment Act of 1887 to the Indian Self-Determination and Education Assistance Act of 1975, Congress has determined Indian needs. It is obvious that creating tribal business committees under the Indian Reorganization Act or under the Alaskan Native Claims Settlement Act can never produce true self-determination. The doctrine of plenary power and the whole nature of the present federal-Indian relationship must be altered from one of paternalism and intervention to true self-government.

Notes

Introduction

1. Peter J. Hugill and D. Bruce Dickson, eds., *The Transfer and Transformation of Ideas and Material Culture* (College Station: Texas A&M University Press, 1988), 76–77. Historian William McNeill's essay "Diffusion in History" cites the case of a mid-seventeenth-century upheaval in East European Jewry and orthodox Christianity which was triggered by ideas of English Puritans. Cultural diffusion does not require that the party of the second part admire or show affection toward the party of the first part. "Sometimes, too, ideological principles required borrowers to deny that they had imitated strangers." Although it is widely accepted that English Puritans influenced a movement in Eastern Europe, it is noteworthy that there is no concrete evidence, no documentary proof, that it happened.

2. George F. Carter, "Cultural, Historical Diffusion, *Transfer and Transformation of Ideas*, eds. Hugill and Dickson, 19.

3. "The diffusion process involves the physical transfer of things or artifacts . . . ; the transfer of techniques for constructing or replicating such artifacts; the transfer of institutionalized systems of relationships . . . ; and the transfer of ideas or complexes of ideas including religious beliefs and political ideologies. Consequently, it is a phenomenon confronted by a host of disciplines besides geography and anthropology. Diffusion figures importantly in the study of history, economics, political science, and sociology. Given this broad relevance, it is surprising that a critical examination from a multidisciplinary perspective of both the concept and the phenomenon of diffusion does not exist." From *Transfer and Transformation of Ideas*, eds. Hugill and Dickson, 263.

4. See Eric M. Jensen, "The Imaginary Connection Between the Great Law of Peace and the United States Constitution: A Reply to Professor Schaaf," *American Indian Law Review* 15, no. 2 (1991): 295–308.

5. Ibid., 299.

6. William McNeill, "Diffusion in History," in *Transfer and Transformation of Ideas*, eds. Hugill and Dickson, 78. McNeill has made significant use of evidence for diffusion in history in *The Rise of the West* (Chicago: University of Chicago Press, 1963).

7. Jensen, "Imaginary Connection," 301.

8. A final objection to the ideas of confederation being Iroquois in origin has been raised: recognition of such origins tends to paint the Iroquois as "superhuman." This objection has not been raised in print, but it seems a particularly disingenuous position. Certainly the Iroquois were significant because of their strategic location at a specific time. If cultural diffusion is legitimate, the Iroquois were also influenced by other Indian peoples, many of which had systems of government and philosophy very similar to their own. No one knows, and no one will probably ever know, which American Indian group originated the principles of democratic thought or American Indian political organization.

1: The American Indian in the Past

1. Paul A. W. Wallace, *The White Roots of Peace* (Port Washington, N.Y.: Ira J. Friedman, Inc., 1968), 30–31.

2. Olive Patricia Dickason, *The Myth of the Savage and the Beginning of French Colonialism in the Americas* (Alberta, Canada: University of Alberta Press, 1984), xiv.

3. Ibid.

4. Jeffrey Goodman, *American Genesis* (New York: Summit Books, 1981), 24.

5. Ibid., 31.

6. Alfred W. Crosby, Jr., *Ecological Imperialism: The Biological Expansion of Europe, 900–1900* (Westport, Conn.: Greenwood Press, 1986), 31.

7. Ibid.

8. Ibid.

9. Ibid., 76.

10. Ibid., 75.

11. Ibid., 82.

12. Alfred W. Crosby, Jr., *The Columbian Exchange: Biological and Cultural Consequences of 1492* (Westport, Conn.: Greenwood Press, 1973), 54–58.

13. Louis M. Hacker, *The Shaping of the American Tradition* (New York: Columbia University Press, 1947), 7.

14. Angie Debo, *A History of the Indians of the United States* (Norman: University of Oklahoma Press, 1985), 34.

15. William H. McNeill, *Plagues and Peoples* (New York: Anchor Books, 1976), 31.

16. Michael Wood, *Domesday: A Search for the Roots of England* (New York: Facts on File Publications, 1988), 201.

17. Arthur H. Johnson, *The Disappearance of the Small Landowner* (London: Merlin Press Ltd., 1963), 65.

18. Karl Polanyi, *The Great Transformation: The Political and Economic Origins of Our Time* (Boston: Beacon Press, 1957), 35.

19. Hacker, *Shaping of American Tradition*, 46.

20. Nicholas P. Canny, *The Elizabethan Conquest of Ireland: A Pattern Established 1565–1576* (New York: Barnes & Noble, 1976), 66.

21. Ibid., 76.

22. Ibid.

23. Ibid., 119.

24. An excellent recounting of English-Indian relations in early New England is found in William Cronon's *Changes in the Land: Indians, Colonists, and the Ecology of New England* (New York: Hill and Wang, 1987).

25. Whether the Indians were or were not Christian was beside the point. Some Indian groups, most notably the so-called civilized tribes, converted to Christianity but were nevertheless forcibly removed from their lands.

26. George F. Willison, *Saints and Strangers* (New York: Reynal & Hitchcock, 1945), 212.

27. Richard Drinnon, *Facing West: The Metaphysics of Indian-Hating and Empire-Building* (Minneapolis: University of Minnesota Press, 1980), 46.

28. Herbert Eugene Bolton, *The Colonization of North America, 1492–1783* (New York: MacMillan Co., 1921), 81.

29. Baron de Lahontan, *New Voyages to North America*, ed. Reuben G. Thwaites, vol. 1 (1703; reprint, Chicago: A. C. McClurg & Co., 1905), 7.

30. McNeill, *Plagues and Peoples*, 288.

31. Howard Zinn, *A People's History of the United States* (New York: Harper & Row, 1980), 53. For more on this subject, see Nicholas P. Canny, "The Permissive Frontier: The Problem of Social Control in English Settlements in Ireland and Virginia," in *The Westward Enterprise: English Activities in Ireland, the Atlantic and America, 1400–1650*, eds. K. R. Andress, N. P. Canny, and P. E. H. Hair (Detroit, Mich.: Wayne State University Press, 1979), 33. Also see James Axtell, *The Invasion Within* (New York: Oxford University Press, 1986), 302–27, for an interesting account of the "white Indians."

32. Christine Bolt, "Return of the Native: Some Reflexions on the History of American Indians," in *Journal of American Studies* 8, no. 2 (1974): 248.

33. Richard D. Heffner, ed. *Democracy in America: Alexis de Tocqueville* (New York: New American Library, 1956), 11.

34. Gregory Schaaf, *Wampum Belts and Peace Tree: George Morgan, Native Americans, and Revolutionary Democracy* (Golden, Colo.: Fulcrum Publishing, 1990), 21–23.

35. See generally Paul A. W. Wallace, *The White Roots of Peace*, for an interpretation of ancient Iroquois political philosophy. See also William N. Fenton, ed., *Parker on the Iroquois* (Syracuse, N.Y.: Syracuse University Press, 1968) for a version of the tradition of "The Constitution of the Five Nations."

36. American anthropologists and historians have been interpreting and reinterpreting the Iroquois tradition of government since it appeared in writing in English. Some have argued that since the Iroquois sometimes went to war, they could not have possessed an ideology of peace, implying that American Indians must be held to a higher standard of behavior than other peoples before we can discuss their ideologies. Who would deny, for example, that although the United States government has often supported, and even created, extremely repressive dictatorships in other countries, it nevertheless still possesses a tradition of individual liberty and collective democracy?

37. Unpublished manuscript of a speech by Chief Robert Cusick of the Six Nations, Grand River County. Chief Cusick made the speech at the Onondaga Indian Reservation in the early 1970s. Manuscript in author's possession.

2: Indians and Democracy: No One Ever Told Us

1. Martin Bernal, *Black Athena: The Afroasiatic Roots of Classical Civilization*, vol. 1 (New Brunswick, N.J.: Rutgers University Press, 1987), 2.

2. Harold Berman, *Law and Revolution: The Formation of the Western Legal Tradition* (Cambridge, Mass.: Harvard University Press, 1983), 3–4.

3. Ibid., 101.

4. Ibid., 94.

5. Ibid., 104.

6. Ibid., 105.

7. Ibid., 113.

8. Lewis Hanke, *The Spanish Struggle for Justice in the Conquest of America* (Philadelphia: University of Philadelphia Press, 1949), 28.

9. For a strong discussion of how American Indians influenced the development of modernity, see Jack Weatherford, *Indian Givers: How the Indians of the Americas Transformed the World* (New York: Crown Publishers, 1988). See also Weatherford's *Native Roots: How the Indians Nourished America* (New York: Crown Publishers, 1991).

10. Tzvetan Todorov, *The Conquest of America* (New York: Harper & Row, 1982), 141.

11. Ibid., 133.

12. Robert F. Berkhofer, Jr., *The White Man's Indian: Images of the American Indian from Columbus to the Present* (New York: Vintage Books, 1979), 34–35.

13. Hanke, *Spanish Struggle for Justice*, 120.

14. Ibid., 122.

15. Ibid., 126.

16. Drinnon offers a useful definition for the term "racism": ". . . racism consists in habitual practice by a people of treating, feeling and viewing physically dissimilar peoples . . . as less than persons." Richard Drinnon, *Facing West: The Metaphysics of Indian-Hating and Empire-Building* (Minneapolis: University of Minnesota Press, 1980), 51.

17. Lewis Hanke, *The First Social Experiments in America: A Study in the Development of Spanish-Indian Policy in the Sixteenth Century* (Gloucester, Mass.: Peter Smith, 1964), 13. "Even in this twentieth century, the excuse given by the Peruvian upper classes for their harsh treatment of the Indian is that they are animals, not men." Quoted from W. E. Hrdenburg, *The Putumayop* (Gloucester, Mass.: Peter Smith, 1912), 37.

18. Todorov, *Conquest of America*, 48–49.

19. Lewis Hanke, *Aristotle and the American Indian: A Study in Race Prejudice in the Modern World* (Bloomington: Indiana University Press, 1970), 17. "Our Christian relation is suitable for and may be adapted to all the nations of the world, and all alike may receive it; and no one may be deprived of his liberty, nor may he be enslaved on the excuse that he is a natural slave. . . ."

20. Lewis Hanke, *Spanish Struggle for Justice*, 124.

Las Casas declared flatly that Sepulveda did not understand Aristotle, in fact that he had absolutely misunderstood "the Philosopher" and his theory of slavery. As one studies the use made by both contestants of Aristotle's theory of slavery, the doubt arises whether either Las Casas or Sepulveda had a firm grasp on the theory, even though each one was absolutely certain he understood it. Even today the theory has its obscurities and, as a modern interpreter declares, "it must be confessed that Aristotle in no place clearly indicates how a true slave may be known from free man." In the absence of any clear definition of a slave, both contestants interpreted Aristotle according to their own lights.

21. Of Sepulveda, Hanke wrote:

[At] a time when the conquistadores were bringing to the notice of the civilized world a whole new continent peopled with strange races, he chose to regard all these new peoples as an inferior type of humanity which should be submitted to the rule of Spaniards. Without having seen or observed their lands and civilization, he felt no hesitation in condemning them as not quite men, above monkeys to be sure, but unworthy of being considered in the same class with the Spaniards. . . . Aristotle believed that the state ought to consist of a single race, for a single race is united in its customs and habits which makes for friendship between citizens by reason of their likeness to one another. Spanish America has never had such unity.

Ibid., 126–27.

22. Lewis Hanke, *Aristotle and the American Indian: A Study in Race Prejudice in the Modern World* (London: Hollis and Carter, 1959), 13.

23. Todorov, *Conquest of America*, 161–62.

24. Berkhofer, *White Man's Indian*, 28–29.

25. Roy Preiswerk and Dominique Perrot, *Ethnocentrism and History: Africa, Asia and Indian America in Western Textbooks* (New York: NOK Publishers, 1978), 61.

26. Ibid., 219.

27. Rev. Charles A. Goodrich, *History of the United States* (Hartford, Conn.: Barber & Robinson, 1823), 17.

28. Ibid., 19.

29. Ibid., 72.

30. Francis Jennings, *The Invasion of America: Indians, Colonialism, and the Cant of Conquest* (New York: W. W. Norton & Co., 1977), 60.

31. At a later date this principle would become enshrined in the plenary power doctrine which essentially ". . . means the United States can do whatever it wishes to Indian nations. . . . Such power is not only plenary but is also the most singular and extensive power of Congress. [The only greater and more unusual power would be the power to declare nuclear war, thereby ending all nations. I think Congress has no such legitimate power.]" Milner S. Ball, "Constitution, Court, Indian Tribes," *American Bar Foundation Research Journal* 1, no. 1 (Winter 1987): 49.

32. Drinnon, *Facing West*, 181.

33. Jennings, *Invasion of America*, 126.

34. George F. Willison, *Saints and Strangers* (New York: Reynal & Hitchcock, 1945), 188–89.

35. Drinnon, *Facing West*, 6. "Among them, 'woe to the youth or maiden who did but dream of a dance.' "

36. Raymond William Stedman, *Shadows of the Indian: Stereotypes in American Culture* (Norman: University of Oklahoma Press, 1982), 255.

37. Edward H. Dance, *History of the Betrayer* (London: Hitchinson, 1967), 12.

38. Jennings, *Invasion of America*, 9.

39. Martin Bernal, *Black Athena*, 281. Bernal provides a lengthy in-depth discussion of how African and Asiatic roots of modern civilization were deliberately purged from the history.

40. Ibid., 387.

41. Ibid., 27–28.

42. Lewis Henry Morgan, *Ancient Society, or Researches in the Lines of Human Progress from Savagery through Barbarism to Civilization*, ed. Eleanor Burke Leacock (Cleveland, Ohio: Meridian Books, 1963), 11–12.

43. Berkhofer, *White Man's Indian*, 53.

44. Ibid., 54.

45. Morgan was unquestionably an "Indian buff," and this is reflected in his writings and other activities which promote Iroquois political organization. His writings also articulate an ideology of progress which helped to promote a scientific method of study of cultures that was used to substantiate an ideology of Aryan racial superiority.

46. Christine Bolt, "Return of the Native: Some Reflexions on the History of American Indians," *Journal of American Studies* 8, no. 2 (1974): 255.

47. Ibid., 252.

48. Frederick J. Fausz, "Anglo-Indian Relations in Colonial North America," in *Scholars and the Indian Experience: Critical Reviews of Recent Writings in the Social Sciences*, ed. W. R. Swagerty (Bloomington: Indiana University Press, 1984), 80.

49. Barrington Moore, Jr., *Social Origins of Dictatorship and Democracy: Lord and Peasant in the Making of the Modern World* (Boston: Beacon Press, 1970), 21.

50. Weatherford, *Indian Givers*, 128.

51. "*Feudalism*, by definition, is a system in which occupants of land hold it as tenants of the sovereign in exchange for military service. In other words, it is an arrangement in which a hierarchy of land-tenure relationships parallels the hierarchy of military relationships. Given the military and political origins of the authority of the lord of the manor, it is scarcely surprising that his authority was as much political as economic." Nathan Rosenberg and L. E. Bridzall, Jr., *How the West Grew Rich: The Economic Transformation of the Industrial World* (New York: Basic Books, 1986), 41.

52. "Both in theory and in practice, the whole system was deeply oppressive, not merely by modern standards, but measured in its own day by the desperation of peasant uprisings, repeated over and over no matter how bloodily repressed." Ibid., 45.

53. Ibid., 41.

54. "As a matter of general political philosophy, the most comprehensive concept of sovereignty treats the personal sovereign or the state as absolute owner of all her, his, or its subjects and of all the property in the realm." Ibid., 61.

55. Ibid., 68.

56. "In England, the House of Commons was elected by townsmen (women were not allowed to vote) and small landowners, and its control of the power to tax was a substantial issue in the civil wars of the seventeenth century." Ibid., 56.

57. Ray Allen Billington, *Land of Savagery, Land of Promise: The European Image of the American Frontier in the Nineteenth Century* (Norman: University of Oklahoma Press, 1985), 2.

58. Ibid., 3.

59. Ibid., 5.

60. Mario Di Nunzio, *American Democracy and the Authoritarian Tradition of the West* (Lanham, Md.: University Press of America, 1987), 25.

61. Ibid., 75. "Enlightenment ideas stimulated long overdue reforms that benefited the modern world, but a review of the cast of thinkers shows clearly that neither democracy nor egalitarianism was among its contributions."

62. Ibid., 20.

63. Ibid., 71. According to Di Nunzio, not even Rousseau can be credited with democratic thinking: "Rousseau did not understand participatory democracy. He discussed democracy, in fact, as a form of government abused by private interests and possible only in very small communities, and always subject to civil strife. 'It is a government suited to gods and not to men.' " Ibid., 69.

64. Ibid., 43

65. Ibid., 53. "All this is not to deny the contribution of Locke's work to democratic ideas later. The right to resist tyrannical rule had been asserted as far back as Aquinas and later by Suarez and Bellarmine in the sixteenth century, but it was Locke's argument that so directly inspired later generations. His eloquence in asserting the essential equality of men, the concept of natural and inalienable rights, the idea of separation of powers, served the American revolutionaries and constitution-makers well. . . . On genuine republicanism, which demands some degree of popular participation in the representative process, Locke and the 'glorious revolution' were silent." Ibid., 54.

66. Ibid., 45. Some of the colonists were aware of this.

67. Billington, *Land of Savagery*, 18.

68. Ibid., 19.

69. Howard Zinn, A People's History of the United States (New York: Harper & Row, 1980), 50–51.

70. Ibid., 47.

71. Di Nunzio, American Democracy, 98.

3: American Indian Influences on the America of the Founding Fathers

1. Kenneth Silverman, A Cultural History of the American Revolution: Painting, Music, Literature, and the Theatre in the Colonies and the United States from the Treaty of Paris to the Inauguration of George Washington, 1763–1789 (New York: T. Y. Crowell, 1976), 585–86.

2. Max Farrand, ed., The Records of the Federal Convention of 1787, 4 vols. (1937; reprint, New Haven, Conn.: Yale University Press, 1966–1967), 1: 533, 536.

3. Ibid., 536.

4. Hugh Honour, The New Golden Land: European Images of America from the Discoveries to the Present Time (New York: Pantheon Books, 1975), 118.

5. Jean Jacques Rousseau, The Social Contract and Discourse on the Origin of Inequality among Mankind, ed. Lester G. Crocer (New York: Washington Square Press, 1967), 244–45.

6. Honour, New Golden Land, 53.

7. Rousseau, Social Contract, 186.

8. Lewis Hanke, All Mankind Is One: A Study of the Disputation between Bartolome de Las Casas and Juan Gines de Sepulveda on the Religious and Intellectual Capacity of the American Indians (DeKalb: Northern Illinois University Press, 1974), 79–107. See also Bartolome de Las Casas, In Defense of the Indians: The Defense of the Most Reverend Lord, Don Fray Bartolome de Las Casas, of the Order of Preachers, Last Bishop of Chiapa, Against the Persecutors and Slanderers of the People of the New World, Discovered Across the Seas, trans. Stafford Poole (DeKalb: Northern Illinois University Press, 1974); Juan Friede and Benjamin Keen, eds., Bartolome de Las Casas in History: Toward an Understanding of the Man and His Work (DeKalb: Northern Illinois University Press, 1971); and Lewis Hanke, Aristotle and the American Indian: A Study in Race Prejudice in the Modern World (Bloomington: University of Indiana Press, 1959).

9. Hugh Honour, The European Vision of America (Cleveland: Cleveland Museum of Art, 1975), Illustration 6.

10. Honour, New Golden Land, 54.

11. John Block Friedman, The Monstrous Races in Medieval Art and Thought (Cambridge: Harvard University Press, 1981), 18.

12. Ibid., 4, 206.

13. Peter Jansen Schaghen to the States-General, 5 November 1626, photograph of the original in Indian Life of Long Ago in the City of New York, Reginald Pelham Bolton, 2d ed. (New York: Harmony Books, 1972), 128, 128a.

14. Farrand, Records, vol. 3, 238.

15. Ibid.

16. Sir Thomas More, Utopia, trans. and ed. Robert M. Adams (New York: W. W. Norton & Company, 1975), 45 [Book Two, "Social and Business Relations"]. The relationship of More's Utopia and the Western Hemisphere is noted by Richard Marius, in his biography Thomas More (New York: Vintage Books, 1984), 153, 159:

Utopia remains mysterious and even perplexing. . . . The tone is cast in the narrative realism typical of books written by voyagers returning from the New World to tell their stories to Europe. . . . It has often been claimed that More's Utopia is part of the literature of the "noble savage" that we find in writing as diverse as the essays of Montaigne, the travels of Lemuel Gulliver, and the adolescent attacks on civilization by J. J. Rousseau. It is a little too simplistic to lump all these writers together. But it is true that they were each stirred by the amazing discovery that many societies did in fact lie out there beyond the great oceans and that they did not share European civilization. Some Europeans, dismayed by the failures of their society, yearned for those other civilizations to be better than their own.

17. Michel de Montaigne, *Essays*, trans. and intro. J. M. Cohen (Hammondsworth, England: Penguin Books, 1958), 373.

18. Ibid., 108–09.

19. Benjamin Franklin, "Remarks Concerning the Savages of North-America," in *Benjamin Franklin: Writings*, ed. J. A. Leo Lemay (New York: The Library of America, 1987), 969.

20. Montaigne, *Essays*, 109–10.

21. Ibid., 113.

22. Ibid., 119.

23. Ibid., 276–77.

24. Ibid., 278–79.

25. Ibid., 279.

26. William Shakespeare, *The Tempest*, eds. Louis B. Wright and Virginia A. LaMar (New York: Folger Library and Washington Square Press, 1961). See also D. G. James, *The Dream of Prospero* (Oxford: Oxford University Press, 1987), 80–81. And see Leo Marx, *The Machine in the Garden* (New York: Oxford University Press, 1974), 35–72; and David Beers Quinn, *England and the Discovery of America, 1481–1620* (New York: Alfred A. Knopf, 1974), 221–22.

27. Alexander Pope, *Pope: Poetical Works*, ed. Herbert Davis (1966; reprint, New York: Oxford University Press, 1985), 244.

28. François-Marie Arouet Voltaire, *Candide*, trans. John Butt (London: Penguin Books, 1988), 62.

29. Ibid., 63.

30. Ibid., 70.

31. Malvina Bolus, "Four Kings Come to Dinner with Their Honours," in *The Beaver* (Autumn 1973): 4–11; and Richmond P. Bond, *Queen Anne's American Kings* (New York: Oxford University Press, 1952), passim.

32. Ibid., 76; and *The Compact Edition of the Oxford English Dictionary: Complete Text Reproduced Micrographically*, 2 vols. (New York: Oxford University Press, 1971), 1: 1830.

33. David H. Corkran, *The Creek Frontier, 1540–1783* (Norman: University of Oklahoma Press, 1967), 87.

34. Helmut von Erffa and Allen Staley, *The Paintings of Benjamin West* (New Haven, Conn.: Yale University Press, 1986), 54–68, 211–16; and Ann Uhry Abrams, *The Valiant Hero: Benjamin West and the Grand-Style History Painting* (Washington, D.C.: Smithsonian Institution Press, 1979), Plates 29, 30.

35. Robert F. Berkhofer, Jr., *The White Man's Indian: Images of the American Indian from Columbus to the Present* (New York: Vintage Books, 1979), 49.

36. Franklin, "Remarks," in *Franklin*, ed. Lemay, 969–70.

37. Ibid., 969, 970–71.

38. Benjamin Franklin, "A Narrative of the Late Massacres, in Lancaster County, of a Number of Indians, Friends of this Province, by Persons Unknown; with Some Observations on the Same," in *Franklin*, ed. Lemay, 553–54.

39. Ibid., 568.

40. Ibid., 635.

41. John Shy, *Toward Lexington: The Role of the British Army in the Coming of the American Revolution* (Princeton, N.J.: Princeton University Press, 1965), 129–30.

42. Arthur B. Tourtellot, *Lexington and Concord* (New York: W. W. Norton & Company, 1959), 89–91.

43. Shy, *Toward Lexington*, 129.

44. Robert Rogers, *Ponteach* (1766) in *Representative Plays by American Dramatists, 1765–1819*, ed. Montrose J. Moses, vol. 1 (1918; reprint, New York: Benjamin Blom, 1964), 132.

45. *Oxford English Dictionary*, vol. 2, 2402; John R. Swanton, *Indians of the Southeastern United States* (Washington, D.C.: Smithsonian Institution Press, 1979), 89–91; George R. Stewart, *American Placenames* (New York: Oxford University Press, 1970), 18–19, 110, 283, 299, 339, 385; and Robert Steven Grumet, *Native American Place Names in New York City* (New York: Museum of the City of New York, 1981), 23–24. See also George R. Stewart, *Names on the Land* (Boston: Houghton Mifflin, 1967).

46. John Adams to Thomas Jefferson, 28 June 1812, in *The Works of John Adams*, ed. Charles Francis Adams, vol. 10 (Boston: Little, Brown and Company, 1856), 19–20.

47. Alexander Starbuck, "History of the American Whale-Fishery from Its Earliest Inception to the Year 1876," 1–779 of the Appendix bound in *United States Commission of Fish and Fisheries, Part IV, Report of the Commissioner for 1875–1876* (Washington, D.C.: U.S. Government Printing Office, 1878), 11; Eduard A. Stackpole, *The Sea Hunters: The New England Whalemen during Two Centuries, 1635–1835* (Philadelphia: J. B. Lippencott, 1953), 15–17; *The Trial of the British Soldiers . . .* , 27 November 1770 [trial transcript] (Boston: Belcher and Armstrong, 1807), 11, 100; Frederic Kidder, ed., *History of the Boston Massacre, March 5, 1770, Consisting of the Narrative of the Town, the Trial of the Soldiers: And a Historical Introduction, Containing Unpublished Documents of John Adams, and Explanatary Notes* (Albany, N.Y.: Joel Munsell, 1870), 29–30, note 3; Benjamin Quarles, *The Negro in the American Revolution* (Chapel Hill: University of North Carolina Press, 1961), 4–7; and Hiller B. Zobel, *The Boston Massacre* (New York: W. W. Norton & Company, 1971), 191.

Samuel Quincy, one of two lawyers for the Crown/prosecution, questioned Edward G. Langford, a member of the town watch, early in the trial on 27 November 1770 (trial transcript, 11): "Q. Did you know the Indian that was killed? A. No."

John Adams, one of the British soldiers' three defense lawyers, referred to Attucks as a "mulatto" and as "Attucks from Framingham." (trial transcript, 100). That Attucks was a mulatto is indicated by the frequent use of the word in the trial—for example, on trial transcript pages 8, 13, 14, 15, 17, and 63. Frederic Kidder, editor of the 1807 collection of documents referred to above describes Attucks at length (29–30, note 3):

> Crispus Attucks is described . . . as a mulatto; he was born in Framingham near the Chochituate Lake and not far from the line of Natick [a Praying Indian

town] . . . his ancestors were probably of the Natic tribe, who had intermarried with Negroes who were slaves, and as their descendants were held as such; he inherited their condition, although it is likely the blood of three races coursed through his veins.

48. John Adams to Abigail Adams, 24 January 1776, in *The Book of Abigail and John: Selected Letters of the Adams Family, 1762–1784*, eds. Lyman H. Butterfield, Marc Friedlaender, and Mary-Jo Kline (Cambridge, Mass.: Harvard University Press, 1975) 114–15.

49. Alexander Hamilton to "Mr. Duche," 7 September 1787, in *Records*, ed. Farrand, vol. 4, 263.

50. John Adams, *A Defence of the Constitutions of Government of the United States of America*, vol. 1 (London: C. Dilly, 1787–1788), xxvi.

51. Jean Jacques Rousseau, *Social Contract*, 221.

52. Timothy Pickering to Rufus King, 4 June 1785, King Papers, Box 1, New York Historical Society, New York, New York. See also Charles King, ed., *The Life and Correspondence of Rufus King*, 6 vols. (New York: G. P. Putnam's Sons, 1894–1899), 1: 107.

53. John Locke, *An Essay Concerning Human Understanding*, 2 vols. (1947; rev. ed., London: J. M. Dent & Sons, 1974), 1: 169.

54. John Locke, *Two Treatises of Government* (1924; reprint, London: J. M. Dent & Sons, 1975), 118.

55. Ibid., 124.

56. Ibid., 171.

57. Ibid.

58. Treaty with the Delawares, 17 September 1778, in *Indian Treaties, 1778–1883*, ed. Charles J. Kappler (1904; reprint, New York: Interland Publishing, 1972), 3–5.

59. Philip B. Kurland and Ralph Lerner, eds., *The Founders' Constitution*, 5 vols. (Chicago: University of Chicago Press, 1987), 1: 624.

60. Farrand, *Records*, vol. 1, 536.

61. John Locke, "Of the Ends of Political Society and Government," in *Locke— Second Treatise of Government*, ed. Richard H. Cox (Arlington Heights: Harlan Davidson, Inc., 1982), 75.

62. Ibid.

63. Samuel Eliot Morison, ed., *Sources and Documents Illustrating the American Revolution, 1764–1788, and the Formation of the Federal Constitution* (Oxford: Oxford University Press, 1961), 178.

64. Adams, *Defence of Constitutions*, vol. 1, xxv.

65. Kurland and Lerner, eds., *The Founders' Constitution*, vol. 1, 49.

66. Ibid., 50.

67. Adams, *Defence of Constitutions*, vol. 1, xxii–xxiii; see also xxvi, 225–26.

68. John Smith, "The General Historie of Virginia by Captain John Smith, 1624: The Fourth Booke," in *Narratives of Early Virginia, 1606–1625*, ed. Lyon Gardiner Tyler (1907; reprint, New York: Barnes and Noble, 1966), 365.

69. Herbert J. Storing, "What the Anti-Federalists Were *For*," in *The Complete Anti-Federalist*, ed. Herbert J. Storing, 5 vols. (Chicago: University of Chicago Press, 1981), 1: 3–6 and passim.

70. Farrand, *Records*, vol. 1, 448.

71. Allan R. Millett and Peter Maslowski, *For the Common Defense: A Military History of the United States* (New York: Macmillan, 1984), 92; Francis P. Prucha, *Sword of the Republic: The United States Army on the Frontier, 1783–1846* (New

York: Macmillan, 1968), 25; and Randolph C. Downes, *Council Fires on the Upper Ohio: A Narrative of Indian Affairs in the Upper Ohio Valley Until 1795* (Pittsburgh: University of Pittsburgh Press, 1940), 318. Millett and Maslowski state that St. Clair's was "the worst defeat ever suffered by an American Army" (92). Downes notes that "St. Clair's defeat was the worst defeat ever suffered by the American Army in proportion to the numbers engaged" (318).

4: Perspectives on American Indian Sovereignty and International Law, 1600 to 1776

1. See *Report of the Working Group on Indigenous Populations on its Fifth Session*, U.N. Doc. E/CN.4/Sub. 27/1987/22 (1987). The Working Group is made up of five members of the United Nations Subcommission on Prevention of Discrimination and Protection of Minorities, which despite its specialized title functions as the comprehensive subordinate body of the Human Rights Commission. The Working Group meets annually as a presessional committee of the subcommission and reports directly to it.

2. The international character of the relationship between Indian nations and the United States forms the conceptual framework of Felix S. Cohen's seminal *Handbook of Federal Indian Law* (Washington, D.C.: U.S. Government Printing Office, 1942). Although intended as a manual for the use of Interior Department personnel, Cohen's work has had a substantial impact on legal argument and judicial decision for decades.

3. Social Darwinism and race theory played a major role in the legitimization of colonialism and in the political and juridical invisibility of indigenous peoples on a global basis. See Reginald Horsman, *Race and Manifest Destiny: The Origins of American Racial Anglo-Saxonism* (Cambridge, Mass.: Harvard University Press, 1981); Richard Drinnon, *Facing West: The Metaphysics of Indian-Hating and Empire-Building* (Minneapolis: University of Minnesota Press, 1980); Henry Reynolds, *Frontier: Aborigines, Settlers, and the Land* (Boston: Allen & Unwin, 1987), 108–30; Eriksson, "Darwinism and Sami Legislation," in *The Sami National Minority in Sweden*, ed. Birgitta Jahreskog (Atlantic Highland, N.J.: Humanities Press, 1982), 89–101; John H. Bodley, *Victims of Progress* (Menlo Park, Calif.: Cummings Publishing Co., 1975); George W. Stocking, Jr., "The Dark Skinned Savage: The Image of Primitive Man in Evolutionary Anthropology," in *Race, Culture, and Evolution: Essays in the History of Anthropology* (New York: Free Press, 1968), 110–32.

Some European writers such as Leopold Ranke went so far as to declare that Afro-Asian peoples were devoid of history, and thus existed in a "legal vacuum." C. H. Alexandrowicz, "Empirical and Doctrinal Positivism in International Law," *British Yearbook of International Law* 47 (1974–1975): 286–89.

4. Western Sahara (Advisory Opinion), 1975 I.C.J. 12. The matter was brought before the International Court of Justice by the United Nations General Assembly seeking guidance as to whether the peoples of the Western Sahara were eligible for decolonization following the withdrawal of Spain as administering power. At the time the case was considered, Spain, Mauritania, and Morocco asserted sovereign rights over the region. See Malcolm N. Shaw, *Title to Territory in Africa: International Legal Issues* (New York: Oxford University Press, 1986), 32–36.

5. See Island of Palmas Case (United States v. The Netherlands), 2 Hague Ct. Rep. 83, 100; (Perm. Ct. Arb. 1928); Case Concerning Right of Passage over Indian Territory (Portugal v. India) 1960 I.C.J. 6; the Minquiers and Ecrehos Case (France

v. United Kingdom) 1953 I.C.J. 47; Elias, "The Doctrine of Intertemporal Law," *American Journal of International Law* 74 (1980): 285–307. Waldock, "Disputed Sovereignty in the Falkland Islands Dependencies," *British Yearbook of International Law* 25 (1948): 311, 320–27. The doctrine continues to evolve. See McWhinney, "The Time Dimension in International Law, Historical Relativism and Intertemporal Law," in *Essays in International Law in Honour of Judge Manfred Lachs*, ed. Jerzy Makarczyk (The Hague: Martinus Nijhoff, 1984), 179–99.

 6. In analyzing the status of the territory and its people, the Court determined that territories inhabited by organized societies could never be considered as *terra nullius* (legally vacant space) open to acquisition by a state on the basis of occupation. The Court further determined that as political communities, the nomadic peoples of the Western Sahara possessed the capacity to enter into relations with other political entities (1975 I.C.J. 12, 64–65, 66–68). D. P. O'Connell observed that "[i]t was only the invention by the late nineteenth-century authors of the doctrine that uncivilized peoples have no capacity in international law that led to the characterization of their territories as *terrae nullius*, and resort to the doctrine of *occupatio* to explain title." D. P. O'Connell, *International Law*, vol. 1 (Dobbs Ferry, N.Y.: Oceana Publications, 1965), 470 and note 17.

 7. Robert F. Berkhofer, *The White Man's Indian: Images of the American Indian from Columbus to the Present* (New York: Alfred A. Knopf, 1978), 3–69; Francis Jennings, *The Invasion of America: Indians, Colonialism, and the Cant of Conquest* (Chapel Hill: University of North Carolina Press, 1975), 3–14, 43–57. Robert A. Williams, *The American Indian in Western Legal Thought: The Discourses of Conquest* (New York: Oxford University Press, 1990). See also Antonello Gerbi, *The Dispute of the New World: The History of a Polemic, 1750–1900* (Pittsburgh: University of Pittsburgh Press, 1973).

 8. Although European treaty-making with non-Christian peoples was an element of diplomatic practice in the Middle Ages, the question of whether Christian peoples could legitimately treat or ally with others was a matter of some doctrinal concern in the fifteenth through seventeenth centuries. The earliest debates were theological in nature, centering on a fifteenth-century alliance between Christian Poland and "pagan" Lithuania against the expansionist Teutonic Order in Prussia. The Polish representative to the Council of Constance, Paulus Vladimiri (Pawel Wlodkowic), eloquently defended the full measure of political rights and international intercourse for non-Christian nations based on natural law principles. Stanislaus F. Belch, *Paulus Vladimiri and His Doctrine Concerning International Law and Politics* (The Hague: Mouton, 1965); C. H. Alexandrowicz, "Paulus Vladimiri and the Development of the Doctrine of Coexistence of Christian and Non-Christian Countries," *British Yearbook of International Law* 39 (1963): 441, 444–47; W. F. Reddaway et al., eds., *The Cambridge History of Poland: From the Origins to Sobieski* (Cambridge: Cambridge University Press, 1950), 125–47. Hugo Grotius gave the question considerable treatment in his treatise *On the Law of War and Peace*, concluding that according to natural law, "the right to enter into treaties is so common to all men that it does not admit to a distinction arising from religion." Hugo Grotius, *De Jure Belli Ac Pacis Libri Tres*, trans. Francis W. Kelsey (1646; reprint, Oxford: Clarendon Press, 1925), 397–402. Vattel endorsed Grotius's view and regarded the issue as long settled. Emer de Vattel, *The Law of Nations, or, the Principles of Natural Law*, trans. C. Fenwick (1758; reprint, Washington, D.C.: Carnegie Institute, 1916), 162, 191. Martens did not mention the issue and included two treaties between Indian nations and Britain in his appended "List of Treaties": Treaty of Peace and Friendship concluded by W. Littleton, English governor of the

province of South Carolina with Attakullakulla, deputy of the Chorokie [sic] nation, Fort Prince George, Dec. 26, 1759, and Preliminary Articles of Peace, Friendship and Alliance entered into between the English and the deputies sent for the whole Seneca nation, 3 Apr. 1764. G. F. von Martens, *Summary of the Law of Nations, Founded on the Treaties and Customs of the Modern Nations of Europe*, trans. W. Corbett (Philadelphia: Thomas Bradford, 1795), 352, 355.

9. Apart from the question of European nations entering into treaty relations with non-Christian peoples, which was well settled by the seventeenth century, a number of jurists were troubled by the issue of military alliances. C. H. Alexandrowicz, *An Introduction to the History of the Law of Nations in the East Indies: 16th, 17th, and 18th Centuries* (Oxford: Clarendon Press, 1967), 85–89. Grotius, for example, believed that such alliances were lawful unless directed at Christian nations or where they would increase the military capacity of non-Christian states. Grotius, *De Jure Belli Ac Pacis*, 397–403. As the present study will demonstrate, neither Britain nor France was squeamish about forming alliances with Indian nations to advance their imperial interests against each other.

10. See generally Charles Tilly, ed., *The Formation of National States in Western Europe* (Princeton, N.J.: Princeton University Press, 1975).

11. For example, John Westlake, *Chapters on the Principles of International Law* (Cambridge, Mass.: Harvard University Press, 1894), 137–55. See also James Lorimer, *The Institutes of the Law of Nations: A Treatise of the Jural Relations of Separate Political Communities*, vol. 1 (Edinburgh and London: W. Blackwood and Sons, 1883–1884), 93–125.

12. Western Sahara (Advisory Opinion) 1975 I.C.J. 35–36; Broms, "Subjects: Entitlement in the International Legal System," in *The Structure and Process of International Law*, eds. R. St. J. Macdonald and Douglas M. Johnston (The Hague: M. Nijhoff, 1983), 383–411; Ian Brownlie, *Principles of Public International Law* (Oxford: Clarendon Press, 1979), 73–82; James Crawford, *The Creation of States in International Law* (New York: Oxford University Press, 1979), 5–10, 31–71; L. Oppenheim (Lauterpacht), *International Law: A Treatise* (New York: Longmans, Green, 1955), 117–19, 259–97. O'Connell noted the relative character of statehood: "The term 'state' is no term of art. . . . The sense in which it is used will depend upon the context, and the inclusion or exclusion of a particular entity from the category of 'state' cannot be presumed from any *a priori* notion of the qualifications of statehood." O'Connell, *International Law*, vol. 1, 303. See also Lissitzyn, "Territorial Entities Other Than Independent States," in *Receuil Des Cours: Collected Courses of the Hague Academy of International Law*, vol. 125 (Leyden: A. W. Sijthoff, 1970), 8–11.

13. Among the sovereign entities cited are the Kingdom of Naples, the Order of Malta, Sicily, Sardinia, the Republic of Genoa, Duchy of Silesia, the Comte of Glatz, the principalities of Monaco, Bouillon, and Henrichemont, the republics of Lucca, San Marino, and Ragusa, each of the Seven United Provinces of the Netherlands, Drenthe, each of the Swiss cantons, Abbi, the town of St. Gal, the Grisons, the Valais, the city of Mulhausen, the principality of Neufchatel, the city of Geneva, the Bishopric of Basel, and numerous "demi-sovereign" entities ruled by the electors of the "Germanic Empire." Martens, *Summary of the Law of Nations*, 23–32. See also J. H. W. Verzijl, *International Law in Historical Perspective*, vol. 2 (Leyden: A. W. Sijthoff, 1968), 17–44.

14. "For a state to be entirely free and sovereign, it must govern itself, and acknowledge no legislative superior but God. Everything which is compatible with this independence is also compatible with sovereignty, so that mere alliances of

protection, tribute, or vassalage which a state may contract with another, do not hinder it from continuing perfectly sovereign, or from being looked upon as occupying its usual place on the great theatre of Europe." Martens, *Summary of the Law of Nations,* 23–24. See also Vattel, *Law of Nations,* 11–12.

15. Alexandrowicz, *Introduction to the History of the Law of Nations;* C. H. Alexandrowicz, *The European-African Confrontation: A Study in Treaty Making* (Leyden: A. W. Sijthoff, 1973).

16. Alexandrowicz, *Introduction to the History of the Law of Nations;* James Brown Scott, *The Discovery of America and Its Influence on International Law: The Four Hundredth Anniversary of Francisco de Vitoria's "De Indis" of 1532: Address of James Brown Scott* (Washington, D.C.: n.p., 1929). Scott focuses largely on the writings and influence of the Spanish theologian Francisco de Vitoria. Vitoria recognized the indigenous nations of the Western Hemisphere as peoples with rights under international law. See Ernest Nys, ed., Francisco de Vitoria, *De Indis et de Ivre Belli Relectiones* (trans. of 1696 edition; reprint, Washington, D.C.: Carnegie Institution of Washington, 1917), 119–49.

17. C. H. Alexandrowicz, "Doctrinal Aspects of the Universality of the Law of Nations," *British Yearbook of International Law* 37 (1961): 506–15. In Mark Frank Lindley's survey of the writings of publicists on the question of indigenous territorial sovereignty, only certain writers of the late nineteenth and early twentieth centuries completely denied the existence of such status. Mark Frank Lindley, *The Acquisition and Government of Backward Territory in International Law: Being a Treatise on the Law and Practice Relating to Colonial Expansion* (London: Longmans, Green and Co., 1926), 10–20.

18. Tilly, *Formation of National States;* Joseph R. Strayer, *On the Medieval Origins of the Modern State* (Princeton, N.J.: Princeton University Press, 1970); Otto Gierke, *Political Theories of the Middle Age,* trans. Frederic William Maitland (Cambridge: Harvard University Press, 1951), 87–100; Julius Goebel, "The Equality of States, II," *Columbia Law Review* 23 (1923): 113–41; Goebel, "The Equality of States, III," ibid., 247–77. A number of writers point to the 1648 Peace of Westphalia ending the Thirty Years' War as marking the emergence of the modern state system. Falk, "A New Paradigm for International Legal Studies," *Yale Law Journal* 84 (1975): 969, 975–92; Gross, "The Peace of Westphalia, 1648–1948," *American Journal of International Law* 42 (1948): 20–41. Despite political developments in this period, however, many European frontiers remained ill-defined through the seventeenth century. See George Norman Clark, *The Seventeenth Century* (1929; reprint, Oxford: Clarendon Press, 1947), 140–52.

19. Grotius described the States-General as a union of equal sovereigns. See Hugo Grotius, *Annales* (1667), cited in Goebel, "The Equality of States, III," 270.

20. Baron de Lahontan, *New Voyages to North America,* ed. Reuben G. Thwaites, vol. 1 (1703; reprint, Chicago: A. C. McClurg, 1905), 58, 59.

21. The barest consensus on the elements of statehood was achieved in Article I of the Montevideo Convention on Rights and Duties of States formulated in 1933. Conference participants agreed that reduced to the most essential criteria, a state must exhibit a permanent population, a defined territory, a government, and the capacity to enter into relations with other states. Convention on the Rights and Duties of States, 49 Stat. 3097, T.S. 881, 165 L.N.T.S. 19. Although formulations reached in 1933 should not be applied indiscriminately through history, they do reflect fundamental attributes most common to the political and territorial entities recognized as international persons through a succession of historic eras.

22. See Jennings, *Invasion of America*, 132–34; W. C. MacLeod, *The American Indian Frontier* (London: Dawsons of Pall Mall, 1968), 195–96.

23. Actual European explorations in the hemisphere were examined in several works by the cultural geographer Carl O. Sauer. Carl O. Sauer, *The Early Spanish Main* (Berkeley: University of California Press, 1966); *Northern Mists* (Berkeley: University of California Press, 1968); and *Sixteenth Century North America* (Berkeley: University of California Press, 1971).

24. Julius Goebel, *The Struggle for the Falkland Islands: A Study in Legal and Diplomatic History* (New Haven, Conn.: Yale University Press, 1927), 94–97; Frances G. Davenport, ed., *European Treaties Bearing on the History of the United States and Its Dependencies*, 4 vols. (Washington, D.C.: Carnegie Institution of Washington, 1917–1937), 1: 1–32, 49, 56–78; Von Der Heydte, "Discovery, Symbolic Annexation and Virtual Effectiveness in International Law," *American Journal of International Law* 29 (1935): 448–60; Cheyney, "International Law Under Queen Elizabeth," *English Historical Review* 20 (1905): 660.

25. Julius Goebel, *Struggle for the Falkland Islands*, 62–119; Williams, "The Medieval and Renaissance Origins of the Status of the American Indian in Western Legal Thought," *Southern California Law Review* 57, no. 1 (1983): 11–36.

26. Goebel, ibid., 63, 97–108, 121–29; Daniel P. O'Connell, *International Law*, vol. 1, 468–70.

27. The so-called papal donation arose from a series of papal bulls in the late fifteenth century. The most famous of them, *Inter Caetera* (Alexander VI) of 4 May 1493 established the "line of demarcation" between the claimed interests of Spain and Portugal. Davenport, ed., *European Treaties*, vol. 1, 71–78; S. Z. Ehler and J. B. Morrall, eds., *Church and State through the Centuries: A Collection of Historic Documents with Commentaries* (Westminster, Md.: The Newman Press, 1954), 144–59. Davenport, following Grotius and others, has characterized the papacy's role in these conflicts as akin to an "arbitrator between nations," an analogy that conveys a more accurate sense of the bilateral nature of the disputes and of the papal function in their resolution. Hugo Grotius, *The Freedom of the Seas* [*Mare Liberum*], trans. R. Magoffin (1608; reprint, New York: Oxford University Press, 1916), 15–17. Indeed, the "line of demarcation" was freely ignored by competitor states in all regions. Max Savelle, *The Origins of American Diplomacy: The International History of Anglo-America, 1942–1763* (New York: Macmillan, 1967), 17–31; Slattery, "French Claims in North America, 1500–1559," *Canadian Historical Review* 59 (1978): 139–69.

28. Goebel has termed "discovery" as "never anything more than a fugitive ·political argument advanced by a chancellery that was unable to find adequate support in accepted international custom." *Struggle for the Falkland Islands*, 86–87. See also Myres S. McDougal, Harold D. Lasswell, and Ivan A. Vlasic, *Law and Public Order in Space* (New Haven, Conn.: Yale University Press, 1963), 828–37; Von der Heydte, "Discovery, Symbolic Annexation and Virtual Effectiveness," 452–53; Slattery, "French Claims." The contention by Keller et al. that discovery combined with symbolic possession was accepted as sufficient to establish title to inhabited territory is not supported by state practice. See Arthur S. Keller, Oliver J. Lissitzyn, and Frederick J. Mann, *Creation of Rights of Sovereignty through Symbolic Acts, 1400–1800* (New York: Columbia University Press, 1938).

29. One of the most secure foundations for a claim of exclusive right recognized in this period was provided by the conquest and subjugation of an enemy in a "just war." Military conquest alone, however, did not give the conquering state sovereign

rights. Sovereignty was the product of three factors in addition to military success: the conquest must have been firmly established—so long as warfare continued, no annexation could be effective in international law; subjugation must have been complete—the enemy must have ceased to exist as a political entity in the territory at issue and the fate of that territory left to the unilateral disposition of the conqueror; a formal annexation must have been effected, amounting to the assimilation of the territory to the dominions of the conquering state. Even total victory would not produce a transfer of sovereignty if the victorious powers disclaimed any intention to annex the occupied territory. L. Oppenheim, *International Law: A Treatise*, vol. 1 (London: Longmans, Green, and Company, 1905), 287–92.

30. R. Y. Jennings, *The Acquisition of Territory in International Law* (New York: Oceana Publications, 1963), 16–19.

31. Ibid.

32. The hinterland claim was also disregarded by European states during the period of African colonization. Uzoigwee, "Spheres of Influence and the Doctrine of the Hinterland in the Partition of Africa," *Journal of African Studies* 3 (1976): 183, 194–97; and Shaw, *Title to Territory*, 48–50.

33. The Confederacy has been known by a number of names throughout recorded history in North America. British documents refer variously to the "Five Nations" or "Six Nations," French to the "Iroquois." Dutch records evidence no knowledge of the political structure of the Confederacy. Most of the anthropological and historical literature following Lewis Henry Morgan's classic study uses "Iroquois." Lewis H. Morgan, *League of the Ho-de-no-sau-nee, or Iroquois* (Rochester, N.Y.: Sage & Brother, 1851). Out of the need for both consistency and respect, this article will employ the terms "Haudenosaunee" and "Confederacy" to identify the people concerned. However, quotations include any of these terms of identification.

34. The Tuscarora Nation formally became the sixth nation of the Confederacy circa 1722.

35. The *Kaianerakoa* remains a vital part of Haudenosaunee oral tradition and has never been committed to writing in its entirety. A few controversial summary texts have been published. See *The Great Law of Peace of the Longhouse People* (Mohawk Nation via Rooseveltown, N.Y.: Akwesasne Notes, 1977); see also Arthur C. Parker, "The Constitution of the Five Nations," in *Parker on the Iroquois*, ed. William N. Fenton (Syracuse, N.Y.: Syracuse University Press, 1968).

36. On the basis of European records, the degree to which the Confederacy functioned as a unitary entity with respect to external relations varied over time. From current practice and Haudenosaunee oral tradition, lack of consensus among the nations as to a particular course of action could result in either inaction or an agreement that one or more nations would exercise its own policy judgment in external affairs. In some instances, one or more nations might be designated as a diplomatic agent of the entire Confederacy or would function as such as a matter of historical tradition. Because European records tell us essentially nothing about the internal discussions of the Confederacy leading to policy decisions, it is difficult to determine the extent of cohesion among the nations in international relations in a particular historical period.

The issue is further complicated by the fact that for much of this era, the Haudenosaunee played a delicate diplomatic game, maneuvering between and among European neighbors and frequently playing one off against another. In this environment, it may have been useful for individual nations to form apparently separate relations. For example, after the 1670s, the Mohawk Nation was physically divided between communities in the Mohawk Valley near Albany allied with the British and Christianized communities relocated to the area of Montreal allied with the French. Despite the apparent radical division, the two groups geographically anchored the important contraband trade between French Montreal and British Albany. In any event, decisions involving war and peace and major treaty arrangements likely involved a high degree of consultation and coordination.

37. The symbolism of the *Guswenta* in Haudenosaunee oral tradition was explained in the Onondaga Nation Longhouse in central New York State at several meetings attended by the author.

38. Hudson's voyage began within days of the formal acknowledgment of the independence of the United Netherlands by Spain in the Treaty of Antwerp of 9 April 1609. Davenport, ed., *European Treaties*, vol. 1, 258–69; see also John Romeyn Brodhead, *History of the State of New York*, 2 vols. (New York: Harper & Brothers, 1853–1871), 1: 38–42.

39. Treaty of Peace and Alliance between the United Netherlands and Great Britain, concluded at Breda, July 21/31, 1667," in *European Treaties*, ed. Davenport, vol. 2, 119–42. The treaty provided that both parties would retain sovereignty and possession of all lands seized from the other during the war. Ibid., 129. The position of the Dutch negotiators is found in *Documents Relative to the Colonial History of the State of New York*, eds. E. B. O'Callaghan and B. Fernow, 15 vols. (Albany: Weed, Parsons & Co., 1853–1887), 2: 379–84, 516–17.

40. "Treaty of Peace between Great Britain and the United Netherlands, concluded at Westminster, February 9/19, 1674," in *European Treaties*, ed. Davenport, vol. 2, 229, 239.

41. "Grant of Exclusive Trade to New Netherland, October 1614," in *Documents Relative to Colonial History*, eds. O'Callaghan and Fernow, vol. 1, 11–12.

42. "Charter of the West India Company," in *History of New Netherland, or New York under the Dutch*, E. B. O'Callaghan, vol. 1 (New York: D. Appleton & Co., 1855), 399–401. On colonizing companies in this period, see Lindley, *Acquisition and Government*, 91–99.

43. Allen W. Trelease, *Indian Affairs in Colonial New York: The Seventeenth Century* (Ithaca, N.Y.: Cornell University Press, 1960), 40.

44. For example, Johnson v. McIntosh, 21 U.S. (8 Wheat) 543, 593–94 (1823). In the decision of the case, the Supreme Court recognized Indian nations and the United States as separate political entities with distinct juridical orders. In order for property interests claimed by American citizens within territories ceded to the United States to be recognized by the federal courts, they had to be derived from either inchoate rights patented prior to the cession (Fletcher v. Peck, 10 U.S. [6 Cranch] 87, 142–143) or from a patent for the actual property issued after the cession. The only exception concerned property rights reserved in a treaty of cession. See Howard R. Berman, "The Concept of Aboriginal Rights in the Early Legal History of the United States," *Buffalo Law Review* 27 (1978): 637, 653–54.

45. See note 42.

46. Trelease, *Indian Affairs*, 37–38.

47. The 1613 treaty was apparently made with a Dutch trading ship and involved an agreement for permission to erect a trading post (possibly for the New Netherland Company). See Hendrik W. Van Loon, "Tawagonshi, Beginning of the Treaty Era," *Indian Historian* 1, no. 3 (1968): 22, 23–26; and Richter, "Rediscovered Links in the Covenant Chain: Previously Unpublished Transcripts of New York Indian Treaty Minutes, 1677–1691," *Proceedings of the American Antiquarian Society* 92, Pt. 1 (1982): 45, 50–53. See also Francis Jennings, *The Ambiguous*

Iroquois Empire: The Covenant Chain Confederation of Indian Tribes with English Colonies from Its Beginnings to the Lancaster Treaty of 1744 (New York: W. W. Norton & Company, 1984), 53–55. Samuel de Champlain reported a Dutch alliance with the Haudenosaunee in the winter of 1615 to 1616. See Henry P. Biggar, *The Early Trading Companies of New France: A Contribution to the History of Commerce and Discovery in North America* (Toronto: University of Toronto Library, 1901), 106.

48. Period records indicate that at least one and possibly two treaties of alliance were negotiated with the Dutch in 1642 or 1643. See O'Callaghan and Fernow, eds., *Documents Relative to Colonial History*, vol. 13, 15, 112.

49. Jennings, *Ambiguous Iroquois Empire*, 55.

50. Ibid., 56.

51. "Report of the Board of Accounts on New Netherland, 1644," in *Documents Relative to Colonial History*, eds. O'Callaghan and Fernow, vol. 1, 149–56; O'Callaghan, *History of New Netherland*, vol. 1, 349–51, 418–24.

52. "Instructions to the Director General and the Council of New Netherland, July 1645," in *Documents Relative to Colonial History*, eds. O'Callaghan and Fernow, vol. 1, 160, 161.

53. Jennings, *Ambiguous Iroquois Empire*, 55–56; O'Callaghan, *History of New Netherland*, vol. 1, 355–57; Brodhead, *History of the State of New York*, vol. 1, 407–09. The Dutch reciprocated in 1664 by acting as mediators between the Mohawks and northern Indian peoples. See "Journal of Jan Dareth and Jacob Lookermans, Commissioners to Negotiate a Peace between the Maquaas and the Northern Indians, May 1664," in *Documents Relative to Colonial History*, eds. O'Callaghan and Fernow, vol. 13, 380–82.

54. "Articles of Peace Concluded in the Presence of the Mohawks Between the Dutch and the River Indians, August 1645," ibid., 18.

55. O'Callaghan and Fernow, eds., *Documents Relative to Colonial History*, vol. 1, 150.

56. At a later stage in their relationship, the Dutch expressed concern about becoming dependent on a Mohawk alliance. During a war with the Esopus Indians, the director and council of New Netherland resisted recommendations from the directors in Holland to encourage the Mohawks to subdue the Esopus. New Netherland officials regarded the plan for Indian assistance as "partly unsafe" and "partly dangerous," particularly with the Mohawks,

> for they are a self-exulting, arrogant and bold tribe made too haughty through their continuous victories and advantages, which they have gained over the French themselves and French Indians in Canada; if we were to ask them hereto and they obtained and gained the desired result, they would exalt themselves and belittle us so much more among the other tribes and in case we should not reward them according to their avidity and appetite and did not continually stand there open-handed, we would constantly hear ourselves upbraided and would have to fear an attack, if we contradicted them. For these and many other considerations, it is best, to stand as far as possible on our own feet and to pray the Good God for a happy result.

"Excerpts from a letter of the Director and Council of New Netherland to the Directors in Holland, Defending Their Course Against the Indians, June 1660," in *Documents Relative to Colonial History*, eds. O'Callaghan and Fernow, vol. 13, 176.

57. For a historical perspective on the international regulation of acts of reprisal, see Spiegel, "Origin and Development of Denial of Justice," *American Journal*

of International Law 32 (1938): 63–81. Spiegel surveyed the writings of Vitoria, Gentili, Grotius, Zouche, Wolff, and Vattel, publicists relevant to the period covered in this article, as well as state practice. See also Julius Goebel,"The International Responsibility of States for Injuries Sustained by Aliens on Account of Mob Violence, Insurrections and Civil Wars," *American Journal of International Law* 8 (1914): 802–52; and Louis B. Sohn and Thomas Buergenthal, *International Protection of Human Rights* (Indianapolis, Ind.: Bobbs-Merrill, 1973), 23–39.

58. Examples of similar provisions in European treaties of the same era can be found in "Treaty between England and the Netherlands, signed at Westminster, 5 April 1654 (Art. XXIV)," in *The Consolidated Treaty Series*, ed. Clive Parry, vol. 3 (Dobbs Ferry, N.Y.: Oceana Publications, 1969), 225, 234–35; and "Treaty of Peace and Alliance between England and the Netherlands, signed at Whitehall, 4 (14) September 1662 (Art. XXIII)," in *Consolidated Treaty Series*, ed. Parry, vol. 7, 193, 207.

59. Trelease, *Indian Affairs*, 148–68. See also "Articles between Col. Cartwright and the New York Indians, September 1664," in *Documents Relative to Colonial History*, eds. O'Callaghan and Fernow, vol. 3, 67–68 and infra text accompanying note 90.

60. "Treaty of Peace Concluded with the Esopus Indians, July 1660," in *Documents Relative to Colonial History*, eds. O'Callaghan and Fernow, vol. 13, 179–81.

61. "Articles of Peace Made with the Esopus Indians, May 1664," ibid., 375–77.

62. "Articles of Agreement between the delegates of the Commissioners of the United Colonies of New England and the Delegates of the Director-General of New Netherland, concluded at Hartford, September 1650," in *European Treaties*, ed. Davenport, vol. 2, 1–6; "Treaty of Amity and Commerce between Virginia and New Netherland, concluded at Jamestown, April 1660," ibid., 53–56; Savelle, *Origins of American Diplomacy*, 157–70.

63. Savelle, *Origins of American Diplomacy*, 170–73; Jennings, *Ambiguous Iroquois Empire*, 99; O'Callaghan and Fernow, eds., *Documents Relative to Colonial History*, vol. 13, 23–24.

64. E. B. O'Callaghan, ed., *The Documentary History of the State of New York*, 4 vols. (Albany, N.Y.: Weed, Parsons & Co., 1850–1851), 1: 46, 47.

65. "Warrant for William Ussling [Usselincx] to Establish a General Company for Trade to Asia, Africa, America and Magellanica (1624)," in *Documents Relative to Colonial History*, eds. O'Callaghan and Fernow, vol. 12, 1–2. At the close of the Thirty Years' War, Sweden was the principal Protestant power in continental Europe. See "Treaty of Peace between Sweden and the Empire, signed at Osnabruck, October 1648," in *Consolidated Treaty Series*, ed. Parry, vol. 1, 198; "Agreement between the Empire and France and Sweden, signed at Münster, January 1649," ibid., 385; "Public Convention between the Empire and Sweden for the execution of the Peace of Westphalia, signed at Nuremberg, June 1649," in *Consolidated Treaty Series*, ed. Parry, vol. 2, 153.

66. "Charter or Privilege, which the Mighty and Most Noble Prince and Lord Gustavus Adolphus, King of Sweden [etc.] Has Graciously Given by Letters—Patent to the Newly Established Swedish South Company (1626)," in *Documents Relative to Colonial History*, eds. O'Callaghan and Fernow, vol. 12, 7, 12–14. The second governor of the colony of New Sweden, Johan Printz, was similarly instructed to maintain peaceful relations with Indian nations. See Amandus Johnson, ed. and trans., *The Instruction for Johan Printz, Governor of New Sweden: The First Constitution or Supreme Law of the States of Pennsylvania and Delaware* (Philadelphia: The Swedish Colonial Society, 1930), 78, 80.

67. The expedition consisted of two ships, the *Kalmar Nyckel* (Key of Calmar) and the *Griffin*. See Brodhead, *History of the State of New York*, vol. 1, 280–81.

68. D. H. Kent, ed., *Early American Indian Documents, Treaties and Laws, 1607–1789: Pennsylvania and Delaware Treaties, 1629–1737*, vol. 1 (Washington, D.C.: University Publications of America, 1979), 11–12; see also "Certificate and Deposition of Certain Antient Sweeds," ibid., 13; and Amandus Johnson, *The Swedish Settlements on the Delaware: Their History and Relation to the Indians, Dutch and English, 1638–1664, with an Account of the South, the New Sweden, and the American Companies, and the Efforts of Sweden to Regain the Colony*, 2 vols. (Philadelphia: University of Pennsylvania Press, 1911), 1: 183–84.

69. Johnson, ed., *Instruction for Johan Printz*, 66, 68. According to the eighteenth-century chronicler Acrelius, land cessions were negotiated with a form of public ratification:

> Purchases of land from the savages were made in this way: Both parties set their names and marks under the purchase-contract. Two witnesses were also taken from among the Christians. When these made their oath that they were present at the transaction, and had seen the payment made, then the purchase was valid. If the kings or chiefs of the Indians signed such an agreement in the presence of a number of their people, then it was legitimate on their side.

From Acrelius, "Account of the Swedish Churches in New Sweden (1769)," in *Early American Indian Documents*, ed. D. H. Kent, 9, 10.

70. "Relation to the Noble West India Company in Old Sweden, despatched from New Sweden on June 11, Anno 1644," in *Instruction for Johan Printz*, ed. Johnson, 105, 116–17; Johnson, *Swedish Settlements on the Delaware*, vol. 1, 375–79.

71. Johnson, *Swedish Settlements on the Delaware*, vol. 2, 563–65.

72. The Swedish overseas enterprise may well have been rooted in "Grotian" principles. The original charter to the Swedish South Company, which required respect for non-European sovereigns and incorporated "just war" concepts, was drafted in 1626—one year after the publication of Grotius's treatise *De Jure Belli Ac Pacis*. It is known that J. Oxenstierna, adviser to the Swedish Crown in this period, respected Grotius's work to the extent of employing him as the Swedish ambassador to France during the Thirty Years' War. See Lee, "Grotius—The Last Phase, 1635–45," *Grotius Society Transactions* 31 (1945): 193–215.

73. Henry P. Biggar, ed., *The Works of Samuel De Champlain*, 6 vols. (Toronto: Champlain Society, 1922–1936), 2: 82–101; 2: 122–34; 3: 56–77; 4: 92–99 (1609); 4: 106–15 (1610); 4: 252–65 (1615); Trelease, *Indian Affairs*, 52; Bruce G. Trigger, "Early Iroquoian Contacts with Europeans," in *Handbook of North American Indians: Northeast*, ed. Bruce G. Trigger, vol. 15 (Washington, D.C.: Smithsonian Institution, 1978), 349.

74. Trelease, *Indian Affairs*, 52; Biggar, ed., *Works of Samuel De Champlain*, vol. 5, 117–19, 130–33; Biggar, *Early Trading Companies*, 124. This treaty was preceded by a French diplomatic mission to the Huron Nation to prevent a commercial alliance between the Hurons and the Haudenosaunee. See Marcel Trudel, *The Beginnings of New France, 1524–1663*, trans. Patricia Claxton (Toronto: McClelland and Stewart, 1973), 147–48.

75. "Treaty of Peace between Great Britain and France concluded at Utrecht, March 31/April 11, 1713," in *European Treaties*, ed. Davenport, vol. 3, 193–214. Jennings takes the position that the French initiated and continued hostilities with the Haudenosaunee as part of a divide and survive strategy in the fur trade. To the extent that this was the case, and it unquestionably was an element of French

policy in certain periods, France paid a heavy subsidy in war losses for the integrity of its trade. Jennings, *Ambiguous Iroquois Empire*, 86–87.

76. A detailed description of the public treaty process is contained in the report of Fr. Barthelmy Vimont, S.J., "Relation of What Occurred in New France in the Years 1644 and 1645," in *The Jesuit Relations and Allied Documents: Travels and Explorations of the Jesuit Missionaries in New France, 1610–1791*, ed. Reuben G. Thwaites, 73 vols. (Cleveland: Burrows Brothers Co., 1896–1901), 27: 123, 247–305. In a private conference with the governor, separately reported in Latin to preserve secrecy, Mohawk envoys demanded that the French abandon the Algonquians as the price for peace with New France and its Huron allies. After initially refusing to consider the proposal, the governor in a second private meeting agreed:

> Monsieur the Governor said that there were two kinds of Algonquins—one like ourselves, recognized as Christians; the other, unlike us. Without the former, it is certain, we do not make a peace; as for the latter, they themselves are the masters of their own actions, nor are they united to us like the others.

From *Jesuit Relations and Allied Documents*, ed. Thwaites, vol. 28, 150–51, 315. See also Francis Jennings et al., eds., *The History and Culture of Iroquois Diplomacy: An Interdisciplinary Guide to the Treaties of the Six Nations and Their League* (Syracuse, N.Y.: Syracuse University Press, 1985), 127–53.

77. Bruce G. Trigger, *The Children of Aataentsic: A History of the Huron People to 1660*, vol. 2 (Montreal: McGill-Queen's University Press, 1976), 725–88; George T. Hunt, *The Wars of the Iroquois: A Study in Intertribal Trade Relations* (Madison: University of Wisconsin Press, 1967), 87–104.

78. "The Council constituted by his Majesty in these Countries ... would willingly desire that commerce, and at the same time the union of hearts and spirits, between your Colonies and ours, but that we should wish to enter at the same time into a *league offensive and defensive with you against the Iroquois, our enemies*, who would impede us in that trade, or would at least render it less advantageous for you and for us." (Emphasis added.) From "Letter of the Council of Quebec to the Commissioners of New England, June 1651," in *Documents Relative to Colonial History*, eds. O'Callaghan and Fernow, vol. 9, 5.

79. Trelease, *Indian Affairs*, 121; Thwaites, ed., *Jesuit Relations*, vol. 40, 157; Trudel, *Beginnings of New France*, 224–27. Trudel notes that the 1653 treaty followed several Mohawk victories.

80. "Memoir of the King to serve as Instruction to Sieur Talon ... March 1665," in *Documents Relative to Colonial History*, eds. O'Callaghan and Fernow, vol. 9, 24, 25.

81. "Treaty of Peace between the Iroquois and Governor de Tracy, December 1665," in ibid., vol. 3, 121–25.

82. Ibid., 121, 122. The French summary record of the position of the Haudenosaunee ambassadors in this regard refers only to a confirmation of earlier treaties of peace and a willingness to overlook previous French and allied violations of those treaties. "Explanation of the Eleven Presents of the Iroquois Ambassadors, December 1665," in *Documents Relative to Colonial History*, eds. O'Callaghan and Fernow, vol. 9, 37.

83. Ibid., 58–59.

84. Oppenheim, writing during the modern colonial era, regarded vassalage as a troublesome concept that could only be considered according to each special case. In general terms, he regarded the status as international rather than constitutional, with the vassal state retaining its sovereignty over domestic affairs, but

giving over to the suzerain state control over external relations. If that control were complete and the vassal state had no relations with other states, Oppenheim considered the state as retaining internal sovereignty, but losing its international personality. He cited a number of examples, however, of vassal states continuing to exercise some aspects of international relations. In either case, all international treaties concluded by the suzerain are ipso facto binding on the vassal unless it is expressly or implicitly excepted from their operation, and war of the suzerain is war of the vassal. Oppenheim, *International Law* (1905), vol. 1, 133–37. For the history of vassal states in Europe and North Africa, see Verzijl, *International Law*, vol. 2, 339–59, 365–412.

Oppenheim described a protectorate as coming into being by a treaty between a weak and a strong state, under which the weaker entity transfers the management of its most important international relations to the protecting state. A protected state of this nature never completely loses its international personality and is not necessarily a party to wars of the protecting state or to its treaties with third states. Oppenheim, *International Law* (1905), vol. 1, 137–39; Verzijl, *International Law*, vol. 2, 412–21. Earlier, more contemporary jurists adopted a more expansive view of the retained status of the vassal or protected entity. Vattel regarded unequal alliances, protectorates, and feudatory states as essentially the same in legal status. So long as these states retained their internal self-government, sovereignty remained intact. Vattel, *Law of Nations*, 11–12. Similarly, Martens considered that "mere alliances of protection, tribute, or vassalage which a state may contract with another, do not hinder it from continuing perfectly sovereign. . . ." Martens, *Summary of the Law of Nations*, 23–24.

85. O'Callaghan and Fernow, eds., *Documents Relative to Colonial History*, vol. 9, 52–54.

86. Ibid., 60.

87. Ibid., vol. 3, 121–25.

88. J. Dumont, *Corps Universel Diplomatique du Droit des Gens: Contenant un Recueil des Traitez d'Alliance, de Paix, de Treve, de Neutralitae, de Commerce, d'Aechange . . . & Autres Contrats, Qui ont Aetae Fait,* 8 vols. (The Hague: Chez P. Husson and Charles Levier, 1726–1731), 6: 112, 113–14, 133–34; ratifications in English translation: Seneca, *Documents Relative to Colonial History*, vol. 3, 125–26; vol. 9, 44–45; Oneida and Mohawk, ibid., vol. 3, 126–27; vol. 9, 45–47. Dumont's collection was a significant achievement in the development of international law and remains an important source for many early treaties. See Mario Toscano, *The History of Treaties and International Politics: An Introduction to the History of Treaties and International Politics, the Documentary and Memoir Sources* (Baltimore: Johns Hopkins University Press, 1966), 59–66.

89. W. J. Eccles, *Frontenac: The Courtier Governor* (Toronto: McClelland and Stewart, 1959), 5.

90. "Articles between Col. Cartwright and the New York Indians, September 1664," in *Documents Relative to Colonial History*, eds. O'Callaghan and Fernow, vol. 3, 67–68.

91. Europeans were required to take an oath of allegiance, later followed by complete integration through the gradual introduction of English laws and institutions:

> I doe sweare by the Almighty God that I will beare faith and allegience to his Majtie of great Brittaine, and that I will obey all such comands as I shall receive from the Governor, Deputy Governor or other officers appointed by his Majties authority soe long as I live in these or any other His Majties Territoryes.

From ibid., 71; see also 74–77.

92. Ibid., 51, 53, 62–64; Jennings, *Invasion of America*, 285–86.

93. O'Callaghan and Fernow, eds., *Documents Relative to Colonial History*, vol. 3, 55–56.

94. Jennings, *Ambiguous Iroquois Empire*, 148–49; Trelease, *Indian Affairs*, 233–37; Robert Livingston, *The Livingston Indian Records, 1666–1723*, ed. Lawrence H. Leder (Stanfordville, N.Y.: E. M. Coleman, 1979), 42–48.

95. Leder, ed., *Livingston Indian Records*, 48–61.

96. Jennings, *Ambiguous Iroquois Empire*, 145–71, 367–75.

97. See generally ibid.

98. Jennings made a brief effort in this direction, but his source for the Great Law of Peace is a summary document. Ibid., 93–95. The actual "Reading of the Great Law" requires many hours over several days of oral recitation.

99. See William N. Fenton, "Structure, Continuity, and Change in the Process of Iroquois Treaty Making," in *History and Culture of Iroquois Diplomacy*, ed. Jennings et al., 3–36. Fenton's idealized composite description of the Haudenosaunee process of treaty-making with the British is very much an anthropologist's construction. Although it only presents procedural elements of diplomatic practice, it does demonstrate some consistency between Haudenosaunee internal social and political relations, particularly systems of kinship and reciprocity, and the conceptualization of international relations.

International diplomacy has always been highly ritualized. See John R. Wood and Jean Serres, *Diplomatic Ceremonial and Protocol: Principles, Procedures & Practices* (New York: Columbia University Press, 1970), 17–20, 81–157; see also Alexandrowicz, *Introduction to the History of the Law of Nations*, 189–223.

100. O'Callaghan and Fernow, eds., *Documents Relative to Colonial History*, vol. 9, 52–54.

101. See text accompanying notes 81–86.

102. Trelease, *Indian Affairs*, 249. He elsewhere described these "submissions" as "in reality no more than a facet of their [Haudenosaunee] independent diplomacy." Ibid., 268.

103. Jennings, *Ambiguous Iroquois Empire*, 182–83, 191–94.

104. Ibid., 194. See also Jennings, *Invasion of America*, 105–27. Jennings seems to have altered this view in a later article:

> Called the Covenant Chain, it was a multiparty alliance of two groupings of members: tribes, under the general leadership of the Iroquois, and English colonies, under the general supervision of New York. As in the modern United Nations, no member gave up its sovereignty. All decisions were made by consultation and treaty, and all were implemented by each member individually.

Jennings, "Iroquois Alliances in American History," in *History and Culture of Iroquois Diplomacy*, 38.

105. See note 84.

106. Treaties of protection and vassalage were negotiated by the British in North America, but their terms stand in sharp contrast to the Anglo-Haudenosaunee relationship. For example, in 1677 British authorities in the Virginia colony negotiated a treaty of vassalage with the "kings and queens" of the Pamunkey, Woanoke (Roanoke), Hottoway, and Naneymond peoples in the aftermath of Bacon's Rebellion. Under the terms of the treaty, the Indian parties recognized their dependence upon and subjection to the king of England, his heirs and successors as a liege lord, and agreed to pay a yearly symbolic tribute in beaver pelts to the governor. Indian territories were formally ceded to the Crown with the agreement that continuing Indian possession would be confirmed by letters patent. In lieu of rents, each people

was required to present three arrows in return for the patents. In line with European feudal practice, the symbolic offerings memorialized recognition that the Indian rulers owed their crowns and their lands to the British monarch ("*pour marque de reconnaissance qu'ils tiennent leurs Couronnes et leurs Terres du Grand Roi d'Angleterre*").

Despite vassal status and certain jurisdictional concessions in intersocietal conflicts, it is quite clear that the Indian parties were not incorporated into the settler colony—they remained distinct, if dependent political entities. No legislative or other jurisdictional authority was ceded to the English over matters internal to each Indian society. Each nation continued to govern itself internally. In external matters, the treaty defined the relationship as a defensive alliance with mutual responsibilities. Moreover, although the governor of Virginia was recognized as an arbitrator in the event of conflict among Indian allies, other inter-Indian relations were unaffected by the treaty. "Treaty of Peace and Alliance between Great Britain and the American Indian Tribes neighboring the Colony of Virginia, 29 May 1677," in *Consolidated Treaty Series*, ed. Parry, vol. 14, 255, 257–63; see also Wilcomb E. Washburn, *The Governor and the Rebel: A History of Bacon's Rebellion in Virginia* (Chapel Hill: University of North Carolina Press, 1957), 19–48, 135–36. Verzijl describes contemporaneous rituals of vassalage in European diplomacy; see Verzijl, *International Law*, vol. 2, 359–61.

107. Trelease, *Indian Affairs*, 242–44.

108. "Secret Treaty between Great Britain and France, concluded at Dover, May 22/June 1, 1670," in *European Treaties*, ed. Davenport, vol. 2, 177–82.

109. "Treaty of Peace between Great Britain and the United Netherlands concluded at Westminster, February 9/19, 1673/4," in ibid., 229–40.

110. In 1675, simultaneous Indian wars against the New England, Maryland, and Virginia colonies shocked the English. Jennings, *Invasion of America*, 300; see also Washburn, *Governor and the Rebel*, 40; and Jennings, *Ambiguous Iroquois Empire*, 145–47.

111. O'Callaghan and Fernow, eds., *Documents Relative to Colonial History*, vol. 3, 254; Trelease, *Indian Affairs*, 249.

112. Leder, ed., *Livingston Indian Records*, 155; Jennings, *Ambiguous Iroquois Empire*, 148–49; Jennings, *Invasion of America*, 313–23; *Documents Relative to Colonial History*, eds. O'Callaghan and Fernow, vol. 3, 254–55; Trelease, *Indian Affairs*, 233–37.

113. Jennings, *Ambiguous Iroquois Empire*, 148–49, 162–64, 180–83; Leder, ed., *Livingston Indian Records*, 42–61; "Treaty of Peace between Maryland and the Five Iroquois Nations," in *Documents Relative to Colonial History*, eds. O'Callaghan and Fernow, vol. 3, 321–28; see also Cadwallader Colden, *The History of the Five Indian Nations Depending on the Province of New York in America* (1727; reprint, Ithaca, N.Y.: Great Seal Books, 1958), 21–35.

114. Trelease, *Indian Affairs*, 230–31, 236; Jennings, *Invasion of America*, 300–02, 307–08. Andros's empty claim of control over the Haudenosaunee prefigured later British efforts to assert Confederacy subjection in order to advance imperial interests in European diplomacy. At one stage, Andros unsuccessfully offered the French his services to mediate a dispute with the Mohawk Nation, proposing to gain "due satisfaction" from the Mohawks if France would agree not to molest them "without Cause." O'Callaghan and Fernow, eds., *Documents Relative to Colonial History*, vol. 13, 483–84; Trelease, *Indian Affairs*, 249.

115. Jennings, *Ambiguous Iroquois Empire*, 162–64, 170–71.

116. Remarking on the importance of maintaining the Haudenosaunee alliance in order to protect British interests from French aggression, Colden noted, "For this reason the Governors of New-York have always, with the greatest Caution, avoided a Breach with these Nations, on account of the little Differences they had with the Neighboring Colonies." Colden, *History of the Five Indian Nations*, 32.

117. Eccles, *Frontenac*, 3.

118. "The King's Instructions to Count de Frontenac," in *Documents Relative to Colonial History*, eds. O'Callaghan and Fernow, vol. 9, 85, 86.

119. Trelease, *Indian Affairs*, 247.

120. O'Callaghan and Fernow, eds., *Documents Relative to Colonial History*, vol. 9, 90–92, 95, 96.

121. "Count de Frontenac to M. Colbert, November 1674," ibid., 117.

122. Ibid., 96–97; Trelease, *Indian Affairs*, 246; Anthony F. C. Wallace, "Origins of Iroquois Neutrality: The Grand Settlement of 1701," *Pennsylvania History* 24 (1957): 223, 225–26.

123. O'Callaghan and Fernow, eds., *Documents Relative to Colonial History*, vol. 9, 103–12. A documentary history of the fort is contained in *Royal Fort Frontenac*, eds. R. Preston and L. Lemontagne (Toronto: Champlain Society, 1958).

124. Eccles, *Frontenac*, 79. In broad outline, Frontenac's diplomatic efforts produced a measure of success. In addition to the establishment of Fort Frontenac (Cadaraqui), French Jesuits actively proselytized and collected intelligence in Confederacy communities during the decade. In 1676, the priests successfully enticed a large contingent of Mohawk people to resettle near Montreal.

125. In 1678, Louis XIV expressly invested La Salle with a mission to explore, construct forts, and conduct trade in regions beyond French commercial reach. La Salle's voyages together with his diplomatic and trade activities in the Great Lakes and Mississippi Valley brought France on collision course with the Haudenosaunee. See O'Callaghan and Fernow, eds., *Documents Relative to Colonial History*, vol. 9, 115, 126, 127.

126. Ibid., 162–63; Hunt, *Wars of the Iroquois*, 149–52. Eccles has characterized the Haudenosaunee and France as "rival imperial powers" as the Confederacy moved into the Ohio Valley and beyond in the 1670s. William J. Eccles, "The Fur Trade and Eighteenth Century Imperialism," in *Essays on New France*, W. J. Eccles (Toronto: Oxford University Press, 1987), 80.

127. "Conference between Count de Frontenac and the Ottawas, August 1682," in *Documents Relative to Colonial History*, eds. O'Callaghan and Fernow, vol. 9, 176–83.

128. "Conference between Count de Frontenac and a Deputy from the Five Nations, September 1682," ibid., 183–89.

129. "Extract of the Instructions to M. de la Barre, May 1682," ibid., 167–68. La Barre was also instructed to resolve British encroachments into the French colony of Acadia by "defining" the boundary for the governor of New England.

130. Ibid., 194–95, 201–02.

131. Summarized records indicate that such a message was communicated by the French ambassador in London and an answer received from the British secretary of state. Ibid., 198. Trelease identified a draft reply claiming British jurisdiction over the Haudenosaunee and requesting that La Barre be instructed to leave them in peace. There is no indication, however, whether this draft was ever transmitted to the French ambassador. Trelease, *Indian Affairs*, 261.

132. "Louis XIV to M. de la Barre, August 1683," in *Documents Relative to Colonial History*, eds. O'Callaghan and Fernow, vol. 9, 200–01. La Barre had also initiated correspondence with New York on general relations. Ibid., 199–200.

133. Ibid., 201–03, 208. La Barre reported that he gave considerable presents to the Haudenosaunee. Ibid., 203–04.

134. Ibid., 226.

135. Although he regarded the Seneca attack as a "declaration of war," Louis XIV was concerned about the strain that a prolonged war would produce:

> In regard to this war, you must observe that, even should you prosecute it with advantage, if you do not find means to do so promptly, it will no less cause the ruin of the colony, the people of which cannot subsist in the continual alarm they will be [sic] of an attack from the savages, and in the impossibility of attending to their trade and agriculture. Therefore, whatever advantage you may be enabled to reap for the glory of my arms and the total destruction of the Indians by the continuance of this war, you ought to prefer a peace which, restoring quiet to my subjects, will place you in a position to increase the Colony. . . .

"Louis XIV to M. de la Barre, July 1684," ibid., 232–33.

136. "Louis XIV to M. de la Barre, July 1684," ibid., 233; "M. de Seignelay to M. Barillon [Ambassador to London], July 1684," ibid., 234.

137. Through Jesuit intelligence reports, La Barre was aware of the killing of English settlers in Maryland and Virginia by Confederacy warriors. He ended the appeal to Dongan with a request for solidarity: "[W]hen they see the Christians united on this subject they will shew them more respect than they have done hitherto." O'Callaghan and Fernow, eds., *Documents Relative to Colonial History*, vol. 3, 447–48.

138. Dongan justified his "protection" on the basis of "His Royal Highness' [Duke of York] patent from His Majestie the King of England and their submitting themselves to this Government as is manifest by our Records." Ibid., 448–49.

139. Ibid., 449. La Barre responded with astonishment:

> I sent . . . to advise you of the vengeance which I was about to wreak for the insult inflicted on the Christian name by the Senecas and Cayugas, and you answer me about pretensions to the possession of lands of which neither you nor I are judges, but our two kings who have sent us, and of which there is no question at present, having no thought of conquering countries but of making the Christian and the French people to be respected.

Ibid., 450.

140. Ibid.

141. In 1683, Dongan asserted his scenario to a deputation of Mohawks, including a claim that all of the region to the south of Lake Ontario and the St. Lawrence River belonged to the New York colony. He also cautioned them to have no diplomatic or commercial contact with the French without his consent. The Mohawks are recorded as paying lip service to the governor's legal theories while, as always, continuing to go their own way. Trelease, *Indian Affairs*, 261–62; O'Callaghan and Fernow, eds., *Documents Relative to Colonial History*, vol. 14, 771–74.

142. Colden, *History of the Five Indian Nations*, 40–42.

143. In an interesting twist, the Seneca speaker noted that the governor of New France also promised to "protect" them. Ibid., 47–49; O'Callaghan and Fernow, eds., *Documents Relative to Colonial History*, vol. 3, 450–51.

144. "M. de la Barre's proceedings with the Five Nations," in *Documents Relative to Colonial History*, eds. O'Callaghan and Fernow, vol. 9, 241; see also ibid., 252–56.

145. Lahontan, *New Voyages*, vol. 1, 66–73.

146. Colden, *History of the Five Indian Nations*, 50.

147. Ibid., 40.

148. Ibid., 50–51. Jean de Lamberville, a Jesuit priest residing at Onondaga, reported the following to La Barre:

> I believe I advised you that Colonel Dongan had the Duke of York's placards of protection (de sauvegardes) affixed to the three Upper Iroquois villages, and that he styled himself Lord of the Iroquois. Here, a drunken man tore these proclamations down and nothing remains but the post to which the Duke of York's escutcheon was attached.

O'Callaghan and Fernow, eds., *Documents Relative to Colonial History*, vol. 9, 257.

149. He ended with an extraordinary flight of fancy fully a match for any of Dongan's: "I wish my words may produce the desired effect," he exhorted, "for if they do not, I am oblig'd to joyn the Governor of New-York, who has orders from the King his Master, to assist me to burn the five Villages, and cut you off." Lahontan, *New Voyages*, vol. 1, 77–79.

150. Bracketed words replace "Onnontio" and "Corlaer" in the original, Haudenosaunee titles for the governors of New France and New York, respectively. Ibid., 81–82.

151. Ibid., 82–83.

152. Ibid., 84.

153. O'Callaghan and Fernow, eds., *Documents Relative to Colonial History*, vol. 9, 244, 247.

154. See text accompanying notes 82, 83.

155. "Instructions to M. de Denonville," in *Documents Relative to Colonial History*, eds. O'Callaghan and Fernow, vol. 9, 271–72.

156. Ibid., 269.

157. Davenport, ed., *European Treaties*, vol. 2, 309–13.

158. "Treaty of Neutrality in America between Great Britain and France, concluded at Whitehall, November 6/16, 1686," ibid., 319–23.

159. Instructions were immediately sent to the governors of New York and New France to publish and observe the terms of the treaty. "Privy Council to Governor Dongan," in *Documents Relative to Colonial History*, eds. O'Callaghan and Fernow, vol.3, 388; see also "Louis XIV to M. de Denonville," ibid., vol. 9, 330.

160. Ibid., 296–303.

161. Ibid., 303–05.

162. "Louis XIV to Messrs. de Denonville and de Champigny," ibid., 322.

163. He declared his possession of the villages "together with all the lands in their vicinity as many as they may be, and how far soever they may extend, conquered in His Majesty's name, and to that end has set up in all the said Villages and Fort His said Majesty's Arms, and has caused to be proclaimed in loud voice: *Vive le Roi.* . . . " "Minute of the taking possession of the County of the Iroquois called Senecas," ibid., 334, 335.

164. "Memoir of the Voyage and Expedition of the Marquis de Denonville, pursuant to the King's order, against the Senecas, enemies of the colony," ibid., 357–69.

165. Leder, ed., *Livingston Indian Records*, 131–32.

166. Ibid., 133–35.

167. "Governor Dongan's Propositions to the Five Nations," in Documents Relative to Colonial History, eds. O'Callaghan and Fernow, vol. 3, 438–39.

168. "Answer of the Five Nations to Governor Dongan," ibid., 441–44.

169. The governor's assessment in the immediate aftermath of the incursion into Seneca country is quite revealing:

> This war, My Lord, was an absolute necessity, for without it all was lost. On the other hand, however, the condition of the country [Canada]—open on all sides, without a single place inclosed by walls—does not require war. In truth, had we to do with people who were aware of their advantages over us, what injury could they not inflict on us. Doubtless, it is God alone who blinds them.

O'Callaghan and Fernow, eds., Documents Relative to Colonial History, vol. 9, 341. See also W. J. Eccles, France in America (New York: Harper & Row, 1972), 90.

170. Frank H. Severance, An Old Frontier of France: The Niagara Region and Adjacent Lakes under French Control, vol. 1 (New York: Dodd, Mead and Company, 1917), 118–19; O'Callaghan and Fernow, eds., Documents Relative to Colonial History, vol. 9, 391; Trelease, Indian Affairs, 283.

171. "Memorials, etc. between the French Ambassador and English Commissioners about New York Affairs," in Documents Relative to Colonial History, eds. O'Callaghan and Fernow, vol. 3, 506–07, 508–09.

Perceiving the utility of adopting the claim for purposes of negotiation, James II quickly issued a warrant to Governor Dongan which described the Haudenosaunee as Indians "who from all times have submitted themselves to our Government and by their acknowledgements of our Sovereignty are become our Subjects. . . . " Dongan was instructed to inform officials of New France "that upon mature consideration we have thought fitt to own the five Nations or Cantons of Indians." Should the Confederacy be attacked by the French, the governor was authorized to defend them with arms. "Warrant authorizing Governor Dongan to protect the Five Nations, November 1687," ibid., 503–04. These instructions and the negotiations toward which they were aimed represented the first instance in which British claims to suzerainty over the Confederacy were expressly manifested as official government policy. Dongan's manipulations involving the Confederacy during 1684 and 1685 were conducted as the representative of the Duke of York, not the Crown. When James II (Duke of York) assumed the throne and united New York with the realm as a royal colony, his governor's rhetoric of Haudenosaunee subjection had not been adopted as a matter of state. Indeed, in negotiating the 1686 treaty of neutrality in North America with France, James had left his would-be "subjects" to the vagaries of war.

172. Ibid., 507. Neither set of commissioners offered arguments based on discovery or the terms of royal charters. The reference to Champlain by the French commissioners involved a claim that the Confederacy had acknowledged and submitted to French authority as early as 1610.

173. "Agreement between France and Great Britain, respecting peace in America, concluded at Whitehall, December 1/11, 1687," in European Treaties, ed. Davenport, vol. 2, 324–29. In the interim, both parties were required to maintain strict peace while assembling their arguments and proofs. Thus Denonville, in the midst of defending New France against Haudenosaunee attacks, was instructed to compile a case for French rights in Iroquoia, Acadia, and Hudson Bay. "Additional Instruction to M. de Denonville," in Documents Relative to Colonial History, eds. O'Callaghan and Fernow, vol. 9, 371–72.

174. "Declaration of Neutrality by three of the Iroquois nations," ibid., 384–85; see also ibid., 390–91; and Trelease, *Indian Affairs*, 290.

175. O'Callaghan and Fernow, eds., *Documents Relative to Colonial History*, vol. 9, 393–94. The suggestion was rejected by the ministry, which continued to follow a policy intended to prevent the Haudenosaunee from "uniting with the English." Ibid., 394.

176. Davenport, ed., *European Treaties*, vol. 2, 350–52; "Order in Council on the State of the Plantations, etc.," in *Documents Relative to Colonial History*, eds. O'Callaghan and Fernow, vol. 3, 573–74.

177. During a treaty conference between commissioners representing Massachusetts and Connecticut and the Haudenosaunee to renew the Covenant Chain, the Confederacy made its independent war policy clear:

> But Ye French and there associates wee are Resolved to warr upon, for . . . when wee took up ye axe against ye French, it was not by Councill or advise of any Body, but our oune Inclination to be Revenged neither did any Soule know of our Intentions for when wee Came to alby [Albany] to acquaint ye Magistrates with our Design, our men had been out 14 days against ye French.

Leder, ed., *Livingston Indian Records*, 157.

178. Colden, *History of the Five Indian Nations*, 93–101; O'Callaghan, ed., *Documentary History of the State of New York*, vol. 2, 76–80; O'Callaghan and Fernow, eds., *Documents Relative to Colonial History*, vol. 9, 464–66.

179. A few months earlier, a party of Mohawks had participated in preliminary discussions with the French. "Propositions of Mohawks and other Indians to Governor Sloughter and his Answer," ibid., vol. 3, 777–80; ibid., vol. 9, 515–17.

180. "Treaty Conference (Haudenosaunee-Great Britain), June, 1691," in *Documents Relative to Colonial History*, eds. O'Callaghan and Fernow, vol. 3, 773–80 (especially page 776).

181. "Propositions of the Commander-in-Chief to the Five Nations," ibid., 840–44; see also O'Callaghan and Fernow, eds., *Documents Relative to Colonial History*, vol. 4, 38–46, 51, 79–83, 85–92, 120–24, 126–27. British efforts to persuade the Haudenosaunee to forebear negotiating a separate peace and the consequent agreement to coordinate diplomacy was a typical feature of unstable wartime alliances in that era. During the War of Spanish Succession in the following decade, Britain attempted to negotiate a similar commitment from its Dutch ally in the face of French diplomatic attempts to break that alliance. See Davenport, ed., *European Treaties*, vol. 3, 135–36.

182. Trelease, *Indian Affairs*, 313–15, 317, 321; "Propositions of the Five Nations at Albany," in *Documents Relative to Colonial History*, eds. O'Callaghan and Fernow, vol. 4, 85–92; "Journal of Governor Fletcher's Visit to Albany," ibid., 235–41. The peace initiative by Governor Frontenac to the Confederacy occurred during the same period as Louis XIV's similar initiatives in Europe. Davenport, ed., *European Treaties*, vol. 2, 353.

183. Charlevoix reported that the Haudenosaunee were "rather stunned than subdued" by Frontenac's invasion and by the spring of 1697 had again taken the field against New France. P. F. D de Charlevoix, *History and General Description of New France*, 6 vols. (1744; reprint, New York: P. O'Shea, 1871), 5: 48, 49–52.

184. Article VII of the treaty required both parties

> to restore . . . all countries, forts, and colonies, wheresoever situated which [they] did possess before the declaration of this present war. And to that end,

immediately after the ratification of this treaty, each of the said king's shall deliver . . . to the other, or to commissioners authorized in his name for that purpose, all acts of concession, instruments, and necessary orders . . . so that they may have their effect.

"Treaty of Peace between Great Britain and France, concluded at Ryswyk, September 10/20, 1697," in *European Treaties,* ed. Davenport, vol. 2, 260, 262–63; English translation, *Consolidated Treaty Series,* ed. Parry, vol. 21, 445, 446–47. For Britain, the most significant result in the treaty concerned European dynastic rivalries. Louis XIV recognized William III as King of England, thus ensuring a Protestant succession to the British throne. See David B. Horn, *Great Britain and Europe in the Eighteenth Century* (Oxford: Clarendon Press, 1967), 41; Mark A. Thomson, "Louis XIV and William III, 1689–97," in *William III and Louis XIV,* eds. Ragnhild Hatton and J. S. Bromley (Toronto: University of Toronto Press, 1968), 24–48.

185. Indian wars continued against both sides. It was not until 1699 that Britain, for example, was able to negotiate peace on the borders of New England with their Abenaki enemies allied with New France. See Davenport, ed., *European Treaties,* vol. 2, 352; "Earl of Bellomont to the Lords of Trade," in *Documents Relative to Colonial History,* eds. O'Callaghan and Fernow, vol. 4, 314–15. See also the Abenaki account of the 1727 Treaty of Casco Bay in which the independence of the Abenaki peoples was recognized by the British, ibid., vol. 9, 955–66, 966–67, 990–95.

186. The French government's position is expressed in the following:

His Majesty has recommended to his Commissioners who are to labor in London in the settlement of said American boundaries, to employ all their care to engage the English to cede that Sovereignty to France; or to declare those people independent both of the one and the other Crown, observing on both sides a reciprocal neutrality; or, finally, ceding, if it be absolutely necessary, the Sovereignty to the English, with the stipulation that the King of England will prevent those people making war and disturbing the French and the Indians who are subjects or allies of France.

"Sovereignty of the King of France over the Iroquois, 1698," in *Documents Relative to Colonial History,* eds. O'Callaghan and Fernow, vol. 9, 689; see also ibid., 677. For the British position, see ibid., vol. 4, 475–78.

187. Ibid., vol. 9, 678–82.

188. Ibid., 690–95.

189. Trelease, *Indian Affairs,* 333–37, 340–43; O'Callaghan and Fernow, eds., *Documents Relative to Colonial History,* vol. 4, 405–09, 487–88, 491–500, 558–65; "Proceedings of the Commissioners and the Five Nations," ibid., 567–73.

190. "Louis XIV to Count de Frontenac, March 1699," in *Documents Relative to Colonial History,* eds. O'Callaghan and Fernow, vol. 9, 697–98.

191. Trelease, *Indian Affairs,* 347; "Propositions of the Five Nations to the Commissioners of Indian Affairs, June 1700," in *Documents Relative to Colonial History,* eds. O'Callaghan and Fernow, vol. 4, 693–95.

192. "Reply of the Count de Frontenac to the Earl of Bellomont, September 1698," ibid., vol. 9, 694–95.

193. Charlevoix, *History and General Description of New France,* vol. 5, 99–103; Leder, ed., *Livingston Indian Records,* 179–80.

194. "Conference between Chevalier de Callières and the Iroquois at Montreal, July 1700," in *Documents Relative to Colonial History,* eds. O'Callaghan and Fernow, vol. 9, 708–11; "Conference between Governor de Callières and the Iroquois,

September 1700," ibid., 715–20; Charlevoix, *History and General Description of New France*, vol. 5, 109–12. Louis XIV warmly endorsed the treaty of neutrality: "It has afforded his Majesty much satisfaction to learn that Peace has been concluded with the Iroquois without any participation of, and in spite of the means employed by, the English, to prevent it." "Louis XIV to Messrs. de Callières and de Champigny," in *Documents Relative to Colonial History*, eds. O'Callaghan and Fernow, vol. 9, 721.

195. "Conference of the Earl of Bellomont with the Indians, August 1700," ibid., vol. 4, 727–43, 745–46 (quote, page 729).

196. "Earl of Bellomont to the Lords of Trade, October 17, 1700," ibid., 714.

197. "We have perused the Conference you had with the Indians at Albany and do agree with your Lordship that the less such things are published to the world, the better; and that therefore it is not fit they should be printed, but rather transmitted to us . . . in writing." "Lords of Trade to the Earl of Bellomont, February 1701," ibid., 840, 842.

198. "Ratification of the Peace between the French and the Indians, August 1701," ibid., vol. 9, 722–25, 736–37; Charlevoix, *History and General Description of New France*, vol. 5, 137, 141–42, 143–54. Trelease reports that 1,300 Indians representing thirty nations attended the treaty ratification, including the Chippewa, Cree, Miami, Ottawa, Sauk and Fox, Illinois, Algonquin, and Abenaki in addition to the Haudenosaunee. Trelease, *Indian Affairs*, 362–63; Wallace, "Origins of Iroquois Neutrality," 229–30. The Haudenosaunee decided to ratify the treaty during a Grand Council the previous June. Charlevoix, *History and General Description of New France*, vol. 5, 138–40. See also Richard Aquila, *The Iroquois Restoration: Indian Diplomacy on the Colonial Frontier, 1701–1754* (Detroit: Wayne State University Press, 1983), 62.

199. "Conference of Lieutenant-Governor Nanfan with the Indians, July 1701," in *Documents Relative to Colonial History*, eds. O'Callaghan and Fernow, vol. 4, 896–911.

200. "Messrs. de Vaudreuil and Beauharnois to M. de Pontchartrain, 1704," ibid., vol. 9, 763; "Louis XIV to M. de Vaudreuil, 1705," ibid., 765; "M. de Vaudreuil to M. de Pontchartrain, 1705," ibid., 766; Yves F. Zoltvany, *Philippe de Rigaud de Vaudreuil: Governor of New France, 1703–1725* (Toronto: McClelland and Stewart, 1974), 46.

201. See Thomson, "Louis XIV and the Origins of the War of the Spanish Succession," in *William III and Louis XIV*, eds. Hatton and Bromley, 140–161.

202. "Conference between M. de Vaudreuil and the Indians, 1703," *Documents Relative to Colonial History*, eds. O'Callaghan and Fernow, vol. 9, 746, 747–48.

203. "Abstract of certain parts of a despatch from Messrs. de Vaudreuil and Beauharnois; with Notes by the Minister, 1703," ibid., 755–56; Zoltvany, *Philippe de Rigaud de Vaudreuil*, 47–48, 49–51; Charlevoix, *History and General Description of New France*, vol. 5, 167–68. An intercolonial treaty of neutrality drafted by Governor Dudley of Massachusetts was unsuccessfully proposed in 1705. "Proposed Treaty between Canada and New England, October 1705," in *Documents Relative to Colonial History*, eds. O'Callaghan and Fernow, vol. 9, 770–72; Zoltvany, *Philippe de Rigaud de Vaudreuil*, 61–62.

204. Colden, "Continuation of Colden's History of the Five Indian Nations, for the years 1707 through 1720," *New York Historical Society Collections* 68 (1935): 359, 376.

205. Ibid., 377–80; Leder, ed., *Livingston Indian Records*, 206–14; Zoltvany, *Philippe de Rigaud de Vaudreuil*, 94–96, 101–103. Charlevoix, *History and General Description of New France*, vol. 5, 300.

206. Oppenheim, *International Law* (1905), vol. 2, 302–03, 305–06, 320; Verzijl, *International Law*, vol. 10, 40–45, 72–76, 85–88, 93–96, 98. Contemporary doctrinal writings all confirm the legitimacy of qualified neutrality. Grotius briefly touched on neutrality, but his views on the question were not influential. Grotius, *De Jure Belli Ac Pacis*, 783–87. A more significant treatment was authored by Cornelius van Bynkershoek in the early eighteenth century, Cornelius van Bynkershoek, *Quaestionum Juris Publici Libri Duo*, trans. Tenney Frank (1737; reprint, Oxford: Clarendon Press, 1930), 60–65. See also Vattel, *Law of Nations*, 268–78, and Martens, *Summary of the Law of Nations*, 312.

207. Leder, ed., *Livingston Indian Records*, 206–10, 211–12; "Conference of Governor Hunter with the Indians, August 1710," in *Documents Relative to Colonial History*, eds. O'Callaghan and Fernow, vol. 5, 217–27. In 1710, the British went so far as to bring four Haudenosaunee "kings" to meet with Queen Anne in London in order to persuade them of Britain's power. See Richmond P. Bond, *Queen Anne's American Kings* (Oxford: Clarendon Press, 1952).

208. The British practice of giving "presents" as a matter of state policy to reinforce the friendship and alliance of the Haudenosaunee began in 1691 in the context of the War of the League of Augsburg. "Instructions for Colonel Henry Sloughter, Governor of New York, 1690," in *Documents Relative to Colonial History*, eds. O'Callaghan and Fernow, vol. 3, 685, 690. In the eighteenth century, the practice assumed considerable importance in Anglo-Haudenosaunee diplomacy. By the time of the intercolonial conference at Albany in 1754, the British government relied heavily on these payments to prevent Haudenosaunee defections to the French interest. "Proceedings of the Colonial Congress held at Albany, June 1754," in *Documents Relative to Colonial History*, eds. O'Callaghan and Fernow, vol. 6, 853, 854–56. For a study of British and French diplomatic gift giving in this latter period, see Wilbur R. Jacobs, ed., *Wilderness Politics and Indian Gifts: The Northern Colonial Frontier, 1748–1763* (Lincoln: University of Nebraska Press, 1950).

209. "Board of Trade to the Queen on the Right of Sovereignty over the Five Nations, June 1709," in *Documents Relative to Colonial History*, eds. O'Callaghan and Fernow, vol. 5, 74–77; "Memoir on the French Dominion in Canada, 1504–1706," ibid., vol. 9, 781–803 (Hudson Bay, Iroquoia, Acadia).

210. Davenport, ed., *European Treaties*, vol. 3, 133–51.

211. The proposed clause read:

Les sujets de la France, habitans de la Canadie et autres, s'abstiendront a l'avenir d'empescher le nègoce réciproque, entre des sujets de la Grande Bretagne, et les natifs des pays de l'Amerique; comme aussi d'inquieter les Cinq Nations, ou cantons Indiens ou autres, qui sont sous l'obeissance, ou dans l'amitié de la Grande Bretagne.

Ibid., 158–59, note 37.

212. Paragraph thirteen of this document read:

13. Galliae subditi Canadam incolentes aliique Quinque Nationes, sive Cantones Indorum Magnae Britanniae imperio subjectas, ut et caeteros Americae indigenas eidem amicitia conjunctos, nullo in posterum impedimento aut molestia afficiant. Magnae autem Britaniae subditi lacus fluviosque Ontario, Eries, Huron, Illinis appellatos, pariter ac regiones omnes iis circumjacentes commercii causa frequentandi libertate plena gaudebunt. Pari quoque cum libertate regionum istarum indigenae colonias Britannicas ad promovendum hinc inde commercium pro lubitu adibunt absque ulla ex parte subditorum Gallicorum molestia aut impedimento.

> 13. French inhabitants of Canada and others shall not molest the Five Nations or cantons of Indians subject to Great Britain, or other American natives bound to her by friendship. British subjects shall enjoy full liberty of frequenting for the sake of trade the places and rivers called Ontario, Erie, Huron, and all the surrounding districts. The natives of these regions shall be equally free to go to the British colonies to promote trade in both directions without being hindered by the French.

Ibid., 197–98.

214. Article 15 of the final treaty text read:
213. Ibid., 199–200.

> 15. *Les habitans du Canada et autres sujets de la France ne molesteront point a l'avenir les Cinq Nations ou cantons des Indiens soumis a La Grande Bretagne, ny les autres nations de l'Amerique amies de cette couronne. Pareillement les sujets de la Grande Bretagne se comporteront pacifiquement envers les Americains sujets ou amis de la France, et les uns et les autres joüiront d'une pleine liberté de se frequenter pour le bien du commerce, et avec la mesme liberté les habitans de ces regions pourront visiter les colonies Françoises et Britanniques pour l'avantage reciproque du commerce sans aucune molestation, ny empechement de part ny d'autre. Au surplus les Commissaires regleront exactement et distinctement quels seront ceux qui seront ou devront estre censez sujets et amis de la France, ou de la Grande Bretagne.*

"Treaty of Peace between Great Britain and France, concluded at Utrecht, March 31/April 11, 1713," ibid., 193, 213.

215. Ibid., 213, note 74; Severance, *An Old Frontier of France*, vol. 1, 256; "Governor Burnet to the Marquis de Beauharnois," in *Documents Relative to Colonial History*, eds. O'Callaghan and Fernow, vol. 5, 829, 831. Charles H. McIlwain described Article 15 of the treaty as vague and ambiguous leading "to much controversy." McIlwaine, "Introduction," in Peter Wraxall, *An Abridgment of the Indian Affairs Contained in Four Folio Volumes, Transacted in the Colony of New York from the Year 1678 to the Year 1751*, ed. Charles H. McIlwain (Cambridge: Harvard University Press, 1915), lxiv.

216. See note 186.

217. Referring to Article 15 of the treaty, Charlevoix noted that "[t]his last article did not deprive us of anything real, or give anything more to the English, as the Cantons renewed their protestations that they had already more than once made against the reciprocal pretentions of their neighbors, and they have succeeded quite well in maintaining possession of their liberty and independence." Charlevoix, *History and General Description of New France*, vol. 5, 266. See also Cadwallader Colden, *The Colden Letter Books, New York Historical Society Collections . . . 1876–1877*, vol. 9 (New York: New York Historical Society, 1877–1878), 272–73.

218. Under classical principles of international law, treaties bind the contracting parties only (*pacta tertiis nec nocent nec prosunt*). As a result, third states which are non-parties acquire neither rights nor duties under the instrument without their express consent. See Oppenheim (Lauterpacht), *International Law*, vol. 1, 925–26; Brownlie, *Principles of Public International Law*, 619–22. The principle has been incorporated into the Vienna Convention on the Law of Treaties (Article 34), U.N. Doc. A/CONF. 39/27 (1969); *American Journal of International Law* 63 (1969): 875, 886; *International Legal Materials* 8 (1969): 679, 693.

219. During a treaty conference in 1715 to renew the relationship, Governor Hunter of New York recapitulated the historic meaning of the Covenant Chain alliance in the following terms:

> And to prevent all mistakes on this head, I must remind you what has ever been meant and understood by you as well as us, by the Covenant Chaine, that is on ye one hand the subjects of his Majestie on this Continent should not only refrain from all Acts of hostility or any thing tending that way toward you, but readly assist you when you were attacked by others or enable you by such methods as were in their power to repell force by force or defend your selves, and on the other hand you were on you part to live in the strictest friendship wth all his Majesties subjects, and in case they should be attacked by any enemy whatsoever, to afford them the readyest and most effectual assistance in your power.

"Conference between Governor Hunter and the Indians, June 1717," in *Documents Relative to Colonial History*, eds. O'Callaghan and Fernow, vol. 5, 484–85.

220. Not only diplomacy, but "presents" as well. In 1712, the British were hard-pressed to retain Haudenosaunee friendship. At a conference at Onondaga, Col. Schuyler, the English envoy, assured the Confederacy that the Crown had no claim to their territories "of wch her Majesty acknowledges them to be the sole and Rightful Proprieters." In reply, the Haudenosaunee reminded Schuyler "[t]hat it is well known the original Foundation of their Alliance with the Christians were the Advantages they received by Trading with them." They expressed approval that the English wished to strengthen the Covenant Chain: "We hope as we have now told you the true and only Method to preserve this Chain inviolable between us namely to let us have goods Cheaper, that this Method will take Place by wch the Chain will be kept firm and we shall live in Peace forever." Wraxall, *Abridgment of the Indian Affairs*, 94–95.

221. Leder, ed., *Livingston Indian Records*, 222–24; "Conference between Governor Hunter and the Indians, June 1717" in *Documents Relative to Colonial History*, eds. O'Callaghan and Fernow, vol. 5, 484, 489–93.

222. Leder, ed., *Livingston Indian Records*, 224, 225. The British definition is quoted in "Conference between Governor Hunter and the Indians, June 1717," in *Documents Relative to Colonial History*, eds. O'Callaghan and Fernow, vol. 5, 484–85. The Confederacy took a similar position during a conflict between Great Britain and Spain in 1740. Haudenosaunee ambassadors declined a request to join New York forces in a British attack on the Spanish in the West Indies. "Extract of the Conference between Lt. Gov. Clarke and the Five Nations, August 1740," ibid., vol. 9, 1062–063; ibid., vol. 6, 170.

223. See, for example, "Conference between Governor Hunter and the Indians, September 1714," ibid., vol. 5, 384; "Conference between Governor Cosby and the Indians, September 1733," ibid., 962, 964.

224. Ibid., 783–804, 815, 818, 820, 821–22, 825–32; ibid., vol. 9, 949–65, 968–88; Savelle, *Origins of American Diplomacy*, 250–56; Severance, *An Old Frontier of France*, vol. 1, 225–63; Colden, *Colden Letter Books*, vol. 9, 273. Haudenosaunee independence is illustrated by an incident in 1725 during maneuverings concerning Niagara and Oswego. The French emissary Longeuil was escorted from Canada to a Confederacy Council meeting at Onondaga by several Haudenosaunee chiefs. Passing through the region of Oswego, Longeuil was stopped by a large company of Englishmen under instructions to refuse transit to any Frenchman not possessing a passport. In response, the Haudenosaunee delegation reminded the British that

they had been permitted to enter the country for purposes of trade only. Other activities would not be tolerated. Moreover, they reaffirmed neutrality in the event of a European war. Once at Onondaga, Longeuil obtained the consent of the Haudenosaunee to replace the bark trading structure at Niagara with an unfortified "stone house," a significant achievement in French diplomacy. See O'Callaghan and Fernow, eds., *Documents Relative to Colonial History*, vol. 9, 949–53; Wraxall, *Abridgment of the Indian Affairs*, 158–59; O'Callaghan and Fernow, eds., *Documents Relative to Colonial History*, vol. 5, 802–03; Severance, *An Old Frontier of France*, vol. 1, 227–29.

225. Trelease criticized the view that Haudenosaunee opposition to the construction of forts was the result of their position as middlemen in the fur trade: "To explain it we need only point to the effect which such establishments would have upon Iroquois independence and territorial integrity. They were not prepared to accept domination by English or other European garrisons, let alone to see a bridgehead established for white settlers in their midst." Trelease, "The Iroquois and the Western Fur Trade: A Problem in Interpretation," *Mississippi Valley Historical Review* 49 (1962): 32, 49.

226. "Conference between Governor Clinton and the Indians, June 1744," in *Documents Relative to Colonial History*, eds. O'Callaghan and Fernow, vol. 6, 262–66.

227. "Conference between Commissioners of the Colonies and the Indians, October 1745," ibid., 289, 297–98, 300. Curiously, Governor Clinton described the French allied "eastern Indians" then at war with the New England colonies as having a few months before "acknowledged their *subjection* to the Crown of Great Britain." (Emphasis added.) Ibid., 298.

228. "Conference between M. de Beauharnois and some of the Five Nations, July 1745," ibid., vol. 10, 22, 22–25.

229. Despite Confederacy neutrality, some Mohawks fought with the British against New France in later stages of the war. French acceptance of the relative character of neutrality in this period is underscored by the fact that New France did not regard the recruitment of Mohawk warriors by the British as a violation of Haudenosaunee international obligations. The French did, however, demand that the Confederacy take corporate responsibility for the prisoner exchange.

Haudenosaunee warriors were also recruited by the French during times of war. See, for example, the complaints of the governors of Pennsylvania and New Jersey to the Seneca and Cayuga nations during negotiations leading to the 1758 Treaty of Easton, "Minutes of Conferences held at Easton, in October 1759," in *Indian Treaties Printed by Benjamin Franklin, 1736–1762*, ed. Julian Boyd (Philadelphia: Historical Society of Pennsylvania, 1938), 213, 220–25.

230. "Governor Shirley to the Marquis de la Galissonière, July 1748," in *Documents Relative to Colonial History*, eds. O'Callaghan and Fernow, vol. 6, 452, 453.

231. "Marquis de la Galissonière to Governor Clinton, December 1748," ibid., 496, 496–97; see also ibid., 488–89.

232. Governor Galissonière read the following British communication to the Confederacy envoys:

Children, I have invited you to-day to inquire if you are subjects of the English, as I have heard they pretend, and as I have been advised by Messrs. Clinton and Shirley, Governors of New-York and of Boston, of whom these are the letters, wherein they write me that you are vassals of the Crown of England, and that you are bound to go to war for the English, whenever they order you so to do.

"Conference between M. de la Galissonière and the Iroquois, November 1748," in *Documents Relative to Colonial History*, eds. O'Callaghan and Fernow, vol. 10, 186, 187.

233. Ibid.

234. William J. Eccles has analogized European sovereign pretentions in this period to the claim of the British monarch to the French throne, a claim not formally relinquished until 1802. William J. Eccles, "A Belated Review of Harold Adams Innis' *The Fur Trade in Canada*," in Eccles, *Essays on New France*, 61, 64.

235. "Conference between Governor Clinton and the Indians, June 1753," in *Documents Relative to Colonial History*, eds. O'Callaghan and Fernow, vol. 6, 781, 788; Francis Jennings, "Iroquois Alliances in American History," in *History and Culture of Iroquois Diplomacy*, eds. Jennings et al., 50–51; see generally Georgiana C. Nammack, *Fraud, Politics, and the Dispossession of the Indians* (Norman: University of Oklahoma Press, 1969).

236. "Lords of Trade to the Governors in America, September 1753," in *Documents Relative to Colonial History*, eds. O'Callaghan and Fernow, vol. 6, 802.

237. "Lords of Trade to Sir Danvers Osborne, September 1753," ibid., 800–01. Although the ensuing intercolonial treaty conference is best known for Benjamin Franklin's "Albany Plan of Union," the primary purpose of the gathering was to reaffirm and strengthen peace and friendship with the Haudenosaunee. "Proceedings of the Colonial Congress held at Albany, June–July 1754," ibid., 853–92.

238. "Treaty of peace between Great Britain, France, and Spain, concluded at Paris, February 10, 1763," in *European Treaties*, ed. Davenport, vol. 4, 92–98. Diplomatic negotiations leading to the treaty are described in E. F. Choiseul-Stainville, *Historical Memorial of the Negotiation of France and England* (1761; reprint, New York: Research Imprints, 1970); and Max Savelle, *The Diplomatic History of the Canadian Boundary, 1749–1763* (New Haven, Conn.: Yale University Press, 1940), 103–46.

239. For example, "Proceedings at a Meeting and Treaty held with the Six Nations at Johnson Hall, April 21, 1762," Sir William Johnson, *The Papers of Sir William Johnson*, ed. J. Sullivan, 14 vols. (Albany: The University of the State of New York, 1921–1965), 690–717.

240. "Sir William Johnson to the Lords of Trade, August 1764," in *Documents Relative to Colonial History*, eds. O'Callaghan and Fernow, vol. 7, 648–650; "Proceedings of the Detroit Indian Congress (1761)," in *Papers of Sir William Johnson*, ed. J. Sullivan, vol. 3, 474–503; "Proceedings with the Indians at Niagara, July–August 1764," in ibid., vol. 4, 466–81; ibid., vol. 11, 262–327; "Journal of Colonel Croghan's Transactions with the Western Indians, November 1765," in *Documents Relative to Colonial History*, eds. O'Callaghan and Fernow, vol. 7, 779–88; "Proceedings of Sir William Johnson with Pondiac [Pontiac] and other Indians, July 1766," ibid., 854–67.

241. Regarding the negotiation of boundaries with the Six Nations, Sir William Johnson stated the following:

> The ascertaining and defining the precise and exact Boundaries of Indian Lands, is a very necessary, but delicate point; I shall do everything in my power towards effecting it when ordered; but I must beg leave to observe, that the Six Nations, Western Indians, etc., having never been conquered, either by the English or French, nor subject to the Laws, consider themselves as a free people. I am therefore induced to think it will require a good deal of caution to point out any boundary, that shall appear to circumscribe their limits too far.

"Sir William Johnson to the Lords of Trade," ibid., 661, 665. The most important of the boundary treaties was negotiated at Fort Stanwix with the Haudenosaunee and nations within its hegemonic influence. "Proceedings of Sir William Johnson with the Indians at Fort Stanwix to Settle a Boundary Line, October–November 1768," ibid., vol. 8, 111–37 (including map); *Papers of Sir William Johnson*, ed. J. Sullivan, vol. 12, 617–29. Earlier boundary treaties negotiated between 1763 and 1766 with the Chickasaw, Choctaw, Creek, Cherokee, and Catawba nations are summarized in *Documents Relative to Colonial History*, eds. O'Callaghan and Fernow, vol. 8, 31, 32, 33–34. See also "Lords of Trade to the King, April 1769," ibid., 158–63.

242. "Sir William Johnson to the Lords of Trade, November 1763," ibid., vol. 7, 572, 575; see also ibid., 573, and Colden, *Colden Letter Books*, vol. 9, 272–74.

243. "Proceedings of the Commissioners of the Twelve United Colonies with the Six Nations, August 1775," in *Documents Relative to Colonial History*, eds. O'Callaghan and Fernow, vol. 8, 605–31.

244. Britain continued to engage in treaty-making with indigenous nations; for treaties in Canada see *Indian Treaties and Surrenders, from 1680 to 1890*, 3 vols. (1891; reprint, Toronto: Coles Publishing Co., 1971); New Zealand, see "Treaty of Waitangi (1840)," in *Consolidated Treaty Series*, ed. Parry, vol. 89, 473; Hawaii, see Ralph S. Kuykendall and A. Grove Day, *Hawaii: A History, from Polynesian Kingdom to American Commonwealth* (New York: Prentice-Hall, 1948), 58–59; Tonga, see Crawford, *Creation of States in International Law*, 177, note 25; and Africa, see E. Hertslet, ed., *The Map of Africa by Treaty*, 3 vols. (London: Harrisons and Sons, 1909), vol. 1, and Shaw, *Title to Territory*.

245. "Treaty with the Six Nations (1784)," in *Indian Affairs, Laws and Treaties*, ed. C. Kappler, 4 vols. (Washington, D.C.: U.S. Government Printing Office, 1904), 2: 5, 7 Stat. 15; "Treaty with the Wyandot, etc. (1785)," ibid., 6, 7 Stat. 16; "Treaty with the Cherokee (1785)," ibid., 8, 7 Stat. 18; "Treaty with the Choctaw (1786)," ibid., 11, 7 Stat. 21; "Treaty with the Chickasaw (1786)," ibid., 14, 7 Stat. 24; "Treaty with the Shawnee (1786)," ibid., 16, 7 Stat. 26; "Treaty with the Wyandot, etc. (1789)," ibid., 18, 7 Stat. 28. The treaties with the Wyandots and Shawnees were not successful in ending conflict with those nations.

246. For example, "Treaty of Peace and Alliance between Spain and the Choctaw and Chickasaw, signed at Bouctouca, May 1793," in *Consolidated Treaty Series*, ed. Parry, vol. 52, 29; "Treaty of Peace and Alliance between Spain and the Cherokee, signed at Los Nogales, Oct. 1793," ibid., 175. Although Spain was notorious for its conquests and oppressions of indigenous nations, it did engage in diplomacy and treaty-making in North America. For British diplomacy in northern areas, see J. Leitch Wright, Jr., *Britain and the American Frontier, 1783–1815* (Athens: University of Georgia Press, 1975).

247. Ralston R. Hayden, *The Senate and Treaties, 1789–1817: The Development of the Treaty-Making Functions of the United States Senate during Their Formative Period* (New York: Macmillan, 1920), 11–39.

248. Worcester v. Georgia, 31 U.S. (6 Pet.), 515, 559–560 (1832).

5: United States–Indian Relations: The Constitutional Basis

1. See, for example, Nell J. Newton, "Federal Power over Indians: Its Sources, Scope, and Limitations," *University of Pennsylvania Law Review* 132 (January

1984): 195–288; Milner S. Ball, "Constitution, Court, Indian Tribes," *1987 American Bar Foundation Research Journal* (Winter 1987): 1–140.

2. "Lords of Trade to Sir Danvers Osborne, September 18, 1753," in *Documents Relative to the Colonial History of the State of New York*, eds. E. B. O'Callaghan and B. Fernow, vol. 6 (Albany: Weed, Parsons & Co., 1853–1887), 800–01.

3. "Lords of Trade to the King," ibid., vol. 7, 477–79.

4. Adam Short and Arthur G. Doughty, eds., *Documents Relating to the Constitutional History of Canada, 1759–1791* (Ottawa: J. de L. Tache, 1918), 119–23.

5. O'Callaghan and Fernow, eds., *Documents Relative to Colonial History*, vol. 6, 889–91.

6. "Proceedings of Sir William Johnson with the Indians at Fort Stanwix to Settle a Boundary Line," in *Documents Relative to Colonial History*, eds. O'Callaghan and Fernow, vol. 8, 111–37.

7. See Francis Jennings, *The Ambiguous Iroquois Empire: The Covenant Chain Confederation of Indian Tribes with English Colonies from Its Beginnings to the Lancaster Treaty of 1744* (New York: W. W. Norton & Company, 1984), 10–11.

8. "Sir William Johnson to Governor Clinton, November 22, 1749," in *Documents Relative to Colonial History*, eds. O'Callaghan and Fernow, vol. 6, 540–42.

9. Letter of 29 December 1748, in *Documents Relative to Colonial History*, eds. O'Callaghan and Fernow, vol. 6, 496–500.

10. Jennings, *Ambiguous Iroquois Empire*, 373.

11. Worthington C. Ford et al., eds., *Journals of the Continental Congress 1774–1789*, vol. 2 (Washington, D.C.: U.S. Government Printing Office, 1904–1937), 1004–005.

12. Ibid., vol. 2, 174.

13. Ibid., 175.

14. Ibid., 183.

15. Ibid., 182.

16. Resolution of 22 November 1775, in ibid., vol. 2, 365.

17. Andrew Allen to Philip Schuyler, 17 March 1776, in *Letters of Members of the Continental Congress*, ed. Edward C. Burnett, vol. 1 (Washington D.C.: Carnegie Institution, 1921–1936), 397–98.

18. Resolution of 15 April 1776, in *Journals of the Continental Congress*, eds. Ford et al., vol. 4, 308–09.

19. 7 Stat. 3.

20. 7 Stat. 3, 4.

21. Ibid.

22. Worcester v. Georgia, 31 U.S. (6 Pet.) 515, 549 (1832).

23. *Journals of the Continental Congress*, eds. Ford et al., vol. 5, 668.

24. Ibid., vol. 5, 753.

25. Resolution of 10 April 1776, in ibid., vol. 4, 266.

26. Ibid., vol. 2, 549.

27. Ibid.

28. Proposal reported by committee on 20 August 1776, in ibid., vol. 5, 549–53.

29. Ibid., vol. 9, 845.

30. Treaty of Galphinton, 12 November 1785, reprinted in *American State Papers*, vol. 1 (Washington, D.C.: U.S. Government Printing Office, 1832), 17.

31. *Journals of the Continental Congress*, eds. Ford et al., vol. 6, 1078.

32. Ibid., vol. 6, 1077.

33. Letter to James Monroe, 27 November 1784, in *The Papers of James Madison*, eds. Robert A. Rutland et al., vol. 8 (Chicago: University of Chicago Press, 1973), 156.

34. *Journals of the Continental Congress,* eds. Ford et al., vol. 9, 844.

35. *The Papers of James Madison,* eds. Rutland et al., vol. 8, 156.

36. Letter of 29 April 1783, in *Pennsylvania Archives,* ed. Samuel Hazard, 1st series, vol. 10 (Philadelphia: Joseph Severns & Co., 1854), 45.

37. "Report of Ephraim Douglas to Secretary of War, August 18, 1783," in *Pennsylvania Archives,* ed. Hazard, vol. 10, 83, 88.

38. Letter of Philip Schuyler to the president of Congress, *Papers of the Continental Congress,* M247, Microfilm Roll 173, 606.

39. Letter to James Duane, 7 September 1783, in *The Writings of George Washington,* ed. John C. Fitzpatrick, vol. 27 (Washington, D.C.: U.S. Government Printing Office, 1938), 135.

40. Proclamation of 22 September 1783, in *Journals of the Continental Congress,* eds. Ford et al., vol. 25, 264.

41. Ibid., vol. 24, 505 (14 August 1783).

42. Ibid., vol. 25, 680–95.

43. Ibid., 693.

44. Ibid., 686.

45. Ibid., 684.

46. Ibid., 684–85.

47. 7 Stat. 15, Articles II, III.

48. "Minutes of the Proceedings at Fort Stanwix, 1784," Wayne Manuscripts, Indian Treaties, 1778–1795, B, extracts from *Journals of the Commissioners of Indian Affairs for the Northern and Middle Departments,* Historical Society of Pennsylvania, 13.

49. Letter from James Madison to Thomas Jefferson, 11 October 1784, in *The Papers of Thomas Jefferson,* ed. Julian P. Boyd, vol. 7 (Princeton, N.J.: Princeton University Press, 1953), 439–41.

50. Franklin Hough, ed., *Proceedings of the Commissioners of Indian Affairs, Appointed by Law for the Extinguishment of Indian Titles in the State of New York,* vol. 1 (Albany, N.Y.: Joel Munsell, 1861), 29–30.

51. Ibid., 63.

52. The account of this transaction is found in *Proceedings of the Commissioners of Indian Affairs,* ed. Hough, vol. 1, 89–118.

53. "Speech of Petrus the Minister to New York Governor Clinton and New York Commissioners, June 25, 1785," reprinted in *Proceedings of the Commissioners of Indian Affairs,* ed. Hough, vol. 1, 106.

54. *Journals of the Continental Congress,* eds. Ford et al., vol. 29, 806.

55. "Committee Report on the State of Indian Affairs in the Southern Department, May 1784," in *Journals of the Continental Congress,* eds. Ford et al., vol. 27, 453–65.

56. Ibid., 459.

57. Article V, 7 Stat. 18, 19 (Cherokee); Article IV, 7 Stat. 21, 22 (Choctaw); and Article IV, 7 Stat. 24, 25 (Chickasaw).

58. 7 Stat. 20, 23, 26, 27.

59. *Journals of the Continental Congress,* eds. Ford et al., vol. 31, 490–93.

60. Ibid., 488.

61. Merrill Jensen, ed., *The Documentary History of the Ratification of the Constitution,* vol. 13 (Madison: State Historical Society of Wisconsin, 1983), 452.

62. Emphasis in original; reprinted in ibid., 72.

63. Letter of 12 April 1786, in *Letters of Members of the Continental Congress,* ed. Burnett, vol. 8, 339–40.

64. Letter to Henry Knox, 5 December 1784, in *The Writings of George Washington*, ed. John C. Fitzpatrick, vol. 28 (Westport, Conn.: Greenwood Press, 1970), 5.

65. Max Farrand, ed., *The Records of the Federal Convention of 1787*, vol. 8 (New Haven, Conn.: Yale University Press, 1966), 14.

66. United States Constitution, Article I, section 8.

67. Leonard Levy et al., eds., *Encyclopedia of the American Constitution*, vol. 1 (New York: Macmillan, 1986), 361.

68. "The Vices of the American Political System," in *Papers of James Madison*, eds. Rutland et al., vol. 9 (Chicago: University of Chicago Press, 1975), 348.

69. Benjamin F. Wright, ed., *The Federalist* (Cambridge, Mass.: Harvard University Press, 1961), 306.

70. Richard B. Morris, *The Forging of the Union, 1781–1789* (New York: Harper & Row, 1987), 270.

71. Letter to James Duane, 7 September 1783, in *Writings of George Washington*, ed. Fitzpatrick, vol. 27, 135.

72. Geoffrey Seed, *James Wilson* (Millwood, N.Y.: KTO Press, 1978), 163.

73. *Journals of the Continental Congress*, eds. Ford et al., vol. 6, 1078.

74. Ibid., 1078–079.

75. Ibid., 1079.

76. Excerpt from *The Federalist Papers*, reprinted in *Documentary History of Ratification*, ed. Jensen, vol. 3, 60.

77. John C. Hamilton, ed., *The Works of Alexander Hamilton, His Correspondence, and His Political and Official Writings, Exclusive of the Federalist, Civil and Military*, vol. 2 (New York: Charles S. Francis & Co., 1851), 273.

78. Albert V. Goodpasture, "William Blount and the Old Southwest Territory," *The American Historical Magazine* 8 (January 1903): 3.

79. Letter to Beverley Randolph, 12 July 1787, in *Supplement to Max Farrand's The Records of the Federal Convention of 1787*, ed. James H. Hutson (New Haven, Conn.: Yale University Press, 1987), 165.

80. Letter to Delegates in Virginia Assembly, 30 May 1783, reprinted in *The Life of George Mason, 1725–1792*, Kate Rowland (New York: Russell & Russell, 1964), 51.

81. Letter to the Republican, 8 November 1787, Federal Farmer, Letter I; in *Documentary History of Ratification*, ed. Jensen, vol. 14 (Madison: State Historical Society of Wisconsin, 1983), 24.

82. Letter from James Gunn to Alexander Hamilton, 11 November 1790, in *The Papers of Alexander Hamilton*, ed. Harold C. Syrett, vol. 7 (New York: Columbia University Press, 1963), 147–48.

83. Letter of Sydney, 13 June 1788; published in the *New York Journal* and reprinted in *Essays on the Constitution Published During Its Discussion by the People, 1787–1788*, ed. Paul L. Ford (New York: The Historical Printing Club of Brooklyn, 1892), 297, 301.

84. *Journals of the Continental Congress*, eds. Ford et al., vol. 33, 455–63.

85. William H. Masterson, *William Blount* (New York: Greenwood Press, 1969), 133.

86. Farrand, ed., *Records of the Federal Convention*, vol. 1, 21.

87. Ibid., 19.

88. Ibid., vol. 3, 601–04, 607.

89. Ibid., vol. 2, 159.

90. Ibid., vol. 1, 45–47.

91. Ibid., 47.

92. Ibid., 164.

93. Ibid., 245.

94. Ibid., 243.

95. Ibid., 297.

96. Ibid., 316–17.

97. Ibid., vol. 2, 157, note 154.

98. Ibid., 143.

99. Ibid., 137, note 6.

100. Ibid., 143.

101. Ibid., vol. 2, 169.

102. *Journals of the Continental Congress*, eds. Ford et al., vol. 33, 455–63.

103. Ibid., 457.

104. Ibid.

105. Ibid.

106. Ibid., 460.

107. Farrand, ed., *Records of the Federal Convention*, vol. 2, 321.

108. Ibid., 324, note 3.

109. Ibid., 308.

110. Ibid., 367.

111. *Supplement to Max Farrand's The Records of the Federal Convention*, ed. Hutson, 253; and Farrand, ed., *Records of the Federal Convention*, vol. 2, 493.

112. Farrand, ed., *Records of the Federal Convention*, vol. 2, 499.

113. Albert S. Abel, "The Commerce Clause in the Constitutional Convention and in Contemporary Comment," *Minnesota Law Review* 25 (1941): 432, 465.

114. *Journals of the Continental Congress*, eds. Ford et al., vol. 33, 458.

115. Lance Banning, "The Practical Sphere of Republic: James Madison, the Constitutional Convention, and the Emergence of Revolutionary Federalism," in *Beyond Confederation: Origins of the Constitution and American National Identity*, eds. Richard Meeman et al. (Chapel Hill: University of North Carolina Press, 1987), 169.

116. Emphasis in original. Letter to Andrew Stevenson, 25 March 1826; reprinted in Farrand, ed., *Records of the Federal Convention*, vol. 3., 473.

117. Jonathan Elliott, ed., *The Debates in the Several State Conventions on the Adoption of the Federal Constitution of 1787*, vol. 4 (Philadelphia: J. B. Lippincott & Co., 1937), 286.

118. 30 May 1787, in *Documentary History of Ratification*, ed. Jensen, vol. 13, 119.

119. Ibid., 116.

120. 28 November 1787; in *Documentary History of Ratification*, ed. Jensen, vol. 14, 245.

121. 2 January 1788, ibid., 230.

122. Article I, section 2.

123. Draft of 12 July 1776; reprinted in part in *The Works of Thomas Jefferson*, ed. Paul L. Ford, vol. 1 (New York: G. P. Putnam's Sons, 1904–1905), 43.

124. Article IX.

125. Reprinted in *The Works of Alexander Hamilton*, ed. Hamilton, vol. 2, 241.

126. Letter of William Grayson (congressional delegate from Virginia) to William Short, 10 November 1787, in *Documentary History of Ratification*, ed. Jensen, vol. 14, 82.

127. Letter of Joseph Clay to John Pierce, 17 October 1787, ibid., vol. 3, 232.

128. Letter of Abraham Baldwin to Nicholas Gilman, 20 December 1787, ibid., 262.

129. 10 June 1790, MSS, Journal of the House of Representatives, Georgia Department of Archives on History, 178.

130. Letter of G. J. A. Ducher to Compte de la Luzerne, 2 February 1787, in *Documentary History of Ratification*, ed. Jensen, vol. 3, 283.

131. *American State Papers*, vol. 1 (Washington, D.C.: U.S. Government Printing Office, 1832), 112–13.

132. Elliott, ed., *Debates in the Several State Conventions*, vol. 1, 329.

133. Ibid., 331.

134. Letter of 4 April 1791, in *Papers of Alexander Hamilton*, ed. Syrett, vol. 8, 241–42.

135. National Farmers Union Ins. Co. v. Crow Tribe, 471 U.S. 845 (1985).

6: Iroquois Political Theory and the Roots of American Democracy

1. "Native Women Send Message," *Wassaja* 4, no. 8 (August 1976): 7.

2. John C. Mohawk, "Prologue," in Paul A. W. Wallace, *White Roots of Peace* (Saranac Lake, N.Y.: Chauncy Press, 1986), 15.

3. Isabel T. Kelsay, *Joseph Brant, 1743–1807* (Syracuse, N.Y.: Syracuse University Press, 1984), 40–41. Actually, alcoholism was pervasive in Euro-American society. David Ramsay, M.D., in his *History of South Carolina*, vol. 2 (Charleston, S.C.: David Longworth, 1809), 391, flatly states that "drunkenness may be called an endemic vice of Carolina." As a physician, Ramsay observed that the majority of the population abused "spirituous liquors." Often the insults to Native American people are more insidious. Bernard Bailyn's recent work, *The Peopling of British North America* (New York: Alfred A. Knopf, 1986), has nothing to do with American Indians. Instead, it examines the English origins of early colonists that came to North America. Such titles imply that either American Indians were subhuman, or that they did not exist in eastern North America.

4. All quotations from Jack D. Forbes, "Americanism Is the Answer," *Akwesasne Notes* 6, no. 1 (April 1974): 37.

5. *The Complete Works of Montesquieu*, vol. 1 (London: T. Evans and W. Davis, 1777), 27, 142.

6. For a fuller discussion of these concepts, see Jack D. Forbes, "Americanism Is the Answer," *Akwesasne Notes* 6, no. 1 (April 1974): 37.

7. Ibid.

8. Finley Peter Dunne, *Mr. Dooley on Ivrything & Evrybody* (New York: Dover Publications, 1963), 207–08.

9. Indeed, some Americans at the time of the ratification of the United States Constitution rejected the notion that the Magna Carta was relevant to them. An editorial in the *Charleston Columbian Herald*, 12 June 1788, states that Americans "have no more to do with Magna Charta than with the Alcoran [Koran] . . . as Americans [we] have no dependence upon this boasted Magna Charta, [since] this government is for the people of the United States."

10. Sidney S. Rider, *The Lands of Rhode Island As They Were Known to Caucounicus and Miantunnomu When Roger Williams Came in 1636* (Providence, R.I.: the author, 1904), 44.

11. James E. Ernest, *The Political Thought of Roger Williams* (New York: Macmillan Co., 1929), 172.

12. Rider, *Lands of Rhode Island*, 9.

13. John Locke, *Second Treatise on Government,* in *The Works of John Locke,* vol. 4 (London: C. & J. Rivington, 1824), 402.

14. See John Mohawk, "Native People and the Right to Survive," *Akwesasne Notes* 9, no. 2 (May 1979): 5.

15. John Locke, *Second Treatise on Civil Government* (1690), chapters 1–4. Reprinted in *The Development of the Democratic Idea,* ed. Charles M. Sherover (New York: New American Library, 1979).

16. Ibid., chapter 6, paragraph 57.

17. Ibid., chapter 7, paragraphs 87–90.

18. Ibid., chapter 15, paragraph 173.

19. Benjamin F. Wright, *American Interpretation of Natural Law* (Cambridge, Mass.: Harvard University Press, 1931), 64–71.

20. Benjamin P. Poore, comp., *The Federal and State Constitutions, Colonial Charters, and Other Organic Laws of the United States,* vol. 2 (Washington, D.C.: U.S. Government Printing Office, 1877), 1389.

21. Adario is probably a fictional character, a literary foil employed by Lahontan to effectively present controversial ideas to Europeans. See Baron Lahontan, *New Voyages to North America,* vol. 2 (London: H. Bonwicke, T. Goodwin et al., 1703), 124; see also Percy G. Adams, "Benjamin Franklin and the Travel-Writing Tradition," in *The Oldest Revolutionary: Essays on Benjamin Franklin,* ed. J. A. Leo Lemay (Philadelphia: University of Pennsylvania Press, 1976).

22. Lahontan, *New Voyages,* 146.

23. Charles M. Sherover, ed., *Annotated Edition of the Social Contract* (New York: Harper & Row, 1984), Book 1, chapters 1, 2.

24. Ibid., passim; see also Bernard Sheehan, *Seeds of Extinction: Jeffersonian Philanthropy and the American Indian* (Chapel Hill: University of North Carolina Press, 1973) for an examination of these themes in a more distinctly American context.

25. Sherover, ed., *The Social Contract,* Book 3, chapter 7.

26. Jean Jacques Rousseau, "A Discourse on the Origin of Inequality," *The Social Contract* (New York: E. P. Dutton, 1950), 242.

27. Sherover, ed., *The Social Contract,* Book 1, chapters 3, 4; Book 3, chapters 4, 5.

28. See "The Huron, or Pupil of Nature," in *The Best Known Works of Voltaire* (New York: Literary Classics of the U.S., 1940), 212.

29. Robert Rogers, *A Concise Account of North America* (New Haven, Conn.: Johnson Reprint, 1966), 233.

30. David Jones, *A Journey of Two Visits Made to Some Nations of Indians on the West Side of the Ohio in the Years 1772 and 1773* (New York: Arno Press, 1971), 73.

31. "John Long's Journal, 1768–1782," in *Early Western Travels,* ed. Reuben G. Thwaites, vol. 2 (Cleveland: Burrows Bros. Co., 1904), 65. For a lengthier discussion of American Indians and freedom, see Leroy V. Eid, "Liberty: The Indian Contribution to the American Revolution," *The Midwest Quarterly* 22, no. 3 (Spring 1981): 279–98.

32. "Abram Charles, Law of the Woman Chief, 21 May 1923," Bureau of American Ethnology MSS #1636, National Anthropological Archives, Smithsonian Institution; Hazel W. Hertzberg, *The Great Tree and the Longhouse: The Culture of the Iroquois* (New York: MacMillan, 1966), 55–60; Lewis Henry Morgan, *Houses and House-Life of the American Aborigines* (Chicago: University of Chicago Press, 1966); Paul Bohannon and William N. Fenton, eds. and intro., "The Iroquois in

History," in *North American Indians in Historical Perspective*, eds. Eleanor B. Leacock and Nancy O. Lurie (New York: Random House, 1971), 138–39.

33. Henry R. Schoolcraft, *Notes on the Iroquois* (New York: AMS Press, 1975), 80; and see William N. Fenton, "Seth Newhouse's Traditional History and Constitution of the Iroquois Confederacy," *Proceedings of the American Philosophical Society* 93, no. 2: 141–58.

34. See John Mohawk, "Origins of Iroquois Political Thought," *Northeast Indian Quarterly* 3, no. 1 (1986). See also William Canfield, *The Legends of the Iroquois: Told by "The Cornplanter"* (New York: A. Wessels, 1902); and Frank H. Severance, ed., *Publications of the Buffalo Historical Society*, vol. 6 (Buffalo, N.Y.: Buffalo Historical Society Publications, 1903), 415–16.

35. Ibid., and James Dean, "Mythology of the Iroquois," MSS #4961, National Anthropological Archives, Smithsonian Institution. See also Anthony F. C. Wallace, *The Death and Rebirth of the Seneca* (New York: Alfred A. Knopf, 1970), 34–38.

36. See Paul A. W. Wallace, *The White Roots of Peace* (Philadelphia: University of Pennsylvania Press, 1946), 4–7.

37. See Tehanetorens, *Wampum Belts* (Onchiota, N.Y.: Six Nations Museum, n.d.), 6–7; and Tehanetorens, *White Roots of Peace: The Great Law of Peace of the Longhouse People* (Rooseveltown, N.Y.: White Roots of Peace, 1971).

38. Wallace, *White Roots*, 29.

39. Ibid.

40. Wilbur R. Jacobs, "Wampum, the Protocol of Indian Diplomacy," *William and Mary Quarterly* 3, no. 4 (1949): 596–604; Hertzberg, *Great Tree*, 104–05; Arthur C. Parker, *The Constitution of the Five Nations* (Albany, N.Y.: State Museum, 1916); and Rev. Joseph F. Lafitau, S. J., *Moeurs de Sauvages Americaines, Comparees aux Premiere Temps*, vol. 1 (Toronto: Champlain Society, 1974–1977), 466–67.

41. Tehanetorens, *White Roots*, sections 1–12.

42. Ibid., section 93; and Cadwallader Colden, *History of the Five Indian Nations*, vol. 1 (New York: New Amsterdam Books, 1902), xvii–xix.

43. Tehanetorens, *White Roots*, section 16.

44. Ibid., section 47.

45. Ibid., section 16. During the debates on the ratification of the Constitution, newspaper editorials used the "rafters" analogy and styled James Wilson as the architect. Wilson was said to state that "the intention was to make a firm and substantial roof by uniting the strength of the thirteen rafters." See *Charleston Columbian Herald*, 24 and 28 April 1788.

46. "Abram Charles, Law of the Woman Chief," Bureau of American Ethnology, MSS #1636, National Anthropological Archives, Smithsonian Institution; George B. Goode, ed., *The Smithsonian Institution* (Washington, D.C.: U.S. Government Printing Office, 1897), 390.

47. "Interview with Oren Lyons," *Akwesasne Notes* 3, no. 7 (September 1971): 6; Felix Cohen, "Americanizing the White Man," *The American Scholar* 21, no. 2 (Spring 1952): 179–80; Bruce Barton, "Iroquois Confederate Law and the Origins of the U.S. Constitution," *Northeast Indian Quarterly* 3, no. 3 (1986): 4–9.

48. William S. Newell, commentary, *Akwesasne Notes* 3, no. 4 (1972): 22–23; and William S. Corwin, "Franklin and the Constitution," *Proceedings of the American Philosophical Society* 100 (1956): 283–88.

49. Colden, *History of the Five Indian Nations*, vol. 2, 18–24.

50. Carl Van Doren and Julian P. Boyd, eds., *Indian Treaties Printed by Benjamin Franklin 1736–1762* (Philadelphia: Historical Society of Pennsylvania, 1938), 75.

51. E. B. O'Callaghan and B. Fernow, eds., *Documents Relative to the Colonial History of the State of New York,* vol. 6 (Albany, N.Y.: Weed, Parsons & Co., 1853–1887), 670–71.

52. Mary E. Fleming Mathur, "Tiyanoga of the Mohawks: Father of the United States," *Indian Historian* 3, no. 2: 59.

53. "To our Great Queen, April 1710," and "The Four Indian Sachems Letter to Rt. Honourable Lords of her Majesty's Council," [April 1710] in Schuyler Indian Papers, Box 13, Manuscript Division, New York Public Library; Richmond P. Bond, *Queen Anne's American Kings* (Oxford: Clarendon Press, 1952).

54. Ibid.

55. Bond, *Kings,* 118.

56. Donald A. Grinde, Jr., *The Iroquois and the Founding of the American Nation* (San Francisco: Indian Historian Press, 1977), 34–36.

57. Ibid., and Bruce E. Johansen, "The Forgotten Founders: Benjamin Franklin, the Iroquois and the Rationale for the American Revolution," *Four Winds* 2, no. 4 (1982): 9–13.

58. One of the items discussed at the Junto (an intellectual club organized by Franklin and the predecessor to the American Philosophical Society) in the 1740s was: "Which is the best form of government and what was that form which first prevailed among mankind?" See "Rules Established for a Club in Philadelphia," Franklin Papers, Library of Congress, Reel 11.

59. Albert H. Smythe, ed., *The Writings of Benjamin Franklin,* vol. 3 (New York: MacMillan Co., 1905–1907), 42.

60. Leonard W. Labaree and Whitfield W. Bell, Jr., eds., *The Papers of Benjamin Franklin,* vol. 4 (New Haven, Conn.: Yale University Press, 1962), 481.

61. Ibid., 482.

62. Van Doren and Boyd, eds., *Indian Treaties,* 128; and Leonard W. Labaree, ed., *The Autobiography of Benjamin Franklin* (New Haven, Conn.: Yale University Press, 1964), 197–99.

63. Van Doren and Boyd, eds., *Indian Treaties,* 128.

64. Ibid., 129.

65. Ibid., 131.

66. Labaree and Bell, eds., *The Papers of Benjamin Franklin,* vol. 5 (New Haven, Conn.: Yale University Press, 1962), 80–81.

67. O'Callaghan and Fernow, eds., *Documents Relative to Colonial History,* vol. 6, 869.

68. *Pennsylvania Colonial Records,* vol. 6 (Harrisburg, Penn.: Theo. Fenn & Company, 1851), 98.

69. Ibid.

70. O'Callaghan and Fernow, eds., *Documents Relative to Colonial History,* 889–91.

71. John Bigelow, ed., *Autobiography of Benjamin Franklin* (Philadelphia: J. P. Lippincott, 1868), 295. There were about one hundred and fifty Iroquois and about twenty-five colonists at the meeting.

72. Labaree and Bell, eds., *Papers of Benjamin Franklin,* vol. 5, 387.

73. Ibid., vol. 5, 387–92.

74. Ibid., vol. 3, 272.

75. Benjamin Franklin to Cadwallader Colden, 25 October 1753, ibid., vol. 5, 80.

76. Henry Steele Commager, *Documents of American History,* 7th ed. (New York: Appleton Century Crofts, 1963), 111.

77. See Clinton Rossiter, "The Political Theory of Benjamin Franklin," in *Benjamin Franklin: A Profile*, ed. Esmond Wright (New York: Hill and Wang, 1970), 179–80.

78. See Julian P. Boyd, "Dr. Franklin: Friend of the Indians," in *Meet Dr. Franklin*, ed. Roy N. Lokken (Philadelphia: Franklin Institute, 1981), 239.

79. Ibid., 238–39.

80. See Wilbur R. Jacobs, *Wilderness Politics and Indian Gifts* (Lincoln: University of Nebraska Press, 1966) for a fuller discussion of these themes.

81. *The Complete Works of Montesquieu*, vol. 1 (London: T. Evans and W. Davis, 1777), Book 1, chapter 3, "Of Positive Laws," 7.

82. Boyd, "Dr. Franklin," 246; and Barton, "Iroquois Confederate Law," *Northeast Indian Quarterly* 3, no. 3 (Fall 1986), passim.

83. John Adams to Abigail Adams, 10 July 1776, in *The Book of Abigail and John: Selected Letters of the Adams Family, 1762–1784*, eds. Lyman H. Butterfield, Marc Friedlaender, and Mary-Jo Kline (Cambridge, Mass.: Harvard University Press, 1975), 143.

84. "Journals of Captain John Montresor 1757–1778," 4 April 1766, *Collections of the New York Historical Society*, vol. 14 (New York: Printed for the Society, 1868–1949), 357.

85. Ibid., 20 May 1766, vol. 14, 367–68. One of the leaders of the Sons of Liberty at this time was "General" Joseph Allicocke, a "mulatto."

86. Ibid., 11 August 1766, vol. 14, 382. For a graphic portrayal of the assembly post and the "Liberty Pole," see *Liberty Pole, New York*—pen and ink drawing, 1770, in P. E. Du Simitiere Papers, Acc. #396.f, vol. 2, Library Company of Philadelphia.

87. Richard Barry, *Mr. Rutledge of South Carolina* (New York: Duell, Sloan & Price, 1942), 338 and chapter 3.

88. See John R. Bartlett, ed., *Records of the Colony of Rhode Island*, vol. 7 (New York: AMS Press, 1968), 192. Since the investigation of the *Gaspee* incident was marked by perjury, it is difficult to ascertain the disguise of the men through the official testimony, but a song composed shortly after the incident claimed that the Sons of Liberty were disguised as sixty-four "Narragansett Indian men." Before the *Gaspee* incident, Rhode Islanders had burned the British revenue sloop *Liberty* on 17 July 1769, to protest Britain's tougher policies on smuggling. I am indebted to Alfred Owen Albridge, Professor of Comparative Literature at the University of Illinois, for calling my attention to an interesting fictional account of the Sons of Liberty dressing as American Indians (circa 1765) in the short story by Nathaniel Hawthorne entitled *My Kinsman: Major Molineaux*.

89. The subsequent investigation of the *Gaspee* incident caused the creation of committees of correspondence by the Virginia House of Burgesses on 12 March 1773. See *Virginia Gazette*, 18 March 1773.

90. *Providence Gazette*, 12 June 1773.

91. *New York Gazetteer*, 2 December 1773, and *New York Journal*, 16 December 1773. It is interesting to note that the New York Tammany Society clearly traced its roots to the Sons of Liberty and the need to create an institution for native rights. For an account of this connection, see "Preface to Constitution" in "Constitution and Roll of Members of the Saint Tammany Society, 1789–1916," Manuscript Division, New York Public Library.

92. *Boston Evening Post*, 6 December 1773.

93. See John Adams to Hezekiah Niles, 10 May 1819, in *Niles Register* 16 (May 1819): 226. Adams stated that the men at the Tea Party were "no ordinary Mohawks." See also "Minutes of the Tea Meetings, 1773," *Proceedings of the Massachusetts*

Historical Society, vol. 20 (Boston: Massachusetts Historical Society, 1882–1883), 16; and see Bruce E. Johansen, "Mohawks, Axes and Taxes: Images of the American Revolution," *History Today* 35 (April 1985): 10–16 for in-depth details of "Mohawk" Bostonians at the Boston Tea Party.

94. *Pennsylvania Colonial Records*, vol. 11, 98; see also Alfred Owen Aldridge, *Man of Reason: The Life of Thomas Paine* (Philadelphia: J. P. Lippincott, 1959), 5. Years after the Easton Treaty, Paine would recall an anecdote told by a chief called "King Lastnight" at the meeting. In criticizing the viability of British naval power on North American soil, the chief said: "The King of England is like a fish, when he is in the water he can wag his tail. When he comes on land he lays down on his side" (*New York Public Advertiser*, 5 August 1807).

95. Moncure D. Conway, ed., *The Writings of Thomas Paine*, vol. 1 (New York: AMS Press, 1967); *Common Sense*, 70; and John P. Reid, *The Concept of Liberty in the Age of the American Revolution* (Chicago: University of Chicago Press, 1988).

96. See Paul W. Conner, *Poor Richard's Politicks* (New York: Oxford University Press, 1965); and Bruce Barton, "Iroquois Confederate Law," *Northeast Indian Quarterly* 3, no. 3 (Fall 1986).

97. "Speech in Convention, January 1775," in *Selected Political Essays of James Wilson*, ed. Randolph G. Adams (New York: Alfred A. Knopf, 1930), 90.

98. Worthington C. Ford et al., eds., *Journals of the Continental Congress*, vol. 2 (Washington, D.C.: U.S. Government Printing Office, 1904–1937), 195–99.

99. "Proceedings of the Commissioners Appointed by the Continental Congress to Negotiate a Treaty with the Six Nations, 1775," *Papers of the Continental Congress, 1774–1789*, National Archives (M247, Roll 144, Item No. 134). See Treaty Council at German Flats, New York, 15 August 1775. The use of the term "island" alludes to the Iroquois term for North America, "Turtle Island."

100. Ibid., 24 August 1775, at Albany, New York.

101. Ibid., 25 August 1775, at Albany, New York.

102. Ibid. Actually, the Americans were using the imagery of section 57 of the Great Law of Peace of the Iroquois. This Iroquois image of an eagle clutching arrows would later become a symbol of strength and sovereignty for the United States, just as it had been for the Iroquois (see J. N. B. Hewitt to Arthur C. Parker, 11 September 1912, J. N. B. Hewitt Letters, Box 2, National Anthropological Archives, Smithsonian Institution).

103. *Papers of the Continental Congress*, 25 August 1775.

104. Ibid., 26 August 1775.

105. Ibid., 28 August 1775.

106. Ibid.

107. Ibid.

108. Ibid., 31 August 1775.

109. Ibid.

110. Ibid.

111. Ibid., 1 September 1775. For Euro-Americans and American Indians of the revolutionary era, this meeting was of enormous significance. See "American Chronology, or list of Important . . . Events," in *The Columbian Magazine* 4, no. 1 (January 1790): 5, where it is considered as one of the most important events leading to the revolution. See also Timothy Pickering Papers in the Massachusetts Historical Society, Reel 62, 5 December 1794, 117, where Stockbridge and Oneida Indians showed Pickering a "talk from Congress by Mr. Hancock" dated 1775.

112. Robert L. Scribner and Brent Tarter, eds., *Revolutionary Virginia: The Road to Independence*, vol. 4 (Charlottesville: University of Virginia Press, 1973–

1983), 175, 187. For an example of James Wilson's depth of knowledge on Iroquois matters, see James Wilson to John Montgomery, 24 August 1775, in *Letters of the Delegates to Congress, 1774–1789*, ed. Paul H. Smith, vol. 1 (Washington, D.C.: Library of Congress, 1976–), 706.

113. Scribner and Tarter, eds., *Revolutionary Virginia*, vol. 4, 188.

114. Gaillard Hunt and James B. Scott, eds., *The Debates in the Federal Convention of 1787 Which Framed the Constitution of the United States of America Reported by James Madison* (New York: Oxford University Press, 1920), 77.

115. See John F. Watson, *Annals of Philadelphia and Pennsylvania in the Olden Time* (Philadelphia: E. Thomas, 1857), 570; Richard K. Matthews, *The Radical Politics of Thomas Jefferson: A Revisionist View* (Lawrence: University of Kansas Press, 1984), 143; and James E. Hendricks, *Charles Thomson and the Making of the New Nation* (Rutherford, N.J.: Fairleigh Dickinson University Press, 1979). A few years after his adoption into the Delaware tribe, Thomson wrote *An Enquiry into the Causes of the Alienation of the Delaware and Shawnee Indians from the British Interest* (London: J. Wilkie, 1759). For Thomson's appendix, see *The Works of Thomas Jefferson*, ed. Paul L. Ford, vol. 3 (New York: G. P. Putnam, 1904–1905), 454–58, 498–504, and 508–09. It is significant that Jefferson wrote *Notes on Virginia* as a result of a request by François de Marbois. In 1784, Marbois and Madison visited the Iroquois while attending the treaty at Fort Stanwix. Madison had taken an interest in American Indians early in life. During his childhood and student years, Madison had a trusted servant with the Saponi Indian name of "Sawney." In 1724, as a young man, "Sawney" had threatened the Virginians with the wrath of the Iroquois. Perhaps "Sawney" talked of the Iroquois League with Madison (see H. R. McIlwaine, ed., *Executive Journals of the Council of Colonial Virginia*, vol. 4 (Richmond, Va.: D. Bottom, 1925–1945), 76–77, 80; William T. Hutchinson and William M. E. Rachal, eds., *The Papers of James Madison*, vol. 1 (Chicago: University of Chicago Press, 1962–1985), 42–43. Madison's papers also contain the earliest known version (20 January 1775) of Logan's speech (Logan was a Mingo or part-Iroquois who had suffered the death of his whole family at the hands of unscrupulous non-Indians). See ibid., vol. 1, 136.

116. Robert Treat Paine to Joseph Palmer, 1 January 1776, in *Letters of Delegates*, ed. Smith, vol. 3, 5.

117. Lyman H. Butterfield, ed., *Diary and Autobiography of John Adams*, vol. 2 (Cambridge, Mass.: Harvard University Press, 1961), 226. Adams also wrote of his dinner to his wife; see John Adams to Abigail Adams, 24 January 1776, in *The Book of Abigail and John*, eds. Butterfield et al., 114. Adams also refers to this letter on 28 April 1776 in another letter to his wife, ibid.

118. Butterfield, ed., *Diary*, vol. 2, 226.

119. Butterfield et al., eds., *Book of Abigail and John*, 114.

120. See John Adams, *Thoughts on Government: Applicable to the Present State of the American Colonies* (Philadelphia: John Dunlap, 1776); and Butterfield et al., eds., *Book of Abigail and John*, 115. In 1787, while musing on restructuring American government, John Adams would mention that collecting the legislation "of the Indians would be well worth the pains." See John Adams, *Defence of the Constitutions of Government of the United States of America* (Philadelphia: Hall & Sellars, 1787), xvii. Adams also remarks on page xv that in the government of "Indians . . . the existence of the three divisions of power is marked with a precision that excludes all controversy." Adams has the Iroquois in mind since he writes extensively about "sachems [and] a great council fire" on page 225. Throughout early 1776, Adams was receiving extensive intelligence about the Iroquois (see Robert

J. Taylor, ed., *Papers of John Adams*, vol. 4 (Cambridge, Mass.: Harvard University Press, 1977–), 129.

121. Labaree and Bell, eds., *Papers of Benjamin Franklin*, vol. 22, 357; and Eric P. Newman, "Franklin Making Money More Plentiful," in *Proceedings of the American Philosophical Society* 115, no. 5: 347. Franklin's knowledge of American Indian ideas was acknowledged by the Tammany Society through the frequent references to "Anecdotes of Franklin" in their early meetings. See "Society of St. Tammany, Constitution and Roll of Members," in Manuscript Division, New York Public Library. The symbol of the silver chain with thirteen links has gone unnoticed as an Iroquois symbol in American history, but the Tammany Society clearly used it in an Indian context. See Benjamin DeWitt, "An Account of the Internment of the Remains of 11,500 American Seamen . . . Who Fell Victim to the Cruelties of the British on Board Their Prison Ships at Wallabout During the American Revolution" (1808), 66, a pamphlet in the Library Company of Philadelphia.

122. Ford, ed., *Journals*, vol. 6, 1086–1088. By July of 1776, the public mind had been prepared for independence by Thomas Paine's *Common Sense*. Franklin had played a key role in "furnishing materials for this work" (see "William Temple Franklin's Notes on Franklin's Life," in Franklin Papers, Manuscript Division, Library of Congress).

123. See "Richard Smith's Diary, March 11, 1776," in *Letters of Delegates*, ed. Smith, vol. 3, 368.

124. Richard Henry Lee to General Charles Lee, Philadelphia, 2 May 1776, in *Collections of the New York Historical Society*, vol. 5 (New York: Printed for the Society, 1872), 46; Caesar Rodney to Thomas Rodney, Philadelphia, 28 May 1776, in *Letters of Delegates*, ed. Smith, vol. 4, 99; ibid., vol. 4, 281; and *Pennsylvania Gazette*, 29 May 1776. Benjamin Rush wrote to his wife (26 May 1776) that this parade was to give the "Indian ambassadors now among us an august idea of the military strength of our province." See Lyman H. Butterfield, ed., *Letters of Benjamin Rush*, vol. 1 (Princeton, N.J.: Princeton University Press, 1951), 97.

125. Ford, ed., *Journals*, vol. 5, 430. James Wilson and Thomas Jefferson were on the standing committee on Indian affairs in the Continental Congress during 1776 (see Ford, ed., *Journals*, vol. 6, 1065). Formal and informal relations with the Iroquois would continue throughout the revolution. An Oneida woman, Polly Cook, served as George Washington's cook during the revolution. The Oneidas also brought corn to Washington's troops during the bitter winter at Valley Forge, thus enabling them to survive. See Cara Richards, *The Oneida People* (Phoenix, Ariz.: Indian Tribal Series, 1974), 53–54.

126. Ford. ed., *Journals*, vol. 5, 430.

127. See Charles Thomson's "History of the Articles of Confederation" (a work that was secret during the revolution), in *Papers of the Continental Congress, 1774–1789* (National Archives M247, Roll 22, Item no. 9) for an 11 June 1776 notation entitled, "Resolved that a committee be appointed to prepare and digest the form of a confederation to be entered into between these Colonies"; on the next day, Thomson noted that committee members were appointed. By 12 July 1776, Thomson notes that Article II of the draft of the Articles of Confederation states that the "Colonies Unite themselves so as to never be divided by any act whatsoever, and hereby severally enter into a firm League of friendship with each other. . . . " This phraseology is similar to the Canassateego speech of 1744 at Lancaster that was reiterated by the Americans at the Albany conference of 1775. Also see *Letters of Delegates*, ed. Smith, vol. 4, 252, editorial note. This editorial note states, ". . . there can be no doubt that the members of the committee began

their work with a copy of Benjamin Franklin's *Proposed Articles of Confederation* before them, for which see *Journals*, ed. Ford, vol. 2, 195–199. Several passages from Franklin's plan can be found verbatim in the Dickenson drafts, and many others survive with slight variations. Indeed, ". . . the 4th, 7th, 8th and 12th of Franklin's Thirteen Articles are conspicuously incorporated into the committee's work."

128. Ford, ed., *Journals*, vol. 6, 1078.

129. Ibid., vol. 5, 690–91.

130. Ibid., vol. 7, 398.

131. See Gordon S. Wood, ed., *The Confederation and the Constitution: The Critical Issues* (Washington, D.C.: American University Press, 1979); and Forrest McDonald, *E Pluribus Unum* (Boston: Houghton Mifflin, 1965) for a deeper analysis of these issues and events. The term "league of friendship" is used in the "Final Draft of the Articles of Confederation" (9 July 1778), Article III in "History of Articles of Confederation," 12 February 1781, *Papers of the Continental Congress, 1774–1789*, National Archives (M247, Roll 22, Item no. 9).

132. See *Apocalypse de Chiokoyhekouy, Chief des Iroquois* (Philadelphia: C. Roberdson, 1777), 93, Library Company of Philadelphia; and Dwight W. Hoover, *The Red and the Black* (Chicago: Rand McNally, 1976), 56–57. The prophet bird *Tsklelei*, or news carrier, was an image used in the rhetoric of Iroquois diplomacy (see Peter Force, ed., *American Archives*, 4th Series, vol. 3, 479, 491, for examples of how this image was used by the American commissioners and the Iroquois at the Albany conference of 1775). One of the American commissioners to France in 1777, Silas Deane, was on a committee of Congress to confer with the Rev. Samuel Kirkland about the "prophet bird" speech with the Iroquois in 1775. It may be surmised that Franklin, Deane, and perhaps Arthur Lee (American commissioners to France) worked on this pamphlet, since they were all familiar with Iroquois ideas and imagery (see *Journals*, ed. Ford, vol. 2, 186). This pamphlet, then, was a clever combination of ideas and images to allay French, Spanish, and Dutch fears about American independence. It also appealed to the "noble savage" sentiments in France that were so ardently advanced by philosophers like Rousseau. In the nineteenth century, the Tuscarora anthropologist J.N.B. Hewitt recorded the Tuscarora story about the prophetic bird-like being that could foresee events important to the survival of the tribe (see J.N.B. Hewitt Collection, MSS #422, National Anthropological Archives, Smithsonian Institution). For a contemporary version of an Iroquois apocalyptic prophecy, see Wallace (Mad Bear) Anderson, "The Lost Brother: An Iroquois Prophecy of the Serpents," in *The Way: An Anthology of American Indian Literature*, eds. Shirley H. Witt and Stan Steiner (New York: Vintage Books, 1972), 243–47.

133. See Richards, *The Oneida People*, 53–54; and the quote from the *Military Journal of George Ewing* (1928) in *The Writings of George Washington*, ed. John C. Fitzpatrick, vol. 2 (Washington, D.C.: U.S. Government Printing Office, 1931–1944), 342, for a fuller explanation of events during the winter and spring of 1778.

134. Treaty with the Delawares of 17 September 1778, 7 Stat. 13. No doubt Charles Thomson (adopted Delaware), secretary to Congress, had a major role in the negotiation and recording of this treaty.

135. George Washington to James Duane, 7 September 1783, in *The Washington Papers*, ed. Saul K. Padover (New York: Harper & Row, 1955), 352; see also Richard B. Morris, *The Forging of the Union, 1781–1789* (New York: Harper & Row, 1987), 270–71. In fact, Washington had been fascinated by the Iroquois since the age of sixteen. See Albert C. Myers, *The Boy Washington, Age 16: His Own Account of An Iroquois Indian Dance, 1748* (Philadelphia: A.C. Myers, 1932).

136. For a general discussion of the origins of the United States Constitution, see Richard Beeman et al., eds., *Beyond Confederation: Origins of the Constitution and American National Identity* (Chapel Hill: University of North Carolina Press, 1987).

137. Madison is quite clear about conditions of the time. He states: "It required but little time after taking my seat in the [Virginia] House of Delegates in May 1784 to discover that, however favorable the general disposition of the state might be towards the Confederacy, the legislature retained the aversion of its predecessors to transfers of power from the state to the government of the union; notwithstanding the urgent demands of the federal treasury, the glaring inadequacy of the authorized mode of supplying it, the rapid growth of anarchy in the federal system, and the animosity kindled among the states by their conflicting regulations" (quoted from *Debates in Federal Convention*, eds. Hunt and Scott, 6). Two other future presidents, Thomas Jefferson and James Monroe, had planned a visit to Iroquois country in 1784, but Jefferson's appointment as ambassador to France prevented him from going on the trip. Monroe went without Jefferson. See Stuart G. Brown, ed., *The Autobiography of James Monroe* (Syracuse, N.Y.: Syracuse University Press, 1959), 38–39.

138. Eugene P. Chase, ed., *Our Revolutionary Forefathers: The Letters of François, Marquis de Barbe-Marbois* (Freeport, N.Y.: Books for Libraries, 1969), 191–93; and Irving Brant, *James Madison*, vol. 1 (Indianapolis: Bobbs-Merrill Co., 1941), 330–31.

139. Chase, ed., *Letters of Marquis de Barbe-Marbois*, 211–12.

140. Brant, *Madison*, vol. 1, chapter 21.

141. Tammany was a Delaware chief and said to be a friend of William Penn. He was supposed to have been sympathetic to the early colonists of Pennsylvania. See *Pennsylvania Chronicle*, 4 May 1772. The twenty-first toast at the 1 May 1772 meeting of the society is interesting. "May the Sons of King Tammany, St. George, St. Andrew, St. Patrick, and St. David love each other as the brethren of one common ancestor, and unite in their hearty endeavors to preserve their native Constitutional American Liberties." By 1775, King George III was no longer popular, so Philadelphians had a mock "canonization" of Tammany and changed the organization's name to the Society of the Sons of Saint Tammany. See "Extracts from the Journal of Miss Sarah Eve, May 1, 1773," *Pennsylvania Magazine of History and Biography* 5, no. 1 (January 1881): 29.

142. On 1 May 1777 (Tammany Day), John Adams described the origins and activities of the Tammany Society in Philadelphia to his wife; see Lyman H. Butterfield, ed., *Adams Family Correspondence*, vol. 2 (Cambridge, Mass.: Harvard University Press, 1963), 229–30.

143. Ibid., 7 May 1783. On 1 May 1783, to celebrate the coming of peace, thirteen "sachems" (Philadelphians dressed as Indians) were invested with supreme authority for the day. Subsequently, the hatchet was buried, and a calumet or peace pipe (the six-foot pipe had thirteen feathers and thirteen stars) was smoked by several hundred people present. Numerous toasts were made to Saint Tammany, the Constitution of Pennsylvania, the union, General Washington, and others.

144. *Pennsylvania Packet*, 6 May 1784, and *Freeman's Journal*, 5 May 1784. Washington was dining with the financier general, Robert Morris (near Fifth and Market streets), at the time of the visit by the Tammany Society. Later in the day, a gentleman also appeared in complete "powwow dress" and performed a Manetta Dance. At this time, it became apparent that the Tammany Society was an artisan/professional political group interested in reform of the government to secure a firm union, hard money, and a bicameral legislature.

145. *Virginia Gazette*, 23 April 1785; and Donald Jackson and Dorothy Twohig, eds., *The Diaries of George Washington*, vol. 4 (Charlottesville: University of Virginia Press, 1976–1979), 132.

146. *Independent Gazetteer*, 22 April 1786.

147. Ibid. The author remembers that several of his Seneca students had commented that crumbs and scraps are still left on the ground for consumption by the dead at funeral feasts today among the Iroquois.

148. Ibid.

149. *Virginia Gazette*, 24 May 1786. Edward Telfair, delegate from Georgia, was present at Cornplanter's speech and, no doubt, was influenced by it. By 1 May 1790, Telfair, as governor of Georgia, was made grand sachem at a Tammany Day celebration in Augusta, Georgia. See *New York Journal*, 16 July 1790, and *Augusta Chronicle* and *Gazette of the State*, 15 May 1790.

150. *Pennsylvania Evening Herald*, 6 May 1786. Apparently Benjamin Franklin was a member of the Constitutional Sons of Saint Tammany; he was frequently toasted as a "brother." On the eve of the Constitutional Convention, the Constitutional Sons of Saint Tammany, like Franklin, supported the concept of a unicameral legislature.

151. *Pennsylvania Packet*, 5 June 1786; and ibid., 11 May 1787. By 1805, the *Freeman's Journal*, 10 April 1805, was calling the New York Tammany Society a votary of "mummery," since it was fast becoming a political machine.

152. *The American Museum* 1 (May 1787): 477; in American Philosophical Society.

153. Adams, *Defence of Constitutions*, xv. Jack P. Greene, in *The Intellectual Heritage of the Constitutional Era: The Delegates Library* (Philadelphia: Library Company of Philadelphia, 1986), 54, calls Adams's *Thoughts on Government* (1776) and his *Defence of Constitutions* "two of the most significant works [in] the discussion of the problem of forming new constitutions." Indeed, Greene states that *Defence of Constitutions* is "massive and learned." *Defence of Constitutions*, published in January 1787, was, of course, available to the delegates of the Constitutional Convention and readily used.

154. Ibid. According to Adams, Turgot and other contemporary French philosophers influenced by Franklin and other travel accounts wanted to renounce monarchies and return to tribal governments like the modern Indians and the ancient Germans. No doubt Franklin's repeated references to the Iroquois in the salons of Paris had an effect on ideas of the times. For a discussion of Franklin's conversations on the Iroquois in Paris during the revolution, see Alfred O. Aldridge, *Benjamin Franklin: Philosopher and Man* (Philadelphia: J. P. Lippincott, 1965), 112–13.

155. See Charles Francis Adams, ed., *The Works of John Adams* (Boston: Little, Brown and Company, 1850–1856), 279, 389–90, 581, for Adams's insights into the association of Turgot and Franklin with unicameral legislatures. Given the fact that Franklin talked of the Iroquois frequently in the French salons, Turgot would have been imbued with certain insights as to the structures of Iroquois government.

156. See Adams, *Defence of Constitutions*, xv–xvi.

157. Ibid., xvii.

158. Ibid., xv–xvi.

159. Ibid., 315.

160. Ibid., 225.

161. Ibid., xi.

162. Ibid., 6–7. Adams reserves special scorn for the work of John Locke. Commenting on Locke's "plan of legislation for Carolina," where Locke gave "whole authority . . . to the . . . proprietors," Adams asked who did Locke "think would live under his government? He should have created a new species of being to govern before he instituted such a government" (quoted from ibid., 365–66).

163. See Hendricks, *Thomson*, for a more detailed examination of some of these questions.

164. For insights into the development of American government, see Gordon S. Wood, *The Creation of the American Republic* (Chapel Hill: University of North Carolina Press, 1969); Jackson T. Main, *The Sovereign States* (New York: New Viewpoints, 1973); Merrill Jensen, *The New Nation* (New York: Alfred A. Knopf, 1950); Forrest McDonald, *We the People* (Chicago: University of Chicago Press, 1958); and Peter S. Onuf, *Statehood and Union: A History of the Northwest Ordinance* (Bloomington: Indiana University Press, 1987).

165. *Charleston Columbian Herald*, 9 June 1788.

166. See Adams, *Defence of Constitutions*, xii–xv, 176, 369.

167. George Mason to George Mason, Jr., Philadelphia, 20 May 1787, in George Mason Papers, Manuscript Division, Library of Congress.

168. George Mason to George Mason, Jr., 1 June 1787, ibid.

169. *The American Museum* 1 (June 1787): 565.

170. Max Farrand, ed., *The Records of the Federal Convention of 1787*, vol. 1 (New Haven: Yale University Press, 1911), 66. The term "confederate republic" had been used in accounts describing the Iroquois in the 1740s (see "Lewis Evans' Brief Account of Pennsylvania," in *Lewis Evans*, ed. Lawrence H. Gipson (Philadelphia: Historical Society of Pennsylvania, 1939). See map insert.

171. Hunt and Scott, eds., *Debates in Federal Convention*, 77. See also Harold C. Syrett, ed., *Papers of Alexander Hamilton*, vol. 4 (New York: Columbia University Press, 1961–1987), 166–67. Hamilton uses "Ind" to mean "Indians" in his 7 June 1787 notes. On the next day, he records "Union basis of our oppos & Ind" in his notes relating to James Wilson's speech of 8 June 1787, but the editors of the Hamilton papers interpret that notation as meaning "independence" a day later, in spite of its use to mean "Indians" a day earlier. Wilson, of course, was thoroughly familiar with Iroquois imagery. In 1775, he had traveled to Pittsburgh to negotiate a treaty with the Iroquois and the western nations. Referring to his experience in 1775, Wilson stated that "the idea of the union of the colonies struck [the Iroquois] forcibly." Just three weeks after independence (26 July 1776), Wilson would argue in debate over the Articles of Confederation that "Indians know the striking benefits of confederation" and they "have an example of it in the union of the Six Nations" (quoted from Ford, ed., *Journals*, vol. 6, 1078).

172. Dumas Malone, ed., *Dictionary of American Biography*, vol. 11 (New York: Scribner's, 1933), 325; see also Leonard Levy et al., eds., *Encyclopedia of the American Constitution* (New York: MacMillan, 1986) for a more complete discussion of the experiences of the Founding Fathers with Native American affairs.

173. Farrand, ed., *Records*, vol. 1, 641.

174. See Benjamin Franklin, "Talk to the Old Chief," 30 June 1787, Franklin Papers, Manuscript Division, Library of Congress. The noted political scientist Clinton Rossiter stated that Franklin's role at the convention was extremely important, and that "Franklin made rich contributions to the theory and practice of federalism . . . he was far ahead of the men around him in abandoning provincialism." See Clinton Rossiter, *Seedtime of the Republic* (New York: Harcourt, Brace, 1953), 306.

175. The Enlightenment historian Peter Gay maintains that Franklin developed a philosophical approach that had abundant references to the Native American societies which he encountered. Indeed, Franklin's combining of Native American thought and European concepts made him America's first philosopher and, in Europe, he was said to be "the philosopher as savage." See Peter Gay, "Enlightenment Thought and the American Revolution," in *The Role of Ideology in the American Revolution*, ed. John R. Howe (New York: Holt, Rinehart and Winston, 1970), 48.

176. Benjamin Franklin to Cornstalk, the Cherokee chief, 30 June 1787, Franklin Papers, Manuscript Division, Library of Congress. Cornstalk is a popular Tammany name, since the real Cornstalk was brutally murdered by the British in 1777 while trying to maintain the neutrality of his tribe. See "Sketch of Cornstalk," *Ohio Archaeological and Historical Society Quarterly* 21 (Fall 1912): 245–62.

177. *The American Museum* 2 (July 1787). Rush maintained an avid interest in American Indians. See Benjamin Rush Papers, MSS #1051, "Commonplace Book, 1792–1813," 127, in American Philosophical Society. See also George W. Conner, ed., *The Autobiography of Benjamin Rush* (Princeton, N.J.: Princeton University Press, 1948), 188, for a conversation in Philadelphia between Rush and the Creek chief Alexander M'Gillvray just two days before M'Gillvray arrived in New York City to negotiate an important treaty with the new federal government. Rush also believed that it was better to teach American students "the Indian languages of our country than to speak or write Latin." See also Butterfield, ed., *Letters of Benjamin Rush*, vol. 1, 607.

178. *The American Museum* 2 (July 1787): 86. George Washington recommended *The American Museum* to his acquaintances. See John C. Fitzpatrick, ed., *Writings of Washington*, vol. 29 (Washington, D.C.: U.S. Government Printing Office, 1931–1944), 521.

179. *Pennsylvania Herald*, 18 August 1787.

180. Barry, *Rutledge*, 338 and chapter 3; and Charles L. Mee, Jr., *The Genius of the People* (New York: Harper & Row, 1987), 237. For an interesting analysis of the relationship of the United States Constitution to the Great Law of Peace of the Iroquois, see Gregory Schaaf, "The Birth of Frontier Democracy from an Eagle's Eye View: The Great Law of Peace to the Constitution of the United States," *Akwesasne Notes* 19, no. 4 (1987): 3–7. Richard Barry, Rutledge's most recent biographer, states that according to family lore, Rutledge was imbued with Iroquois political theory from the time of the Stamp Act. Unfortunately, most of Rutledge's papers were destroyed in a house fire in the nineteenth century. Rutledge brought up some of the points about American Indian government that Adams had discussed in his *Defence of Constitutions*.

181. "Propositions, Objections &c in Debates on Adoption of the Constitution," James Wilson Papers, vol. 2, 61–68, Manuscript Division, Historical Society of Pennsylvania.

182. Tehanetorens, *White Roots*, section 57.

183. *The American Museum* 2 (August 1787): 201. The Founding Fathers had ample access to Cadwallader Colden's *History of the Five Indian Nations* and James Adair's *The History of the American Indians* (London: E. & C. Dills, 1776). See Greene, *Intellectual Heritage of the Constitutional Era*, 56. Here, we see a popular expression of Adams's ideas about American Indian governments from his *Defence of Constitutions*.

184. *The American Museum* 2 (August 1787): 181. In this issue, the Northwest Ordinance of 1787 (done 13 July 1787) was reprinted. According to Jayne K. Kribs in *Bibliography of American Literary Periodicals, 1741–1850* (Boston: G.K. Hall

& Co., 1977), 12, ". . . *The Columbian Magazine* [and] *The American Museum* share the distinction of being the first successful American magazines. Subscribers included Washington, Franklin, Hamilton, Jefferson, Madison, Edmund Randolph, Thomas Allibone, Francis Hopkinson, Jared Ingersoll, and Benjamin Rush."

185. Farrand, ed., *Records,* vol. 3, 138–40. Early in the debates on the United States Constitution, James Wilson "opposed the annihilation of the state governments, and he represented that the freedom of the people . . . depended on their existence in full vigour." See ibid., 411. For a detailed analysis of the importance of unity in the eighteenth century, see Harry M. Ward, *Unite or Die: Intercolonial Relations, 1690–1754* (Port Washington, N.Y.: Kennikat Press, 1971).

186. ". . . of a Plan concerning the new states," Wilson Papers, Manuscript Division, Historical Society of Pennsylvania, vol. 2, 132; and "Notes from Mr. Wilson's Lectures by Joseph Hopkinson, 1791," in Joseph Hopkinson Papers, Manuscript Division, Historical Society of Pennsylvania (lecture was delivered at the University of Pennsylvania); see also Geoffrey Seed, *James Wilson* (1978).

187. See *Charleston Columbian Herald,* 3 July 1788. The "Unite or Die" slogan was directly attributed to Franklin in a poem published in *The American Museum* 4 (July 1788): 193–95. It was entitled "Union or Only Hope: A Federal Poem." The poem, in part, asserted: "Unite or Die—arouse or fall, / Is rev'rend Franklin's dying call."

188. *The Columbian Magazine* 2, no. 10 (November 1788): 578–82.

189. David Ramsay, "An address to the Freemen of South Carolina on the Subject of the Federal Constitution . . . 1788 by Civis," in *Pamphlets on the Constitution of the United States,* ed. Paul L. Ford (Brooklyn, N.Y.: Library of American Civilization, 1888), 373.

190. *The American Museum* 5, nos. 1, 2 (January/February 1789); see "Albany Papers."

191. Ibid., no. 3 (March 1789): 285.

192. See Treaty at Hopewell, Article XII, 7 Stat. 18.

193. Robert Beverley, *The History and Present State of Virginia* (Chapel Hill: University of North Carolina Press, 1947), 9. A recent article on Robert Beverley states that the main question in his discourse is "natural liberty versus authority." (See Robert D. Arner, "The Quest for Freedom: Style and Meaning in Robert Beverley's *The History and Present State of Virginia,*" *The Southern Literary Journal* 8, no. 1 (Spring 1978): 98.

194. *New York Journal,* 23 July 1790.

195. Ibid., 10 August 1790.

196. Ibid.

197. Ibid.

198. Ibid., 3 August 1790. Apparently, the Saint Tammany Society was widespread by this time. Obviously the symbols of the Iroquois and their relationship to the Constitution had become idiomatic through the spread of the Saint Tammany Society throughout the United States. Jefferson and Madison continued their interest in Native American ideas by examining Indian languages on Long Island, New York (see "Unquahog tribe, Puspatuck Settlement, Brookhaven, Long Island, N.Y. taken by Thomas Jefferson, 13 June 1791, in the presence of James Madison and General Wm. Floyd," in Indian Boxes, Box 1, Manuscript Division, New York Public Library.

199. See De Witt Clinton, "A Discourse Delivered Before the New York Historical Society, 1811," in *Early America Imprints,* 2nd. Series, no. 38779 (New York: Van Winkle & Wiley, 1814), 50. See also "Constitution and Roll of Members of the

Saint Tammany Society, 1789–1916," Manuscript Division, New York Public Library, for a record of De Witt Clinton's membership in the Tammany Society.

200. See William B. Campbell, ed., *The Life and Writings of De Witt Clinton* (New York: Baker & Scribner, 1849).

201. *Freneau's National Gazette,* 5 April 1792.

202. De Witt Clinton, "Discourse . . . Before the New York Historical Society," 16.

203. Thomas Jefferson to John Adams, 11 June 1812, in *The Writings of Thomas Jefferson,* ed. Albert E. Bergh, vol. 11 (Washington, D.C.: Jefferson Memorial Association, 1904–1905), 160. In this letter, Jefferson was quite critical of "Indian experts" like Joseph F. Lafitau, S.J., and James Adair, who reflected on American Indian governments and customs. He stated that Lafitau had a "preconceived theory . . . of the ancient nations of Europe, Asia and Africa" and kept up a perpetual "parallel . . . between Indians of America and the ancients of other quarters of the globe." Jefferson also thought Adair had "his kink," since he believed "all the Indians of America to be descended from the Jews."

204. John Adams to Thomas Jefferson, 28 June 1813; ibid., 288. Adams was critical like Jefferson of European observers of American Indians, and said their representations of Indian governments resembled the "philosophy of Plato, more than the genuine system of Indianism."

205. William Brandon, *The American Heritage Book of Indians* (New York: Simon and Schuster, 1961), 241.

206. Richard K. Cralle, ed., *The Works of John C. Calhoun,* vol. 1 (New York: Appleton & Co., 1851), 71–72. Calhoun, of course, had dealt with the Iroquois as secretary of war; see John C. Calhoun to David Ogden, 14 May 1818, in Indian Boxes, Box 1, Manuscript Division, New York Public Library.

207. Quoted in *Akwesasne Notes* 2, no. 6 (1969): 24.

208. "Onondaga Indians," *Harper's Weekly,* 17 February 1872. This story also contains a good written account of the "White Dog Sacrifice," and an illustration.

209. Lewis Henry Morgan, *Houses and House-Life of the American Aborigines* (Chicago: University of Chicago Press, 1965), 32; see also Thomas R. Trautmann, *Lewis Henry Morgan and the Invention of Kinship* (Berkeley: University of California Press, 1987) for a recent evaluation of the importance of Morgan's work.

210. See Sally Roesch Wagner, "The Iroquois Confederacy: A Native American Model for Non-sexist Men," *Changing Men* 19 (Spring/Summer 1988): 32–34; and Matilda Jocelyn Gage, "The Matriarchate: Or, Woman in the Past," *Twentieth Century,* 25 December 1890.

211. "Indians of New York," *Utica Morning Herald,* 9 May 1894.

212. "The Six Nations," in *Encyclopedia Americana,* vol. 14 (New York: Americana Corporation, 1896). (Copy in J.N.B. Hewitt Papers, National Anthropological Archives, Smithsonian Institution.)

213. Matthew W. Stirling, "America's First Settlers, the Indians," *National Geographic* 62, no. 5 (November 1937). Matthew Stirling was head of the Bureau of Ethnology during the years that William N. Fenton, anthropologist of the Iroquois, worked there.

214. *Washington Post,* 7 February 1950.

215. Felix Cohen, "Americanizing the White Man," *The American Scholar* 21, no. 2 (1952): 179–80. For a detailed analysis of the influence of American Indian ideas on colonial Americans, see Bruce E. Johansen, *Forgotten Founders* (Ipswich, Mass.: Gambit, 1982).

216. William N. Fenton, "Iroquois in History," in *North American Indians in Historical Perspective,* eds. Leacock and Lurie, 151.

217. Francis Jennings, *The Invasion of America: Indians, Colonialism, and the Cant of Conquest* (Chapel Hill: University of North Carolina Press, 1975), 171.

218. Ibid.

219. See Elbridge Gerry to John Adams, 11 November 1775, in *Papers of John Adams*, ed. Taylor, vol. 3, 287–92. As early as 1753 commentators on the Iroquois noted that the Iroquois ". . . chuse their War Captain" (see "Lewis Evans' Brief Account of Pennsylvania," in *Lewis Evans*, ed. Gipson, 92).

220. Ethan Allen to Indians of Canada, 24 May 1775, Q11 Public Archives of Canada, 193–94. Methods of American Indian warfare were widely known in America. See Marc Lescarbot, *History of New France*, trans. W. L. Grant, vol. 3 (Toronto: Champlain Society, 1914), 11; and Michael Alexander, ed., *Discovering the New World: Jacques LeMoyne's Account* (New York: Harper & Row, 1976), 29–30, for early accounts of Indian warfare and tactics.

221. Jennings, *Invasion*, 173.

222. Ibid., 173–74. In Francis Jennings, *The Ambiguous Iroquois Empire: The Covenant Chain Confederation of Indian Tribes with English Colonies from Its Beginnings to the Lancaster Treaty of 1744* (New York: W. W. Norton & Company, 1984), Iroquois diplomacy with the colonials is viewed as an evolving bicultural phenomenon. The intellectual impact of the interchange on the American colonials is not emphasized, since Jennings is interested in the dynamics of the colonial system.

223. James Axtell, *The European and the Indian* (New York: Oxford University Press, 1981), 10. Axtell has even ignored American Indians in a historical context. Rather than deal with Euro-American and Native American interaction, he preferred to postulate an America without American Indians in order to vaguely argue that some things in America have Native American roots. For his counterfactual argument concerning history without Indians, see "Colonial America without the Indians: Counterfactual Reflections," *Journal of American History* 73, no. 4 (March 1987): 981–96.

224. See James Axtell to William N. Fenton, 10 September 1975, in William N. Fenton Papers, MSS Collection #20, Correspondence Box 1979–1982 in American Philosophical Society.

225. Elisabeth Tooker, "The United States Constitution and the Iroquois League," *Ethnohistory* 35, no. 4 (Fall 1988): 305.

226. See ibid., 306–10 for Tooker's outline of the historical evidence upon which she bases her argument (only about ten percent of the article actually addresses historical documentary fact); also see Van Doren and Boyd, eds., *Indian Treaties*, 128, and Labaree and Bell, eds., *Papers of Benjamin Franklin*, vol. 4, 481–82.

227. Tooker, "The United States Constitution and the Iroquois League," 309–10.

228. Ibid., 327.

229. For the naming ceremony, see Ford, ed., *Journals*, vol. 6, 430. For an analysis of Franklin's Albany Plan being derived from the Iroquois, see Boyd, "Dr. Franklin," 239. For a more complete analysis of how Franklin's revised Albany Plan was used in Congress, see Smith, ed., *Letters of Delegates*, vol. 4, 252. In fact, a member of the Confederation Committee noted on 12 July 1776 that "the Plan of Confederation [was] by the Albany Plan" (see ibid., vol. 4, 199–201).

230. See *Apocalypse de Chiokoyhekoy, Chief des Iroquois* (Issued By Order of the Continental Congress, 1777) for an interesting use of Iroquois prophecy as propaganda to bring European powers into the war on the side of Americans.

231. See Adams, *Defence of Constitutions*, xv–xvii.

232. See *The American Museum* 2 (August 1787): 201 for the use of the "bundle of arrows" imagery in a statement to the "Federal Constitution."

233. For a discussion of the evolution of the United States Constitution and the nature of the New Jersey Plan, see Leonard Levy, ed., *Essays on the Making of the Constitution* (New York: Oxford University Press, 1989); J.R. Pole, ed., *The American Constitution* (New York: Hill and Wang, 1987); and Clinton Rossiter, *The Grand Convention* (New York: MacMillan, 1966).

234. See *New York Journal,* 10 August 1790, for an example of the synthesis concept by the Tammany Society.

235. Vine Deloria, Jr., and Clifford M. Lytle, *American Indians, American Justice* (Austin: University of Texas Press, 1983), 82.

236. Quoted from Bernard DeVoto's introduction to Joseph K. Howard, *Strange Empire* (New York: William Morrow, 1952), 8.

237. Virgil Vogel, "The Indian in American History," *Akwesasne Notes* 4, no. 4 (1972): 31.

238. Vine Deloria, Jr., "Some Thoughts," *Akwesasne Notes* 4, no. 4 (1972): 31. For a more comprehensive examination of American Indian ideas of freedom and democracy, see Donald A. Grinde, Jr., and Bruce E. Johansen, *Exemplar of Liberty: Native America and the Evolution of Democracy* (Los Angeles: University of California Regents and UCLA American Indian Studies Center, 1991).

239. "Onondaga Council of Chiefs of the Iroquois Confederacy," *Akwesasne Notes* 3, no. 2 (1971): 36.

7: The Application of the Constitution to American Indians

1. Alexander Hamilton, "Federalist No. 24," in *The Federalist Papers,* ed. Henry Cabot Lodge (New York: G.P. Putnam & Sons, 1884), 147.

2. 34 Op. A.G. 186–89 (1924)—discontinued 44 Stat. 1347.

3. Worcester v. Georgia, 31 U.S. (6 Pet.) 515, 559 (1832).

4. "The Six Nations, Wyandots, and Others," in *American State Papers, Indian Affairs,* 1st Cong., vol. 1, no. 6 (17 September 1789), 58.

5. "The Cherokees," in *American State Papers, Indian Affairs,* 1st Cong., vol. 1, no. 13 (11 August 1790), 83.

6. *Congressional Globe* (1 March 1871), U.S. Senate, 1824.

7. 16 Stat. 544, 566.

8. 5 Wall 755 (1866).

9. *Congressional Globe* (1 March 1871), U.S. Senate, 1824.

10. Ibid., 1824–825.

11. Ibid., 1825.

12. Ibid., 1822.

13. Ibid.

14. See Roy Meyer, *History of the Santee Sioux* (Lincoln: University of Nebraska Press, 1967), 127–28.

15. United States v. Kagama, 118 U.S. 375, 378–379 (1885).

16. Ibid., 379–380.

17. United States Constitution, Article IV, Section 3, clause 2.

18. Johnson v. McIntosh, 8 Wheat 543, 572–573 (1823).

19. Ibid., 574.

20. Ibid., 591–592.

21. Francis P. Prucha, *The Great Father: The United States Government and the American Indians*, vol. 1 (Lincoln: University of Nebraska Press, 1984), 519.

22. Ibid.

23. Ibid., 523.

24. Ibid., 514–25.

25. Quick Bear v. Leupp, 210 U.S. 50, 76–77 (1908).

26. Missouri, Kansas and Texas Railway Co. v. Roberts, 152 U.S. 114 (1894).

27. Ibid., 117–118.

28. Felix Cohen, *Handbook of Federal Indian Law* (Washington, D.C.: U.S. Government Printing Office, 1942), 175.

29. Connors v. United States, 33 Ct. Cls. 317, 323–324 (1898).

30. Colliflower v. Garland, 342 P.2d. 369, 378–379 (1965).

31. Fort Berthold Reservation v. United States, 390 F.2d. 686, 691 (1968).

32. 14 Stat. 755, 756 (21 March 1866).

33. Cohen, *Handbook*, 340.

34. *Senate Report No. 268*, 41st Cong., 3d. Sess., SS 1443 (14 December 1870), 10.

35. United States v. Nice, 241 U.S. 591, 598 (1916).

36. Talton v. Mayes, 163 U.S. 376, 384 (1896).

37. Native American Church v. Navajo Tribal Council, 272 F.2d. 131, 134 (1959).

8: Congress, Plenary Power, and the American Indian, 1870 to 1992

1. See, for example, Vine Deloria, Jr., *Behind the Trail of Broken Treaties* (New York: Dell Publishing Co., 1974).

2. Alvin J. Ziontz, "Indian Litigation," in *The Aggressions of Civilization*, eds. Vine Deloria, Jr., and Sandra Cadwalader (Philadelphia: Temple University Press, 1984), 156–57.

3. Cherokee Tobacco, 78 U.S. 616 (1870).

4. Ex Parte Crow Dog, 109 U.S. 556 (1883).

5. 23 Stat. 362 (1885).

6. Francis P. Prucha, *The Great Father: The United States Government and the American Indians*, vol. 2 (Lincoln: University of Nebraska Press, 1984), 679.

7. United States v. Kagama, 118 U.S. 375 (1886).

8. Russell L. Barsh and James Y. Henderson, *The Road: Indian Tribes and Political Liberty* (Berkeley: University of California Press, 1980), 83.

9. 118 U.S. 375 (1886).

10. Barsh and Henderson, *The Road*, 83.

11. Ann L. Estin, "Lone Wolf v. Hitchcock: The Long Shadow," in *The Aggressions of Civilization*, eds. Deloria and Cadwalader, 216–45.

12. Lone Wolf v. Hitchcock, 187 U.S. 535 (1903).

13. Ibid.

14. Ibid.

15. Ziontz, "Indian Litigation," 158. Two examples include United States v. Winans, 198 U.S. 371 (1905), relating to Indian fishing rights; and Winters v. United States, 207 U.S. 564 (1908), relating to Indian water rights.

16. 24 Stat. 388 (1887).

17. Francis P. Prucha, ed., *Americanizing the American Indian: Writings of 'Friends' of the Indian* (Cambridge, Mass.: Harvard University Press, 1973), 164.

18. Michael T. Smith, "The History of Indian Citizenship," *Great Plains Journal* 10 (1970): 30–31.

19. See D. S. Otis, *The Dawes Act and the Allotment of Indian Lands,* ed. Francis P. Prucha (Norman: University of Oklahoma Press, 1973). For the impact on one Indian nation, the Oneida, see Laurence M. Hauptman, *The Iroquois and the New Deal* (Syracuse, N.Y.: Syracuse University Press, 1981), 70–77. Some of the results in native communities, such as the White Earth Reservation, were separation from land and homes, malnutrition and even starvation, extreme depression, alcohol abuse, family break-up, scattering of people, and suicide.

20. 26 Stat. 81, 99–100 (1890).

21. 34 Stat. 182 (1906).

22. 41 Stat. 350 (1919).

23. Vine Deloria, Jr., and Clifford M. Lytle, *American Indians, American Justice* (Austin: University of Texas Press, 1983), 220–25.

24. Hauptman, *Iroquois and the New Deal,* chapter 1; Barbara Graymont, ed., *Fighting Tuscarora: The Autobiography of Chief Clinton Rickard* (Syracuse, N.Y.: Syracuse University Press, 1973), 53.

25. 43 Stat. 253 (1924).

26. Ibid.

27. Gary C. Stein, "The Indian Citizenship Act of 1924," *New Mexico Historical Review* 47 (1972): 268.

28. Ibid., 266.

29. Linda S. Parker, "The Indian Citizenship Act of 1924," in *Between Two Worlds: The Survival of Twentieth Century Indians,* ed. Arrell M. Gibson (Oklahoma City: Oklahoma Historical Society, 1986), 49.

30. Laurence M. Hauptman, *The Iroquois Struggle for Survival: World War II to Red Power* (Syracuse, N.Y.: Syracuse University Press, 1986), 5–6.

31. Ex Parte Green, 123 F.2d. 862 (1941).

32. United States v. Claus, 63 F. Supp. 433 (1944); Albany v. United States, 152 F.2d. 267 (1945).

33. Hauptman, *Iroquois Struggle for Survival,* chapter 1.

34. Graymont, *Fighting Tuscarora,* 53.

35. 48 Stat. 984 (1934).

36. Hauptman, *Iroquois and the New Deal,* chapter 5.

37. Robert Burnette and John Koster, *The Road to Wounded Knee* (New York: Bantam Books, 1974), 115, 117, 132, 168–69, 182–87.

38. American Indian Policy Review Commission, *Final Report,* vol. 1 (Washington, D.C.: U.S. Government Printing Office, 1977), 309–10.

39. 48 Stat. 984 (1934).

40. Ibid.

41. Ibid.

42. "Tribal Government and the Indian Reorganization Act of 1934," *Michigan Law Review* 70 (1972): 966.

43. Russell L. Barsh, "The BIA Reorganization Follies of 1978: A Lesson in Bureaucratic Self-Defense," *American Indian Law Review* 7 (1979): 12.

44. Barsh and Henderson, *The Road,* 105–06.

45. Ibid.

46. Burnette and Koster, *Road to Wounded Knee,* 16.

47. Harry Conroy to Ben Dwight, 16 October 1946, National Congress of American Indians MSS, National Anthropological Archives, Smithsonian Institution.

48. Vine Deloria, Jr., *Custer Died for Your Sins* (New York: Macmillan Co., 1969), 147.

49. Prucha, *The Great Father*, vol. 2, 1013–059; C. F. Wilkinson and E. R. Biggs, "The Evolution of the Termination Policy," *American Indian Law Review* 5 (1980): 139–84.

50. Oscar Chapman to Harry Truman, 18 March 1950, Truman MSS, 6–C, Truman Library, Independence, Missouri.

51. Report of the Committee on Indian Affairs of the Hoover Commission, Philleo Nash MSS, Box 44, Truman Library, Independence, Missouri.

52. 67 Stat. B132 (1953). For the Menominee Termination Act, see 68 Stat. 250–252 (1954).

53. 67 Stat. 588–590. For the earlier transfer of criminal and civil jurisdiction in New York, see Hauptman, *Iroquois Struggle for Survival*, chapters 3 and 4.

54. Michael Lawson, *Dammed Indians* (Norman: University of Oklahoma Press, 1982), xxi–xxii, 179–200.

55. Hauptman, *Iroquois Struggle for Survival*, 85–122.

56. Ibid., 100–01.

57. Excerpts from Department of Justice Memorandum of Law with respect to taking of Indian lands for the Allegheny Reservoir, 15 July 1957, John S. Bragdon MSS, Box 51, Eisenhower Library, Abilene, Kansas.

58. Seneca Nation of Indians v. Wilbur M. Brucker et al., 162 F.Supp. 580 (1958).

59. Seneca Nation of Indians v. Wilbur M. Brucker et al., 262 F.2d. 27 (1958).

60. Laurence M. Hauptman, interview with Edward O'Neill (former attorney for Seneca Nation), 10 January 1984, Washington, D.C.

61. Seneca Nation of Indians v. Wilbur M. Brucker et al., 162 F.2d. 27 (1958).

62. Seneca Nation of Indians v. Wilbur M. Brucker et al., 262 F.2d. 27 (1958).

63. Oneida Indian Nation et al. v. County of Oneida, New York, et al., 94 S.Ct. 772 (1974); County of Oneida, New York, et al. v. Oneida Indian Nation et al.; New York v. Oneida Indian Nation, U.S. Sup. Ct.—83–1065; 83–1240—opinion (4 March 1985).

64. For the provisions of the Maine settlement, see 94 Stat. 1785–1797.

65. See, for example, Susan Chira, "Pequot Indians Prevail in Battle Begun in 1637," *New York Times*, 20 October 1972.

66. For the Menominee Restoration Act, see 87 Stat. 770–773 (1973).

67. United States v. Washington, 384 F.Supp. 312 (1974).

68. Laurence M. Hauptman, interview with Larry Kinley (Lummi Business Council), 11 October 1987, Philadelphia, Pennsylvania.

69. United States Congress, Senate, Select Committee on Indian Affairs, Hearings on S. 2084: Ancient Indian Land Claims, 97th Cong., 2d. Sess., Washington, D.C., 1982.

70. 85 Stat. 688–716 (1971).

71. Thomas R. Berger, *Village Journey* (New York: Hill and Wang, 1985), 6.

72. Ibid.

73. 88 Stat. 1712–1723 (1974). See also Jerry Kammer, *The Second Long Walk: The Navajo-Hopi Land Dispute* (Albuquerque: University of New Mexico Press, 1980).

74. "Navajos' Leader Tells Congress Abuses Mar Relocation Plan," *New York Times*, 13 December 1987.

75. 88 Stat. 2213–2217 (1975).

Index

The Authors

Oren R. Lyons is a traditional chief of the Turtle Clan, Onondaga Nation, Iroquois Confederacy, and Associate Professor of American Studies at the State University of New York at Buffalo. He is the publisher of *Daybreak*, a national Indian news magazine, and has represented American Indian interests at the United Nations and other international forums.

John C. Mohawk, a member of the Seneca Nation, was editor-in-chief of *Akwesasne Notes* from 1976 to 1983, then the country's largest English-language indigenous publication, and currently serves as editor of *Daybreak*. He is presently a lecturer in American Studies at SUNY, Buffalo.

Robert W. Venables currently teaches in the American Indian Studies program at Cornell University and serves as a consultant for the Smithsonian Institution National Museum of the American Indian. He has written or coauthored several books, including *American Indian Environments*.

Howard R. Berman is an associate professor at California Western School of Law in San Diego, where he specializes in international and comparative law. He has written numerous articles on Indian rights and has represented American Indian nations before domestic and international forums.

Curtis G. Berkey is director of the Indian Law Resource Center in Washington, D.C. Among his clients is the Iroquois Six Nations Confederacy. He pioneered the use of international human rights procedures for Native American rights in the United Nations and the Organization of American States.

Donald A. Grinde, Jr., a professor of history at California Polytechnic State University, San Luis Obispo, is the author of several books, including *The Iroquois and the Founding of the American Nation* and *Exemplar of Liberty: Native America and the Evolution of Democracy*.

Vine Deloria, Jr., of the Standing Rock Sioux tribe, is the author of several books, including *Custer Died for Your Sins, God Is Red,* and *Behind the Trail of Broken Treaties*. He is currently a professor of law, religious studies, political science, and history at the University of Colorado in Boulder.

Laurence M. Hauptman, a professor of history at SUNY, New Paltz, is the author/editor of seven books, including *The Iroquois and the New Deal, The Iroquois Struggle for Survival,* and *The Pequots in Southern New England*. He has testified before Congress on behalf of Native American land claims.